William Goyen

Selected

Letters

from a

Writer's

Life

WILLIAM GOYEN

Selected

Letters

from a

Writer's

Life

EDITED AND WITH AN
INTRODUCTION BY
Robert Phillips

AFTERWORD BY
Sir Stephen Spender

University of Texas Press
AUSTIN

Published in conjunction with TriQuarterly magazine

Library of Congress Cataloging-in-Publication Data

Goyen, William.
    [Correspondence. Selections]
    William Goyen : selected letters from a writer's life / edited and with an
introduction by Robert Phillips.
        p.   cm.
    Includes index.
    ISBN 0-292-72773-9
    1. Goyen, William—Correspondence. 2. Novelists, American—20th
century—Correspondence. I. Phillips, Robert S. II. Title.
PS3513.O97Z48 1995
813'.54—dc20
[B]   94-8789

For

Doris

Roberts

CONTENTS

INTRODUCTION

"I did not describe William Goyen's visit one evening," Anaïs Nin wrote in her diary. "A man in pain—gray-haired but with a youthfulness of gestures and face, a young man upon whose body age could only imprint a few lines and would never weigh down. A softness of voice, a gentleness of manner. He had gestures of disturbance, his hands made efforts to erase the lines of anxiety. What came to the surface was the injuries received, the disappointments, the injustices, the brutalities of the press. A wounded man. The ones who expected great love and are wounded at the beginning later cannot register the love they receive in the present, only the one denied them. The groove is made to receive only the insults and betrayals."

Truman Capote based a fictional character upon Goyen, and that man also is described as having "wounded eyes. Injured and insulted." In *Answered Prayers* Capote wrote of a young fiction writer, P. B. Jones, who had an affair with a much older Southern novelist, Alice Lee Longman. There are many parallels between this and Goyen's two-year infatuation with Katherine Anne Porter, or more correctly, as these letters reveal, her infatuation with him. The unflattering portrait of Goyen was possibly an act of revenge on Capote's part. He did not speak to his friend for years after Goyen savaged Capote's *Breakfast at Tiffany's* in a review (titled "That Old Valentine Maker") in the *New York Times Book Review* in 1958. Elsewhere Capote bragged that all the characters in the novel were based on his friends: "The plot—or rather plots—was true, and all the characters were real: it wasn't difficult to keep it all in mind, for I hadn't invented anything." As the saying goes, with friends like that, who needs enemies?

Anaïs Nin is correct to record Goyen's psychic wounds. One instance of his hurt and outrage was how—in Nin's words—he was "ruthlessly handled by *Time* magazine." Nin recounts what Goyen reported to her: "Random House refused to publish his last book after sending it for approval to a *Time* magazine literary critic. They paid him $175 for reading it, and as he said 'No' [to publication], Random House turned it down. A new kind of rigged game in publishing. Since *Time* has the power to make or break a writer, the publisher might as well know in advance. These critics make as much as 2,000 dollars a week in this way."

This story of Goyen and the *Time* critic may be apocryphal; he had a way of stretching reality, especially when his career was involved. It is undeniable, however, that he was another fatality in the world of publication. As Nin has written, his fiction was composed of subtle poetry and symbols, fantasy and reverie. In a marketplace where the novels of Jacqueline Susann, Harold Robbins, and Sidney Sheldon sold by the millions, Goyen was attempting to place fictions in which atmosphere and suggestion were more important than plot, illusion more important than reality, the unconscious as important as the conscious. A very deliberated style, based on regional speech, was his fictional vehicle, not a standard-speak language.

Consequently, his books did not sell in big numbers. And just as consequently, he was dropped by publishers. In his journals he wrote on the failure of his work to find a life even when published:

> *Something that was so full of life—so beautiful and pure and free while it was being created—to fall into oblivion, to be dismissed, to be befouled. A kind of murder. The humiliation of pure and instinctive and beautiful work. The heartbreak. The threatening bitterness. The bleak emptiness. The loneliness.*
>
> *Some publishers are book-killers. When they publish a book they kill it. For them, to publish a book is to kill it, is **an act of violence** (on a book). Publication is killing.*
>
> *My work has always hurt me. Tears have fallen upon everything I've written. Hurt at the conception, hurt in the creation of it, hurt by the lack of acknowledgment it brings, at its poor life and obscurity in the world. Yet the joy in the vision of it is unequalled. And there is the sense of **having** to do my work, of simple total commitment; it is simply my way.*

In the early part of his career, Goyen could be thought of as one of those writers with an "underground" reputation. But he never surfaced aboveground. Even today, after publishing five novels, four collections of stories, and a nonfiction book—as well as having several plays produced— he still is not as well known as he should be, given the extraordinary nature of his work. When his last novel, *Arcadio*, was published in 1983, the reviewer in the *New York Times Book Review* proclaimed him "one of the great American writers of short fiction." And when his final collection, *Had I a Hundred Mouths* (1985), was reviewed in the same publication, the reviewer concluded that it contained pieces that belonged "among the great short stories of the century." Yet despite such assessments by some of his contemporaries, Goyen is not often enough mentioned in the same breath as William Faulkner, Katherine Anne Porter, Eudora Welty, or Flannery O'Connor. What he had in common with those four figures was more than a masterful way with a tale and Southernness. Actually he repudiated being a Southern writer. In a note appended to his second published novel, *In a Farther Country* (1955), he wrote:

> *I am tired of being called a young Southern writer . . . and am fully forty, from Texas, which is the Southwest, and have had little to do with what has been called "the Southern Literary Revival." Though my father and his family are from Mississippi, I have never lived in that or any other Southern state, only passed through them on a train. The language of my work up to the present novel . . . where it has been regional idiom, has been based on that of Texas, which I know and speak and carry in my ears; it is not Southern. The themes of my work have no affinity with the eccentricities of Southern personality or Gothic bizarreries, though my work has been attracted to that category through spurious association.*

What Goyen does share with Faulkner, Porter, Welty, and O'Connor is a distinct literary style and subject matter from which he did not waver at any point in his writing career. Look, for instance, at Goyen's whole-cloth oeuvre beside that of his contemporary with whom he was sometimes mistakenly compared, Truman Capote. Capote's first novel, *Other Voices, Other Rooms*, was an integration of poetry and prose, as was his second, *The Grass Harp*, which Goyen felt owed a debt to his own subject matter and themes. Afterward, Capote tried to capture a large popular audience, as evidenced by the trendiness of *Breakfast at Tiffany's*, the commercialism of *House of Flowers*, the sensationalism of *In Cold Blood*, and the high-society gossip of *Answered Prayers*. But as Nin wrote, "William Goyen matured without betraying his sensitivity, he became stronger without surrendering the qualities which made him both human and subtle, able to handle overtones in relationships without destroying them in the process. The balanced, harmonious maturity of sensitiveness is a rare quality in our culture, for it usually does not have the endurance to survive."

Endurance is what Goyen's life was about. Physical endurance, yes: These letters chronicle decades of poverty and numerous ailments of body and mind, including pleurisy, migraine headaches, hay fever, and back spasms; operations on the hand, the knee, the eye; alcoholism, depression, and the lymphoma which eventually was to claim his life. In his letters he frequently wrote "abcession" for "obsession"—either a pun or a Freudian slip. Despite all this, it was artistic endurance which took the greater courage. As the letters document, his books were hard to place; his editors and some agents and play producers were often insensitive. He made exactly $57 from the production of his first New York play. One book-royalty check totaled $3.94. His publishers quickly remaindered or shredded his books. (See Goyen's letter of September 8, 1981, to Robin Moody concerning Doubleday's destruction of two thousand copies of *Come, the Restorer*.) Ultimately he found himself totally out of print in this country, although translations of his works sold well in Europe. In his early years even his own mother was not supportive of either his work or his life-style; see his letter dated June 3, 1948, to his former Houston schoolmate William M. Hart. Eventually both parents came to be very proud of his career, and their meetings back in Texas were quite amicable. Once during a game at the Houston Astrodome they all saw WELCOME HOME, BILL GOYEN, flashed on the Dome's giant screen.

In the course of locating, reading, and annotating these letters, I have come to think of William Goyen as a prototype for the sensitive artist or poet in America today. It is for this reason, as well as for reasons of space, that this volume is devoted somewhat exclusively to letters about his writing, the writing of others, and art and literature in general. Of course, there are other subjects and concerns, such as familial matters and affairs of the heart. But transcending even these relationships is William Goyen on Writing. The letters reveal the difficulty of the artist in this country; the killing effect of war on the human spirit; the therapy of doing translations; the effect of travel on the imagination; the necessity for talking to other creative people; the evil of literary politics; the importance of place to the creative imagination; Goyen's generosity to younger writers; and the debilitating effect on the artist of a job in commerce.

"What I wanted was to make splendor," he wrote in retrospect of his life. "I can't imagine *not* writing. Writing simply is a way of life for me. The older I get, the more of a way of life it is. At the beginning, it was totally a way of life excluding everything else. Now it's gathered to it marriage and children and other responsibilities. But still, it is simply a way of life before all other ways, a way to observe the world and to move through life, among human beings, and to record it all above all and to shape it, to give it sense, and to express something of myself in it. Writing is something I cannot imagine living without, nor scarcely would want to."

Goyen himself addressed the idea of the writer in America in a speech that he prepared, called "The Position of the Creative Writer in the Social Milieu," which began with a little joke. The position, he said, is generally "a seated position before a piece of paper, alone, in some room." He defined "milieu" as the world outside, the world around the writer; in other words, the contemporary American scene, which he called "an age of intense and various experience." If the writer lived in a large city, he was surrounded not only by an excess of impressions of people, places, and scenes but also by an intense awareness of success, possibilities, and pressures, such as TV, films, theater, the commercial attitude of publishers. Goyen saw American cities as progenitors of panic, fostering the quest for success, materialism, expensive apartments, weekend houses, and the like. In this sense he predicted the Yuppie Generation of the 1980s. For him the builders of the new Manhattan were a primitive force. He rails on the same subject at the conclusion of his August 18, 1946, letter to his first agent, Toni Strassman.

On the other hand, Goyen found life in a small town "deadly" and life in the American countryside a hiding away, a kind of hiding that parents do not understand in their hopes for their offspring to be "successful" in the "entertainment" or "communications" worlds. In one note he re-marks, "The style of America is 'success.'"

He wrote, "I have lived in all these varieties of the American social milieu, and it had appeared to me, as I grew older as a writer, that the basic situation of the writer—and perhaps I speak of the artist-writer—is isolation." He declared to one of his editors, "I am an exile, but at home, where every exile should be." Yet perhaps because he felt uncomfortable in both town and city, Goyen moved about a great deal, as the seven sections of this book reveal. He even fled Germany prematurely when asked by the American government to give readings there, fearing that he was suffering cultural claustrophobia and was potentially in danger of a nervous breakdown. He wrote one friend, "Trouble with people like us is that one place is not enough in this world."

Politics, with the possible exception of racial relations in *The Fair Sister* (1963), played little role in Goyen's fiction or his life. When invited to attend the inauguration of President John F. Kennedy, he refused. An excerpt from his unpublished journals reads:

Could it be true that:

*In such a time as this, when the world is chaotic and complex and men no longer trust men, nor have faith in each other nor in values—suspicion, envy, treachery, hatred—can not the best possible way for the artist be to go on his way, at great odds, and by the force of example as a human being, work as an **individual** to maintain the values that are corrupted, keep clear and clean the truth, honest, etc., in the world he tries constantly to fashion and preserve and keep from destruction—by serving (?) and holding to these, as an **individual** in the midst of mass thinking and agitation against him and his values—to steadfastly serve the values and the truths of his world and do this in his **individual** life and in his work. Is not this the artist's way of proclaiming truth, of **influencing** men, of enlightening them?*

This rather than joining a group, rather than acting as missionary or preacher or speaker or radical agitator—this in preference to political men?

*Is not this the function and service of **art** in society? Can we abandon art in such a time? Is it of so little power and worth?*

Throughout his life Goyen never cared for the idea of the artist in society or, for that matter, the artist in action—i.e., espousing social or political concerns, and especially if it was "for the sake of accumulating material for writing or 'experience' out of which to write." For whom does one write? he asked. Either writing is a dialogue with the deepest, truest part of oneself (or one's beloved), or it is an address to an audience, in order to impress it or change it. Clearly he held the former view. He claimed never to have been touched by those American writers who were socially active in the world, nor did he feel he had anything in common with them:

I have never identified my work with any cause, nor sought causes, political or social, as sources, stimuli, material for my work. And, thankfully, have no aims or needs to instruct or change ways of political or social action in order to identify, justify, or liberate myself.

*The literature of self-regarding—subjective, autobiographical, etc.— seems to me to be no different or not as subjective and autobiographical as that of the group of that generation which made itself active in tempestuous areas of the world in order to write about **their** feelings in it, in order to report **their** eye's view of it, and to, at the same time, lament home and safety . . .*

*Words like materialism, democracy, socialism, do not work any force in literature. They only state, date, and document. For me, literature documents **lust**.*

It is no wonder we find him, in one letter, expressing lack of sympathy with the novels of Joan Didion. His view was that the writer must be concerned with human behavior in the real world as it exists—not so much with the surface causes, but with the deeper psychological ones. In the act of story-telling, he felt, the writer recovered "our ancient line and heritage of national spirit of a country—and all have a common source: legends, myth, human experience." The artist must "relate the past to the present and see the future through the meaning of this relationship— delved for and set down—a continuity under the temporal variations of human behavior: the larger, permanent meanings of daily fact and daily event and human daily action."

Goyen, who had lived in Europe, was especially concerned with the few provisions made in this country for the true artist, particularly one who is slow or is temporarily blocked: What is he or she to do in the meantime? What kind of jobs are provided? He saw both teaching and fellowship-chasing as "dangerous." Yet he realized that things were much the same for artists in other parts of the world as well, and he thought one should recognize it, accept it, and go on with his or her "true work." Above all, the artist should not let it make him become eccentric, "special," rebellious, precious, or "arty." These conclusions are somewhat ironic, in that the criticism most leveled at Goyen's fiction by his detractors was that it was too affected, too delicate, too refined.

He concluded that the writer must accept that his basic situation is isolation and, finally, alienation—"Not answering the knock at the door, not looking out the window, but alone in his bed, at his work of construction and reconstruction." His thoughts about the artist's need for privacy are vented in a letter to his friend Dorothy Brett, dated January 20, 1954. Elsewhere, in a letter to Zoë Léger of June 9, 1948, he says, "One doesn't create in a crowd."

I alluded earlier to problems of space. The reader should be aware of the quantity of Goyen correspondence which, over the decades, was released like a torrent from his pen and typewriter. The letters rarely are brief. One of the first printed here, to Archibald MacLeish, is fully four single-spaced typewritten pages long. Another, to an editor who had questioned the working title of one of Goyen's books, is an eight-page, single-spaced typewritten defense of the title (letter to Robert Linscott, March 14, 1951). And there literally are thousands of letters. A few figures will demonstrate. When I first wrote the Fondren Library at Rice University, Goyen's alma mater, to inquire whether the library had any

Goyen correspondence, the director replied, "I am enclosing a 16-page description and inventory of the Goyen letters in Rice's collection. As you will see, there are 582 letters to his family, 171 to William Hart, and 16 to Zoë Léger." When I queried the Harry Ransom Humanities Research Center, the research librarian conveyed that the center had "fifteen boxes of uncatalogued correspondence." These included 133 letters to Dorothy Brett and 47 to Willard "Spud" Johnson. And when I wrote the University of Maryland Library, the librarian reported that they had "138 photocopying images" of letters from Goyen to Katherine Anne Porter. Columbia University Library held, among other things, 93 Goyen letters and telegrams to agents, editors, and friends.

These figures are from only four of the many extant collections. I was to find other large collections in this country, letters to Margo Jones, James Laughlin, even myself. (Goyen and I were friends, or, as he put it in one letter, "best friends," from our first meeting on July 8, 1969, until his death on August 30, 1983.) In addition, there were large collections in Europe—in France (Patrice Repusseau, Maurice Coindreau), Switzerland (Elisabeth Schnack), and Germany (Ernst Robert Curtius).

Since nearly six hundred letters to his family are on file, one might ask why more of them are not represented here. The answer is found in the focus of this book. After having been rebuked by his family for allegedly writing *of* family in *The House of Breath* (1950), Goyen loyally wrote home about his finances, his travels, his health, even the weather. But rarely did he discuss his art after having to defend his first novel.

For all the availability of material, there nevertheless are certain regrettable lapses. Among these is a representation of Goyen's letters to his friend and mentor Stephen Spender. Sir Stephen initially wrote me, "I did have a lot of letters from Bill Goyen, but I think they were all destroyed or were lost." Later he wrote, "Bill's letters to me are certainly destroyed. We went through all the files of letters I have at home recently and found none from William Goyen, I am sorry to say." To compensate for that loss, Sir Stephen graciously agreed to write an afterword to this volume.

A second lost collection is that of letters to Goyen's wartime friend and postwar companion, Walter Berns. Professor Berns has written that theirs was not an epistolary friendship, and letters he had were of no interest. He has discarded them, feeling that his own memory of Goyen is best preserved in photographs and copies of Goyen's published work. Another companion, Joseph Glasco, says that he has no Goyen letters. One of Goyen's translators, Elisabeth Schnack, fell too ill to collaborate during the time letters were being gathered.

Letters to such celebrities as Samuel Barber, Truman Capote, Carson McCullers, Tennessee Williams, and Eudora Welty existed, but not one has been found. One explanation could be the hectic life-styles led by most of these people, life-styles which may have precluded the saving of archives. But that does not explain the absence of Goyen letters among Miss Welty's papers in the Mississippi State Archives. There are numerous mentions of letters to and from Miss Welty in this volume. And Goyen himself was distraught when he discovered in 1974 that his hundreds of letters to Frieda Lawrence had apparently been lost. Goyen had written to Angelo Ravagli, Frieda Lawrence's widower, to inquire about the location of his letters. Ravagli replied from Spotorno that he had given all of Frieda's material to E. W. Tedlock, Jr., who was researching a book. Goyen then contacted Tedlock, who responded: "I've never seen your letters—they were not among the papers Angie turned over to me, papers that were truly jumbled, as if he in his shock and despair had thrown them together very carelessly. I wonder if he might have burned or thrown away some of her papers without realizing their potential value, or, again, in a nihilistic gesture." Nor are there any letters which chronicle Goyen's feelings about her death in August 1956, though surely he must have written about it to others. Finally, another regrettable omission is the absence of letters to his wife, the actress Doris Roberts. These were all lost in a move from Manhattan to Los Angeles in 1978. The boxes of correspondence, together with boxes of Miss Roberts's phonograph record collection, were lost or stolen from the moving van.

But rather than lament what is missing, we should celebrate what has been saved. We have God's own plenty of William Goyen letters. This book begins with one to a young Houston friend, written when Goyen was a young student; it ends with a letter to a Houston friend written a month before Goyen's death. Two-thirds of the letters are from the period 1946 to 1954. After that time, Goyen became less of a correspondent. A number of factors account for this. In 1960, at the age of forty-five, he decided to begin teaching again, a job he stuck with until 1966, when he became an editor at the McGraw-Hill Book Publishing Company. Teaching, editing, depression, and alcoholism all took their toll. He published nothing during the McGraw-Hill years, which lasted until the latter part of 1971. Even his correspondence was greatly curtailed during this period. Then in the 1970s, when Goyen became visiting professor in the writing program at Brown University, the pace of writing and correspondence accelerated. In accepting that position he revised some of his earlier views on the role of the writer.

Goyen began as a modernist. There was something deeply modernist

(yet archaic) about his attitude toward the artist. No better example can
be found than in his extraordinary letter to Robert Linscott of March 14,
1951. He later revised some of these elitist views when he actively joined
the creative writing revolution taking place in universities across the
country. He accepted teaching positions at Hollins, Brown, Princeton,
the University of Houston, and the University of Southern California.
These positions gave him an audience and a sense of belonging at a time
when his books were out of print. In one letter he relates that he
autographed "Xerox copies" of his work at public readings because none
of his books could be found.

These letters reveal another undocumented aspect of Goyen's work—
his theatrical career. His plays and teleplays have not been published and
largely went unreviewed. Yet, especially in the 1950s, he devoted a great
deal of time and energy to these media.

Throughout his life and work and these letters, Goyen's sense of
humor prevailed. Even in his last years, knowing he was dying, he was
writing a comic novel about a Tex-Mex Tiresias, a "Mescan" who talks
about himself and other outcasts who pursue "escape." It was his humor
and his work and his music which preserved him so long as he lived. And
in these selected letters Goyen sings arias about art and spirit, loss and
recovery, dignity and beauty, the mystery in each of us which is waiting in
the night by the river that we will all surely come to.

---

insults and betrayals: Anaïs Nin, *The Diary of Anaïs Nin*, vol. 6, 1955–1966, ed. and with
a preface by Gunther Stuhlmann (New York: Harcourt Brace Jovanovich, 1977), p. 79.
injured and insulted: Truman Capote, *Answered Prayers* (New York: Random House,
1987), p. 60.
hadn't invented anything: Truman Capote, Preface to *Music for Chameleons* (New York:
Random House, 1980), p. xvi.
by Time *magazine:* Nin, *Diary*, p. 79.
2,000 dollars a week: Ibid., p. 63. The novel under discussion was *Half a Look of Cain*
(Evanston, Ill.: TriQuarterly Books, 1994).
my way: Mid-American Review 13, no. 1 (1992): 138.
writers of short fiction: Reginald Gibbons, "Redeemed in the Telling," *New York Times
Book Review*, November 6, 1983, p. 14.
stories of the century: Vance Bourjaily, "Words for a World," *New York Times Book
Review*, June 9, 1985, p. 28.
spurious association: William Goyen, "About the Author," in *In a Farther Country* (New
York: Random House, 1955), p. 184. This outburst may have been prompted by editor
Bennett Cerf's comparisons of Goyen with Capote. Random House published both.
See Goyen's letter of July 17, 1951, to Katherine Anne Porter.
endurance to survive: The Novel of the Future (New York: Macmillan, 1968), p. 182.

scarcely would want to: Robert Phillips, *William Goyen* (Boston: G. K. Hall, 1979), p. 32.

alone, in some room: Quotations and paraphrases taken from Goyen's notes under this title, housed at the Harry Ransom Humanities Research Center, University of Texas at Austin. Quoted with permission.

of which to write: Ibid.

documents lust: Ibid.

to Zoë Léger: Letter from Nancy L. Boothe, Director, Woodson Research Center, to R.P., June 14, 1989.

to Willard "Spud" Johnson: Letter from Cathy Henderson, Research Librarian, to R.P., April 25, 1989.

to Katherine Anne Porter: Letter from Blanche T. Ebeling-Koning, Curator for Rare Books and Literary Manuscripts, College Park Libraries, to R.P., May 25, 1989.

93 Goyen letters and telegrams: Letter from Bernard R. Crystal, Assistant Librarian for Manuscripts, to R.P., May 6, 1989.

destroyed or were lost: Letter to R.P., May 22, 1989.

sorry to say: Letter to R.P., June 10, 1990.

of no interest: Letter from Walter Berns to R.P., September 29, 1990.

no Goyen letters: Note from Joseph Glasco to R.P., December 17, 1990.

nihilistic gesture: Letter from E. W. Tedlock, Jr., to W.G., May 20, 1974.

the moving van: Letter from Doris Roberts to R.P., June 16, 1990.

surely come to: My closing paragraph is a paraphrase of Goyen's concluding paragraph in the last public speech he made, "Recovering: Writing and Healing," a paper presented at New York University, April 13, 1983. It was published under that title in the Writer at Work Series, Gallatin Division, New York University (1983).

NOTES ON THE TEXT

In the preparation of these letters for publication, the following guidelines have been used. Every letter but one is reproduced from an original, or from microfilm or a photostat of an original. The exception is the letter to Anaïs Nin, quoted from her published *Diary;* the original appears to have been lost.

Most letters are reproduced in their entirety, without editorial abridgement, except for many salutations and closings. Some deletions have been made for reasons of privacy of living persons. Where material is deleted, it is indicated by ellipses within editorial brackets. (Ellipses are a form of punctuation alien to Goyen's own letter writing.) Where clarity demands, abbreviations have been spelled out. In some letters repetitious closings have been silently deleted.

Each letter is preceded by an editorial headnote which gives its physical form and the number of pages. The following standard abbreviations have been used: TLS (typed letter signed), TL (typed letter unsigned), ALS (autograph letter signed), AL (autograph letter unsigned), TCS (typed card signed), and ACS (autograph card signed). Telegrams have been reproduced in their all-capitalized form.

Letters have been standardized: Positions of addresses, dates, salutations, closings, and signatures are regularized. Goyen's handwritten corrections and additions have been silently added. Italics have been used for all book, play, and magazine titles. Titles of shorter works—poems, stories, essays, speeches—appear within quotation marks. Goyen always capitalized and underlined the names of publishers. It becomes apparent that this was not always meant as an expression of respect. Publishers' names here have been printed in normal capitals and lowercase. Typographical errors have been corrected. Goyen was a good speller.

Occasional slips—usually in individuals' given and surnames—have been corrected. Editorial insertions appear within square brackets.

A small number of letters in the present edition have been published previously. These include letters to Zoë Léger and to Maurice Coindreau, in *Delta* 9 (November 1979): 49–99; letters to John Igo, in *Pax* 1 and 2 (1985–1986): 41–59; and letters to diverse individuals in *Mid-American Review* 13, no. 1 (1992): 109–126. A fourth group appeared in the fall of last year (1994) in *Shenandoah*, and two in *Gulf Coast* the same year. The other letters have not appeared in print. It has been my pleasure to bring them together.

ACKNOWLEDGMENTS

My greatest debt is to Reginald Gibbons, Literary Executor for the Estate of William Goyen, who suggested that I attempt this book in the first place, did footwork for me in Texas, compared my typescripts with the originals, and gave blanket permission to quote from the letters and unpublished journals.

Matthew Kutcher, Ed Ernst, and Fred Shafer provided me with hundreds of hours of fact checking, manuscript comparing, and word processing. This book would not appear in its present form without them. They and Dr. Gibbons have my utmost thanks.

Doris Roberts, Goyen's widow and heiress, has answered countless queries with patience and good humor and has subsidized the considerable cost of all photoduplication and microfilming of the letters.

Special thanks also go to the Research Council, the Limited Grant-in-Aid Committee, and the Office of Sponsored Programs of the University of Houston for a grant that made possible the indexing of this volume.

I wish to express my gratitude to the following persons and institutions for granting access to letters which they own or which are part of their holdings, and to those listed below who provided letters and photographs or information on the whereabouts of such items, or who identified correspondents and allusions or otherwise assisted in the annotation:

Daria Ague, Public Services, Beinecke Rare Book and Manuscript Library, Yale University; Beth Alvarez, Curator of Literary Manuscripts, Archives and Manuscripts, Papers of Katherine Anne Porter, University of Maryland at College Park Libraries; Gillian B. Anderson, Music Specialist, Library of Congress; Bridget Ascenderg, International Creative Management, Inc.; Elise Atkatz, Corporation of Yaddo; James Atlas, New York City; Don Bacardy, Santa Monica, California; Thomas W. Baker, Santa Monica, California; Walter Berns, John M. Olin University

Professor, Georgetown University; the late Leonard Bernstein, New York City; Nancy L. Boothe, Director, Woodson Research Center, Rice University; Kenneth Botnick, Red Ozier Press; Vance Bourjaily, Professor of English, Louisiana State University; Patricia Bozeman, Head, Special Collections, University of Houston Libraries; Dorothy Brett Papers, Center for Southwest Research, University of New Mexico General Library; Andreas Brown, Proprietor, Gotham Book Mart; Lynn Buck, Hampton Bays, New York; Paul Cadmus, Weston, Connecticut; Anne Caiger, Manuscripts Libraries, The University Library, University of California, Los Angeles; Hortense Calisher, New York City; Charlotte Capers, former Director, Mississippi State Archives, Jackson; Eve Caram, Los Angeles; Nione Carlson, Houston; Eleanor Clark, Redding, Connecticut; Walter Clemons, Long Island City, New York; William Rossa Cole, New York City; Stephen Connelly, Professor, Indiana State University; Bernard R. Crystal, Assistant Librarian for Manuscripts, The Libraries, Columbia University; Patricia Dale, Coordinator for Special Projects, Corporation of Yaddo; William Darried, Sherman Oaks, California; Carolyn A. Davis, Reader Services Librarian, George Arents Research Library, Syracuse University; Rodney G. Dennis, Curator of Manuscripts, The Houghton Library, Harvard University; Mitch Douglas, International Creative Management, Inc.; Erika Duncan, Sag Harbor and New York City; Robert Eason, Margo Jones Collection and Fine Arts Archivist, Dallas Public Library; Blanche T. Ebeling-Koning, Curator for Rare Books and Literary Manuscripts, University of Maryland, College Park; the late Albert Erskine, Random House, Inc.; Alexandra M. Eylie, Syracuse; the late Doris Frankel, New York City; Joan Seeger Fry, Duarte, California; Dana Gioia, Hastings-on-Hudson, New York; Robert Giroux, Farrar, Straus, and Giroux, Inc.; Joan Givner, Regina, Saskatchewan; Adrian Hall, Artistic Director, Trinity Repertory Company, Providence, Rhode Island; Wynn Handman, Director, American Place Theatre; Harcourt Brace Jovanovich, for permission to print a letter from William Goyen to Anaïs Nin; Charles Harman, Archivist, Amberson Enterprises; Thomas S. Hart, Thomas S. Hart Literary Enterprises; June Havoc, Wilton, Connecticut; Cathy Henderson, Research Librarian, Harry Ransom Humanities Research Center, University of Texas at Austin; the late James Leo Herlihy, Los Angeles; William Herrick, East Nassau, New York; William Heyen, Professor of English, State University of New York at Brockport; Dr. Barbara Heyman, Professor, Brooklyn College, City University of New York; Mary-Pat Hoffman, Dallas; Jeffrey Hoover, Curtis Brown, Ltd.; Patrick Houlihan, Executive Director, Millicent Rogers Museum, Taos, New

Mexico; Peter Howard, Serendipity Books, Berkeley, California; James Hutson, Chief, Manuscript Division, Library of Congress; John Igo, San Antonio; Rebecca Jabdow, Photocopy Office, University of California, Berkeley; Victoria Jones, Manuscript Curator, Special Collections, The Library, University of Oregon; B. Kelber, Dipl.-Bib., Universitäts-bibliothek, Bonn, Germany; Perry Knowlton, President, Curtis Brown, Ltd.; Michael Kowal, Professor, Department of English, Queens College; Floria V. Lasky, Fitelson, Lasky, Aslan, and Couture; James Laughlin, New Directions Publishing Corporation; Claude Le Moine, Public Service Branch, National Library of Canada; Leonard E. Le Sourd, Associate Publisher, Chosen Books; Lyle Leverich, New York City; Shelley List, CBS Entertainment, Studio City, California; Linda J. Long, Public Services Manager, Department of Special Collections, Stanford University Libraries; David M. Markson, New York City; Special Collections, University of Maryland at College Park Libraries; Allen Maxwell, Southern Methodist University; William Maxwell, New York City; Kenneth McCormack, Doubleday and Company; Steve Miller, Red Ozier Press; Rosemary Mirurelli, Corporation of Yaddo; Robin Moody, Daedalus Books; Timothy D. Murray, Associate Librarian, Special Collections, University Library, University of Delaware; Naomi Shihab Nye, San Antonio; Joyce Carol Oates, Roger Berliner Professor, Princeton University; Helen Olson, Research Librarian, Katonah Village Library, Katonah, New York; Edward J. Osowski, Houston; Peter Owen, London, England; Palaemon Press, Ltd.; Paul Peralta-Ramos, Taos, New Mexico; Francesca Pitaro, Manuscripts Specialist, Rare Books and Manuscripts Division, New York Public Library; Anatole Pohorilank, Philadelphia; Laurence Pollinger, London; Jean F. Preston, Curator of Manuscripts, The Library, Princeton University; Roberta Pryor, Literary Agent, New York City; James Ragan, Director, Professional Writing Program, University of Southern California; John Rechy, Los Angeles; Rex Reed, New York City; Professor Patrice Repusseau, Laval, France; Stewart Richardson, New York City; Carol Roark, Archivist, Texas/Dallas History and Archives Division, Dallas Public Library; Anne Roiphe, New York City; Ned Rorem, New York City; Frank Rosengren, San Antonio; the late Michael Rubin, San Francisco; Raphael Rudnik, New York City; Sheila Ryan, Curator of Manuscripts, Morris Library, Southern Illinois University; James Scheville, Providence, Rhode Island; Frau Dr. Elisabeth Schnack, Zürich, Switzerland; Douglas Schwartz, Witter Bynner Foundation; Barbara Sheffert, Special Collections Assistant, Woodson Research Center, The Fondren Library, Rice University; Steven Siegel, Library Director and Archivist, Ninety-second Street

YMHA, New York City; Anne Simmons, Lexington, Massachusetts; Del Singleton, Library Director, William Inge Collection, Independence Community College, Independence, Kansas; the late Oliver Smith, Brooklyn and North Salem, New York; Raymond J. Smith, Publisher, Ontario Review Press, Princeton, New Jersey; Cindy Smolovik, Margo Jones Collection, Dallas Public Library; Carol Southern, Editor, Clarkson A. Potter; Elizabeth Spencer, Chapel Hill, North Carolina; Sir Stephen Spender, London, England, and Maussane, France; Albert Stadler, Executor, Estate of Howard Moss; Max Steele, Chapel Hill, North Carolina; Daniel Stern, Houston; Marion Strode, Assistant Librarian, Chester County Historical Society, West Chester, Pennsylvania; Gunther Stuhlmann, Author's Representative, Becket, Massachusetts; Barbara Unger, Rockland County (New York) Community College; Jack Valenti, President, Motion Picture Association of America, Inc.; Cynthia Vartan, New York City; Samuel S. Vaughan, Senior Vice President and Editor, Random House, Inc.; Ralph F. Voss, University of Alabama, Tuscaloosa; Christine Weidlick, Bibl.-Amtm., Universitätsbibliothek, Bonn; Eudora Welty, Jackson, Mississippi; Frankie W. Westbrook, former Sponsoring Editor, University of Texas Press; James P. White, Writing Program, University of Southern California; Patricia C. Willis, Curator of Literature, Beinecke Rare Book and Manuscript Library, Yale University; Melanie Yolles, Manuscripts Specialist, The Research Libraries, Rare Books and Manuscripts Division, New York Public Library; Marguerite Young, New York City; Lois Parkinson Zamora, Houston; and Mark Zipoli, Los Angeles. Special thanks to Dr. David Stam and Mark Weimer, Bird Library, Syracuse University.

Letters to Dorothy Brett on pages 316–317, 320–321, and 325–326 are from Dorothy Brett Papers (MSS 494 BC, Box 1, Folder 44), Center for Southwest Research, General Library, University of New Mexico.

Two books have been especially helpful in the identification of certain individuals in Goyen's circle. These are Helen Sheehy's *Margo: The Life and Theatre of Margo Jones* (Dallas: Southern Methodist University Press, 1989), and E. W. Tedlock, Jr.'s *Frieda Lawrence: The Memoirs and Correspondence* (New York: Alfred A. Knopf, 1964).

In the location of elusive letters, I have had the remarkable energies of Kathleen Manwaring, Archives and Manuscripts Supervisor, George Arents Research Library, Syracuse University. Additional material was located by Edwin Gallaher, former Program Coordinator, Creative Writing Program, University of Houston. Special appreciation goes to Jan McInroy, Manuscript Editor, University of Texas Press. Thanks to all.

R.P.

CHRONOLOGY

This chronology builds upon that compiled by Reginald Gibbons, published in *William Goyen: A Study of the Short Fiction* (Boston: Twayne Publishers, 1991). It in turn was based, in part, on the chronology in my *William Goyen* (Boston: Twayne Publishers, 1979). The reader will notice numerous discrepancies from both, however. In accumulating and studying Goyen's letters—almost all of which were dated—I became aware that certain dates and events had been misrepresented or misremembered in earlier conversations with the author. For example, Goyen's translation of Albert Cossery's *The Lazy Ones* (which was published without a copyright date) had been dated by me as 1949 and by Gibbons as 1950. It is now apparent that the book was published in 1952. Gibbons had Goyen living "off and on for a year" in London in 1949, when actually the writer did not arrive there until the autumn of that year. The film version of "The White Rooster" premiered in 1953, not 1955 or 1957 as previously cited. Goyen wrote his lyrics for the film *The Left-Handed Gun* in 1957, not 1955. And both earlier chronologies had Goyen traveling to Germany in 1961 and not returning until 1963. His correspondence reveals that he was there a much briefer time. In conversation, Goyen liked to mythologize his German experience; it was perhaps important to him to feel so well accepted in that country, since he felt so ill-treated in this one.

1894	Birth of father, Charles Provine Goyen, in Crystal Springs, Mississippi.
1896	Birth of mother, Mary Inez (Emma) Trow, in Trinity, Texas.
1915	(Charles) William Goyen born April 24 in Trinity, Texas.
1923	Father moves family briefly to Shreveport, Louisiana, then to 614 Merrill Street, Houston, where Goyen will grow up.

1928–1932   Attends Sam Houston High School.

1932–1937   Attends Rice Institute, works part-time at Houston Public Library.

1936   Meets Margo Jones in the fall, joins the Houston Players, performs in dramas under her direction.

1937   Receives B.A. in literature from Rice, having taken prizes in both playwriting and short-story writing.

1937–1939   Pursues graduate studies at Rice Institute.

1939   Receives M.A. in comparative literature from Rice. Enrolls in Ph.D. program at University of Iowa, drops out after three months. Returns to Houston and teaches at University of Houston. Receives draft notice, enlists in the Navy.

1940   Serves in Houston in a Navy recruitment office. Attends Midshipmen's School at Columbia University in New York City.

1941–1945   Serves as officer on the aircraft carrier *Casablanca* in the South Pacific. Begins writing first novel. Is hospitalized in 1945.

1945   Receives discharge from service. Leaves for California by car with Walter Berns, friend from the Navy. Stops at Taos, New Mexico, in March and meets Frieda Lawrence. Stays in Taos, builds house on land in El Prado given him by Frieda Lawrence.

1946   Devotes full time to writing. First acceptance of fiction for publication, "The Evil," which appeared in *The Illiterati* 5 (1948): 3–4.

1947   Acceptances of "The White Rooster" and "A Parable of Perez." Meets James Laughlin. Travels to California with Berns. Meets Katherine Anne Porter in August.

1948   Works part-time as script reader in Dallas for Margo Jones. "Four American Portraits as Elegy" published in *Accent*. Meets Stephen Spender. Moves to Napa, California, in August, intending to teach at Reed College. Job falls through. Meets Eudora Welty in the autumn. Receives *Southwest Review* literary fellowship. Returns to Taos.

1949   Lives in London in the autumn, visits Paris. Completes first novel, *The House of Breath*. Is hospitalized at end of year for knee injury.

1950–1951   Leaves British hospital in February, returns to New York. Lives in New York, Chicago, and Houston while writing stories for *Ghost and Flesh*. Publication of *The House of Breath* on August 9, 1950. Receives MacMurray Prize for best first novel by a Texan. Fellow at Yaddo. Beginning of affair with Katherine Anne Porter.

1952   *Ghost and Flesh* published. Wins a Guggenheim Fellowship. End of affair with Porter. Translation of *Les Fainéants* (*The Lazy Ones*) published. Meets the painter Joseph Glasco.

1953   Finishes *Half a Look of Cain*. Film version of "The White Rooster" premieres in Princeton. Publishes "The People of Joseph Glasco," text for an exhibition catalog, Catherine Viviano Gallery, Manhattan.

1954   Stage adaptation of *The House of Breath* produced off-Broadway. Wins second Guggenheim Fellowship, lives in Rome and Naples.

1955   *In a Farther Country*, second published novel. Lives in New York. Play, *The Diamond Rattler*, produced in Boston. *Whisper to Me*, play adaptation of his story "The Letter in the Cedarchest," adapted by Greer Johnson, produced by Margo Jones in Dallas and New York. Begins five-year teaching stint at the New School for Social Research. Death of Margo Jones.

1956   Death of Frieda Lawrence.

1957   *The House of Breath* (play) produced in Manhattan at Circle in the Square. Moves to Bucks County, Pennsylvania. Travels to Hollywood to write lyrics for the film *The Left-Handed Gun*.

1958   Release of *The Left-Handed Gun*. Sells his house in Taos.

1960   *The Faces of Blood Kindred*, second story collection, published. *The Diamond Rattler* produced in Boston. Quits teaching job at the New School.

1961   Travels in Germany as guest of State Department. Two television plays produced, *A Possibility of Oil* on CBS TV and *The Mind* on ABC TV.

1962   Begins teaching position at university in Kiel, West Germany. Suddenly returns to United States in the spring.

1963   Receives Ford Foundation Grant for Theatre Writing. Fourth play, *Christy*, produced in New York with actress Doris Roberts. Marries Roberts on November 10. *The Fair Sister*, third novel, published.

1964–1965   Teaches at Columbia University.

1965   Begins book of memoirs, *Six Women*.

1966   Publishes two critical commentaries, *My Antonia* and *Ralph*

Ellison's Invisible Man. Assumes duties as Senior Trade Editor for McGraw-Hill publishers.

1968   Death of father on July 11.

1969   Playwright in residence, Trinity Square Repertory Company, Providence, Rhode Island. *The House of Breath, Black/White* produced.

1970   Visiting professor in the writing program, Brown University.

1971   On staff of Southwest Writers' Conference, Houston, in July. Begins *A Book of Jesus*. Leaves McGraw-Hill on October 29 to write full-time.

1972   Residency at Brown University.

1973   *A Book of Jesus* published. Again at Southwest Writers' Conference and Brown University.

1974   Fourth novel (*Come, the Restorer*) and *Selected Writings of William Goyen* published. Musical *Aimee!* (based on the life of Aimee Semple McPherson), with book and lyrics by Goyen, produced in Providence. Visits Paris and Madrid in September with wife and stepson. Teaches at Brown.

1975   *The Collected Stories* and Twenty-fifth Anniversary Edition of *The House of Breath* published. Gives address at Trinity University in San Antonio. Moves to Los Angeles from Manhattan in June.

1976   *Nine Poems* published in limited edition of 226 copies. Undergoes operation for detached retina. Writer in residence at Princeton University. *Paris Review* interview published.

1977   Receives Distinguished Alumni Award from Rice University. Returns to Princeton to teach.

1978   "William Goyen: A Bibliographic Chronicle," by Clyde Grimm, published. Terminates teaching at Princeton. Divides time between New York and Los Angeles. Undergoes operation for dupetrends. Delivers lecture at Houston Public Library, sponsored by the National Endowment for the Humanities.

1979   *Arthur Bond* published in limited edition of 230 copies. Special William Goyen Issue of *Delta*. *William Goyen*, by Robert Phillips, published. Is diagnosed as having lymphoma.

1980   *Wonderful Plant* published in limited edition of 160 copies. Has operation on left hand. Death of Katherine Anne Porter.

1981   *Precious Door* published in limited edition of 115 copies. Teaches in spring semester at University of Houston.

1982   Is hospitalized in Los Angeles and released in remission. *TriQuarterly* interview published.

1983   Lectures in April at New York University on "Recovering." *New Work and Work in Progress* published in limited edition of 200 copies. Is hospitalized again in Los Angeles in summer. Dies on August 29. *Arcadio,* fourth novel, published in October.

1985   *Had I a Hundred Mouths: New and Selected Stories 1947–1983* published.

1986   *William Goyen: A Descriptive Bibliography, 1938–1985,* by Stuart Wright, published by Meckler Publishing. "A propos de 'Suite Funèbre I' de Francis Mockel" published in exhibition catalog, *Francis Mockel, Gravures,* Centre de Développement Culturel de Boulogne-Sur-Mer.

1991   *William Goyen: A Study of the Short Fiction,* by Reginald Gibbons, published. *William Goyen. Cahier coordonné par Patrice Repusseau,* with a preface by Claude Mettra, published by Le Castor astral in France. "Marvello" chapter of *Half a Look of Cain* published in spring issue of *Southern Review.*

1992   William Goyen Issue of *Mid-American Review* published, including excerpts from *The Diamond Rattler* and three essays by Goyen.

1994   *Half a Look of Cain* published and *Arcadio* reissued.

1995   *William Goyen: Selected Letters from a Writer's Life* published.

Goyen as a miserable, unshaven ensign, early 1940s. Courtesy of Walter Berns.

Goyen and Walter Berns in
Taos, late 1940s. Courtesy of
Walter Berns.

Goyen's adobe house in Taos.

Stephen Spender, Frieda Lawrence, and Goyen at the Lawrence Ranch.

Dorothy Brett.

Dorothy Robinson,
Frieda Lawrence,
Walter Berns, and
Goyen in Taos.

Dorothy Robinson and
Goyen, 1949. Courtesy
of Walter Berns.

Margo Jones, "The Texas Tornado." Courtesy of the Jones Family Archives, Richard and Bea Jones and Charles Jones, Houston, Texas.

The jacket photograph, later cropped, for **The House of Breath** *(1949).*

Joe Glasco in Alphonso Ossario's Paris studio, 1950. Courtesy of Contemporary Arts Museum, Houston, Texas.

Goyen in a 1952 publicity shot. Photograph by Edward A. Bourdon. Courtesy of Random House, Inc.

Katherine Anne Porter and Goyen in 1951. Photograph by Arthur Long. Courtesy of Special Collections, University of Maryland Libraries.

Goyen in Manhattan studio, 1952. Opposite page, top left: Goyen's German translator, Ernst Robert Curtius, June 1952. Top right: Goyen's French translator, Maurice Edgar Coindreau. Bottom: Doris Roberts and Goyen at the time of their marriage in November 1963. Photograph by Ben McCall. Courtesy of Doris Roberts.

Goyen in his Los Angeles backyard, 1983. Photograph by J. Gary Dontzig. Courtesy of Doris Roberts.

William Goyen

Selected

Letters

from a

Writer's

Life

ONE

Houston, Texas
Wed. afternoon
[March 3, 1937]

Dear Bill:

[. . .] These are words I have to constantly pound into my mind: "Be yourself!" I have never known how to conduct myself around people; I am just beginning to learn. I like people, I need them—yet when I am with them I become timorous, afraid, incapable. One of my experiences in "combatting" people has been the desire to assert myself strongly, either in the disguise of what I am not, or in the guise of MYSELF, exalted, omnipotent—egotism. These two reactions are the most commonplace ever indulged in. I watch people with inferiority complexes, people who are abnormal in various ways, people who are introverted by some strange quirk of nature or incident. They all react in either of these two guises.

Bill, it's so simple to be one's self. Now, I'm writing this to myself as well as to you; I often preach, for my own good as well as for my object's. I have all the problems you have; every-one does. It's up to you, to me, whether you and I will go down with these problems, or rise above them. That's what living is: it is a dynamic process, a constant building, destruction, birth, death. Bewildered at times, I have a tendency to give up the whole thing and drift along with the current. But I always drift into a barrier, an obstacle that knocks me to my senses and sets me immediately swimming in the opposite direction with all my mad strength. Thank God for that! I want to be in the swim of things, not sitting on the outside, aloof from all that's going on. And that's what we are doing when we hold ourselves away from people—the common people—the man on the street. We've got to get right in the middle of things and touch and mix with everyone concerned. It's only then that we can know what's real and true about this business we call living. Then we are capable of understanding life; then we are human.

I want to do more than be able to get along with people: I want to be one of them, one with them. I've tried to exist apart from them and I've found no peace; it won't work for me. It's true they are prejudiced, critical, narrow. But am I not prejudiced, critical, narrow if I isolate myself?

It's almost unfair that some of us were made different from the general run of people. It hurts deeply; it's a wound that's always fresh and certainly not self-inflicted. But wounds can be healed. Have you ever seen a dumb cat or dog humbly lick his horrid wounds for hours after someone has inflicted that wound with brutish hatred or ignorance? Those wounds have healed. Yes, there are scars always left, but, oh, I had rather be one of those kind, not so dumb as even cats or dogs, who strive assiduously to heal their wounds, silently and alone in some dark secret place, than to be as some who never allow their wounds to heal. Those kind keep their wounds open and raw. They expose them to the dull wind and to passersby, shouting to them, "Here, I have a wound; it stings, it bleeds!"

And what's so crazy about the whole business is the fact that we are not compelled to do a thing. It's up to us to do as we like, or choose. That's where intelligence comes in. Perhaps that's where religion plays a part, also.

All of which says that I, too, am fighting Indians every day, just as you, Bill. But it's not going to be a blind fight if I have anything to do with it, and most certainly I do have very much to do with it. We've got to know where we are going, know what we would have ourselves be, and then go after it with all the power and madness that's in us. And think how much greater a victory it will be when we have achieved something, even with our petty handicaps and frailties! It's something glorious that can be fashioned out of something crawling and hideous. I'm going to see what my hands can make out of it.

Thanks very much for the Gauguin. You know how much I like his things. It was very nice of you to denude your portfolio for me. My play which has been so often promised you is now being read by a committee of the Current Literature Society (!) with the possibility of being produced by them sometime in April. I'm afraid they will question the subject matter. Anyway, when it is returned, I swear you'll get it.

Plato

William M. Hart: (1916–1986). Goyen's good friend and coworker at the Houston Public Library, where Goyen worked during some of his years at Rice University. After he left the library, Hart worked at Brown's Book Shop. Goyen's correspondence with Hart was voluminous; there are 171 letters from Goyen to Hart in the Fondren Library, Rice University, from 1937 to 1973, only a few letters having been written after 1960.
1937: Goyen was a senior majoring in literature and languages at Rice University (then Rice Institute). He was twenty-two.
my play: Unidentified.

Tuesday evening
Ten minutes to eleven
[March 31, 1937]

Dear Bill:

I suppose you are thinking that you are not going to hear from me. I have been busy; tonight I went to a French lecture (which was very interesting: I love French) and now that I am home, I must study for a few hours. However, if I do not write tonight I don't [know] when I shall get to it for I have loads to dispense with before the week is through.

Your play is beautiful as I told you over the phone. It's poignant, exquisitely beautiful like the flowing of a tiny, clear brooklet off from the noise and monotony of big, slow, ugly rivers. And it's just as musical. But I'm afraid many people wouldn't say that, outside your circle or peculiar (not in the derogatory sense) friends. I should love to see it danced; then it would be truly beautiful, and for most anyone. I suppose all this reverts to just what one believes a play should do and say through what medium.

I don't know just yet what my medium would be if I were to write. Yes, I say, "if I were to write." For perhaps if I can live wholly and fully I shan't *have* to write. Then what I do write will be truly real and easy flowing: it will be life itself. Why does one write? To disgorge burning emotion? perhaps; to ease a longing, to reach a dream? perhaps. But surely and principally, one writes to help people, to inspire people, to teach people, to ennoble people: a thing which does not always come about through the indigent functioning of life. Your play is to be dreamed, but not spoken. See life, Bill; *know* life. Then what you write will be incisive, it will be straightforward, it will mean something to the poor brute who has not your intelligence but who does have some of your imagination, some of the stuff of your dreams. To dream, to long for something is a universal attribute of man; but to translate that intangible into something real, placable tenets—words, that is only the attribute, the gift, the ability of a few.

Right now I want to learn what living means; the more you think about it the greater a thing it becomes. The borders of life are always shifting for the intelligent, the thinking person. They can expand to infinity; they can shrink to the size of an egg so that they cramp the very brain that will not think. Somebody said, "*You* are the window through which you see the world." Think of it! These are two eyes: my passport to this world. And if I look through the eyes of someone else? If I see blindly?—don't you see the tremendous responsibility that exists in just living? So I want to take advantage of it; so few people do, Bill. What is worse than to live deluded, mistaken, under misapprehension?

Why all this? For what end? I'll swear I can't say. To write? To create? Perhaps, but not positively. I don't know, yet. But to *know*, that's what comes first.

Bill I wish you could read French. Sometimes I just sit down and write for a long time in French; it just seems that I can express things I feel only in French at times. I wrote two or three pages once on the refutation of the saying "La vie n'est pas belle" which says that life is not beautiful. I wish you could read it. Why can't I believe that life is ugly? To me, if to anybody, it should be; in fact it appears so many times. But something won't let me believe that. I find that in spite of my awful predicament, my tragedies and disillusions, I am, at bottom, full of infinite hope. That I must admit, though I am usually very melancholy and doubtful and superficially skeptical.

What is the meaning of all this digression and rambling? It's the best way of telling you what sort of person I am; I can't mechanically relate autobiography. So I'll stop and let you catch your breath and scratch your head [. . .]

B.

———————————————————

your play: Unidentified.

To Joe O'Rillion
TLS-2

614 Merrill Avenue
Houston, TX
May 26, 1940

Dear Joe:

To write so soon is probably both an insult and an indecorum; I had thought to wait until I heard from you, for you said you were to write me "right away." Excuse my not waiting.

I have felt wretched since Friday evening when I refused to allow you to go along with me and my friend to the recital. Even fifteen minutes after you left me at Texas Avenue and Main, I felt it. Seeing you the next evening extenuated, briefly, that compunction, but it returned again.

Now, that feeling has attracted to it diverse kinds of feelings and emotions, and a whole wretched cluster gnaw at me. I am not sure, but I believe your fine and melancholy singing Saturday night has had something to do with it. Also, of course, many things we said together at Alt Wien.

You see, I am an emotional person, too intensely so for my own good. I am the victim of feelings, sharp poignant incidents, and the like. Not for a long time have I felt any thing so poignantly as that meeting and its implications. I had foresworn ever mentioning it—at least until a little time could pass over and so attenuate it and draw out a little of its poignancy, its power. But, you see, unfortunately I have not waited. For I am a terribly confused person, awfully confused, one who whirls around in an anguishing vertigo most of the time. I need a few fine people to clutch me, stay me briefly, allow me to gain my equilibrium and draw things out of me. I do not have enough such fine people. I think you did that for me Friday evening. Now I have begun to whirl again. And I am obsessed [*sic*] with the fear that what little I have that is good may be dissipated by that vertigo, for it wears one down until he is no good. Everywhere I look for stays. I believe teaching will be a great and relatively permanent stay if I can but get into it before I reach eternal dizziness and aberrance. Then I can write, but it is so hard now. It's like turning round and round for long minutes on end and then attempting to study the reflection of something beautiful in a clear pool: though your body is still, your head and mind are still revolving and you only see confusion, vague figures and muddled colors. Everything else is whirling round and so you realize the danger of finally coming to the conviction that all is chaos and vertigo. For I and you and the other person are the *primum mobile* which sets the whole world, all the other spheres, in motion. *They take their motion from us,* and the motion can be beautiful and good and true only insofar as our impelling motion is beautiful and good and true. Do you see what I mean? [. . .]

Joe O'Rillion: Houston friend who later became a clergyman on the West Coast.
614 Merrill Street: Goyen's family home in Houston since 1923. He had attended Rice University in Houston (1932–1937), took an M.A. there in 1939, and enrolled in the Ph.D. program at Iowa. After three months he returned to Houston (see letter of January 16, 1946). He currently was teaching at the University of Houston.
my friend: William M. Hart.
Alt Wien: Restaurant in Houston.

[Houston, TX]
June 1940

Mr. MacLeish:

We are the young men who aspire to the profession of letters in our time, the young men who, at this period, are yet in the preparatory stages for that position in the world. Perhaps you would like to hear from us, who walked the campuses and sat in the lecture halls and the libraries of the universities while the rumble of the world, riding by on rotten wheels, was deafened by the calm unshaken words of the scholars echoing the voices of the irrelevant past. Since you mention, and indeed, gravely indict the scholars in the universities, lament the absence of the man of letters in our time, perhaps the position in which we find ourselves as potential scholars and writers will serve to throw some light on the dilemma which now exists and which promises to continue, and clarify its failure. For we are the scholars of tomorrow, inchoate men of letters, if there are to be any. We are those who depend upon the academies of learning for preparation for the profession to which we aspire. Let us tell you about ourselves.

Desiring to prepare ourselves for the position of letters, we naturally sought the universities. For within us, Mr. MacLeish, lay the burning urge to write and to teach. Within us, early, came the call to keep the fires of the mind burning and exuding warmth. As scholars we would redis-cover and lay bare the work of man's mind lying up from the past, for by acquainting ourselves with the past we could equip ourselves to question the present which grows out of it, and make roads toward the future. As writers, we would make articulate unwritten human experience, perpetu-ate the work of man by elucidating it. By use of the word we would give permanence to man's hope, man's struggle on a darkling plain, and contribute to the preservation and enhancement of man's inherent dignity, which is threatened in every age and most direly in our own. As teachers, we would train those behind us to take our places and thus fortify the reliances of mankind against ignorance and error, destruction and defamation. As scholar, writer, teacher, then, we would act as the antennae of the race. And we felt the gloriousness of our task and the awfulness of it, and the terrible obligation it entailed.

So we came to the colleges, Mr. MacLeish. Before us, crowned with the calm cool laurels of scholarship, stood the professors, reading out to us the cold dry lecture notes, warning us of imminent examinations. There was blasphemy of faiths, slaughter of innocents, terrorization of truth and justice in the world outside, but the breath of the infirm world did not penetrate the walls of our citadel. It was cold in the classrooms, Mr. MacLeish; cold, and we were lonely and hungry. We were on an island lost in the sea, a fortress whose moats drew up disdainfully when the importunate footsteps of the world were heard approaching. Surely, we thought, these men, these minds before us and around us will turn themselves to the beast and of their power and vision give combat and fury. They gave no fury, Mr. MacLeish, they gave no combat. They turned themselves to the peaceful anodyne of research and dispassionate study. For it seemed their hands were tied; it seemed they were afraid of betraying their sacred manuscripts and their traditional quietude. Was this the scholar? We turned away, disillusioned and bewildered. We pondered.

But we went on, Mr. MacLeish, past the Master's thesis and oral, up the path leading to the Ph.D. For we want to write, Mr. MacLeish. We feel that we have something to say, something that will not be hushed. Why choose the universities, then? Why choose the teacher's chair? The ivory tower has never appealed to us—not, at least, since we were sophomores. We wish to be men of action, and, having no interest or faith in the field of politics, nor ambition for the pulpit, we feel that the universities and the teaching chairs offer the greatest and most fruitful opportunity for action. And so we have continued. But we are troubled, profoundly troubled. Why?

We find little encouragement for the writer, the artist, and a preponderant bias for the pure scholar within the universities. And remember, we are that group, however small, which, as scholars and writers, wishes to profess letters. They are trying to teach us silence and dispassion but we will not be silent and dispassionate. And so—many of us are falling away. Falling away, disillusioned, bitter, intransigent. Many of us are seeking jobs elsewhere so that we may write. We feel that many of our writers of today whom you justly attack as deserters of the profession of letters have broken away just this way and for just this reason. They have a feeling of revulsion for the pure scholarship of the academies and have become, instead of men of letters, simply novelists and eremite poets and popular essayists. We do not desire this, yet how can we spend a year, two years, gathering and collating data and information on *Metascopy in Elizabethan England* when beyond the parapets of our institutions the souls of men are atrophying and their minds vitiating in lies and injustice, and we are burning to say something to them, something with the form of art and of its power and magnificence? For the ministers have failed, the legislators have failed, the philosophers have failed, and the social theorists have failed or compromised. Research in the seventeenth century gave us a feeling of paralysis. We could feel an invisible shell gradually enveloping us and we were mortally afraid that soon we would walk in the world like the deaf and the dumb and the blind, oblivious and insensitive to sight and sound. For we are anxious, Mr. MacLeish, to preserve the freshness of mind and heart; we are determined never to lose our consciousness, our awareness of ourselves and the world about us and its people; what we are, what we are about, what we are becoming. It is very hard, Mr. MacLeish, to descend the long dark well of scholarship down down full fathom five to the English Renaissance and return to the terrible face of the twentieth century with twentieth-century sensibilities and responsibilities. And so many have returned to the surface equipped with sixteenth-century sensibilities and respond like anachronistic mechanisms—hence their utter inadequacy and uselessness. Most of them have remained below, on the dark silent floors of the well, and for so long that cries of "hallo!" and "are you there?" from the surface can never reach or rouse them, our scholars whom you attack, our scholars who have failed. Perhaps the defeat and failure of the scholars is the result of the belief among them that it is their duty only to act as a bellows to keep the flame burning. But it is difficult to believe that one who feeds a flame and gives his life to its preservation could have no enduring love for that flame, could stand by and allow some evil Prometheus to rape it from him for a pernicious end: to snuff it out into utter darkness. We refuse to ally ourselves with those.

We find little stimulation in the world of the writers of our time. We emulate and respect very few. The majority of them are serving those of our time who inhabit the vacuums of the office buildings, the vertigos of the nightclubs, and the ivory towers of isolationism and complete indifference to man's fate and future. These writers are rooted in nothing deeper than their own shallow ambience, and in time they will slough off easily and wither away. Others whirl around in their own private orbits and evolve magnificent works of detachment—authors who stand at arm's length from the world and its creatures, their hands unsullied, neither laughing nor deriding. They simply write, and write splendidly, but we will have none of these, either. They are the other half of the man divided, of whom you speak, Mr. MacLeish, having nothing of the scholar in them, standing across the chasm from the scholar. We would bridge this chasm if we could, and so, some of us cling to the scholar's world.

Yet many of us have been driven from the universities, some to work with our hands, simply and quietly, others to labor free and uninhibited in the oil fields, and others to sit behind the drab desks in the offices. These dare not return to the institutions of learning. One of them says: "I am touching life now, moving among men of our time. And I am writing now. That is enough, as things are." This is the attitude of many of us. But there still remain those who will stay and fight for a future reunion of scholar and writer within the cloisters of the universities.

What about us, Mr. MacLeish? What about us? We feel acutely the division in the man of letters, the severance of the whole man into two opposing camps, scholar and writer. What hope is there for us in the universities? Until the two can be reunited we choose the artist, and from us will come the novels, dramas and poetry, created out of desperation and desolation. We shall expect little from the world of the scholars. And we shall look for men of letters among those like some of ourselves who have sought escape from the universities in order to keep scholarship alive in order to feed scholarship with art and life and so flower into a reunion that will produce men of letters; among the courageous and stubborn aliens living in strange out-of-the-way places and engaging in incongruous means of livelihood. We predict novels from the offices, poetry from oil-field riggers, and plays from civil service workers. We predict longer and duller articles in the learned periodicals. And we will not tremble when the scholars come into our theatres or turn the pages of our novels. For they will not be with us; they will not give up their souls to us, and we would have men surrender body and soul to us when they come into our created world. We cannot, we now know, be scholar *and* artist and continue to work in our institutions of learning, and if there is to be division we would not stand on the side of the pure scholars, for our world and our time are being shattered and shorn naked of all its splendid accomplishment because of their, the scholars' lassitude, lethargy, and complacency. And if our work goes down with our civilization, or if our civilization is destroyed before we have reached flower and maturity, we can go down in full knowledge that we were not on the side of those who chose not to choose and thereby chose and contributed to our destruction.

We believe, Mr. MacLeish, that the scholars of our time once felt as we do now, but they have forgotten, they forgot too easily what was their function and their service and so have failed and left us who come after them lonely and deserted. If it is not too late, Mr. MacLeish, we, the radicals, the liberals, the fifth-column traitors within the universities, will do something to rectify the scholar's error and to restore a lost and desecrated profession. If it is not too late.

William Goyen

1940: Goyen left his teaching job at the University of Houston. He enlisted in the
Navy and was working in a Houston Navy recruitment office.
Archibald MacLeish: (1892–1982). American poet and playwright who was the Librarian
of Congress, and an Assistant Secretary of State when this letter was written.
Since you mention: An open letter, perhaps unsent, titled "A Letter to Archibald
MacLeish/ After reading *The Irresponsibles*" and written in direct response to
MacLeish's book *The Irresponsibles: A Declaration* (New York: Duell, Sloan, and Pierce,
1940), in which MacLeish argued that the scholars and writers of his generation had
abdicated their responsibility to fight fascism and thus unwittingly had helped to
disarm and demoralize Western democracies.
little encouragement for the writer: Goyen was writing before the development of
creative writing programs within English departments.
fifth-column traitors: Reference to a group of secret subversives who attempt to impair a
nation's solidarity by any means at their disposal. The term had recently originated
during the Spanish Civil War (1936–1939).

To William M. Hart
ALS-2

Balboa, Canal Zone
Jan. 11, 1943

My dear Billy:

Your two letters came today, dated Dec. 6 and Dec. 21. I had my first
mail two days ago, and I have been here almost 3 weeks and away from
home (after my leave) over a month. The waiting was desperate.

What I have seen and suffered I cannot tell you now, but there will be
the time. In the meantime there are words, hard crystal words that fell
like hail the very first day I went aboard ship and began to wait until we
departed. The most miraculous thing has been happening in my mind
since that day I left for the sea: words have flowed so torrentially that I
have scarcely been able to find enough paper to catch them on. Something has been tapped.

Yes, there have been desperate and lonely days; some deadly quiet
hours in the night on the sea spent in fear and a feeling of cold isolation.
During those times my mind has performed such beautiful things: Long
continuous "movies" of remembering; the fingers of my mind have been
performing such delicate patchwork, piecing together the fragments of
past days. And there is a pattern to it all, Billy, although now our world is
such a shambles and so ruined. Thank God for my bitter nights long ago
and for my black despair, for out of that so much was sown, such a
foundation laid that no one could ever destroy. And now I am building on

it, painfully, oh how painfully, but building. One night as I lay on the ship in port I wrote you a long and candid letter, pouring out everything inside me, for I was afraid and despairing in a calm, controlled sort of way. Only when I finished did I realize that the Censors would not let it pass. I have kept it and one day you will read it.

Life here, on the surface, is mild and the country is beautiful, almost paradisal. I live in comfortable quarters and my work promises to be acceptable, although my duties are not clearly defined yet. There will be the sea, no doubt, but no one must know, and that means a hard, rough life. For the time being I have quite some leisure; indeed there is a leisurely existence here which calms me a little.

Christmas was strange and not Christmas, of course. I was not allowed to contact my family in any way until two days after Christmas, and that was anguish, for they had no idea where I was.

Did you find something for us at La Jolla? It is to be found, Billy, for I have caught it in so many places. It must be held, wildly, and it must be preserved. A final even flow will come, for there must be some meaning to what I have felt and seen. I say there *must* be meaning there, and I will find words. This is all such a great great thing.

You must write and tell me what you do, what you see. I shall need your letters.

Love,
Billy

Ens. Charles William Goyen, U.S.N.R.

Canal Zone: Goyen had received his commission in the U.S. Navy in Riverside Church, New York City, at the end of November 1942. On December 2 he flew home to visit his parents while on leave, and in late December he boarded the USS *Casablanca*, the ship he would serve on for the next two years.

"movies" of remembering: Goyen describes the origin of *The House of Breath* in his *Paris Review* interview: "I thought I was going to die in the war. I was on a terrible ship. It was the Casablanca, the first baby flattop. There were always holes in it, and people dying and it was just the worst place for me to be. I really was desperate. I just wanted to jump off. I thought I was going to die anyway, be killed, and I wanted to die because I couldn't endure what looked like an endless way of life with which I had nothing to do—the war, the ship, and the water. . . . I have been terrified of water all my life. I would have fits when I got close to it.

"Suddenly—it was out on a deck in the cold—I saw the breath that came from me. And I thought that the simplest thing that I know is what I belong to and where I came from and I just called out to my family as I stood there that night, and it just . . . I saw this breath come from me and I thought—in that breath, in that call, is *their* existence,

is that reality . . . and I must shape that and I must write about them—*The House of
Breath*" (*Paris Review* 68 [Winter 1976]: 64–65).
Billy: Hart was one of the few correspondents to whom Goyen signed his letters in this
way. The others were Spud Johnson, Margo Jones, Zoë Léger, and Peggy Bennett.
Even to his parents he was "Bill."

To Charles Provine Goyen
ALS-5

Thursday morn., July 1, 1943

My dearest Dad:

Received your letter yesterday afternoon and I am so sorry you feel so
blue and down. Those days come to all of us, dad, and I know how you
feel. But I want you to remember, when you feel this way, that you and all
of us have so much to be thankful for. The war hasn't really hurt any of
us, you know, and we are still safe and unharmed.

You have done your part already, Dad. After all, you have sacrificed
and slaved to get Sis and me and Jim through school, and now we are all
on our own, except Jim, and it looks like he, too, will soon be able to take
care of himself. You are certainly not an old man. But there's no reason to
believe that you should be doing something active in this war. This war is
for young fellows, very young fellows. Even I feel too old, sometimes, for
what it takes. It's up to you to hold things for us who are away, so we can
have something to come home to. When I think of all the suffering and
hardships these men and boys I know and talk to every day, have to go
through with, then I am a little ashamed of you when you complain, Dad.
I know life is dull there and that there's little to do at the office, but you
must be patient and try to realize that it won't always be this way. You
couldn't have done any more for me and the others if you had been a
millionaire, for what you did for me had nothing to do with money. We
never really needed anything we didn't have, and with all our misfortunes,
I think we came out very well. And now just because we are having a hard
time for a little while, you must remember how fortunate we have been,
and are, and try not to let it get you down. After all, Dad, I could really
complain if I allowed myself to, for I have certainly given up everything.
You know only too well that I am not cut out for the military life, and I
hate it. But I try to bear up under it and do my best. And all for you and
Mom. If I didn't have you two, then I simply couldn't go on. So remember how much I depend upon you, and remember that this is not the end
at all, but that we have a lot of living to do together yet. [. . .]

According to present plans, we do not expect to go to sea before *April 1944*, if we remain a training ship. So don't worry.

We have a fine group of officers aboard. There are about 60 of us, and we have about 800 enlisted men in our crew. So you see it is really a big ship. I have several good friends aboard, and you'd be pleased to know how they all fought and argued to get a room with me on the ship. Riordan, a Lt. from San Francisco, will be my roommate. My other good friends are: Ed Ferguson, a flier, from Chicago (he will be head of our "fighter plane" squadron); Marshall Cook, from Lansing, Mich.; Andy, of course; Bob Engram, from Palm Beach, Fla.; Bob Pyle, from Jersey City, and a graduate of Princeton. So you see, I am doing all right.

Now, Dad, please keep your chin up for me. Try to keep busy; play golf, work in the yard, and keep moving. *Don't* sit around and brood. And always remember that we have so much to be thankful for.

Take care of mom and Jim and Sis and the kids—and tell Sis it hurts me because she hasn't written in so long.

Be sweet and don't worry. I love you more than you realize and I'll always depend on your judgment and advice, for I'd be lost without you. Thanks for the help—and write me often. I love you, Dad.

Bill

Sis: Goyen's sister, Kathryn Goyen Stevenson (b. 1917), now of Arlington, Texas.
Jim: Goyen's brother, Jim (b. 1928), now of Richardson, Texas.
Riordan: Emmet F. Riordan was Goyen's shipmate on the USS *Casablanca*. He and his wife, Ann, became Goyen correspondents in 1946.

To William M. Hart
ALS-2

USS Casablanca
September 14, 1943

My dear Billy:

So much to say, so little time. And our letters are so few these days.

I am working very hard and under a terrific strain. And what I want to say cannot be written. I am no longer a letter-writer (if ever I was one).

I am very much interested in your comment on religion. I want you to find something, whatever it be. My faith has become even more intangible, but certainly more stolid (a contradiction perhaps, but then it is). Humility (ah bitter burden), goodness, kindness, and beauty take all manner of faces, but they have the same soul.

I have a thing in my head to write. I have words, many of which I have thrown down on paper, like a wrestler his opponent, which I want to use. But God how this ship imprisons the mind. I have seen some exquisite places, clouds, waters, mountains. And it is very cold where I have been. I have forgotten summer.

My future is dreadfully uncertain. I cannot say where I shall go or what I shall be doing.

But, you must write. I am simply speechless. And, anyway, you know what I am feeling and trying to do.

Take care, Billy, and write.

Love to you,
Billy

To William M. Hart
ALS-2

USS Casablanca
At Sea
Tues. evening, Feb. 22, 1944

My dear Bill:

Still plowing the waters and watching the planes in the sky. I have been anxious to get some word from you about your new station. I imagine you to be busy adjusting yourself—changes are always bad, yet we are a part of a vast change.

All day and last night I have been moving under a heavy burden on the mind, and since only you know the roots and blood of my relationship with Sterling Price, I must write you tonight that, after having been listed as missing after being shot down over Germany on Nov. 19, word has come that he is a prisoner of the Germans. I received the news last night. Today I have been remembering every word, glance and action of him as I knew and adored him, and it has been hard. For there is something in a relationship like ours, something in a first friendship, sordid and aborted and defeated and heartbreaking though it may have been, that will not let it be kicked in the face like a dead enemy, and keeps it rather sacred and inviolately beautiful and tender. You remember I kept dreaming of Sterling—dreamt so terribly of a disaster that I finally sought his address and found him in New York just preparatory to leaving for England. We exchanged three letters, two from over there, in which we somehow reestablished a friendship—or pulled it out of the debris, both anxious to keep something of it. My fourth letter, written in December, was never answered. There is no reason to be dramatic about a thing like this, but, simply and honestly, there is a part of me, star-eyed and completely unselfish, in a prison camp in Germany, and it hurts and I am restless and concerned for him. I must write his mother tonight, and if I can write him, I will. Now, now if I ever gave Sterling anything he will know it and remember it, as I often remember the little paste-jewels he gave me, which still sometimes glitter like diamonds.

And Velte's ship has been hit and no word from him since early December. This thing keeps hitting at one, over and over, and now the blows are coming home. And I would sing out something of it, but it must be poetry for there is no time for anything else and the words are too molten for sentences and the heart too wild for composition. More and more I realize that there is nothing but human relationship and without that there can be no greatness, no vision, no life. I am so full of heavy, rock-bedded words, Bill, that will not rise to be plucked out. More than that, I *see* so much now, see the symbols and the nature of things, yet I am still so blind and groping.

You would scarcely know me now, Bill. At times I am so irascible and will tolerate absolutely no compromise of those around me and I fling myself into muttering rages of attacks on tyrants and bigots. And through these recurring ordeals I have come, or am coming to a statement, at long last, of how I feel about this war, and what I believe it to mean. It may change again and again, but only in intensity, for that—in degree—is the only manner in which it has changed since last we talked about our beliefs and our convictions.

Please write me soon, Billy, and keep the faith.

Love to you,
Billy

At Sea: The aircraft carrier *Casablanca* sailed in the Pacific.
your new station: Hart was also in the service at this time.
Sterling Price: A Houston companion with whom Goyen apparently was involved before enlistment.
paste-jewels: Perhaps the genesis of Goyen's imagery for Folner in *The House of Breath*. In the funeral sermon, Folner is called "a jewel (a sequin! a rhinestone! a parure of great price!)" (New York: Random House, 1950), p. 126.
Velte: W. E. Velte, a fellow sailor from Upper Darby, Pennsylvania.

To Charles Provine Goyen
ALS-2

Nov. 25, 1944

My dearest Dad:
    How are all of you? Have had your letters and so glad to get them.
Have been way down under, but believe I am on the up-grade now. Guess
the combination of everything put together got me down to where I
couldn't fight back for awhile. Didn't want you and Mom to know, but
you seemed to guess it by my letters. Just keep Mom believing that I am
fine; if I ever know that she is worrying over me then I will break. There
for awhile I was in pretty bad shape. I'll have to tell you now. Had the Dr.
with me for several days—that terrible headache again—haven't had it for
several months. He says it's just nervous condition. All he could do was to
shoot me full of morphine and knock me out. Believe I'll be O.K. now.
Just can't afford to break this late in the game, and I *won't*. So please don't
worry. The worst is past and I wouldn't tell you if it weren't. Even passed
out cold one morning, right on the deck. That was when I really got
worried. Now be assured that I am O.K. now, and *don't dare mention* it to
Mom, or I'll never tell you anything again. I can't bear to think of
worrying you and her. I'll see this thing through, so help me.
    I'm wondering if we shouldn't start buying a bond every month. Can we
spare it from the monthly $75.00? Would sort of like to have something
put away, *yet I want to keep not less than $200* on hand in the bank at all
times. What do you think? Let me know and let's do what you think is best.
    Now remember, Dad, I'm no kid and I can take it, so if you get
emotional and worried over me, I'll just not tell you anything more. Your
health and Mom's, and your happiness, are the only things that matter to
me in this hell of a life. Be sweet, take care of everybody, and don't worry.

I love you,
Bill

To Toni Strassman
TLS-1

July 6, 1945

My dear Miss Strassman:
    I just received your letter and of course I am simply leaping with joy,
can hardly contain myself.

I hope you mean what you say, for, in reality, I am naive and open-mouthed concerning these matters. All I do know is that I can write and must, must, must, and if you can only help me (I mean, of course, only if I *deserve* help), then my God you will save my life.

I have been working terrifically hard for you and Armytage. I have just about finished a pretty long thing which I love very much and think good writing. I also have several other things which I am going to send along to you immediately.

Thank you so much for the things you and the others said. I just can't say what it means to me, for to write is everything, and if I fail there, then I fail in everything, everywhere.

I'll be waiting to hear more.

Sincerely,
William Goyen
Lt (J.G.) USNR
USS Casablanca

Toni Strassman: New York literary agent who agreed to represent Goyen. The Goyen-Strassman correspondence, held at the Columbia University Library, is extensive, from June 1946 to September 1947.
Armytage: Flora Armytage, author, a mutual friend who referred Goyen to Strassman.
a pretty long thing: This short unpublished work, titled "The Bright Burning Prize, Maria," is in the Harry Ransom Humanities Research Center, University of Texas, Austin.

To Toni Strassman
TLS-2

USS Casablanca
July 21, 1945

Dear Miss Strassman:
After four months' work on *Maria* I am through with her (and quite proud of her, withal). I am sending her right along as soon as we hit any kind of port way down here and God how I hope you like the story and can do something good with it. I am also enclosing another little thing which you may be able to use some way.

Needless to say, I am positively working my head off these days in a kind of demented ecstasy, and I really believe things are happening. I assure you that there will be a constant flow of stuff from me to you as long as you will have me.

One thing—I must ask you to excuse the few errors in typing, for you see I have to do it all by myself, under the most extreme conditions: temperatures over 100 degrees in a little reeking office, a wallowing ship, people looking over my shoulder, etc. I tell myself that if I can do anything at all under these wretched circumstances, then certainly I shall be able to do wonders once I am my own man again, and to hell with everybody else. [. . .]

So—I'll be eagerly awaiting word from you. Every time we hit a port, I shake until the mail arrives. Thanks so much for all you have done for me so far.

Sincerely,
William Goyen

To Toni Strassman
ALS-4

U.S. Naval Hospital
Ward 66-B
Oakland, Calif.
Sept. 25, 1945

Dear Toni:

I trust I may retaliate in calling you this; it is much better, less business-like.

Three of your letters finally found me yesterday—one of them containing the long-awaited word on Walt's stuff. I called him in Chicago immediately and read what has been said. He is learning, Toni, and he must have time and more writing behind him. But God he is powerful.

As for me, I have the infirmary blues! I am here for a rest and sort of check-up, preparatory, I hope, to leaving the Navy. It will probably be, as I see it, a few months before I am freed. I set Dec. 1 as the date, but it may be sooner. In the meantime, I have much free time in a quiet beautiful place on San Francisco Bay, and I shall get a lot of work done. The food is unbelievable—*milk* and everything! I shall emerge from the hospital grounds like a lion.

Thanks for all the good things you and others are saying. As for the magazines, wonder if somebody like *Horizon* or *Circle*, etc. wouldn't take some of the "experimental" stuff? I loathe the eccentric, arty, abstract publications. I feel dirty when I read them. They are off the track; they've lost contact with real things. I abominate them. We shall keep trying, and if they do not want me yet, then one day they will, for I have something to say and nothing can stop it.

As for *Maria*, whatever it be, prose poem (I hate appellations and tag descriptions of writing) or what, I knew what I wanted to do and, for one of the few times, I feel I did it there. I did not want characterization, for only feeling and reaction, vague and disturbed, mattered to me. I did not want even as much dialogue as the story has, which is sparse enough, for they (John and Maria) *felt* and spoke to *themselves* more than they did to each other or anybody. You know that sort of thing—when a relationship (not particularly amorous: it may be one of comrades, etc.) is made up of silences and wordless agitation. That is what I wanted to show. Maybe I didn't succeed. But I learned a lot.

I have a new thing, ready to be typed up in its final form, if I can only find a typewriter here. It is about a gypsy named Jandro, two chickens, and an old lonely man named Tom. And oh yes—many grasshoppers leap through it. I'll get it to you, soon.

Now—the novel. You shall have it shortly. It will not be finished; but you can see what it will be like. God I must do it right. Don't give me up—I'll get it to you.

When I am free—I don't know. There will definitely be no teaching again. That's out. I'd like to stay out here, work a little and mostly write—maybe in San Francisco, maybe in lower California. Maybe even Mexico. I'd like, as Flora has probably told you, to live in N.Y. awhile. But wherever it is, I shall write. So it doesn't really matter, I guess. [. . .]

Oakland, Calif.: After more than two years aboard the USS *Casablanca*, Goyen had been placed in a naval hospital. He was diagnosed as suffering from migraines. See letter to Toni Strassman, November 28, 1945.

Walt's stuff: Goyen had asked Strassman to consider representing his shipmate Walter Berns (b. 1919). Although frequently mentioned in Goyen's letters and sometimes co-signing these letters over the next two years, as they travel and live together in Taos, Los Angeles, San Francisco, Portland, London, New York, and Chicago, Berns does not figure as a correspondent in this volume. See Introduction.

Dec. 1 as the date: Goyen was released from the Navy in mid-December.

a new thing: "Grasshoppers," an unpublished, lost manuscript apparently not related to the much later story "The Grasshopper's Burden."

the novel: Goyen had begun an unpublished and never-to-be-completed novel, *Icarus*. See letter to Toni Strassman, November 22, 1945.

Oakland, California
September 29, 1945

My dear Billy:

Pardon the violent yellow—it's all I have.

I am supine on a very quiet bed here tonight, the cool breeze in my face, not sleepy at all, and pondering very hard my future.

As for my immediate future I cannot say much. After a week here, and many tests, there seems to be no real source of my disturbance evident in blood, urine, X-ray, etc. I am sure in my own mind that the famous and age-old headaches (remember them?) came so violently and so frequently (about one day out of five, toward the last) because of the terrific strain I had been under. The doctor seems to think so, too. It appears I shall eventually be recommended for shore duty stateside, for my point total is, as of Sept. 15, 45 1/2, and I need 49. But—I shall be moved up to Medford, Oregon on Oct. 2 for further rest and rehabilitation, since Oak Knoll Hospital has become an evacuation center for prisoners of war. I am very fond of Oregon and I shall enjoy my stay there, I feel sure. I count on at least another month, then leave, then new duty, until around Christmas, when I expect to be released. What will happen after that, is my concern now.

I have several possibilities. All of them are related to opportunities for writing. 1) Hollywood—(you will shrink at this)—mainly its theatre. I have a new and good friend there who has many good connections and wants very much to help me. But you are well aware of all the attendant ills and evils of that messy place. 2) New York. You no doubt heard of Toni Strassman's attempts to help me. Through Flora I got some stuff to her and she has had some encouraging success with the seven stories of mine. She was once with Viking Press and they say they want to see my novel, etc. 3) Teaching—which is a very weak third. It is a compromise, I feel, and I cannot allow it to drain me as it once did. I know, now, that I must go all out.

I want to know where Margo is and how I may reach her by letter. Will you please send me her address, or find it out for me?

And Billy, let us wait until we meet to talk about your late discharge. I am afraid you are taking it too strongly. I have tried to avoid discussing it, since I prefer to wait to talk to you. It only matters that you are fine, now, and that you must get fast to work.

I love San Francisco, but I have had only one chance to get over.

Tomorrow I shall go again. I should like to live there or in Southern California for awhile. But the family—you know all that. However, I have them somewhat prepared, if that is possible. Jimmy is away at school now, and they call to me in every letter. But I am strong now, virile and all my own, and I must keep it that way, Billy.

Please write again—but wait until you are sure of my new address. You might call mother after Oct. 2 if you have not heard from me. God I want to be free, but it is frightening. I have waited so long. This first week has been a bit bewildering. I keep seeking the womb again—that wretched, beloved, old crazy ship. God I have so much to say about all that—and I have a lot of it down. *The principle thing* is to stay *real* and alive and keen—not get distorted, perverse, exotic or unhuman.

Always,
Billy

---

terrific strain: Of being officer on a ship where men were always dying. Goyen was also terrified of water. See *Paris Review* interview.
new and good friend: Emmet F. Riordan was then living in Los Angeles.
Margo: Margo Jones (1911–1955). "The Texas Tornado," who was founder of the first modern professional theatre-in-the-round and first professional resident theatre in this country. According to her letter in support of a grant application for Goyen, he first met her in Houston about 1928, when he was in junior high school and she was producing William Saroyan's *My Heart's in the Highlands*. Goyen performed in the play, but according to Jones, "his real need then was contact with creative people." In 1936, Goyen joined her Community Players in Houston, and in the late 1940s when his courage and finances were both low, she employed him as a play reader for her theatre in Dallas. At that time they spent much time together. See Helen Sheehy's *Margo: The Life and Theatre of Margo Jones* (Dallas: Southern Methodist University Press, 1989).
Jimmy: Goyen's younger brother, Jim.

To William M. Hart
ALS-5

U.S.N. Hospital
Ward A-9
Medford, Oregon
Oct. 16, 1945

Dear Billy:
The ms. arrived safely and I signed the receipt, which you should have by now. Thanks very much.

By this time you should have my letter. There was no other possible answer, and, indeed, that answer was excessive. I should like to believe that what one says in such high passion he means and believes conclusively. Else I should never again be able to believe *anything* he said in the fires of passion and conviction. There was such an air of finality and finish about those words of yours. You have not changed, nor have your words. The same old wonder boy vocabulary.

That just about puts me alone, Willy. Alone except for one. His friendship was forged in the violent smithy of war and fear and shipboard craze. He stood by my bunk and held my body with his giant's hands when I was pretty goddamned ill and almost out of control. He *stood* there *one* complete night, and I don't know how many other hours of other days and nights. And he is fine and noble and right, and he believes unyieldingly in me. He would give his life for me. And, my friend, he is no lover (to use the vernacular); he is—have you ever really *known* the definition of this word?—a comrade. And that is worth all the lovers, men and women, I have ever known.

Did you think to sit your little self down in a chair somewhere and ask what might be "wrong" with Billy? Is he really in hospital "between stations"? Could it be that something has happened to the poor chap? After all, my dear that *is* right—he *has* been 26 months on a ship. Instead you whine and mewl and groan pity me, pity me, pity me. For Christ's sake, Bill, is Houston the *only* refuge for you? Why did you allow yourself to be drawn back to that morass? Are not your friends rotten there like driftwood long lain on the beach? And what in God's name are you doing at Feather and Feather? Is it a wispy feather-like thing that will save you? Plush and pseudo art and dilettantes? *Must* you *continue* to go about with your shirt collar open at the neck and an art magazine under your arm? I had hoped your brilliant (and here I am serious) critical acumen would be sharpened by your years of war agony, that your marvelous gentleness and your aspic tongue would be so transformed with blood, blood of other donors, that you would be mighty and magnificent. Instead you run back to the flabby breasts of your infant suckling days to pull from them what curded sustenance you may.

I am willing to stand by you all the way, Billy. All the way up or all the way down. But I must leave you if you are moving neither way. If you are crawling sidewise in the old crab's game, I hurry by you, on *my* way up, or on my way *down*. I tell you I have waited long enough. And I don't give one good goddamn what you or your fine prattling friends have to say from their nests of security and silky comfort. Have to say about my actions, my deeds, my ambiguous experiments, my violence, etc. I should know what I am doing by this time, and if not, then I do not ask for your grappling hooks to pull me out. Let me go under, Bill, let me go under but for God's sake let me *move move move*. I have learned so much I could not tell you in a hundred years. You want to put the little China Billy back in the shop where you found him. You want him to be the same trembling confused hermit-child that you used to bring books to walk at midnight with and dry his tears away. For Christ's sake, we grow, Billy, and we grow by learning and seeking and suffering error. And I have learned alone, without a single goddamned sop of aid thrown to me by anyone. I have been out alone and I return with one or two to follow me and a big heart full of pain and a head huge with discovery. No one to run to, no one to come running to me. Alone, I tried. Because I must know and discover how and why men live and do what they do, and fail to do what they fail to do. I love the streets and the life in the streets, where before I was afraid and sat in my room and denied life. I want to grow but in all directions like an octopus' tentacles crawling, unfolding OUT. Then I want to draw in all I can and put it in a heap and study it and watch it and wonder at it—and *interpret* it. If you want to keep beating the drums in your own little sideshow then more power to you. Beat those goddamned drums. But respect my three-ringed circus, and you come to my show and I'll come to yours. There's no reason why we can't ever collaborate.

I have not compromised. The only difference in what I believed then and what I believe now is intensity. Volcanic intensity.

If you remember, I had, always, more offers for help than I wanted. I was always rejecting help. You gave to me because you believed in me. Why not let it go at that and forget it. Who else did I ask for help—really *ask*? Was it too much to ask you and Nione to keep a miserable heap of disordered packages for me? Was it a great source of trouble to you? Tell me, did they gather dust, attract mice, smell? If so, I am abashedly sorry and please forgive me. You may either throw the stuff into the alley and burn the lousy bundles, or give them to the Salvation Army for scrap. I have much more to do, just like that, except more sure of itself and— perhaps—less . . . "disordered."

Now you calm your tousled head, my child, and no more of this nonsense. No more of this "I have come through" crap and no more, please, of this war-weary bitterness which is just too much like what everyone "back home" expects of returning veterans. If you have not compromised yourself, if you have not, through all of it, "let yourself down," then I say bravo bravo, I expected just that of you. Why moan and grovel over an apparently successful and unswerving period of action. If you are ill, physically, that is another question. I really don't know, for you have never told me specifically. If so, for God's sake be careful, Bill, and take things slowly.

I am fine fine fine. As the result of my brilliant naval career, my fortitude, my refusal to quit, I am now blessed with a slightly incurable malady donated to me gratis by the war and I am waiting a Medical Discharge. No one else yet knows this and you will not tell them—I want to do it myself, in the most pitiful, the most miserable, the most lamentable leper-like voice ever heard, excepting St. Julian. And then I shall go directly to work. So now, my Billy boy, you may dispel all fears of my "I have come through" return.

Yours,
Billy

---

except for one: Walter Berns.
Nione: Nione Carlson (b. 1918). An artist living in Houston and a close friend of Margo Jones.
I have come through: Allusion to D. H. Lawrence's volume of poems *Look! We Have Come Through* (1917).

To William M. Hart
ALS-6

Oct. 19 [1945]—Friday night

Dear Billy,

I shall try to scrawl from my bed, albeit not too happy a position from which to write. I have been in a pretty bad state since yesterday morning, when I had a severe attack of migraine at 0900, and it had its ruthless way with me right through until this afternoon about 1500. I can feel it subsiding, now.

This, as I intimated to you, is what I am left with. How long it will last, no one knows. Since its cause is strain and tension, the only treatment is rest and anesthetic when it comes. Otherwise, nothing can be done to "cure" it. You know I have always been bothered by the headaches, but never never like this. During the past nine months they recurred so frequently and so violently that I was near insanity, and the only palliation to be given at sea (under unforgettable conditions) was morphine by the bungling hands of a neurotic doctor. So much morphine made a ghost out of me. I got to be unsure of time and incidents [eventually or this or ?????] existed in trance and trauma, and I was alternately madman and nymph. For the last two months, July to September, I am not sure what I did. I do remember standing on the forecastle night after night sobbing hysterically because I could not bear to look at the moonlight upon the sea. Because I had lost my beloved comrade and he, for awhile, had been the only one who could make me still. I remember not saying a word for days and nights, being speechless and paralyzed.

Some of them on the ship, toward the last, thought me mad and they really kept their distance from me. There were others who actually understood and told me so as I left the ship that memorable day, Sept. 21, when, of all things, an ambulance was standing waiting for me at the gangway to deliver me from something like one of Dante's circles, I am not certain which. I think of myself during these last few months as something livid, as firebrand, as demon, as saint, as prophet, as black-guard. God I was mean, Bill; I was pure evil, I was the Devil. People fled before me. And one man, so much like Velte, who was searching—not for something to believe—but for something to feel, felt something. I saw him crumble down on a table and weep and thank God for his tears.

It was all fantasy, Bill. And if, in the midst of all that, my cries out to those I knew, waiting on the periphery of my chasm, were, as you said, "in high passion" and other things I cannot recall, then perhaps that was why. Like Othello, I can say (I was mad, I was afraid, I was fighting desperately to keep what little I had left in my vision)—"that was the only witchcraft that I used."

The doctors say that an earlier (really adolescent—I suffered head-aches most frequently then) condition, which was probably outgrown because I had developed resistance to it, has been uncovered and brought to the surface again, and that I shall have to again develop a resistance to it. That is not a very pleasant future to look to, but I accept it. During the past months I have suffered only two two-day attacks. Your long letter came at the height of one of them.

Enough of all that. Between headaches I feel marvellous now. My God I tell you Billy some of the most incredibly miraculous and wonderful things happened on that ship. Day and night inside it, strange and fantastic life and death and miracle. It is an idiot tale; no one will believe it. Nothing nothing can wash it out of my mind. I have been aberrated by it, thrown away, but I must not allow that, I must hold myself still again, and I will, I will. It is trying to get into everything I write, like contamination, but it will not. There again—Art will save it from corruption; and save me from distortion. Art will liberate it from me and purify my sullied brain.

Velte has been silent for over a year—except for one brief sentence tossed to me one torrid day in August. "If I have not insulted our friendship by my long silence, please write to me and I will tell you the story at length—otherwise, I shall understand." I have not yet been able to say anything to him, for he is playing his rôle for me just as I expected. Such a feeling as I have for him can never be changed by any human vicissitude. It is grander than human.

All the broken fragments of human beings are here. Most of them are very fine people, kind and gentle and brokenhearted. What will heal them?

I expect to be granted 30 days' leave around the first week in November. Since I have to return here for orders around Dec. 1 (to inactive duty), I do not know what I shall do. To come home is a long trip and a hazardous risk, in my condition (unknown to my family—please). Yet they are so impatient to see me—it has been 16 months. It depends on my condition.

What in God's name am I going to do when I am free, Billy? I mean how to make a living? Who will have me, doomed to at least 4 or 5 days out of every month—and maybe more, depending upon the nature of the work? Who would have thought that *I* would be cursed with such an affliction? I cannot stay in Houston; that would shortly kill me. Where? Where?

You are improving daily. I can see it in your letters. When I get home you will be much improved, I know. I feel I should not ask you to write me about yourself. But when you are ready, you will, and I shall wait. Whatever it be, you need not defend yourself before me. If you will only stop shouting a moment, perhaps you can hear my thin voice murmuring just what you expect it to utter.

As ever,
Billy

To Toni Strassman
TLS-2

U.S.N. Hospital
Ward A-9
Medford, Oregon
Nov. 4, 1945

Dear Toni:
Your letter about receiving the three manuscripts, etc. No, I am not at

home and I shall remain here until somewhere around Dec. 1 or so, then go home as civilian, praise be to God.

During the next month I shall be more or less a free man, waiting only for discharge papers from Washington, and I promise you I shall work furiously, woman. I am full of the old fire and things are hot and coming out like magic, so I must keep them coming like that.

Since I do not have the novel to work on, and in spite of the fact that I am working on additions to it, I have, some time ago, begun a short novel, novella, something, which is shaping up very much to my liking and I should like, soon, to have your opinion on it. It is, inevitably, about the weird ship of mine, the fantastic events and the unhuman human beings with whom I lived and fought and struggled through madness and fear and even hate. I do not want it to be one of these things we see so much on the reading lists these days—accounts of shipboard life and such nonsense; rather I do hope it to be a fantasy of feelings and motives, with the lives of men, great and petty, woven all through it, like a drugged dream. After doing a sheaf of pages on it, I found that one character, whom I call the Pink Giant, later the Golden Giant, dominated most of it. In order to avoid that, I have added several other characters, all fantastic and taken from hard reality, and now I have a notion to call it *The Idiot Ship*—which might get me in some trouble, for it is violently condemnatory of people, events, and actions, but only in the sense that these things are blights on the human soul, cankers of human feeling. In it are so many of the things which I must get out of my consciousness, and for me art is, as always, the only means to liberate these things. I hope to send you some of it soon, just for comment and criticism.

What do you really think is the matter with my stuff that causes it to be sent back to you by the editors? What do your friends say, for instance, of things like *Maria* and "Grasshoppers" and "Lace"? Sometimes I wonder if it would be possible and salable to put several of the things together with one or two other long things I have which have to be brushed up, and trying to get them printed that way. But do writers ever start with a collection of stories, or do they have to go the long way of getting one thing published here, another there, etc.? Of course, I know the opportunities are greater for novels, but there are so many little things I want to get out of me, it seems, before I give all myself to one big thing. That's strange—maybe I am only for shorter things, but I refuse to believe that. As a reader of many manuscripts, what do you think is lacking, for you, in the things of mine you have read?

I am furiously trying to get decided on what I want to do for a liveli- hood, beginning with the first of the year. Teaching is tempting me again, for it is the only certain means I have of going right to work. And I don't believe I can just sit someplace and write—yet. I am too full of energy and I want too much to be a part of some organized activity with people, in the stream of everyday life. For I believe that is what one writes out of. Too, I am typically unwealthy, don't have much money with which to just sit and write.

The country up here is ideal for me, I believe. It is tremendously stimulating and so very beautiful; and quiet, where the mind can work, free from the distractions of too much city life around. I feel too strongly, and when I am in the traffic of many human beings and personalities, I get led this way and that, so fascinated and infatuated with people and their lives and their confusion. Yet I cannot stay away from them.

You know I have thought of coming to New York for awhile. But would that really be to my advantage? Flora advises, in spite of the fact that she hesitates to advise, that it might be wise to come there. Yet it might stop the flow of my work and run me out on a limb, isolated from the great creative trunk. I feel that this move is the most important one I will ever make, for it is a new beginning, and it *must* be right. Yet I guess the really important thing is to keep writing, wherever I go, and that I shall do, for there is nothing else for me, it has to be done, and it will be done well and powerfully, I assure you. [. . .]

Please keep writing me here until I give you notice of change of address. And count on me, Toni. I'll put rings on your fingers one of these days.

As ever,
Bill

---

weird ship: USS *Casablanca*.
The Idiot Ship: Later titled *Section Two,* this is an unpublished manuscript authored, according to the title page, by both Goyen and Walter Berns (in the Harry Ransom Humanities Research Center).
the matter with my stuff: Strassman replied that Goyen's stories struck her as "incomplete"—a charge he answers in his letter to her of January 30, 1946.
"Lace": Unidentified manuscript.

U.S. Naval Hospital
Ward A-11
Medford, Oregon
Nov. 20, 1945

My dear Toni:

All right, I will take it easy. I just finished reading the longest and kindest letter you have ever written me, and just when I needed it most. It took me something like two hours to read it, not because of its length, please, but because, you see, I have had an eye treatment today and I am practically blind as a result. My vision lasts about two minutes, then fades away; so I read frantically, groping over the lines, rested, then began again. I have just finished.

How fortunate I am to find an agent like you, who are so much more than an agent. I appreciate your trying to help me at this most critical time, I sincerely do. Please understand my perhaps childlike, fanatical impatience, which grows and grows. It has a firm and real origin, and it is not to be compared, please, with the anxiety of old-maid "writers" and phony small-town authors to get in print and then start a lecture tour. My God, not that. It is a mature and well-grounded impatience I have. If matters could ever work out ideally, which they don't, and if I were God or somebody on the same level with him, I think I would see fit to pull a little trick about this time in M. Goyen's life and time and say, yes, surely this is the time to let him do something with his work, just the ripe and opportune time, for it will turn a tide, set a whole destiny, and give the boy a little push which will set him running, running all the way. He is a little afraid, not of himself, for he seems to have immense faith in his art, but he is shy, and by that I mean shy because he will have to desert a doting family, strike out on a blazed trail (which has been done many many times before and therefore is not at all heroic) and stick his neck *way* out. Briefly, I had so hoped to come out of this Navy shell into the light with something in print, just enough to say at home, "here, see, I can do it, and farewell."

Please don't do to me what you thought about doing to Berns—shelve me until I have "liberated" some things. My dear, whether I sell or not, I shall always be "liberating," for my consciousness is just that kind of consciousness. There may be and certainly are many jobs of editing to be done in my things; I have written, so far, in the white heat of feeling, when there were no nightingales chanting outside my porthole, only the g . . . d . . . ed ocean and kamikazes. Therefore things have got in some stories which should be got out, and that will be done. As for "furiously" trying to make decisions (excuse the many errors—I can't *see!*), that, yes, is bad and not to be done, but every decision for me is an imperative one, of the moment, and I am no logician.

All right, we'll be patient. Just keep telling me the truth and let me know what happens, what people who read me say, what you think, etc. Thanks so much for the article; it discouraged me, for too often I feel that the people who write *about* writing, know too little of *writing*. But alas! they are our judges and the people who buy the manuscripts. The clipping helps me a great deal; I shall use it.

Of course "The Evil" is "precious"—precisely the right adjective to apply to it. I was most "precious" when I wrote it—five years ago. I sent it along because I wanted you to get a better perspective of my total work, from way back. It is easy to see how I have moved away from that kind of style and perception, or shall I say conception of things. Some things I shall always send you (maybe it isn't necessary) which you won't find salable, but which I shall want you to see so that you may better understand what I am doing and have done. Some little things may throw an illuminating glare on some bigger and more complete ones. As for fantasy, don't jump the gun on me. Wait until you see what I am doing. Of course you don't let personal taste influence your putting things before the market. I agree, Pink Giant is not so good as Golden Giant, and I have long since changed it to that, which it was originally. Anything that is real and is drama, is *art*, whether it be fantasy or realism—and a heck of a lot of life, my dear, is sheer and unadulterated fantasy, take it or leave it. Some bad writers (and my God, how do they get in print—who are their agents, their publishers?) have so corrupted fantasy that they have almost done a permanent evil—I mean Benet and Gallico and Robert Nathan and so many damn fools in Hollywood. But do you know E. E. Cummings (*The Enormous Room*), the early Joyce, Eudora Welty, and their like? Ah, God bless 'em, they *know*, they *know*. [. . .]

"*The Evil*": Short story, later published by William Stafford and William Everhart in *The Illiterati* (Oswego, Oregon), no. 5 (1948): 3–4. Originally published in French in *Le Bayou* (Houston), 1939–1940.

Benet: Stephen Vincent Benét (1898–1943). American poet.

Gallico: Paul Gallico (1887–1976). American author.

Robert Nathan: (1894–1985). American author.

The Enormous Room: e. e. cummings (1894–1962). New York: Boni and Liveright, 1922.

U.S.N. Hospital
Ward A-11
Medford, Oregon
Nov. 22, 1945

Dear Toni:

Pleasant Thanksgiving to you. I had a long walk through the golden valley, saw turkeys and doves and pheasants, snow on the golden mountains, air pure as spring water.

I am so happy about the novel. I have got it pretty well sketched through now, despite the heart of it being in Houston. I have, the past few days, after a painful struggle, seen it clear and as a whole. Spent one whole afternoon in the woods, fighting to get a perspective. I have it.

I want to know how you would like to see what I have done—in what form, I mean? A synopsis, yes, and pieces of writing from each of the parts (there will be three parts), and something of some of the characters. Christopher, Emily, Waldo and Klaus. I have an idea about what would give you a feeling and telescopic sight of the whole, but do tell me what *you* want, what the publishers you mention would want to see, to get them interested in it, to show it to best advantage.

I am about arrived at a decision for future action. I hesitate to commit myself to you and Flora now (Walt does not even know, yet), but it means sticking my neck *way* out for at least a year—no compromise. If I could have some little goad, some encouragement to continue and complete the *Icarus* Ms. (novel), then there'd be no question. Think I can scrape up (borrow or steal) enough money to try it. It *must must* be done; I'll be dead otherwise.

Give me your opinion as to what to send, and I'll promise it by Jan. 1. I have had a marvelous feeling of *seeing, discovering,* the past week. I've battled inside myself a long time for it, and I believe, Toni, it has come.

Don't be so soft as to believe people are going to stop writing about the war as quickly as one snaps off a light. My God, they're still writing about the *Greek* and *Trojan* wars! I agree in this respect—no more trench and fox-hole and hand-grenade stuff—no more battle-God miracles and all that. Experience, to be art, must be transformed by the artist into much more—all we have had in the magazines here has been the recounting of battles, invasion, and beachhead suffering. Throw that away, yes!

The American public, stupid as goats, never really knew the war, and now they are quickly and facilely ready to "forget" it, to run into the stores for, at last, nylons, to pick up a new automobile, to buy meat without points. Was the tragedy of war so puerile, so ephemeral, that we can push it out of our minds the day after demobilization? False, false, false. The whole spirit and soul of a people, a nation, a world, is changed by such a war as we've had. We cannot destroy it. Sweetness and light, "love, cheerfulness and laughter" is what they want, so the newspaper clipping says. Fine, fine! Leave that to the potboilers, the plotmakers, Maugham and S. Lewis and Winsor and all these novel-every-six-months millionaires.

Of course, in reality, these demands are made by the *magazines*, mainly the *Colliers, Saturday Evening Post, New Yorker, Variety*—and we are trying to sell something to make a start. So we must know and recognize the market. You are right. Let's be sensible and businesslike. But Toni, watch out—the main body of my work, of what I have to say, is for much greater channels; it will be violent and big, very big. I can't help *that*—for that's what is in me.

Bill

---

the novel: Goyen's novel project at the time was *Christopher Icarus*. Never published; three sections of manuscript—"Christopher Icarus," "Christopher's Apostrophe to the Body," and "Christopher's Prayer"—are in the Harry Ransom Humanities Research Center.
demobilization: World War II concluded when Japan ceased fighting on August 14, 1945, and formally surrendered on September 2.
Maugham: W. Somerset Maugham (1874–1965). English novelist.
S. Lewis: Sinclair Lewis (1885–1951). American novelist and Nobel Prize winner.
Winsor: Kathleen Winsor (b. 1919). American novelist.

To Toni Strassman
TLS-5

U.S. Naval Hospital
Ward A-11
Medford, Oregon
Nov. 28, 1945

Dear Toni:
    There is no reason for this volubility of recent correspondence between us—we are both very busy—except that just as my letter "both-

ered" you, so does yours upset—extremely upset—me. In fact, I have
been ill with the first migraine in three weeks, all last night and today,
because of the combination of the letter and the visit of my friend from
Waldport, Oregon.

If I have not told you outright, you would have found out for yourself,
whether it matters or not, that I suffer from an acute, morbid sense of loss
of time and personal physical strength, and that I *am* impatient, intense,
whether that be good or bad. When you have been held by the hands and
arms, writhing to be free for vengeance, for a long long time, watching
them rape the values like beasts, day after day, it is only human to run to
club the rapists when you are free, not to stand by and say, "Oh I will wait
a little while, there is time." THERE IS *NOT* TIME. I have been told
that in letters coming to me from the Pacific, week after bitter week, for
four years. I have something to say, I have ALWAYS had something to
say, and unfortunately it is a physically true fact that, in order to say
something to a number of people whom you can't reach orally, it is
necessary to use an old medium, in our hands now since 1456, the
printing press. There might be other media, in our hands only a comparatively short time—the radio, the television, the motion pictures—but
it happens to be true that I have chosen the written word. FACT NO. 1.

FACT NO. 2 is that I must decide whether I shall eat or just write
without eating until I fall exhausted from hunger. And that is unreason-
able, since it is a rather true thing that the longer one lives the more he
will be able to produce and say. That means making money. It follows,
then, that I have been, so painfully and incessantly, trying to decide
whether it will be better to take a job and write when the job will allow
me to, or to say to hell with any two-horsed affair, from now on I write
furiously and nothing else. Some people may be able to do this and that,
and write, but I am not some people, I am W.G., and I accrue no benefits
from others' *modus vivendi*s, however apropos they may be. If the time
ever comes when it can be said that I "create," then I will say that I do not
"create" for profit. I have no commercial axe to grind. I want no literary
teas, no literary groups, no big-time grandeur. All I ask is to eat, and to be
able to speak, to learn, day by day, how to say it with more strength, more
clarity, more defiance.

Again it follows that, feeling inadequate to handle the machinery of
dealing with publishers or people who put your stuff into print, I have
long felt the need and wisdom of getting someone with some soul, with
some understanding of what I am and what I must do, to help. Flora
helped me find you (although at first I sent my things to you with some
misgivings, for I felt like a potboiler or a story-seller), and I feel very

fortunate to have you, and I want to stay with you, as you say you will
stick with me. If I lost you now, most of my bright hope, which is all I
have, would be gone.

When you tell me to "let writing be more important than publishing,"
I get a little angry—that is an understatement. It really upsets me so, I
sort of went haywire for about 24 hours. For that makes me feel that even
yet you don't know what I am about. And that *is* necessary, Toni, for if
you don't, then you cannot help me, and I am so counting on your help.
As for Steinbeck's having "no interest in his stuff after he has gotten it out
of his system," alas, he might as well take a good laxative once a week and
have the same result. The people I care about are those who *never* really
get "it" out of their system, and so keep trying over and over again to
liberate it. So that when they are not writing it or painting it, they are
talking about it, everywhere; they are, indeed, *living* it. A "story" is not a
little thing one gets out of himself then forgets it. That may be true for
Steinbeck, but not for me, nor for many others I know, or know of. But
be that as it may.

As I have told you over and over again, Toni, my dear, I have had an
explicit and deliberate reason for wanting to get something into print as
soon as possible. Not in order "to tell my family"—they have no idea that
I am writing, that I am going to do nothing else but write. If they *did*
know, they would not understand.

Well, let us forget this definition of purposes, and, as you say, go on
writing—and, of course, there is nothing else for me.

My friend, Tom Miller, from the C.O. Camp at Waldport, was here
over the weekend, brought numerous publications, humble things, from
The Untide Press, with whom he hopes to work, and also some copies of
a little organ printed by "The Illiterati," a rather wet-behind-the-ears
group who intend to grow. His thesis is that there should be some
mouthpieces like *Illiterati* for people who have things to say which will
not find publishers in the commercial press. This is basically good, but
you will agree with me when I say that I am afraid such an enterprise
encourages a lot of crap which is extreme, short-lived, bizarre, and of no
artistic value. However, the Illiterati are getting their little publication
before discerning people—Gotham Book Shop takes something like 200
each printing—and that is good. Too, of course, one reaches a lot of people
this way. But you know I will not stand for a perversion of standards, and
I'd rather sell my stuff from door to door like Walt Whitman, than surrender to sloppy dilettantism. Tom Miller disturbed me terrifically.

I have several essays and sort of long talking things on a variety of
subjects which I feel something about and which I want to tell people.

They are all pieces off the great big hunk of the never-changing thing I want to say. One is a little thing, an essay on D. H. Lawrence. There are a few on the bastard-writers, the eclectics of our time (some of them I have mentioned to you), whom I not only loathe, but would beat with my walking stick if ever I met them on any street. I don't know whether you handle stuff like this; it needs to be said; it preserves the integrity and purity of those few who are fighting for what they have to say, who are guarding the art of literature from the jaws of the marauding hounds of "writers" who always roam the alleys. Miller wants some of these things for possible publication in some of the "little" publications in Waldport, which have a rather wide circulation in the non-commercial press. Now we would make no money on them, but their being born, as it were, would serve as a clearing-house for some of my ideas, and a stimulation which I need while doing my other work. I want to sound you out on this score. What do you say? If I sent them to you, would you consider looking them over and sending them along to some of these little magazines if you desire?

As for the stories, no. We will keep them until they find a home, if ever. "The Evil" I sent to you as a kind of indication of one of my tangents; I regard it as not bad, but just not for everybody, really. "The Doll" I have no doubts about being a very fine and fresh piece of writing, for *me*, whether anyone else thinks so or not. Same for "The Wind." You see, Toni (and you know it), one writes in order to *communicate*, else he is doing nothing more than self-fertilization, a kind of indecent masturbation, which ends up in nothing more (excuse the bizarre symbol) than one's going about very fat and heavy with his own child, undelivered. "The Siegfried Idyll" and some other pieces of music, as well as prose and poetry, may have been originally written for the artists' children or a small group at home, but because they were art, and art needs more than a group or a drawing room of people to take it, they finally broke through the confines of group or drawing room and flooded out through the big world and the world took them for its own. See what I mean?

But enough of mutual attempts at "justification." The result, the finished product, the deed, *action* is the only justification. All else is only desire and purpose and intent. I am now thinking about returning to northern California, near San Francisco, to roost and work. I regard my work as a full-time job, as a cause, and *that* it shall be. [. . .]

Thanks, Toni, for your warm desire to "square me away" (Navy) and your gentle indignance. You're keen. Stay with me—

Sincerely,
Bill

friend from Waldport: Thomas P. Miller, an editor with the Untide Press when it was located in Cascade Locks, Oregon.

Steinbeck: John Steinbeck (1902–1968). American novelist and Nobel Prize winner.

the Untide Press: Founded by Kemper Nomland, William Everson, Kermit Sheets, and William B. Eshelman in 1943, this press was located in a camp of conscientious objectors in Waldport, Oregon. Its avowed purpose was to protest World War II; the name originated as an opposition to the camp official weekly, *The Tide.* The press later moved to Cascade Locks, Oregon, and after the war, to Los Angeles.

The Illiterati: Name of a group of writers who later founded a little magazine of the same name when the Untide Press moved to Los Angeles. They also produced attractive, hand-set books by poets and writers who later would form the nucleus of the San Francisco literary renaissance.

Gotham Book Shop: Properly "Mart," one of the country's most distinguished independent bookstores, located at 41 W. 47th Street, New York. It was founded by Frances Steloff (1897–1989).

"The Doll": Possibly an early title for "The Storm Doll."

"The Wind": Unidentified. There are four stories with "wind" in the title at the Harry Ransom Humanities Research Center: "The Wind at San Cristobal," "The Wind at Sewanto," "The Wind in the Shutter," and "Wind upon Water."

"The Siegfried Idyll": By the German composer Richard Wagner (1813–1883).

To Reginald Francis Arragon
TLS-2

614 Merrill Avenue
Houston 9, Texas
January 16, 1946

Dear Professor Arragon:

[. . .] I now understand that there is a possibility of an opening in the Humanities Division for the spring semester, on a part-time, temporary basis. This would be a well-nigh perfect way to begin again because I am a bit rusty and unoiled, pedagogically speaking, and yet tired and a little scared of a full-time anything. I do not feel physically qualified to carry a heavy teaching load at this point, and it is only fair to make that clear to you. I do feel that to get into the current again might be the best way to start functioning once more.

I should like to tell you of my training and experience in the hope that I might qualify for whatever opening you have there. I took the B.A. and M.A. (English) Degrees at Rice Institute, where I acted as an assistant in the English and French Departments during my senior and graduate years. I did a lot of work in the Renaissance Period, wrote my thesis on "Literary Criticism in the Renaissance," was active in creative writing at

Rice and published in a French magazine, *Le Bayou*, and in the few paltry publications of the Institute (in 1939 I won the *Axson* Award in Writing for the year). In the autumn of 1939 I proceeded to the University of Iowa to work, as a fellow, for the Doctor's Degree. I locked horns with the theories of Norman Foerster, was utterly discontent, left within a month. Returning to Houston, I began teaching as an assistant in the English Department at the University of Houston, a small place trying to get its feet on the ground, and there I was able to progress rather rapidly. In that peculiar institution, although I was never awarded any higher rank than that of "Assistant Instructor," I was loaded down with five courses— and this fortunately for I gained invaluable experience—and by the summer of 1940 I was teaching courses in Modern Poetry, Creative Writing (which became my forte there), Romantic Poetry, Sophomore and Freshman English. I continued these courses until the War took me in January, 1941. [. . .]

I might add, in closing, that my supreme interest is in creative writing, and this I add humbly. I have some work in progress and I hope to be able to have sufficient time to finish it, and much other, wherever I go. [. . .]

Reginald Francis Arragon: Chairman, Division of Humanities, Reed College. Goyen had visited Reed, where two former Rice Institute professors had relocated, while at the Navy Hospital in Medford.

614 Merrill Avenue: Goyen was released from the U.S. Navy in mid-December 1945 and was living with his parents.

Le Bayou: French-language review published by the University of Houston—not Rice Institute, as his letter would imply. Also, these works were published in 1941 and not the late 1930s when he was at Rice. They include translations of "Angoisse," "Autour du Lac," and "Icare aux Champs," all in *Le Bayou* 5 (1941): 61–62. Goyen did publish "The Children" in *The Thresher* (a Rice student publication), February 11, 1938, p. 3. It was reprinted in *Soundings: Writings from the Rice Institute*, ed. George Williams (Houston: Anson Jones Press, 1953), pp. 150–154.

Norman Foerster: (1887–1972). Leader of the "New Humanities," professor of American literature at the University of North Carolina from 1914 until 1930, and director of the School of Letters at the University of Iowa, 1930–1944.

within a month: Goyen had enrolled in the Ph.D. program at Iowa in 1939, but he returned to Houston after three months.

To Toni Strassman
TLS-2

614 Merrill Ave.
Houston, 9, Texas
January 21, 1946

Dear Toni:

You've been as quiet as somebody getting seduced in the back room; what's the matter? Christ this is a hard time for me, Toni, and not a thing from you. Of course, you think I am on the road and maybe that's why I have heard nothing. But then, too, it means that nothing is happening, naturally.

Mother's illness has become acute, we take her to the hospital today, tomorrow a critical operation, and so the trip has been aborted for another two weeks. Walter is sitting high and dry out in L.A. waiting for me and things are generally up in the air. Add to that the severe illness of one of my dearest friends, almost died, and my shaky physical condition, plus the terror of trying to get out into the civilian streets again like any man, and God you have it.

Nevertheless, I work when I can, at odd times, here and there. That I have to be kept from my novel (and this is a selfish thought, even unkind) is driving me crazy. Toni, it is developing into a terrific thing. Often I am so afraid you will not want to handle it, because it is a "serious" (that is your word, not mine) novel. But it deals with a thing which must be articulated, and my few serious friends here say it must be done and that if done well and artfully it will make a mark. I just wonder if you still want to handle it. We shall see. At any rate, you must do some talking, if you believe in it, when you show it around. I have not got it quite in shape yet, I mean the several chapters and the resume, because I want to be *sure* when it leaves here, and I know you want me to be.

I have turned down a teaching job at Reed College, after much gnashing of teeth, because I am determined to get to work on my own job, sink or swim. No more justifying; either I succeed or fail. You are with me, I know, inasmuch as you can be. Just do all you can to help me, and know that I am adamant to make a go of it.

What of *Cross-Section*? I investigated, found a review in *Newsweek*, found a friend or two who have heard about it. Have you tried *Southern Review* or *Kenyon Review* (are they still in print?)? I am corresponding with Eudora Welty again. Would it be amiss to show her some of my later stuff? Tell me, now; I don't want to be indiscreet. But often other writers can help. She helped me a great deal, once. Tell me. Tom Miller wrote that he had received the two stories, and thank you so much. Maybe I ask too damned much of you, to be a little nobody and nothing at all. Maybe I'm just too eager. Quell me, if I am. God, you are my only hope, I mean you buttress my courage, and Jesus it takes a hell of a lot of courage to do what I'm on the verge of doing. Stick with me, Toni, if you believe in me. But don't tell me stories. Sometimes I get so mad with you I could come up there and pull your nose, but then you've done the same with me.

Have two little stories, "The Crimes of Mirensky" and "The White Rooster." Will send them along soon. Health is trying to be better, if circumstances will only give it a chance. [. . .]

Cross-Section: A magazine published between 1944 and 1948 (New York: P. Fischer) that was "a collection of new American writing."

Welty: Eudora Welty (b. 1909). American author. Goyen had a significant correspondence with Welty, none of which has survived in the possession of either correspondent.

"The Crimes of Mirensky": This manuscript has apparently not survived.

"The White Rooster": Subsequent letters reveal the path to publication of this, Goyen's first commercially published short story.

To Toni Strassman
TLS-2

614 Merrill Avenue
Houston, Texas
January 30, 1946

Dear Toni:

Bless you, I love you good. Your wonderful long letter made me feel like an old cat being stroked. And God I have needed a few strokes these past few weeks. [. . .]

But I have three stories in progress, and they grow even while I am away from them. I water them over each morning during the hour that is mine before leaving for the hospital, and they sprout. I am determined to keep them from being "incomplete," which *is* a valid criticism, I feel, for the most part. The feeling I have is this: I am often afraid to carry a thing, particularly a thing of feeling, too far; I want to stop it when I get to a certain point, for fear of drawing it out too far; something says, Hurry, quit, this is enough; all else will be counter-climax and a falling away. But this time, particularly on "The White Rooster," I shall go on, past what I feel is the stopping point, and we shall see what happens. I am certain that the real trouble is in communication; I fail, many times, to communicate fully and clearly. The symbols are too much my own. I see them so clearly that I forget I must be simple as ABC in order to help the reader see them as clearly as I do. With this in mind and as an experiment, I wrote on a little on "Grasshoppers." I am enclosing the addition to see if you think that it makes the story less incomplete.

Wish I could sit across from you and talk to you. Believe I could make you see something. We are meant to see each other's faces, watch their eyes, hands, when we talk. Letters are bad; a fool can many times write a good letter—just as a rhetorical Insurance Salesman can make a beautifully convincing speech over the radio or via telephone, but alas, when he calls at your front door, he has nothing to give you but a twenty-year pay policy.

I had another magnificent letter from Welty. She must be a tremendous woman; her letters make me feel she is constantly working with experience, with her craft, and that every moment she learns something new and valuable. She says she has wondered about me often, is anxious to see how I have developed since the early things I sent her last year. "I wish we could help each other," she says; "it is meant to be that way. Yet trivialities always interfere, and we must not allow them to become obstacles to mutual help." She and Katherine Anne Porter are among the few writers I respect; most of the rest I cannot even read.

Did Tom tell you about "The Evil"? Makes me feel a little good to know that somebody wants me in black and white. How do you feel about it, Toni? I agree with what they said about "The Doll." They want an explanation! And brother, I gave them one, admitting my apparent failure at communication of an idea. They are right, you are right, Welty was right a year and a half ago about that story. Indeed, it was so personal a thing that it had to remain locked in me, I guess. But we learn. Tell me what you think about the Untide Group's taking "Evil."

I hope to have a few hours each morning to myself from tomorrow on. In that time I shall continue shaping up the book, dabble with the stories, and let you have what is ready as soon as possible. Thanks so much for the arduous work you are doing with my stuff, and I couldn't help believing in you. I know you are with me, and God knows, in the many black moments, that's what keeps me going. Stay with me, Toni.

Sincerely,
Bill

---

leaving for the hospital: To visit his mother.
Tom: Tom Miller.

El Fidel Hotel
Sante Fe, N.M.
March 4, 1946

Dear Billy:

A fantastic two days, yesterday and today, really fantasy. Walter and I have found Taos and want to stay if we can. This afternoon we took a little adobe apartment—quite primitive and quite large—for a month. Taos is like another world, my God how beautiful.

Yesterday we walked two miles up a mountain to see William Hawk, owner of Del Monte Ranch. It was like climbing up to the top of the world, all blue and snowy. And Hawk came out to greet us, strange and shy and almost inarticulate. We talked with him over his fence, he twice asked us in, but I confess I was too frightened, and so we left. I intend to go again. We saw Lawrence's little log cabin, it was sort of sad, somehow.

Today I went into the Harwood Foundation, a branch of the University of New Mexico, to meet Spud Johnson, a veteran of Taos. You remember he went to Mexico with Frieda and Lawrence. He is most humble and kind, took my name, wanted us to take his place for a month when he goes on vacation, said he might find a kind of job for me in the library, if I get to starving. Of course he talked of Frieda, said "She is a grand old girl," expects her back at San Cristobal (20 miles up the road) next month. And of course Mabel Dodge struts about (with the fantastic Indian husband, Tony). But none of that interests me. We have a place to live, it is quiet and so beautiful, and I must work. And I feel I can. [. . .]

Before I left Houston I had a rave letter from Strassman about the Rooster story. This is it, she said. You know I also sent her "Christopher's Prayer" and "Apostrophe," and she went wild—as Toni can do. She said she was going to Viking immediately to try to squeeze out the option. We shall see. [. . .]

God I hope we will not be disappointed at Taos. Write me there, General Delivery. Give Zoë my love.

It has been strange, Willy, and often so frightening. God how strange . . . Tell no one where I am.

Love,
Billy

found Taos: Goyen and Walter Berns had left Houston for California by car. On the way they stopped in Taos, New Mexico, where Goyen fell in love with the landscape, and they decided to stay, living in a rented adobe house.

little log cabin: D. H. Lawrence's (1885–1930) cabin was built on Kiowa Ranch, elevation 12,000 feet and 300 acres around, which was located fifteen miles from Goyen's and Frieda Lawrence's homes. It was given to Frieda by Mabel Dodge Luhan in exchange for the manuscript of *Sons and Lovers;* because Lawrence did not want to own property, the ranch was always in Frieda's name. "Except she never took *Sons and Lovers* away," according to Goyen, "so that the manuscript and many others, *Women in Love,* all holograph . . . were there in a little cupboard at the ranch. I could read them and look at them in amazement" (interview with Robert Phillips, *Paris Review* 68 [Winter 1976]: 69). See also *Frieda Lawrence: The Memoirs and Correspondence,* ed. E. W. Tedlock, Jr. (New York: Alfred A. Knopf, 1964), pp. 334–335.

Spud Johnson: Willard Johnson (1897–1968), nicknamed both "Spud" and "Spoodle," had been a student in Witter Bynner's poetry writing class at the University of California. As an editor of the campus literary magazine, he published D. H. Lawrence and was expelled for it. Later he stayed with Bynner in Sante Fe, ran a bookshop in Taos, and edited a literary magazine, *Laughing Horse.*

Mabel Dodge: Mabel (Ganson) Dodge Luhan (1879–1962), who first married Edwin Dodge, a wealthy Boston architect, and lived at Villa Curonia near Florence. In 1931 she returned to New York and established a famous salon at 23 Fifth Avenue. It was frequented by John Reed, Edwin Arlington Robinson, Margaret Sanger, Emma Goldman, Walter Lippmann, Lincoln Steffens, and Carl Van Vechten, among others. (See *Staying On Alone: Letters of Alice B. Toklas,* ed. Edward Burns [Liveright, 1973], p. 87.) In 1916 she divorced Dodge and married Maurice Sterne, a painter. In 1918 they settled in an adobe house in Taos, and in 1924 she and Sterne were divorced. She then married Tony Luhan.

Tony: Antonio Luhan, Mabel Dodge's third husband, a full-blooded Pueblo Indian.

the Rooster story: "The White Rooster."

"Christopher's Prayer" and "Apostrophe": Portions of *Christopher Icarus.*

Zoë: Zoë Léger. She was a stenographer for Humble Oil in Houston. Hart introduced her to Goyen, and they used to go to her house and listen to music. According to Patrice Repusseau, she was a dark and very beautiful Cajun woman with a motherly quality that caused Goyen to open up with her, much as he did with Margo Jones.

To Toni Strassman
TLS-2

Taos, New Mexico
March 12, 1946

My Dear Toni:

Yesterday I wrote you a rascally letter, read it aloud to Berns, wept, put it aside, today decided not to mail it. I have lost sleep two nights over your last two letters; I have waked cursing you [. . .] exclaiming,

"Whitmanesque!" "Preoccupied with words!" It has been hard to get the rancour out of my mind, but today I am O.K.

We have some strokes of bad luck, for Walter has been pretty ill, the house has been cold and dirty, and we have had to learn arduously how to make fires in our three oil and wood stoves, etc. But still I love it, love it, and I shall stay here as long as I can eat. It is very quiet, the sun shines brilliantly every day, sometimes it snows at night, the mountains circle us all around and have snow and a blue haze over their crests. Our adobe house has many big windows and a skylight in our bedroom, an old church rings its bells just around the corner, and we have met a few good humble people. I was at the point of physical and emotional exhaustion when I left Houston; you never knew that. If I had stayed there I should have collapsed right in the streets and I certainly could have done no work. I know that.

Now, once and for all, I have not come here to be arty, to "be a writer," or any of that nonsense. Please respect me more than that. This is a quiet place, the climate, the air, is what I need for the migraine. I have Walter with me, and some way I shall make enough money to go on working. Christ I have so much to work out of me.

Spud Johnson has been by twice, both times to see about Walter, who until yesterday was confined to his bed with an internal infection of some kind, miserable and terribly frightening to me. Johnson, so far, is much more genuine than most people who have had anything behind them. He is kind and quiet and modest. He has offered me a chance to work in the library at the Harwood Foundation and also wants me to sit for a woman painter over there. I shall do this and anything else required to buy food for the house. I am here to work, to find myself or rather to save myself from dementia. You don't seem to realize that. And so I have these *abasedly* discouraging letters, two of them, telling me that what I have done so far is not publishable, that I have not yet learned to write, etc. etc. We shall see, my dear. Frankly, I am incensed, absolutely infuriated out of my mind because the *Maria* story, an unspeakably fine piece of writing, a rare piece, should have been so abused and mishandled. If the letter you received from *Sewanee Review* said what you quoted, why, then, that is ground for some money from them in payment for the five months during which they held the story and so prevented it from being sold to anyone else. If I am not right, set me aright. I may be naive and so you may be, but Christ, honey, let's use our heads. You just don't do that sort of thing in a business. I think you should get up on your haunches, or let me. Now I may be an amateur, a nothing, but for Christ's sake, I am not to be kicked around, am I? Protect me, my dear, for God's sake, I depend on you. Those things you have are blood right out of my veins, and some day they will be something, mark my word.

Toni, I don't want to hurt you or be ungrateful—God knows I have no one but you, really, who can help—and for some goddamned inexplicable reason, I am terrifically fond of you, feel so close to you—I mean this. But Jesus you make me mad. [. . .]

Some pieces of the novel will come to you shortly, I promise. It is vast in my mind and keeps getting away from me. I have put so much in it it terrifies me. If it fails, well then. It is nevertheless valid.

Promise to keep you posted and thanks for everything you do. I challenge the things Covici said about "The White Rooster," but then he is only Covici. And "Whitmanesque"—oh Christ oh Christ oh Christ, it is unfair to say that about such a piece of writing, and in saying it infers that such a comparison invalidates the power and worth of the writing. Some day, my girl, some day you will see.

Love to you, really,
Bill

Covici: Pascal (Pat) Covici (1885–1964). An editor at Viking Press.

To Toni Strassman
TLS-3

Taos, New Mexico
April 4, 1946

My dear Toni:
   I have been trying to get to an answer to your last for some time, but my God we are working our heels off these days. When we get home we are so exhausted we can do little more than listen to some music, read a little, and then to bed. We hope we shall be able to learn how to conserve our energy soon so that we'll be able to work when we take our two hours off in the morning, three in the afternoons. We shall see. If not, then the job must go, much as we like it.

   We are waiters in an elegant little dining room at a well-known place on the Sante Fe Road called Sagebrush Inn. Walter and I have made quite a hit there, dashing among the tables, serving Brett and her coterie, this elite and that, Charles Nordhoff, etc. We make pretty good tips and we get our meals, so that helps.

I started typing the novel manuscript ten days ago, did several pages, then stopped dead. Something awful has frozen me inside, and most of the time I go about not caring at all whether I do anything or not. It has been a terror to me, Toni, a horrible willessness has got into me again, a lethal despondency which makes me want to quit everything, everything. It is not Taos, it is not the discouraging news I get from you, I swear it is not because of the repeated rejection notes you send me (although they are, as you know, very hard to take—but I can take them, really). It may be the land here, something that won't come alive. Every day I stand hoping it will start in me and I can begin work again; but something stops cold again, and on I go. This is my test, and it is up to me to withstand it, if I can care enough, if I can care enough.

You see, the same thing which got into me on the ship has driven itself into me again out here, and Christ knows if I can stand it again. Most of the time I think I simply cannot endure, and I have even prayed that I may endure, and that I may see the thing through to its end, as I have preached so often to others, as I say in the book, over and over again. This is *my* test. And God, Toni, burn candles for me or do whatever has to be done to give me courage, a unique kind of courage which tells one over and over that he cannot have which is to him the most priceless gift in the world, that he cannot have it, ever, never.

In the midst of all this rubbled life and absolute deadness came a wonderful letter from Welty. She had been reading several of my things— and her letter, so human and glowing, said some things which under other circumstances would have sent me flying. But her words did nothing to me; I just sat and read them and stared. She said she thought I have "an exciting talent, indeed," and that it was only a matter of time until the breaks should come for me, etc. etc.

Then Angoff's little note, which I thank you for initiating. I appreciate it, but I don't quite understand it. He said he thought I had "considerable talent" and he had hoped I would someday write something which "would fit into the scheme of *American Mercury*." Thanks for that, Toni. [. . .]

Don't think you are brutal with me. Sometimes I just feel that you don't quite understand what I am trying to do, or perhaps I am not for your kind of market. Be honest with me. Of course I want honesty from you, if it is all bad, it is up to me to take it. But I do not like vacillation or commercial hodge-podge when it is not necessary. Don't try to make a purse out of my sow's ears, or vice versa. Handle me with care, please, for if what I do is not right for publication, at least it is my own blood and bones, I love it with all my soul and heart, it is all I have. I am awfully lonely with my little pieces, and I always want them to be protected.

The book I know is great. Because there is too much anguish in it, my own anguish, to be a little thing. It must come slowly, but God it is bitter to have it come to me, alone, and with no one to share it with me. That's why I must get someone to look at it, someone who will say yes, get it out, I will help you.

I promise to try to get some of it to you as soon as I can, as I have promised before.

Thanks for all you do, and let me hear from you when you have a second.

Love to you,
Bill

Brett: Dorothy Brett (1883–1977). Daughter of Viscount Esher and heiress to a great fortune, who had chosen to become a painter rather than a socialite. Of all Lawrence's English friends, she alone came to America with him. She had met him in 1915, followed him to New Mexico in 1922, and never left. She gave the Lawrences her ranch on the Sacred Mountain above Taos. She typed Lawrence's manuscripts on a typewriter borrowed from Mabel Dodge Luhan. At the time Goyen knew her, she was eccentric and deaf. Her fierce loyalty to Lawrence was the cause of frequent conflicts with Frieda. For her side of the story, see her book, *Lawrence and Brett, a Friendship* (Philadelphia: J. B. Lippincott, 1933). See also W. G. Rogers's *Ladies Bountiful* (New York: Harcourt, Brace, and World, 1968).
Charles Nordhoff: (1887–1947). American author of popular novels, including *Mutiny on the Bounty* (1932).
Angoff: Charles Angoff (b. 1902). The editor of *American Mercury* magazine.

To William M. Hart
TLS-1

Taos, New Mexico
April 5, 1946

My dear Billy:
I have hoped to hear from you a little more regularly, yet I cannot ask too much since certainly I have not been upholding my end of the correspondence—that is, I have had much to say to you, always holding it back, saving it back, either hoping it won't have to be written or waiting

for another letter from you like your first and only one, which was so fine a letter and more of which I need as fast as you can send them to me.

Neither am I able to make articulate what I have been feeling and experiencing nor do I wish to try to make it so, to put it down in the word, for fear it will betray me and so strike back. I have not written one single word that counts since I have been in Taos; but perhaps, as I have said before, if one lives intensely then there is no need for art, for creativity (awful awful word), until a long time later, when the intensity has cooled and one is a long long way off, cool and at some peace, then looks at the past experience and says, "ah, but I see its meaning now, now I know its significance."

There is challenge every living minute; I am alternately terrified and ecstatic, and always, in proportion, deranged. Most of the time it is too much, many times much too little. And this time I am utterly alone with the challenge. But I shall ride it through, I swear it; ride it through to whatever end we ride to, riding hard, as I promised myself I would do.

Please send me kind letters, tell me what you need of me and let me give it to you, my Billy. Your words in that last little paragraph of the first letter I read over and over again; and I fight like a madman to live up to them. But I have learned that what one does is always in proportion to the amplitude and the scope of the vision he has of what to do, and so that comforts me a little.

I hope you are working hard; let me know what you do. And I hope it is not too hard for you there, that you are serving and functioning some way, as you will. You have been hard with me, often I feel like a brute who has kicked too many people out of his way as he strides blindly—to where God knows. You and some others have made me feel that so strongly that every time I make a mistake with Walter I shudder and tremble for fear that I am acting the savage again. And that is very hard to bear.

But write. And to Zoë my love. Please have no conversation with people about Billy in Taos and that sort of thing. Let me be here and do what I can, then we shall all talk—of my abysmal failure or of a little something done.

I love you Billy.

Billy

Taos, New Mexico
April 17, 1946

My dear Toni:

I have waited and waited to hear from you before writing this letter, but today, after no word from you since 15 March, it must be written.

To begin, I have for a long time been discontent with the way things have gone with my work, and Walter as well. I have tried to be patient and console myself by saying I was not "ready" and that sort of thing, by telling myself that I must move slowly, that you were fully aware of what I was trying to do, etc. The first few rebuffs from you I took squarely and with comparative equanimity, although they hurt to the bone. But when you began to intimate that I had not written anything publishable yet, then I began to lose faith; particularly when word to the contrary was coming to me from others who knew and who had a good sense of what I was doing in my work. I am afraid for that reason I have been so dull and desultory with the novel manuscript. Perhaps I have been a little afraid to let you have it. A few times I felt you exhibited somewhat of a lack of knowledge of my kind of market, for you wrote that you had submitted my things to some pretty low-class magazines, the readers of which could never feel the need of reading the sort of thing I want to communicate. And some of Walter's things, particularly the non-fiction things, brilliant work, were mishandled and left by the wayside because we felt you were not aware of what they said and of their power. And then the awful anti-climax of "The White Rooster" (preceded by the mishandling of *Maria*)—that fine letter saying, "This is it, we must work carefully, any magazine would be glad to have this piece," then not one single word about the story after that *to this date* except the curt note that Covici had said something about somebody killing somebody else in the story. I and Walt are truly disappointed and ready to try somebody new, Toni.

Eudora Welty has some time since offered me her agent. She highly recommends him "if I should ever want to change agents," says he looks for anything that is good writing regardless of subject-matter (war or no war); and some other fine things she says about him. Since I respect her extremely highly, since I am trying to do the same kind of work she and Porter and some others whose stories would never be peddled to this magazine and that, I give a great deal of credence to her recommendation. Her last letter reads, "I think you write with an exciting talent indeed . . . I hope your agent is good. I don't know any agents except mine, who is very fine indeed and if you should ever have cause to want to talk to another one, write to him. He is the best, I think, and it was my good luck to be sent to him without going through any of the usual troubles people have finding the right agent. I also know little of the publishing world but think it is generally honest and anxious to find talent like yours." Etc. Etc.

God knows how much Walt and I appreciate what you have done for us, Toni, but we feel it is high time we had some results, and when things have come to such a pass as our present status, then it is time to make a change. We have been very fortunate to begin with someone like you who have been so intimate and like a personal friend, and we always speak of you as such. But don't you think if you were in our shoes you would try someone else? No hard feelings, we assure you; we are just abysmally discouraged and eager to take action.

I have today written Diarmuid Russell, of Russell and Volkening, asking him if he will look at some of our things, upon recommendation of Welty.

Let us hear from you immediately, please Toni, and we hope you will understand. Maybe this will be the impetus we need, maybe it will be a fresh beginning.

Love to you,
Bill and Walt

---

her agent: Diarmuid Russell (1902–1973). Welty's agent until his death and cofounder of the literary agency Russell and Volkening.

To William M. Hart
TLS-1

Taos, New Mexico
April 29 & May 4, 1946

My dearest Billy,
So much to tell you and so little time in which to put down any kind of sensible sentence. I think of you often, often I wonder what your comment would be on any current or of the moment incident. It is like a whirling line, all tangled with itself, which has slowly and steadily begun to straighten itself and move in a direction. Always there is the feeling of

impermanency, of imminent falling away, but the moment, which in its intensity can never be held as it is, is unspeakably magnificent and really always unbearably tragic. But the lesson is not to throw a beautiful thing into the future like a ball into the air, but to keep bouncing it right now, in the present, right now. And I know a little of what it is to ride a thing along, as I have told you, to stay on its back and ride it where it goes. God it will take you places undreamt of, Willy.

We, of course, have met an innumerable number of people at the Inn; most of them socialites, but some of them delightful. Brett we have come to love and she is simply magnificent, so kind and childlike. We have visited her quaint little place several times. Frieda has been out three times and we have had, unfortunately, only one little chat with her; but we have an invitation to visit her next Monday afternoon. Oh Billy, she is a grand old woman, like a peasant Queen, a marvelous smiling face and a deep husky Germanic voice, and she answers every question with a lusty and throaty, "Ya!" You see, this Spud Johnson, who was such a trusty friend to D.H. and Frieda, has been splendid to us—he comes by often (yesterday, Walt's birthday, he knocked at the door, presented Walt with one of his own snapshots of Lawrence, a keen thing—that's the way he is). So, in spite of innumerable invitations to this and that, we have rejected them all and we make only occasional visits to Johnson's and Brett's little mud places out under the mountain. Spud and Brett love to talk about Lawrence, and what I like is the way they speak of him as though he were just coming around the corner and very shortly would arrive to where you are sitting and join the conversation. How they loved him! And another keen and rare thing among these rare few is the way they accept one for what he is and take for granted that he is trying to do something in all humility. I have many things to tell you which I cannot get in a letter.

You know I have had this confused mess with Strassman and this person Angoff with *American Mercury*. He sent me a letter saying how much he liked my work, and that he was hoping to be the first to introduce me (whatever that is), etc., then on the heels of his letter came a pack of *American Mercury*s for me to study so that I might better understand "the pattern of the magazine." All this, plus more Strassman bungling and misunderstanding has so confused and desolated me that I feel I can no longer go on with the woman. I sent a letter telling her this, she wept and moaned, said when I published, regardless of my agent, it would be because of her groundwork for me, etc. etc. In the meantime, I had a letter from Welty saying some wonderful things about the stories I sent her, suggesting that I write her agent, Diarmuid Russell (Porter's agent also), for she felt that he could best handle "talent like mine." Oh she said some fine things, Willy. Everything is in such a mess and I feel it is necessary (and wise) to look Strassman and Angoff in the face and talk; you know how, after a certain point, letters can do nothing more. So Walt and I are going to New York next week to stay for the month of May. We have made much money at the Inn and our employers are willing to give us time off, if we return, which we certainly shall have to do. What do you think? I have *Section Two* all finished and I think it is powerful; also some half of the novel practically ready. Will carry these along. This may be a silly venture, but I like to think I am free to do this sort of thing if I really want to badly enough, and if I feel honestly that there is the need for it. I shall keep you posted.

Much more to tell you when we can talk. Take care, work hard, have faith, and remember I think of you, Billy. Suddenly the other afternoon, I looked up from my work and knew that I really missed you; I could hear you talking to me, see you walking about your living room. I want to see you again before very long, somehow. Endure, Billy, as I am trying so hard to do.

Love to you,
Billy

---

the Inn: Goyen and Berns were still working as waiters at the Sagebrush Inn. "I met Frieda who came in one night and I waited on her. The whole Lawrence world came to dinner there—Dorothy Brett and Mabel Dodge, Spud Johnson, Tennessee Williams: He was living up at the Ranch. They all came to my table. . . . Frieda said, 'You must come and have tea with me.' She said it right away. I went and from that moment, we just hit it off. It was almost a love affair. It was the whole world" (*Paris Review* interview, p. 66).

To William M. Hart
TLS-5

Taos, N.M.
July 15, 1946

My dear Billy:
Your letter yesterday and pleased to find you alone in a house on the bay instead of in California—how dreadful. You know I had wondered where you would be during the two weeks—hope you found my last letter when you returned home.

Since that letter we have been more or less ordained to the Lawrencian world out here, and all unasked for and sort of gratuitously, I promise you. July 4th we were astonished by an invitation from Mabel Dodge (Luhan) to come to supper at her little place at Embudo, some thirty miles away on the Rio Grande. It was our first chance to get to know her, and I was relatively unimpressed—until the next morning when I startled Walt at breakfast by shouting out unannouncedly, "I know what she is like—a kind of bird creature!" But it is more than that. Mabel Dodge Luhan received us like an old simple country woman, lay on a couch, spoke softly and with not very good diction, read a book while Walt, Spud Johnson and I shelled innumerable green peas, and spoke to us occasionally over the top of the book. We had a most plebeian supper and the conversation was completely this and that, no questions asked about ourselves, no literary comments, simply pedestrian dialogue. We left at 8:30 P.M. The next morning we received another astonishing invitation (actually the third invitation out since we have been in Taos since the last day of February!) to have dinner with the Vanderbilts (yes, they are of *the* Vanderbilts) who have taken one of the many houses in "Mabeltown"— Mabel's own "Big House." My God what a magnificent place! We went reluctantly with what tried to be an open and receptive mind. Ollie Vanderbilt was entertaining two dreadful guests from Dallas—one was the Marcus woman of the Neiman-Marcus thing. God knows who the other was. But Mabel was there, fell on our necks, was jocular, got sort of tight, talked much. After dinner, she pulled out some seven of her many albums and showed us all the pictures of her past—that incredible legend of people and places. She is now 68, small, debauchedly wrinkled and lined, quite clever, and mean and little in the face. About ten o'clock a rain and hail storm came in from the Sacred Mountain and we went up to the third story glassed-in gazebo and watched it. It was much more magnificent, much more terrifying, than Mabel Dodge Luhan.

Then—last Thursday we found as we were washing our breakfast dishes, a quaint little note plastered to our kitchen window screen. It was from Brett, who had come stealthily and quietly, and an invitation to supper with Frieda Lawrence that night. We were ecstatic. We went, had a simple little peasant-like meal in her kitchen, Frieda powerful as a lioness, really just a sort of gross old German peasant woman, but ah! her face! Like a little girl's, and so beautiful and full of life. She talked incessantly about "Lawrence." We were shy about the subject, but she went on and on, once tears were in her eyes when she said in the indescribable husky voice of hers, "Oh, those were wonderful days." Brett sat in a dream, so quiet and faded. Then she asked if we would like to look at some of the Lawrence manuscripts. We sat in her living room with D.H.'s notebooks, immaculate and clear, in our hands—*Kangaroo, The Trespasser,* some of the plays, and *The Woman Who Rode Away.* Frieda Lawrence was really inspired several times; and once, as a kind of valedictory, she leaned her head back, looked up toward the ceiling and said, "And now . . . I am old and you are young. I say to you that you must fight and refuse to compromise, refuse absolutely to compromise. I lived with a fighter and I know what it is to fight . . ." Then she was eager to hear about the Navy, wanted to know what kind of life one lives on a ship, asked us to tell her the day's routine. She listened like a child, occasionally becoming so excited that she would strike the arms of the chair with her fists and shout, like a lioness, some oath or exclamation. Then she asked if we should like to hear a preface which she had just written to another book on Lawrence. She wanted to know our candid opinion. She read four little pages of clear, direct and powerful praise to Lawrence, and we could not say a word. And as we left, she gave us a copy of a Hollywood script of *Lady Chatterley's Lover,* asked us to read it and give her an opinion. She said, "If I go to my grave soon, it will be because of Lady Chatterley . . . she is driving me to the grave." It seems that all the boys are playing with the novel, some bad plays have been adapted from it, now the movie script. I have read it and find it unspeakably bad and shall tell her so. She seems so vulnerable, so defenseless; someone should protect her and D.H. through her. She should have a literary advisor and I am surprised she does not. I should think Aldous Huxley would do that for her.

Before leaving, we mentioned that we were going up to Kiowa Ranch the next day upon invitation of Bob and Kit Nowe. Straight-away she insisted we stay over the weekend, take her other house—newly built, a Swiss Chalet type. It sits right next to the humble little cabin that she and Lawrence lived in. And she asked us to go into Lawrence's chapel and replace the greenery with fresh cedar and pine boughs. That was an unforgettable experience. Indeed the weekend was one Walt and I shall never forget. I shall simply have to wait until I can tell you with my hands and face—I have been trying to put it down since we returned, but it won't come yet. Suffice it to say that the first night was one of the weirdest I have ever known. It *is* true that there is a *feeling*, alternately fierce and gentle, which one gets up there. It is some ten thousand feet up, you are on the top of a mountain and you look down over miles and miles of sweeping uninhabited desert and mesa, all brown and ghostly blue. The room in which we slept had three of the savage Lawrence paintings on the walls, the most fierce of which hung next to our bed. What those paintings do to a room, one cannot describe, but they are certainly not meant to be slept with. I lay next to it all night in a kind of trance, not sleeping, in a kind of peaceful suspension, except for moments of absolute terror. Through three huge open windows I could see the night and hear the wind in the pines, and wild creatures of every kind ran, scrambled over the roof, gnawed, screamed and skittered; once, what must have been a whole herd of quarreling coyote fought for five minutes in a nightmare of a battle. Some were apparently wounded, for they screamed like women; others were vicious and they moaned and whined and howled. Then in a flash they were stilled, and not another sound. And all night there was a muted drumming in the distance, as though someone were rapping on a door, first five raps, then six: I counted them throughout the night. The next day we learned it was an Indian ritual up on another nearby mountain. We were there Friday afternoon, Saturday and Sunday, and the days were like sleepwalking, serene and brilliant. Yet at times everything would suddenly go stark and hard, and a kind of terror came over everything. All that is in *Icarus*, and I had the manuscript up there with me. There is so much more to tell but we shall wait. *Icarus* is moving, at last, and today I read some four chapters to Walt.

I will not know what I have until I first put it away from me today when I read it. I feel somewhat satisfied with it, although God knows it is a brutal struggle. I shall send the finished portion off to Covici this week, and then we shall see. I had a letter from him yesterday and he sent me two new Viking portables, Mark Twain and Rabelais. If he is not satisfied with this I have done I shall be terribly disappointed. I want you to know it, what I have done, but I meant to wait until I have finished the whole thing, then put the manuscript in your lap for better or for worse.

Section Two is at Viking now. We shall see. A letter from Rinehart was most flattering and said some fine things, but they are afraid of it. Same for Dutton. Both houses say they are "eager to see" our next piece of work.

I am learning so much, discipline is hard, but it is good to be at one's work consistently and with continuity. We shall see what it produces.

I am glad you are working, Billy; let me know how it moves and comes through. And now, to bed, for I am tired. Today we acquired a little dog, one month old, and he has had us fussing with him every minute, trying to help him adjust himself to a new and motherless environment.

Take care, Billy, and you shall hear from me. Stay in touch. Give my love to Zoë, read her the parts about Lawrence—and anyone else you think I might like to tell it to. I can't write many such lengthy letters as this, so pass it on, with discrimination.

Love to you,
Billy

the Vanderbilts: Ollie and Joseph Vanderbilt.
the Marcus woman: Mrs. Herbert Stanley Marcus, also known as Minnie (Lichtenstein) Marcus.
Aldous Huxley: (1894–1963). English novelist and man of letters.

To Toni Strassman
TLS-3

Taos, New Mexico
August 18, 1946

My dear Toni:

If Walt and I appear to be "getting panicky," then let's attribute the correct cause to the panic. "Agents," "author's representatives," "publishers," "editors," and all those have, for years, tried to tell the writer how to write, what to write, when to write, etc. Once you wrote me, "write what you have to write, what is in you." I think your own words explain *Section Two.* Let's get this straight: I am a mature man, one grounded in literature and things written creatively, I have fought like hell to get that way, I have a little aesthetic integrity, and, put this down, NOBODY IS GOING TO TELL ME WHAT TO WRITE. That's the first point. The second is, NO ONE, NO ONE, IS GOING TO TELL ME HOW TO LIVE. And I take the consequences of these two statements.

Let's not worry our little heads about my "income" any longer. I write as hard as I can and as close to what I feel and see as I have the gift and power to do so. When it is finished, it comes to you and you do your best to get it through to print. You have hounded me about this novel until I am a wreck. You have written, "there are all kinds of things I can get for you, but first I must have these three chapters and an outline." You have been against any other piece of work except *Icarus* from the start. And because I believe in you so and listen so intently to what you have to say, I have sweated blood with *Icarus,* but it is on its way now. What about the fellowship, which you said you could ask for at the same time you sent the ms. to Covici? I have not had one word about that since I sent you *Icarus.*

You people all profess to have interest in the "struggling young and unpublished writers," yet unless he writes a potboiler or a second *Rebecca* like little Flora's, you kick him around, use him as you please, and tell him he is not yet anything, he must be this, do that, live this way, write this kind of thing not that, no "conventional plot," no "war" (what is war, really—do you know?), books, and all that. Christ, Toni, I want to do something with my work *because* of you, not *in spite of* you.

I want to ask you a question: you deprecate the "influence" of people, you say good works do not need influence. I believe that; most of my past actions in life have illustrated that belief of mine. I would never take a job as a young fellow when my father sent me along with a recommendation. In this wise you sort of cast aside the offered help of a woman like Frieda—or anyone else for that matter. Yet, how often do you ask for, rely on, or simply spiritually count on, the influence and aid of your former friends in the publishing world? Think about that. And I wonder over and over again about this dratted "war-book" stigma which you attach to *Section Two.* Is it a war book in the jargon of your profession up there in Manhattan? We have talked to many people here, visitors, villagers, etc., and there has not been a one who has not been, at that very moment, extremely interested in "the war," what happened to men like ourselves, etc. Does that mean anything, or do you think these people happen not to be readers of books? And the discerning readers here who have carefully and enthusiastically read the book find it strange that the book is dubbed "war book." Have you read it carefully enough to detect that? I wonder. You see, we resent the fact that you have consistently been so dubious and twisting about *Section Two,* afraid of it without really looking it in the face, coming back at us with petty little objections like those of anti-Semitism. *That* has been the cause, and the only cause, of our rancor, our "panicky" state.

As for my present state of living, it is a dare and a stark challenge and a very hard one, Toni. Who among us can *really* presume to offer advice as to how one must live, request or demand justification for one's ways? Now, we are not children nor are we just "boys," and we are certainly not completely ignorant of the publishing business. I think we are well enough informed. I thought the letter you sent today was one of the few really first-rate, hard and real letters, and your stock went up 30% in my camp. Of course it's hard on you, we don't mean to persecute you, but when the time comes to start defining positions, let's do it straight forwardly and directly, and no hedging or pussy-cat-in-the-corner business.

I believe, and Walt along with me, that one must live as he writes, if he is writing anything at all, and it is impossible to create what I believe in and want to say in the midst of the silly and dehumanized clamor of the civilization of the cities and streets, of the offices and the daily neighing concourse of false-faced men and stuffed women. We have made a choice, we have paid a price. Our work will come out of that. There are people who cry to me that I have a responsibility to teaching, but then I don't turn and start a discussion of "responsibilities," for I do not want to embarrass them by asking a question or two of *their* "responsibilities." So let me alone, all of you. If I dig my grave, then give me a Christian burial and walk away murmuring *fini*. Judge me only by my works, and when works come up, give them a fair and honest chance, not a facile, stereotyped appraisal. It is not that simple, and you should know that, Toni.

I believe in you, Toni, as you believe in me. Know that.

Love to you,
Bill

---

a second Rebecca: Apparently an allusion to *Rebecca*, the best-selling novel by Daphne du Maurier (1907–1989), published in 1938, and to a later book by Flora Armytage.

To Toni Strassman
TLS-2

Taos, New Mexico
August 23, 1946

Dear Toni:

Finally the word came through, yesterday. How glibly, how, with a deprecatory wave of the hand, it came to our mailbox.

I think the aspect of the whole rotten mess which hurt me most was the admirable Mr. Pascal Covici's conscienceless dismissal of me, after his "letter," his warm, paternal phrases uttered in his office on that significant May morning in New York. It seems, unless he was dissimulating that day, that he could at least have written to me. But then I take it that the bit of manuscript, those "three chapters and an outline" which had been begged for so long, for which you pleaded and howled and extortionately exhorted me to send, who "am on the threshold of my career," I take it that these fifty little pages and the synopsis proved once and for all that I am not worth any more time to Viking. For, "Ballou thinks *Flora* will be a major writer." The innuendo of this laconic sentence is not very pretty.

But enough of your Covici. And your Mr. Ballou—he *is* somewhat of a genius, who can judge a man's "publishability" (five years—like a prison sentence) after reading half-a-hundred pages of his writing.

Toni, you are so old and sage and so seasoned with "experience"— Tucson, Sante Fe, Greenwich Village, I shall henceforth be afraid to say much of what I am thinking before you. It *is* a tragedy to be "young," but, one *must* be, I suppose. How hard the life of the experienced, the wise old ones, those who have lived, must be, always having to put up with the young ones.

What are your plans with the *Icarus* segment, after Dial? Let me know. As for Dial, it was your own confusion which caused all that confusion. That was the point of the costly long-distance call to you—to get an understanding about Frieda's letter. You said plainly not to mail it until we heard from Viking, which advice we carried out. *That* is why Phillips never received the letter. It was, however, mailed last night.

Toni I am not going to have any more words with you. We've had enough. I blame this dilemma on you for the most part, although I and Walt have certainly contributed our share to the hectic quality of the affair. If you hadn't pressed me so hard for the three chapters and outline, promising options, advances, fellowships, etc., I should have never let you see *Icarus* until it was finished and done. If Covici was so "interested" in me, how could he have dropped me so easily? I think *you*, too, have learned a thing or two from this fracas. Be honest.

At any rate, none of this tin-horn blowing has affected *Icarus*. It goes right on. I am thinking about this "introvert" business—a dangerous word to level against anyone; and this thing of not "having lived enough." I am thinking about that humbly and open-mindedly. I am never as bigoted as you think. After all, one has to get a new start after spending five years of his young life in a war he never made, and I'm trying so hard to get that start.

And now—I have other people to attend to. One or two of them are nearing seventy and their past "experience" has only served to make them younger. Irony, isn't it?

Bill

---

word came through: Pascal Covici had rejected the portions of *Christopher Icarus* which Strassman had submitted to Viking.
after Dial: Strassman had submitted the portion and outline next to Dial Press.
Phillips: An editor at Dial Press. No relation to the editor of this volume.

Taos, New Mexico
Aug. 30, 1946

Toni, my dear:

At last I can take a deep breath, I have really been abysmally miserable since the beginning of our "poisonous" and torrential correspondence, and thank God we are simmering down to sanity and easy breathing. It has been on my mind (and conscience) night and day, and I just can't live and write like that. Please let's be friends, real ones, and not lose a sharing faith in each other. If I should find out that you had lost the bright faith which I once felt you had in me, I think it would do a thing to my work and self-confidence which would be really destructive.

I hadn't realized what your faith in me has meant until I began to fear that I might be destroying it in you. You must believe in me, and I in you (I know that), else we simply can't work together. And, Toni, I *know* I will come through. I am sure of it—some way. Just help me, be patient with me, go along with me, and believe in me.

It has been so wretchedly miserable this last month, really low on my belly, and I just can't go on like that. And since Flora has sort of discarded me, in a spiritual, intangible, abstract sort of way, I have felt groveling for any rock to clutch to. Remember, I am pretty much alone here, doubts come all flooding in, a feeling that I am nothing, nothing and that it is all a farce and I a tinseled fool.

Let's love one another, honestly, and then if, finally one of us is a failure, we cannot impute it to pettiness, lack of faith, and distrust. If this thing goes all unhealthy and morbid and cunning, then I am destroyed. Forgive me and Walt, God bless him, he is errant and so dependent on me; and let's just work and try to hold on to a thing that won't wither and leave us with a weed in our hands when we have thought it an immortal-blooming flower. I really love you, Toni, in one of those indestructible kind of ways, because we came together when you were hope amid hopelessness and, sentimental, spinster-like though it may be, I just can't drop you, ignore you, or ever really "slough you off." And I know you know that.

The Covici thing is a kind of permanent hurt, it deranges a thing that was wholesome in me, it can't be explained to myself, deep down inside. But then, what to do but to go on working?

Something *will* come out of this, for Walt and for you and for me. Else there's something crazy in courage and belief and all that. Basically I suppose Walt and I are just orphans at your doorstep with no one else to cry to but you; therefore all the letters, mawkish some of them, mean and savage some of them. We've just made the mistake of telling you every-thing we think and feel, having few others to listen to us. But try to think of us as being mature, not just kids, maybe it's the intensity of what we are experiencing that makes us seem adolescent and alone in our experience.

We love you,
Bill

To Emmet Riordan
TLS-3

P.O. Box 1522
Taos, New Mexico
Thursday, September 26, 1946

Dear Emmet:
     [. . .] I always told you back there in that deranged neurasthenic cave called Mole Hill on that Idiot Ship that one day we would form a colony and live like something out of Rousseau or a Dorothy LaManure picture. For me, and for Walt, certainly, these parts are almost all one could ask for as a region in which to try to find a way of life that doesn't entail becoming a part of that asinine and silly human clamor of the cities. I don't mean to be snobbish, Emmet, certainly I am striving as hard as I have ever strived to go humble and see things straight in the eye. But I simply feel that I cannot allow myself to become for long part and parcel of the amok and schedule and pattern of the kind of life one finds in most places. Perhaps I am too highly strung to stand the rush and run, or perhaps I don't agree with the way people have to live in most places; and I don't find it possible to do much good work in those places. Out here we are certainly not removed from "reality," as people call it; indeed it seems to me that the realest reality is everywhere about. This land stuns me every time I take a look at it: Most of all I like its untouchedness, its refusal to be anything more than mountain, desert and sky. It does much to me, and so long as it does I shall remain in it. One thing I miss is the sea; often I really long for the ocean, just to look out at it or hear it. That's the only flaw here. But I want you and Ann to see it. I'd love to

have you see it with me. Taos is quiet, sort of primitive, unlike any other place I have ever known. There are a lot of interesting, active, and stimulating people here and some fakes, but one can easily steer clear of those bozos. The few people we know are all hard workers, mostly painters, and they stand for no crap. One of our favorites was Walter Van Tilburg Clark, a regular real fellow if ever there was one, and it is a pity he and his family had to leave last week. There are not very many young people around, and that's one of the lacks. So much could be done in and with Taos. There should be a stronger community feeling, I feel sometimes, but then I would probably spurn that, fearing a division of energy in myself. There is a little music about; there are few "groups" or coteries—and that's good for the most part. But there is the need of a strong, sensible, alert and energetic group of young people, intent on getting a thing done and standing for no poppycock. I should like to have Tom bring the Illiterati Press here, it would be the ideal place, but alas the machinery is already installed in Pasadena.

Seems to me that, granted a person has a thing to get done, a thing which he must, with all his heart get out of him, Taos or environs offers just what he needs: Quiet, reality, a feeling of being a part of the earth, a kind of touch with anciency, and a chance to get one's feet solidly on the ground and look about him and within him. That, you know, is what I was looking for when I left you last year, it had to come. I believe I have found it for a little while. Oh, don't get the idea I am all squared away and settled and set; always there are the doubtings and questionings and often loneliness, etc. But I *must* find a way of living which will allow me to be every bit of what I am, whatever that be, and I am looking for it. I love the country and I want to find a way of living in it without isolating myself from life and the action of life. I have many critics; I am severely maligned by most of my oldest friends because they think I have removed myself, "set myself apart" from the rest of the world to reside on a mountain and look down on them like ants swarming below. That is a great injustice and it hurts terribly. [. . .]

Dorothy LaManure: Pun on film actress Dorothy Lamour's name.
Walter Van Tilburg Clark: (1909–1971). Popular American novelist.
Tom: Tom Miller.

To Margarita G. Smith
TLS-1

P.O. Box 1522
Taos, N.M.
October 25, 1946

Dear Miss Smith:
I had your letter yesterday via Miss Strassman, and I am eager to see what can be done with "The White Rooster" in the light of your criticism and suggestions for revision.

I take your statement, "It seems to us that the story would be more believable if the rooster got away; and since the rooster is a symbol of the grandfather, it would be clear to the reader that the grandfather would live on . . ." to mean that you feel that the death of grandpa renders the story less credible and that you suggest my allowing him to live on, as the rooster, who escapes the trap, lives on, and I am proceeding with that understanding. And I agree about the change in viewpoint, it suddenly shifted on me, but I had hoped that the shift would give a kind of double-jointed power to the latter half of the story. I shall try to clear that up.

Thanks for your help and opinions. I shall do my best and we shall see what happens.

With best wishes,

Sincerely,
William Goyen

Margarita G. Smith: (1923–1983). Sister of Carson McCullers and, at the time, an assistant fiction editor of *Mademoiselle*.
the grandfather would live on: In the published version of the story, the grandfather dies on the last page.

To William M. Hart
TLS-2

Taos, New Mexico
Nov. 19, 1946

Dear Bill:
Your letter, and thanks for the festoons of rosaries. Here, we go about

with fingers crossed, silent and hoping: one gets to where he builds up possibilities, even slight ones, to mountainous proportions, and that is not good. Back in the summer when we thought surely something would come of *Section Two*, we spent some unforgettably miserable days waiting, only to find an empty mailbox for many many days, and then ugly news therein. No more of that. The revised version of the "Rooster" has been mailed some ten days now; I felt, after finishing it (and while working on it I found it, for me, still very much alive, and that was encouraging), that it was and is a much better, stronger (technically) story, and perhaps more credible—so I was indeed thankful for the *Mademoiselle* criticism and suggestions. And much impressed with the comments of their literary editor—her (I met her in New York: young, about 25, and rather keen) comments showed a lot of thought and insight, and I had felt that perhaps what is a "magazine for smart women" would probably have no sense of what tries to be earnest and serious writing. Whether they accept the story or not, I have learned something, I believe. We shall see.

Incidentally, this might amuse you—we have in our yard every day a strange white cock of the same variety as my white rooster. He comes from a neighbor's yard and struts about, almost as a symbol or presentiment. He utterly fascinates me. We bless him, praise him, throw him sops of extravagant food these days. He may help us.

It is so magnificent here. I love the mornings when we wake to find it trembling white outside, and so quiet, and sort of terribly proud to display itself to us, so white. Then the sun comes and everything glistens. We are quite warm and comfortable, the stoves all work, and I love (so far) bringing in wood and pumping water in the late afternoons. I polluted the damn well last week with my washing—dumped all the soapy stuff right back down through the top of the well, not thinking, and so we had to use water from the little river for a while. All Taos knew about the stunt and we were ridiculed. Someone even called (for although we carry water and excrete in an outhouse, we have a telephone) and asked if we "were blowing bubbles at both ends."

I struggle hard with *Icarus*. So I go slowly and try not to rush it. It is beginning to be possible for me to read again—for so long I have not been able to read more than a few pages of *anything*. My infernal weakness of just sitting and analyzing and ordering, trying to get the real honest import of what is, has robbed me of reading and kept me within myself. I believe that weakness has something to do with "discipline," so I am trying to control it. But *Icarus*, although the first draft has for some time been finished, balks and goes frozen in places. It says some terrifying things, for me; and perhaps that is why I find myself fleeing from its perfection at times. A strangest kind of psychology is bound with this; I am trying to understand it. Alas, if only those first fifty pages had never been sent to the agent—what an eager fool I was. For the book is getting judged on the basis of that pittance of writing. All reports say the writing is excellent, that I have an uncommon ability with "words," sensitive, etc. etc., but always they level against my "formlessness" "thinness of plot" etc. I, in defense of myself, feel that "they" don't see what I am trying to do, which probably means I have failed, communicatively, to do what I want to do. It must be a legend, practically all narrative, little dialogue—for why talk?

But oh I love living like this, Bill. It's not for you; I know that. But we make different demands, you and I. At home this time I found you growing, as ever—against odds. I think you are meant to grow like that—as a flower or something in the shade and not able to get any sunlight, but growing along. I love things like washing our own clothing and things like hanging them out in the sun, like stacking wood, like feeling the land and the mountains all around and seeing them through the window. Why oh why do I want to throw off the civilization of my time like a cloak from my shoulders? I am afraid of it, it is a deep and terrible fear. Perhaps because I saw my civilization for the first time, really, during those closing years of the war, and was terrified. Hell, I don't look for "serenity"—who among us can *afford* to?—but I feel that if I don't feel a relation, a living relation with the *permanence*, the uncorruptibility, the secret flow, or whatever it is (the *quidditas* I remember Joyce called it, using, I believe, St. Augustine's definition) in things, then, there is no meaning (and, for me, there *must* be a meaning—that is my flaw) and we all run brainless and careless and there is nothing but orgasm and laughter and despair. This FEAR—it's got to be sublimated, dissolved. [. . .]

And the times when the insidious and weary doubt crawls to where I am sitting and glowers at me like that hideous fat green worm, called the Tatzlwurm, in one of Bachstein's fairy tales. And then I am afraid, afraid for me, afraid for Walt, afraid for all of us. [. . .]

---

their literary editor: Margarita G. Smith.
Tatzlwurm: Precursor of Ole Fuzz in *The House of Breath* and the worm in "Arthur Bond."

To Emmet Riordan
TLS-2

Taos
Sunday, Dec. 1 [1946]

Rear:

[. . .] And now I will tell you another thing—since May, Walt and I have been trying to peddle a book we have done on the ship, to little avail, since publishers, some of whom have been terrifically interested, are still afraid of "war books"—which it certainly is *not*. From the first we have hoped to get you to do some illustrations for it; we wanted to use one, which I have, and more which you shall do. I am now revising the book—called *Section Two*—and I believe this will do it. We must discuss this when you come. DO NOT TELL A SOUL ABOUT THE BOOK—PROMISE ME THIS. We shall probably get in a lot of trouble with it, but I think it will one day be truly a great thing. [. . .]

To Emmet and Ann Riordan
TLS-2

Taos, N.M.
Dec. 6, 1946

Dear Riordans:

[. . .] We have been working very hard; you know, it's a day's work every day to do all the chores and one's own work, too. We have discovered that writing is a slow, tough business, but we are determined. Once you get in line, the thing is not to get out again. And it all comes from *a way of life*. If we sell the story which *Mademoiselle* wants and now has, after some revisions, we shall be somewhat in the money when you arrive—and how we shall celebrate! We plan to buy a bottle of whiskey right off, if the sale comes through—a luxury which we have not been able to afford some months now. So say your aves for the story. [. . .]

Taos, N.M.
Thursday, Dec. 12, 1946

Dear Anne and Emmet:

Another of a countless number of fairy-tale days, with golden technicolor sunshine, deep-blue, purplish hills and mountains, and spectacular sunsets. We are praying for snow, and, indeed, it is unusual that we haven't had any more since the deluge of a month ago. But surely we shall have it shortly, or at least during your time here. Very cold, bitter cold, ice and icicles everywhere, but still the blue skies.

To further prepare you for the primitive, unshed life which you shall enter and partake of shortly, I mention here that as I look out our window I see grubbing under the trees the following: a swinish looking pig, grunting and groveling; an enormous rooster and his two concubines of hens, all pecking, cackling and crowing; two stray horses who will be shortly chased away by Walter, since they muddy up our little river, and an erstwhile gay little rabbit, who escapes from the pen next door periodically. On the clotheslines hangs our bedding, out for a sunning this bright day, the lines having just been relieved yesterday of an enormous washing.

You will come to us at Spud's house in Placita. Frieda has postponed her departure until sometime in January. That is a pity, for we had hoped to have her nice large house when you come; but it is great, too, for it means that we shall have Frieda here for the Holidays, and we love her dearly. Too, you shall get to meet her, and that will be a rare experience for you. We shall be cozy here in this ancient little mud house, we shall teach you how to manage without running water in the house, the outside W.C., etc. Come prepared to have a delectable bath in the old copper bathtub in the kitchen, filled with many buckets of water carried from the pump at the well and from the river. We shall make you comfortable and we think you will be delighted to live like roughshod westerners for several days. [...]

We are making plans, getting excited. Yesterday in the town, chimes, of all things, were ringing out, "Oh Little Town of Bethlehem" to give us the spirit. Taos trying to be sophisticated and city-like. But it thrilled us a little. How I hope we can trudge through snow for a fir tree in the mountains with you. We shall all decorate it most gayly. [...]

If there is something else, write or wire and we shall respond. Just hurry and come, we are waiting for you. Love to you both, see you soon.

Willy and Walt

Taos, N.M.
Jan. 13, 1947

Dear Riordans:

[. . .] We missed you after you had left, were sort of at loose ends. It was a glorious and unforgettable time we had of it, a really memorable Christmas. Among the latest events: A fist fight with MDL on New Year's Eve at Brett's turkey party (which we prepared, lavishly). Then came a letter from her a few days later telling us we should join the UNO or something, that art is dead, etc. Frieda joined in with her great bellowing voice, etc., so the old old feud is on again, with Walt and me whirling around in the center. Kind of flattering, but disturbing, too. And, we have a gorgeous hunk of land given us by Frieda and Angie. Is about two square acres, borders on Indian land, is the plot next to Brett. We are excited beyond measure. Tom drew us some plans for the imaginary house, and will send along completed drawings shortly. We are to have the land surveyed this week, the deed drawn up, etc. Now isn't that wonderful? Forever and ever we shall own a piece of this wonderful land! Details as they progress, will come to you. At least we can build one huge room this spring and gradually add on to it as we go on. Frieda and Angie leave this week for Port Isabel and we are very sad about that. But they'll be back in April. Brett is still raging up and down the roads, bursting in at daily intervals to tell us something is wonderful, and bringing eggs, bacon, etc. She is so excited about having us as neighbors. [. . .]

MDL: Mabel Dodge Luhan.
UNO: United Nations Organization.

Box 1522
Taos, N.M.
Jan. 20, 1947

Dear Toni:

Your word came through late this afternoon and we are leaping with joy. It *is* wonderful, isn't it? As I told Walter, somehow more than a story was sold—and it was all enhanced by the interminable waiting period.

Thank you so much for your hard work, Toni. We feel you did a fine job and we are so grateful to you. And we are happy that at last you are getting returns for all you have done for us these last eighteen months. Perhaps things will move a little faster and a little less painfully now.

We are working terribly hard and slowly we are carving out a method and a discipline, which is the most important thing. It is a magnificent life we have here, and we are not going to give it up without a fight. We were pretty blue over the weekend, money dwindling and we don't want to interrupt our work. The call helped immensely.

I feel so grateful to Margarita Smith. I feel she worked hard for us and I want you to tell her how much I appreciate her work with me and her desire to help.

So congratulations to you, too, Toni, and let's all keep plugging and holding on. Walter sends regards.

Love,
Bill

When will it appear?

Your word: Strassman had informed Goyen that *Mademoiselle* had bought "The White Rooster." The story appeared in the issue of July 24, 1947.

To William M. Hart
TLS-2

Taos
Sat., March 23 [1947]

My dear Billy:
   [. . .] You speak of one's (particularly your) "effect on the world." Therein lies the eternal and searing choice, it seems to me. One chooses a way of life which will permit of the greatest and most potent effect on the world; and the problem, is it by creating, is it by moving among the people of the world and touching them in the various ways and being touched (and crushed and whirled and mauled and muddled) by them, is it by a combination of both these actions? comes up before him if he is

alive and restlessly questioning and being urged on and on by that inner thing like targets in a shooting gallery. We must, I suppose, try all these, subject ourselves to the agonies of all [of] them to find out. Not one is easy (who asks it to be "easy"), nor sure nor complete. There is always something lacking, something half-finished, not all done, wanting and begging and yearning to be whole, but never that. No circles are complete. Oh Jesus Christ it gets so tortured, this trying to make one's way through doubt and catechism. Somedays one is nothing, absolutely nothing; and there is nothing created or uncreated that can take him and shake him alive. There is rarely serenity. But then I believe I know now, although it rarely does me any good when I sink down low, that the achievement of a thing that urges is never complete or *fait accompli*—it is like the clothes I wash in bad water and with second-rate soap: they are not "clean," but "cleaner."

This world here, this mere physical world of so much beauty, means so much to me—the little road I walk on and watch things, the tinkling little river, the beasts in the pastures, the magic colors over mesa and mountain—that too often I feel selfish and want to share it. The greater sharing of it should be through what I write, but then often I wish for a more direct kind of sharing. [...]

To Emmet and Anne Riordan
TLS-2

Taos, N.M.
June 6, 1947

My dear Rears:

The work is finished, we have been living in the little house for about ten days now, and slowly it is becoming a house and we three are getting to be friends. We hadn't realized how exhausted we were until we were in a few days, then the letdown came and we sat like two stones—went up to the Ranch for three days to recuperate (is simply indescribable; spring has just touched that high place, the fruit trees are in bloom, everything shining green, really magnificent), then came down. The house we are very proud of, it is cozy and comfortable, there are still countless projects to be done inside and out. Walter has proved a genius of a carpenter, has made a great cupboard, two very fine desks, thousands of shelves, etc. Will send pictures as soon as can get them developed.

It is beautiful living out here at El Prado. Many wild calls and cries during the night, the early mornings are serene and full of many smells of young alfalfa in the fields just below us, and the odor of the sage which clusters all about us fills the room at night. We can see all round the world out here. My folks sent six young chickens via the mails, they will come here to roost soon as I can make their pen. We've had an offer of a lovely old goat (who is heavily pregnant), but turned that down.

No lights yet, but we burn Brett's lamps and they are adequate. However the electric light men have just appeared, so in several hours we shall be able to turn on the phonograph and have la musique once more and hear those quiz programs on the radio.

Still coldish here, spring is very shy about coming up to these mountains, but the aspens are turning in the mountains now, and by July we should know that summer is in the world. [. . .]

Frieda is bouncing and as booming as ever, Brett as hectic and screaming and excited over trivialities as ever. What wonderful friends all these, and Spud, have been to us. They have helped us in every possible way. We had a combination warming-house (Angie's term) and celebration of Spud's 50th birthday last Wednesday night. Big supper cooked in our new pressure cooker sent by Mrs. Berns, much good talk around our new little fireplace.

Mabel came furiously by after we first moved in with a truck following her—in it were two great Renaissance chairs, called Bill and Walt, and an ancient Mexican carved box—gifts for us. Then she sped away. We took a picture of Frieda sitting like a queen in one of the chairs and will send a copy to you as soon as it comes from the developers.

What the summer holds for us we don't know. Money is very low and manuscripts don't sell. A hard, tough racket, but we stick to it. We wait word on Walter's novel and many of my stories.

Now what is the late news with you? Oh Rear, wish you could find a way—but you are scrambling, as we are, and maybe that's a good sign. Have a small short piece in the summer issue of *Southwest Review*, an annual issue devoted to New Mexico each summer. Is on Rio Grande, very tiny, for which I received five dollars—will buy sugar and butter with it.

As I look before me into our washroom-closet, I see the gargantuan nude form of Berns, which is descending upon a pan of hot water—commonly called sitz bath—the building, heavy lifting, straining, etc., has brought down upon the poor chap that deadly affliction which I suffered on the Casa and for which I was ridiculed by the entire crew—remember?

Many stories to tell you about the building, would give the family jewels to see you two, need you, want to compare notes, ask questions.

Taos in the summer is so different from the winter Taos. Many tourists snapping their little boxes, millions of hoodlum art students, etc. But we are safe from it all this time.

Are fighting a trip to Houston, where my family cry for me. Much loot there for the house, so we may go shortly, just for a week. Then here through the summer, living like misers. Total cost of the house (built in a month and three days): $555.45.

Now don't be blue—send us word more regularly now, keep up the spirits, don't forget us, we'll all come through if we don't sell ourselves in the streets like those women in Tacoma. Spud, Brett, Frieda and Angie ask of you often, you made quite a hit here, you must come back. Take care, write us quickly. Pictures will come your way shortly. Walter sends love from the hot water pan, and you know I love you.

As always,
Bill

---

small short piece: "River's Procession," *Southwest Review* 32, no. 3 (Summer 1947): 316–317. This was the first of Goyen's many contributions to the magazine.
affliction: hemorrhoids.

To James Laughlin
TLS-1

P.O. Box 1522
Taos, New Mexico
July 2, 1947

Dear James Laughlin:
Here are some things of mine and a story by Berns, and believe me it takes a lot of courage to send them up to you. I suppose of all the criticism I have suffered since I have been out here scrambling to write, that which I had from you last summer, via the wretched agent, hit me the hardest and took most out of me. I wonder if what you said then still applies? The things you said about those pieces of mine which were shown you are the things I most loathe in writing, the qualities (if they are that) I will not countenance.

I hope I have not sent along too much, but when I put one piece on a pile for you, I felt the urge to try to balance it with another kind of a thing, always with your past criticism in mind.

I don't know—it may be that I have to go through the dipping vat of some of these sort of dirty things to get, finally, to something clean. I do feel (and this feeling certainly is not unique, I am sure) that I am going to something, slowly, that will be right, for me.

Your sudden appearance here was a peak from which we can't easily and quickly descend. It stimulated us tremendously, particularly the opportunity to *talk* and so throw all one had been feeling, in a kind of solitude, out into a wider area. I think we made it clear to you that we and our writing friends have for a long time counted on New Directions as a strong hope for writing in the U.S., and that should mean something to you. Quite humanly, I labored under the guilt of inferiority and failure for a while.

Again, we enjoyed your visit more than we can say—and if the offer of the work on the translation still goes, please let us help. That would be a great boost—particularly at this low ebb. Let us hear, if you care. With all best wishes.

Sincerely yours,
William Goyen

Enc.: "A Parable of Perez," "The Doll," "Pavane for the Seaslugs," "Observations of Sam Sparks" (poem), "Boy of the Weed," "The Evil" (Fr., from *Le Bayou*), "Notes on a Day," "The Geranium," "Morning Herald."

James Laughlin: (b. 1914). Poet and founder of New Directions Publishing Corporation, a leading publisher of modernists.

the translation: Laughlin had offered Goyen the job of translating Albert Cossery's *The House of Certain Death* for publication by New Directions. Cossery was a Cairo-born fiction writer who wrote in French.

Enc.: Laughlin accepted only "A Parable of Perez." "The Geranium" is the only one of the three stories that Goyen included in *The Collected Stories* (pp. 204–207).

To Toni Strassman
TLS-1

P.O. Box 1522
Taos, New Mexico
July 3, 1947

Dear Toni:

Now I must sincerely beg your pardon for waiting so long to say anything to you, but you see I have really had nothing to say. I have been extremely busy, night and day (this is not an easy, idyllic life), trying to write and trying to keep some kind of living going. Now both of us know what it is like to haunt the mailbox, wait and wait, and find nothing.

Toni, you know I am going to write regardless of what happens, despite you, despite the commercial market, despite the current discouragement of young new writers, despite all those transient, and finally, insignificant facts, I am going to write. And I am going to have to write as best I know how, as faithfully to what I feel and see and know I must say, as faithfully and as honestly as I can. If I have to write "the kind of stories as such-and-such a magazine *requires* and *wants*," then I'll simply try to make my living by other means. I'd rather. I have little respect for your client who decides not to write what he must and "slants" towards *Good Housekeeping*. He is a whore; on every page of the *New York Times Literary Supplement* is the story or picture of a literary whore, all the women with three names, all the sickly, craven, slick plots—they are dross, nothing; they amuse, entertain the sloppy and the half-alive. Such is not my mission nor my way, and before I'll stoop to such corruption I'll go to work in a butcher shop, anything. I'm not arguing with you. I'm not being "poisonous with my pen." I'm simply stating what I believe and what I will and what I won't do.

Slowly I have come to the decision that I don't really need an agent, *any* agent. Maybe I'd rather go on writing in silence, through these desperately hard and bitter times, and just wait, trying occasionally, alone, to get someone to print me. This doesn't mean that I kick you in the pants as a failure, that I lay blame on you, that I reject you, Toni. God knows I am grateful for all the sweat and shoe-leather you have given for me and I think I understand why we have had such a hard time. But it's not over, Toni; it's only begun. But I mean I am tired, exhausted of sitting around waiting for someone else to do the job for me. I want to go alone, now. Literature is not a racket, for me; it is not a trade or an occupation: it is a way of life, and I must write towards that end. I am not a snob; I just have standards and principles and a sense of rightness which I *must* believe in.

Bless you, Toni, and a heart full of thanks to you for what you have done in the past three years. Let me go alone, now, just sit out here and write and learn and try my own hand on publishers and editors when I think something is right. I'll look for all my manuscripts to come from you shortly, please—send them collect. My love and gratitude to you, and no hard feelings. So far as I know, Walter will go on with you and I know you will help him all you can. Let me hear from you and I promise to keep you posted. Best of luck to you, and all best wishes.

Love to you,
Bill

New York Times Literary Supplement: Goyen conflates the *Times Literary Supplement* and the *New York Times Book Review*, perhaps for satirical effect.

To William M. Hart
TLS-2

P.O. Box 1522
Taos, N.M.
July 8, 1947

My dear Billy:
　[. . .] Since last I wrote to you I have, as a kind of apprentice to Walter, built a little cabin. At Christmastime Frieda gave us a bit of land, almost two acres, just across the road from her house and within calling distance of Brett. We determined to construct some kind of lowly dwelling upon it when the spring came, despite our dwindling funds. Tom Miller sent us nice plans, but sort of too-nice they were; so we modified them to fit the land and our resources and, for five hundred dollars, practically all our remaining funds, and in a month and three days—with the help of Trinidad, the Indian, we built with our own hands this house and here it stands. We are very very proud of it, all Taos comes to look at it, and some kind friends have given this and that in the way of rugs, a table, an old chest, a stove, and we are a house. It consists of one long room, one end of which is subdivided into a little cooking-and-eating place and a wash-place. We carry water from Brett's well, live primitively and most penuriously. We may be able to last out the summer; that is doubtful at the moment. [. . .]
　There may be a change coming for me in my work. I had to grow so tired, really so drained, of all I had been wrestling to say; that may be happening. Attitudes toward writing, writing as life, as a way of life, as a "vocation" (preposterous, for me)—all these shift and glimmer and reveal their true significance if one stares at them constantly, patiently. One can know about these in no other way. One speaks with a kind of authority. You know.
　I am determined not to fall back into the march toward greed and possession and anaesthesia; I have gone this far, I want to follow through until the logical conclusion to it comes—but who knows, that may come tomorrow? But I want to know that I have stayed with it right to the end, to tomorrow. But there must be some way of making a living. James Laughlin of New Directions was here (to visit Frieda) a month ago, we

met him, he came to the little house and we drank at a bar in town and talked. I liked him, liked him much more than I had expected to like him—some of his criticisms of my work have been savage and merciless; and I had never been sure just what "new directions" meant or what "new writing" was or what Mr. Laughlin really wanted or was trying to do. But I think he has courage and intelligence; I think he knows something about writing. I think he is one of the few hopes in America for people who are trying to *write*. (If only I could tell you of the crap that comes to me out of New York from the agent about what one must write, what the magazines want, what the publisher wants [and I have letters from publishers and editors, too]—but none of that really matters except to show one that in America writing and *writing* are two different things). Laughlin seemed interested. He took pictures of the house and of us in the doorway; he seemed to want to help us go on. He asked for things to read and offered to give me a translation job on a French novel which he is publishing this fall. That may mean a little money and certainly it will open up a new field for me. I am still waiting to hear from him. We shall see.

Toni the agent has been kissed off. It was rather ridiculous (and a bit pompous, really) for me to have an agent—I am no pulp-machine for *Ladies Home Journal*. She has been very kind to me—really too kind—and God knows I love her for all she has done and tried to do. But there was no sense in our going on together. I want to go alone, silently, for a long time now, and no more of this high-pressure thing. Walter will remain for her for awhile, since she has not long ago received his novel and he wants to see what she can do with it.

Again and again I return to stories. That may be all I can do, need to do. Maybe I'm not meant to lie with whatever the Muse is every night—maybe I don't have enough stamina; maybe I'm supposed only to give her a damned good rustle every now and then, one she won't quickly forget, maybe never. But *Icarus* goes weaving on and on, changing color, but on and on. It grows as I grow. Around January I got so deep down in myself that I couldn't see light at all and I thought I would never come up. No more of that. It becomes negative then, becomes masturbation, what one writes when he is like that is swank and glitter and strut and wail. [. . .]

P.O. Box 1522
Taos, N.M.
July 11, 1947

Dear James Laughlin:

Our manuscripts and your nice letter have just come to us and I want right away to acknowledge their receipt and to thank you for such a prompt and kindly handling of them. I am happy that you even halfway liked "Perez" and sorry that Walter's story seemed the way it did to you. We are both feeling our way along, and the things you say do help.

I can't deny that what you say about my "pedestaling" my material and then sort of approaching it in genuflexion has something in it. I don't mean to be patronizing and soft and all that when I agree with you, in part; but somewhere deep down I always feel it, a kind of little wrongness somewhere, a kind of little diabolical twist in what comes out. Then, when I discover that, I re-work; and re-work until sometimes it's holystoned to death. Language excites the hell out of me, and maybe it leads me astray. There is so much I want to do, to get down—but too often it's like punching a punching bag when the punches don't quite follow through, don't quite hit with the strong blow you direct at it. This, the meaning or cause of this, I shall have to find out, and I will; it is agony of half-release and I swear to God I can't break open yet, to save my life I can't. Yes, I believe your willingness to help by running "Perez" will be a right thing, and it excites me. I only hope your desire to use the piece is motivated some by your caring a bit for it. I am grateful for your help.

I'll wait for your word on Cossery. It would be fun and a lesson to do translation; both Walter and I are eager.

I should like very much to know the stories of Williams. I know his poems, his *In the American Grain*, and here and there I have seen a story of his, but I should like to see your edition of them and study them more carefully.

Thanks again for your kindness, we sincerely appreciate your help.

Cordially,
Bill Goyen

---

by running "Perez": "A Parable of Perez." This marked the third acceptance of a Goyen short story by a national publication.

Williams: William Carlos Williams (1883–1963). American poet, playwright, and fiction writer published by Laughlin.
your edition: Williams's story collection, *Life along the Passaic River* (Norfolk, Conn.: New Directions, 1938).

To James Laughlin
TLS-1

P.O. Box 1522
Taos, New Mexico
Monday, July 20, 1947

Dear James:
    Here are a few pages of the Cossery ms., and I must say I like him and will enjoy getting into him. I find him pretty powerful in places, and he does make one *feel*.
    Honestly, I believe de Mauny's translation does not help Cossery; it is so literal and faithful in most places; it steals away the warmth, the color, sometimes the terror of the French language and pretty well vitiates Cossery's starkness and power. Better some of it stay in French. Some is like Jane Austen.
    I believe I can do it, but you must see. I'd like to get the thing as communicable to English readers as Cossery would make it if he were writing it in that language. I don't mean to overwrite it, nor rewrite it; but I do feel that in a translation some imaginative liberty must be taken, in order not to betray the original feeling, tone and images. If you want me to go along more rigidly faithful to the original text, let me know and I'll do that.
    Yes, I can do it and want very much to. As for what I'd ask for the work, I leave that to you. Whatever comes will help, like alms. I'd like you to set a kind of deadline for me so that I can work towards that. Tell me when you'd like to have it finished and I'll tally up to that.
    In all probability we shall be leaving here soon. Money is low and we may need a change of air and personalities. We are thinking about San Francisco seriously. We would try to work there for a bit of money to live on and continue our own work. Then come back here when we can afford it.
    If you find my handling of Cossery acceptable and want me to do a whole new translation of it—and I really think that necessary—please let me know and I'll get it to you when you want it. In the meantime I am

going on with it and expect to have a sizable portion of it under way by the time I hear from you again. Thanks so much for wanting to help; it's really a great boost.

Best wishes,
Bill Goyen

---

the Cossery ms.: Goyen had begun to translate *The House of Certain Death*. One can only speculate whether this title influenced that of his own first novel, *The House of Breath*. He may also have encountered the phrase "the house of breath" in Eunice Tietjens's poem "The Drug Clerk" from *Body and Raiment* (New York: Alfred A. Knopf, 1926), pp. 25–26.

To James Laughlin
TLS-1

Box 1522
Taos
Aug. 2, 1947

Dear Laughlin:
    That's bad news about Caresse Crosby and the Italian fellow, and I'm blue about it; particularly since I was having such a high time with *La Maison*. I fell for Bayoumi (le montreur des singes).
    Is it really all off? Shall I hold the galleys and the de Mauny translation until I get final hands-off from you? I have done about half the ms in a rough draught translation.
    I liked doing translation. Have done a little before, but mostly poetry and short pieces. This time I found it a kind of *deus ex machina* to save me from devouring myself out here in these mountains. It was often like doing mathematics: a clearheaded, concrete piece of work to be done. Then it sent me back to my own work with sharper claws. I'd like to do more. Don't you have something else I could try my hand at for you? I see you are planning to do Valéry, and I am happy, for I have searched around for some definitive edition of him. Could I help there—he means a lot to me. And I see somebody is doing Corbière. Now what about Laforgue? One would even like to see a group of de Maupassant stories done right (forgetting the many bad ones done of him). You know I read your Flaubert at sea during the war and was quite unhappy with the translation. I mentioned it to Frieda once, and she had felt the same. I love those stories.

New York and thereabouts must be dreadful now. We are hot here, too, at midday. But the early mornings and evenings are redemptions. Just now we are thrilled with the vast flocks of big primroses which open morning and evening in the fields just below us. And the alfalfa next to us has just been cut and baled and lies out there like a bit of the mid-west. Hate to leave all this, but we leave only so that we can come back. We leave on a leash.

I'll be eager to see Rexroth. There are other friends and friends of friends in San Francisco, and we are looking forward to some kind of life there for a little while. No word yet from Jean Garrigue. Wonder if she would care to take our little place for several months? I'll be glad to help her if I can.

Angie today showed us the broken bowl. He was terribly sad about it. Seems his clay is bad, for lately he's had trouble with his things.

I'll wait for more news on Cossery and further instructions. We probably shan't be leaving [for California] for another ten days or so. Thanks again for wanting to help, and best wishes from Walt and me.

Bill Goyen

I have seen a copy of C. Crosby's new *Portfolio*. Think it a bit la-la—but there's a keen photograph of D.H.L. in it, looking pale and ill and wasted.

---

bad news: Evidently Laughlin had heard of another translation of the Cossery in progress.
Caresse Crosby: (1892–1970).Writer and wife of Harry Crosby (1898–1929). Together they were publishers of the Black Sun Press.
La Maison: Cossery's *The House of Certain Death*.
Valéry: Paul Valéry (1871–1945). French poet and critic.
Corbière: Édouard Joachim Corbière (1845–1875). French Symbolist poet.
Laforgue: Jules Laforgue (1860–1887). Another French Symbolist poet.
your Flaubert: Laughlin had published a translation of Flaubert's *Three Tales* in his New Classics Series.
Rexroth: Kenneth Rexroth (1905–1982). West Coast poet published by Laughlin.
Jean Garrigue: (1913–1972). American lyric poet. Laughlin had published her in *Five Young American Poets*, Third Series (1944).
Angie: Angelo Ravagli, who brought Lawrence's ashes from Europe in a pot to give to Frieda Lawrence. He abandoned his family in Italy and, twenty years after Lawrence's death, became Frieda's husband.

Katherine Anne Porter
ALS-2

10250 Wilshire Boulevard
Los Angeles 24, California
(Care of E. F. Riordan)
August 12, 1947

Dear Miss Porter:

I must—and it may seem like too much of a thing, but I don't mean it to—ask to see you again before Walter and I depart for San Francisco. There are so many things I want and need to talk about or hear talked about concerning writing as a way of life. Our visit last night was certainly exciting and I feel I can't leave without a kind of enlargement upon some of the things said.

Often I am afraid of talk, etc., but then I feel that the younger ones must, when they can (humbly and seriously), meet and talk with the older ones.

If I may, I'd like to come along as soon as you can have me. I mean I want to come not for any of the bad reasons a lot of people probably come, or want to come, to you. Somehow I feel I have to explain this.

If you'll just send a note here telling me when I may appear, I'll be grateful.

Sincerely,
William Goyen
Tel.: Crestview 65043.

Katherine Anne Porter: (1890–1980). Fiction writer, author of *Flowering Judas* (1930) and *Pale Horse, Pale Rider* (1939); later the winner of the National Book Award and the Pulitzer Prize. Goyen's first meeting with her was August 11, 1947, in Los Angeles. But his published version of their introduction states: "She lived in a four-story brownstone house on East 65th Street (the house is now destroyed) when I first met her. It was in 1950, in the summer, and she'd invited me to come have a drink on the occasion of the recent publication of my first novel, *The House of Breath*. In fact she'd just written a fine and serious review of the book for *The New York Times*" ("Katherine Anne Porter: An Appreciation," *Dallas Morning News*, September 28, 1980, p. G1). Perhaps he misdated their meeting in order to obscure the fact that she knew him at the time she wrote her highly laudatory review of his novel.

At the time of their first meeting, he was thirty-two and she was fifty-seven. Later, a romance was to follow. It lasted two years. Goyen said in conversations with Robert Phillips that he knew she was older than he, but he never knew how *much* older. The

Goyen-Porter correspondence, which begins with this letter and is held with the Porter papers at the University of Maryland, is considerable, especially in 1951 and 1952.

To Spud Johnson
ALS-2

10250 Wilshire Boulevard
Los Angeles 24, Cal.
August 12, 1947

Spoodle:

We came along as quietly and uneventfully as if we were driving up to Sante Fe to buy vegetables—no trouble. Arrived here Sunday night at nine. Now we are comfortably installed in the plush Riordan apartment, a bit rusty feeling, like an old bottle top, in the midst of this shining, gleaming, colored world. Wilshire Boulevard is like Halley's Comet going past, night and day. There is a shock on every corner.

One feels like a covered wagon.

Yesterday, in the afternoon, we visited Knud Merrild. He's a bit sad, for me, and his wife has been ill for a long time. We sat and talked and I was not sure of what he was; but when we left, he walked out to the car with us and said, wanly, "You two remind me of the early days." Then I knew him. I feel sure he is unhappy here, doesn't belong.

Last night we spent a few hours with Katherine Anne Porter. It was exciting; she spoke quickly and straight out of a wisdom. I found her powerful and full of integrity—one feels the *cleanliness* of writing in her. I must see her again before we leave. She loathes the Lawrence legend. Also Laughlin.

This morning out to UCLA to get information on San Francisco schools. There *is* a University of San Francisco. Also an Extension Bureau there. But it depresses me; I don't feel good or right about it.

All this *is* exciting, and I feel *correct*, somewhere—I mean not nasty or wrong. I believe it is going to be good. Occasionally a forlorn feeling comes over me when I see our old Taos work shoes in a corner, or our forsaken dungarees. A whole life, unspeakable, is in them when I look at them. [. . .]

We'll stay another few days, then away. Will keep you posted. Take care. We miss and love you.

Billy

Spud Johnson: Walter Johnson. There are forty-seven letters from Goyen to Johnson at the Harry Ransom Humanities Research Center (HRC).
Knud Merrild: (1894–1954). Danish painter and author who was a friend of Lawrence's and part of his inner circle since the 1920s. At this time he was reduced to painting houses to make a living.
depresses me: Goyen and Berns were considering taking teaching jobs to make a living.

To Spud Johnson
ALS-7

Berkeley
Aug. 25, 1947

Dear Spoodle:

[. . .] Today the decision was made and Walter signed a contract with the Union High School at Napa. It seems good and right—and of course I am beaming proud of the Boy. I had feared jobs in offices. Now he'll have the chance for a new experience—one that might show him a way not too alien to his own work.

Napa seems nicer and prettier each time we revisit it: smooth, gentle hills—sort of Tuscan-like (like the backgrounds in Italian Renaissance paintings), some mist always forming or being scattered over the hills, rich sun (but not gaudy and technicolored like Southern California's), and the feeling of water not far away. It's not idyllic or any of that, but nice and rather soft feeling.

The problem is a house. Walt's principal, a good Methodist, Lion's Clubber of a kind soul, and genuine, is working to find a place for us. It will be a bit difficult, but it is early and we needn't rush, except for the expense of hotel room and meals out. But for the nonce I am enjoying Berkeley (the University puts something in the air) and—when we can get to it—San Francisco.

We were across the bay last night for dinner with ex-Navy friend Steve Wessels. The thrill of San Francisco is still there, for me; and that old insidious glamour, high swank, misery, grandeur, evil and fear that I knew during the war still lingers over these hills and hotels and bridges. This may not be good—and San Francisco means more than all these—and it is a sensualist's retrogression; but I must admit it, and I believe it will never really be wiped out of my sense's memory. The crown of sorrow on the tragic head of all of it is (and this is a thing I feel always when I revisit places of past powerful experiences) that alas, a thing is *gone*, irretrievable. To not always be wanting to call things back; not to grieve, in really a resigned way, the loss of what one later knows had to be only an ephemeral, fleeting parcel of a greater, steadier, and really unchangeable whole—this must be something like the serenity that lies in something like renunciation. Enough.

Now what shall I do for bread and money? In another several days I shall probably have let myself get hired as a teacher at Napa—which would pay me quite a nice sum for 12 months—enough, if sensibly saved, to keep Walt and me in our little house in Taos for another year. But I don't *want* to teach. I want to *write*. Why can't the world see that? The world, of course, don't care. [. . .]

---

a sensualist's retrogression: Accurate description of Goyen's story set in San Francisco, "Nests in a Stone Image."

To Katherine Anne Porter
TLS-2

General Delivery
Berkeley, Calif.
Aug. 26, 1947

Dear Miss Porter:

I had, at last, your letter yesterday, forwarded on to me by my friend Riordan, and it was really a great pleasure to hear from you—but a disappointment and an embarrassment to know that you had called and called vainly. Indeed, we were right there, we stayed over two extra days so that I might see you again; but lately there had been a change of telephone numbers and that may have caused the trouble. I'm terribly sorry it didn't work out, and it was kind of you to try and try.

But, as you say, there will probably be trips down to Los Angeles, and then I hope we can meet again and talk, or listen.

I was feeling very much stripped and bare when we came to visit you, rather like a shelled pea, podless and snatched off its vine. Coming into Los Angeles from the mud village of Taos was exactly like suffering shock, there was that awful numbness and paralysis of certain faculties, only the senses were working—and then only to confound any clarity— and when we sat together that night there was suddenly and briefly a clear and clean vision of a kind of whole, and it was natural that I should want to try to achieve that again with you.

Of course places in the world—like Taos or San Francisco or New York—never "solve" the problem, if it is that, which one carries around in him (how ridiculous to assume such), for the thing he wrestled with is totally inside—and it may be that the main value and function of the Taoses, the San Franciscos and the New Yorks, is that of a ready mouth into which to thrust the thermometer which will register the degree of intensity of one's inner fever.

But we are here, and San Francisco and the Bay places are lovely. My good comrade Walter Berns has decided to try his hand and wits at teaching and yesterday he took a position in a nice little school up at Napa, Calif., which is some forty miles north. I have found in the past that I can't *genuinely* or *authentically* continue my own work and teach school—there is a kind of conflict or warring of the two patterns, for me. But I have learned, in Taos, that it is not right, for me, to make one's creative work carry the burden and strain of "making a living" for one. It gets rather like a stubborn ass who finally refuses to move at all under such a load.

Yet I believe, like the Hen, that if an egg has got to be laid, either a nest will be made or out it will come on the bare earth.

To be young and really having and wanting to do something is a pretty bad mess these days, don't you think? There are so many gangs. If you go alone you are "not in the world," and if you join up you have to carry a card and a number. There seems not to be any good families of people— relations between people seem to be incestuous, depraved, mutually masturbatory; it's like a Hall of Mirrors where everybody reflects every-body, in distortion. The derangement or perversion of some of the simplest, cleanest little verities or beauties is so wanton that you have to get off in corners constantly and check yourself like an algebraic problem. One's need of steady, whole human beings is as craving, almost, as hunger.

I don't mean this little bit to sound like platitude or rhetoric—for me it is all as important as life and I can't leave it alone.

Thanks again for the letter, and I hope to be able to see you again before too much time has passed. In the meantime, I'd like to write to you again, if I may.

Best wishes,
William Goyen

Berkeley, California
August 27, 1947

Dear Laughlin:

We are here, have been here for a week now, quite a leap from the mountains to the sea, but it is lovely and thrilling. Looks like we'll be here for some time (since we can't afford to go back), and we'll probably be living up in Napa Valley, north of here.

While in Los Angeles had a keen visit with Katherine Anne Porter, found her well now and at work again.

Have met and talked with Everson and Duncan; tried Rexroth twice but found him away. Shall try again tomorrow.

Am wondering about things, about Cossery. Since my mail has had to be forwarded from Taos, everything is awry. Would like to hear from you when there is time. You may write to me c/o General Delivery, Berkeley, until I send further address.

Naturally we miss the adobe and the sagebrush terribly, and we yearn for dear old Frieda and the good Angie. But we'll be back.

Hope to hear—
Bill Goyen

---

at work again: Among Porter's projects in 1947 was an adaptation, with Robert Rossen, producer at Columbia Records, of Chekhov's "La Cigale."

Everson: William Everson (1912–1994). Dominican brother known as Brother Antoninus. Laughlin published his poetry.

Duncan: Robert Duncan (1919–1988). Poet published by Laughlin.

TWO

Napa

Dallas

Portland

1947–1949

To Toni Strassman
ALS-2

Napa, California
Sept. 4, 1947

My dear Toni:

This morning came the ms.—forwarded from faraway Taos—like a returned love letter unopened. It is sad. I won't let it be like a failure—it was never that, we know.

And the good reassuring things you said in the letter—they give me courage.

Now, for a while, Toni, I want to work carefully and slowly, be like a grape in the sun, to learn discipline and exorbitant care. It has all been so *nervous*, so quick and something like hysteria, so deeply felt, like grief or like low-down pain, that I had to get the words for it *out*, spewed or vomited.

In L.A. I had a memorable visit with K. A. Porter. She will help me. I am going down again.

Writing and life are lovers, illicit or matrimonialized, but they mean to go together. The damned unholy problem is the life, how to keep it in a direction, keep it open and right and real and kicking. I've got to take a job (why whine over this? I'm not, honestly)—what? I've only a few dollars. I may try teaching a bit.

Let's go on as though I were sending you a story a month. Let's write, talk about the show, and keep close friends. I've a kind of love for you, Toni.

Bill

---

the ms.: Strassman returned the novel *Section Two*.

To William M. Hart
TLS-2

1949 Main Street
Napa, California
November 10, 1947

My dear Billy:

Again the wrong in waiting so long to write curses this letter, tries to force it into saying all things that have happened since the departure from

Taos. "We came here, we went there, we saw this . . . and then . . ." I do not want to write all this little history; a letter from me to you is always a reaching out to touch you and by touching say that none or nothing has changed, only shifting of place.

The intensive seeping absorption in my work, and life as my work, has made me alienate friends and family, even if for a time; occasionally, as today, I look up and see out beyond my work and find that it has been like a long soaking. For me, Billy, that is the only way; I have shown it, proved it to myself. It may mean nothing, but that is not true, because it already means something, very much.

Every day I contemplate Taos like a whirling little world through an astronomer's tube: I will know its meaning and its value. Taos, like many things loved, fought for and achieved, had to be shamed by turning from it. I suppose I worked as wildly, as irrepressibly, as intensely, as I have ever worked in any place. Only a few good little things came out of it—as writing, I mean—but there are millions of words, all elations or agonies, put down.

Here, you know, I tried teaching again—this time junior high school. It was wrong, wrong, a betrayal, a kind of crime, great abuse. I could not stand it. I worked a month then stood one day before the principal (who was baffled) and told him it was wrong for me and resigned. I was physically and emotionally very ill. I chose, finally, to starve, to die—anything—rather than to live out what was for me a defamation of my way. I have to write—I am ruined that way now, like a whore; I cannot reform. Nothing can take away my use of myself to that end; if it tries I go sick and scattered and useless. I *know* this.

Now I take the risk again, gladly, exultantly—up here with only a steadfast friend, among strangers (but these are everywhere), with very few dollars. I am writing, so deeply absorbed in the things I want to tell. I am trying to learn calmness and incessant care; to go very slowly and carefully. This does not mean, and never has meant, a putting away of the world, or humanity, but a fuller, closer taking in of these, close close to one's very core.

I meditate so often, Billy, the courage to unflinchingly lie down with certain leprous truths to keep them warm with my life and heart, like our Saint Julien. That's the kind of courage one must have. I am finding out whether I have it. Any other is like the false bravado of *un seducteur jusqu'au bord du lit*—and that is not enough, it gets no pleasure or sin, robs the terror of orgasm, which is mean. Everywhere there are these seducers who never finish it off, *right*—only go on using their hand. Billy, this is hard and full of agony, but it is *right*, and time is passing over us and we are going on farther and farther, and dalliance and waste grow more and more profligate. We *must*, even if it means losing jobs, heads, *everything* outside our real valuable useful selves, surrender more and more and more to what we feel to be our work. How often you and I used to speak of all this.

I brought no books here, but sent for two and they recently arrived: the letters of Rilke and *Dear Theo*. Now they mean more to me than ever before (and this does not mean any claiming of kinship, naturally). Rilke keeps speaking of "work," of the "workday"—the daily going into a *work*, like a labor, with one's hands, keenly, ardent and calm, holding the world not far away but holding it just outside one's door, to keep it out of the world of one's work. You know I do not mean by this escape or retreat; but it seems to me that even a little story is a world with its people, and that to bring other bigger worlds into this little one is to show no respect for one's little people he works with; it terrifies them or shies them and, finally, they will not speak for you honestly or clearly, will be like self-conscious children brought into a drawing room where there are grownups. You know I had a wonderful visit with Katherine Anne Porter in Los Angeles a few months ago, and we talked of this. She sat very beautiful and intense and spoke clearly and simply but always with fire and a stinging castigation of what she calls "the muddlers": those who "scum everything up" with their half-values, with their glib comments, and who will not give up much but want life and art to be somewhat easy and glamorous and quick. When she spoke of her *craft* it was like listening to a deft mechanic. She is a little like Frieda; in some way they have that same rare *hold* on visions and common sense.

Then Eudora Welty has been in San Francisco and of course I have spent some time with her—we are old friends since early in the war, if only by what came rapidly to be a kind of intimate correspondence. She is very simple, homely, so quiet one can scarcely hear her words; she responds like an animal. She quoted me a letter she has recently had from E. M. Forster (who, as you know, was until a month or so ago visiting in this country), which praised her beautiful work and set it apart as the freshest and finest American story writing. We had some walks through old parts of San Francisco and one night went together to see *Tristan and Isolde* performed by the San Francisco Opera Company with the splendid Traubel as Isolde. She returned to Mississippi last week.

Walt goes on teaching at the Junior College here and seems quite adjusted and satisfied. He sends his love. Rilke says this somewhere (it is in my notebook): "A togetherness between two people is an impossibility, and where it seems, nevertheless, to exist, it is a narrowing, a reciprocal agreement which robs either one party or both of his fullest freedom and development. But, once the realization is accepted that even between the closest human beings infinite distances continue to exist, a wonderful living side by side can grow up, if they succeed in loving the distance between them which makes it possible for each to see the other *whole* against a wide sky."

I rarely care what others say now; I try to care not even that often. Yet friendship is never really broken, keeps forming again like scarred skin; and often I think of those like Flora, and some others, and yearn a little for them, loving them still, and want to be near them. Silence is never a measure of any kind of alienation between close people. There are, as the years go, only one or two who remain any kind of challenge to my life or my work (have there ever really been more than one or two, ever, at any time?). You are one, Billy. We are beyond justification or inquisition— except always to ourselves. If one can get past himself, then he can appear serenely before those he loves.

So let me hear when there is time and a thing to say; and remember I love you.

As ever,
Billy

Saint Julien: Throughout his life, Goyen liked to allude to a favorite tale by Flaubert, "La légende de Saint Julien l'hospitalier" from *Trois Contes* (1877).
steadfast friend: Walter Berns.
letters of Rilke: Rainer Maria Rilke (1875–1926). Prague-born German poet.
Dear Theo: Edited by Irving Stone (Garden City, N.Y.: Doubleday, 1946), a volume of letters from Vincent van Gogh to his brother.
E. M. Forster: (1879–1970). English novelist and author of *A Passage to India.*
Traubel: Helen Traubel (1899–1972). Opera singer.
Flora: Flora Armytage.

To Katherine Anne Porter
ALS-3

1949 Main Street
Napa, Calif.
Jan. 29, 1948

Dear Miss Porter:
Since Christmas I've been wanting to write to say that one of my real delights of the Holidays was the reading of your matchless article on Miss

G. Stein—a quick, courageous and expert interment of that rusty casket. Your handling of that whole messy genre—and how rancourless I thought it was done!—of scummer-uppers made me once again very grateful that you and your craft and the standards of your art are in the world and functioning. Too many shards off that old flint, alas, are still flashing and sparkling up here. These people are slopping paint and egg-whites over canvases and ready easy ink on page after page of poetry and an anarchistic prose.

Before you finish, I hope you will handle one other—if very minor— muddler: Our Queen of Taos, M.D.L. She must be tagged and shipped away, you know.

Early this fall Eudora Welty was here—or in San Francisco—and at last I had the pleasure of meeting her, after several years of letter-changing. We had some good talks and times together. She has taught me very much and my esteem for her consummate art just can't be shaken.

Best wishes to you in the New Year.

Sincerely yours,
William Goyen

---

article on Miss G. Stein: "Gertrude Stein: A Self Portrait," *Harper's* 195 (December 1947): 519–528.
M.D.L.: Mabel Dodge Luhan.

To Margo Jones
TLS-2

McMurray's
The Personal Bookshop
1330 Commerce Street
Dallas, Texas
Wed., April 7, 1948

My dear Margo:
Your wire came yesterday and your letter today. Of course I was sorry that it could not go on as we had hoped, but I understand and Heaven knows I thank you for the check and the wonderful words and your belief in me. If I could only say, straight off, what all this has meant to me— finding you here, being able to be of some help to you and your theatre,

having you to say quick things to, here and there, on the run, and all that
. . . but gratitude for many things is never spoken, and better that it isn't.
You know, anyway.

I feel guilty at taking so large a check for work I did not do, and I don't
know what to say about it except that I will try to repay you in the ways
you would have me repay you. I have worked my way along, so far, by
hook or crook, scratching and struggling and hanging on by my very
teeth; and I will go on that way. The terrible terrible hurts I feel, like
something abused or violated inside me, when I kick aside my own vision
and fall to the world and run for the money and possessions and the easy
dead life which some people would have me yoke my life to like some
stumbling brutish ox—this hurt makes me know that I am what I am and
that I must take the consequences. The real and ultimate blossoming
which I long ago knew wanted to come, and would, has taken longer than
I thought and it has asked for harder labor and anxiety and even suffering
than I ever dreamed to give, but I say again, and I know I do not have to
say it to you, that I would do it all over again, as I may have to, for it must
be done.

My finding you again in Dallas was a refreshing of many tired things,
for me, but I think the most wonderful thing of all about it was that we
were able to let each other know that we are still in the world and alive
for the purposes we swore to years ago.

Now Margo I want to help you in any way I can. If I can be of service
and help out in Taos, then I must; if you want me to come back to Dallas
in the summer, I'll come. Just let me know. [. . .] I want you to know that
I *believe* in this theatre here in Dallas, that I feel a part of it, and that I will
help in any way when you need me. We leave for Taos probably Friday or
Saturday. You can write me there Care of Dorothy Brett, Box 214, Taos,
New Mex. As soon as I return I'll get a box of my own and send you the
number. I'll be waiting to hear that you need me. [. . .]

Again, thank you from the bottom of my heart for everything that
happened here in Dallas, and I know Walter says the same; and let me
help you in any way I can, whenever you need me. Walt sends warm
regards and I my love. Our greetings to Manning—

Bill Goyen

P.S. I want you to see the whole of my work on East Texas, and as soon as
I can sew it all together in one bundle, I'll send it along to you. I am
going to give everything I have to finishing it this summer in the mountains—it is my one big project. As for the novel which John Selby saw (it

is the war book which Walt and I wrote together), you might mention it to him if you see him—he was extremely nice to us and seemed interested in our outcome. Walter plans to do more revision on the book this summer, then we'll send it back to Selby.

And thanks for giving us friends like Lon Tinkle and Eliz. Ann. Already Elizabeth Ann seems like a lifetime friend, and thank goodness for the clearheadedness, good sense, and integrity of Tinkle. Bless you—

B.

P.P.S. And oh yes—we read Mary McCarthy's discussion of *Streetcar*. There seems little justification for such a slaughterous and really destructive piece of criticism—one feels there is more behind these dirty words than the mere accusation that Williams is "firmly rooted in pay dirt." Whatever the defects of the play, whatever the motives Williams has for writing for the theatre (and I think I know), there is simply *no* justification for such cheap, stinking, biased criticism. To hell with her; forget it and chalk up one black mark against *Partisan Review*.

Goyen's correspondence with Jones runs from 1948 to 1955, and is preserved in the Dallas Public Library.

McMurray's: Successful Dallas bookstore that promised: "Books! Every title—Every author—Every publisher!"

it could not go on: Jones had been giving him cash stipends for play reading.

Manning: Manning Gurian, company manager for Margo Jones's Dallas theatre.

my work on East Texas: The first mention of what would become *The House of Breath*.

John Selby: (b. 1905). An editor at Rinehart and Company, publishers.

the war book: Section Two.

Lon Tinkle: (1906–1980). The editor of the book section of the *Dallas Morning News* and chairman of the French department at Southern Methodist University.

Elizabeth Ann: Elizabeth Ann McMurray, (d. 1994), owner of McMurray's Bookshop.

McCarthy's discussion: McCarthy characterized Williams's play as one about a man's difficulty in getting into his bathroom because his sister-in-law is always occupying it. She wrote, "If art, as Mr. Williams appears to believe, is a lie, then anything goes; but Mr. Williams' lies, like Blanche's, are so garish and ugly . . . his work reeks of literary ambition as the apartment reeks of cheap perfume" (*Partisan Review*, March 1945; reprinted in Mary McCarthy's *Theatre Chronicles, 1937–1962* [New York: Farrar Straus, 1963], p. 82).

To James Laughlin
TLS-2

Taos, N.M.
April 17 [1948]

Dear Jim:
Wherever you are, I hope this reaches you before you leave there. I have been in Texas for some time, working with Margo Jones and her theatre there—script reading, etc. It was an exhilarating experience, indeed, and a great encouragement too, for I was rather low in spirits and money. Margo and I have been friends for years, I had worked with her down in Houston where she started. I hope to be able to do more work for her during the summer and next fall. At present, as you probably know, she is in N.Y. making preparations for *Summer and Smoke*.

Walter and I returned to Taos early this week and it is strange and beautiful here; spring hasn't shown its face yet, but there are rumblings. The mountains are still snow-covered. Taos had a brutal winter—the cruelty of it is still in the air. I came back with an inexplicable feeling of resistance to this place, but it seemed the only place in the world to come to—and there is the little house—and one can live so cheaply—and quietly—and do hard work. I am working well and hard, still "writing art" as you call it—i.e., I am not "slanting" towards *Good Housekeeping*. I'm just not good enough for those mags, I really stink when I try to write for them, it's no good. Will hang on here by the flying trapeze and try to put down well and honestly what comes out of me and hope it says something and means something.

I have waited and waited for *N.D. 10*—where is it? Will it appear? I trust there is no difficulty with the press or paper or some such. Since it means a little money coming in—and, above all, since it means being in print—I am eager to see. Tell me when I may expect to see it and whether I'll get enough money to go on being anxious about.

Frieda arrives next week. Then we shall have some kind of life here. I never cared for the rest of Taos (with one or two exceptions—people); it's shabby and pseudo and second-rate, I feel. Something about the town and those people scares me; I can't go down the streets without fear, without cringing. But out here in the desert I love; there is hard work to do inside the house and outside on the land—and next door there's the good Brett and across the road beloved old Frieda and Angie—and Spud up the road a bit.

But one needs the world often, and the world stays away from El Prado—only the crazy fragments and odd remnants of it come by our houses, usually Frieda's. Dallas I liked very much, good people, genuine, good work there, and some spirit. May try to settle there for a while.

I must say *Partisan Review* makes me sick lately, more and more. Those damned people are so intelligent, they make one feel dull and stupid; they *know* so much. I am about through with the whole outfit. How do you feel about them? I remember I asked you that when you were here—and you said you didn't care for *PR*'s kind of "intellectation"—that was your word. I know what it means. I can never figure out whether they like you and *ND* or hate you, are envious, or what. Mary McCarthy, whom I usually admire extremely, goes vulgarly haywire and smart-alecky too often lately. Her essay on T. Williams and *Streetcar,* while very right and true in places, was, overall, nasty and vindictive and just plain ornery— what do you think, and if you haven't read it, do by all means—it's in the current issue (March, I mean).

Must say I like the little Lawrence of yours, despite some of our friend Rexroth's deep leaps into nonsense. He disappointed me a little in the preface—a lot of people I have talked to feel the same.

Will you return to the U.S. this summer? I have some work I'd like to get your opinion on—it's a collection of pieces on East Texas. A portion of it will come out in *Accent* in the summer. I want to work out a whole group of things on Texas, which I know and must put down.

Hope your work comes along. I enjoyed your letter, written a long time ago, and thank you for sending it. I need money, I have none, and I'm still trying to work out a way by which I can write and think and keep things straight—and earn some money, too. Please let me hear as soon as you have time to write, and luck to you. Walter sends greetings.

Best wishes,
Bill Goyen

---

little Lawrence of yours: Laughlin had published Lawrence's *Selected Poems* (New Directions, 1948) in his New Classics Series, with a preface by Kenneth Rexroth. Laughlin also published Lawrence's *The Man Who Died* (1928).

pieces on East Texas: The germ of *The House of Breath*, "Four American Portraits as Elegy (Charity, Aunty, Folner, Granny Ganchion)," would appear in *Accent* 7, no. 3 (Spring 1948): 131–141.

To Allen Maxwell
TLS-1

Taos, New Mexico
April 25, 1948

Dear Alan [sic] *Maxwell:*

As you probably know, I left Dallas some two weeks ago for this place, after having no luck at finding a job there. Somehow it seemed the right thing to do, since I at least have a little adobe hut here and living is easier and cheaper. Too, I can continue my writing full-time—by the skin of my teeth—and, with less tension, hold out here in the mountains for a little while longer.

I enjoyed our brief little visit and I'm sorry I never got back to see you; but the time was short and harried and, in the end, I was working for Margo Jones some twelve hours a day. I do appreciate your interest, though, and I hope when I am in Dallas again we may have more of a talk.

I am sending you 3 stories in the hope that you might want one of them. Please let me know what you think, when you have the time; and thanks for whatever you can do. All you folks in Dallas were so very nice and hospitable—I certainly mean to return there at the end of the summer.

Best wishes,
William Goyen

My return address is simply Taos, N.M.

Alan Maxwell: Allen Maxwell (b. 1905). Goyen's correspondence with Maxwell and Margaret L. Hartley (1909–1983), editors of the *Southwest Review*, was very full from 1948 to 1955, and then resumes in the 1970s. Goyen dedicated his 1975 *Collected Stories* to them.

3 stories: Goyen submitted "Boy of the Weed," "At the Graveyard," and "Year of the Grasshoppers." Maxwell found them inferior to Goyen's "Four American Portraits as Elegy," which he read in *Accent,* and wrote that he was "going to have to be insistent on getting something up to that standard" (A.M. to W.G., August 24, 1948).

Taos
Sat. night
May 8, 1948

My dear Zoë:

   Your letter a few days ago—and yes indeed spring comes late here, it
has scarcely shown its green face; but since Mayday the cottonwoods have
put out lime-green feathers and the little orchards down in Taos Valley
have burst into bloom, so lovely—we have some in the house and it
smells so good—and all around the desert out here where we live in El
Prado the little pink and white wild flowers have sprung up everywhere.
And the birds! such beautiful wild ones are coming in—I am up between
5:30 and 6:00 every morning and the calls of the birds are like human
voices, a glittering chorus of them. And all day long we hear the mourn-
ing doves in the distance, and yesterday we saw some wild canaries, two
pheasants were on the top of our woodpile, and a yellow-breasted Oriole
was down on the fence. Oh it is lovely here now. May and September-
October are the most beautiful times—but during the past two days we
have had cold and very windy days and nights, the wind's about to drive
us all crazy. Of course out here on the desert it is worse since we have no
trees to protect us; but everywhere there is heavy wind and blowing dust.
   I have, in the past days, dug and planted a rather impressive little
garden down the slope from the house. Last year a garden was out of the
question—we couldn't even plant flowers—because of the extreme
scarcity of water. There was an irrigation ditch running on the land below
our place, but we had no rights to it. But this year there's gallons and
gallons of water for everyone because of the heavy winter snows; and the
irrigation ditch has been diverted through our property so that it may
irrigate a big bean crop planted by the Spaniard who owns a strip of land
next to ours—and we may use all the water from this ditch we wish.
When I learned of this new privilege, I promptly started digging and
planting. Now my little garden lies right along the swiftly flowing ditch
in some very rich soil, and there I have planted beans, peas, carrots,
onions, lettuce, turnips and mustard greens. They are already coming up.
And I have made a few flower beds around the house; some iris, some
poppies, morning glories and petunias—we'll see what they do. You know
how I love planting and gardening, my mother gave me that. Now, after a
hard morning's work inside at my desk, I go out on the land and work
hard in the brilliant sunshine and pure air for two or three hours—makes

all the difference in the world, keeps a clear head and gives time for thinking and meditation.

Zoë I am terribly excited over my work, I am full of it, it has really come alive for me. A portion of it will appear in *Accent* shortly in the Spring issue—I corrected and returned the galleys about three weeks ago. I don't know whether you can get a hold of a copy there or not, but please try to if you can, for I want you to see what I have done there and what I am doing. Surely some more of it will be taken by someone—I believe in it so—I *know* what I am doing. As for New Directions, I am just about through with that bird Laughlin and his crew. I had a letter from him in January saying the anthology would be out "soon"—and to this date I cannot get any information about it, either from him, whom I've written again recently, or from bookstores. I don't know what's happened, but I'd sure as hell like to have my money. We'll just keep waiting.

Make up your mind about this summer and let me know. I still can't say whether I'll be here or not, but then if not here then where? Of course I want to stay here and will hang on to the very last cent (and then probably borrow some if no money has come in); it's a constant scrape and scramble, but then it is right, it is the only way, the *only* reality for me and I know that for myself; so I go on in that faith and belief. I have only just begun. But you come on if you can manage it; I know you'll love it and consider it a real discovery of a place to be quiet and simple in and in which to do good work. It really isn't arty as most people think—life is too damned hard here, you have to work too hard just to eat and be clean. That may be, finally, my objection to it—one spends so much of his time with the necessities like cooking, getting fuel, getting food, keeping house, fighting the elements, etc. But then it seems to me that a creative life might demand just this: a kind of elemental life far away from sophistication and superficiality. Yet sometimes I feel that perhaps a one-room efficiency apartment in a city with the world just outside one's door might be the best way. But, strange thing, Zoë, I can't stay away too long from the woods and the land and nature—so I suppose that's where I belong.

Enough for tonight—I am tired of fighting this brutal wind and must get to my bed. Hope your work is going well, keep whittling at it, that's the way, go at it your own way and to hell with authority and this and that. Send me news when there is any and when you decide what you'll do, let me know and I'll help any way I can. Thanks for the Margo clipping and birthday greeting. Walter sends best wishes, and let us hear—

Yours,
Billy

A portion of it: "Four American Portraits as Elegy."
As for New Directions: After Laughlin accepted Goyen's "A Parable of Perez" for publication in his *New Directions Annual* in 1948, he wrote that the volume was too large and he could not "squeeze in" the story. Goyen felt humiliated and wrote Laughlin on December 6 retracting the story. Laughlin apologized, and it eventually appeared the following year in *Annual* 11: 240–243—its only appearance in print to date.

To William M. Hart
ALS-3

Taos, N.M.
May 26, 1948

My dear Billy:

Thank God for that bright clear and steadfast Eye of yours that hangs over and perceives the *whole* of all this that is happening and has happened. There is nowhere any other such eye, and whether you *want* to see or not, you *do* and can't help it—for you have been in on all this— whatever it be—from the beginning, know its roots, and traditions—and now you see its *direction*. I cannot tell you how valuable you, my Eye, are to me.

I've not even seen *Accent* yet and it is a little terrifying to know that these people are now out beyond me in the world. Somehow I feel, a bit, as though I've betrayed Sue Emma and Folner and Granny and Aunty; but we just couldn't live together so secretly any longer. But they are not at all abandoned, for I go on with them—and the others.

I understand your questioning some parts of Folner's validity as a human being, but I disagree—not that I think I have completely succeeded in putting him down—because I feel that what is not clear is *my* failure, not *his*. By "wild like a creature" I mean untamed, somewhere undomesticated, un*civilized* in the real meaning of the word. Not wild as in *savage* or unrestrained, but like a *creature*—beast, animal—elemental.

Everywhere the *religious* sense of *sin* works in these people. *Of course* they turned, finally, to Beulah Land and memory and to the subterranean world of the cellar. Oh I think and think of these people, live in a stern meditation of them. They have their meaning and by learning it I may know *mine*, and put that down.

You have a responsibility to me—and I have to you—whether we will or like it or not [*sic*]. Bless you for what you say—and my God don't let that starry Eye go blind.

What is the quotation? Thanks for the aye sign. *Accent* had been extraordinary in its praise of this work, but still I did not know what those who know Boy Ganchion and all the rest would think.

Love to you
Billy
and from Walt

---

perceives the whole: Hart had written Goyen in response to seeing the four sections of *The House of Breath* in *Accent*.
Sue Emma . . . and Aunty: The names of the four characters in the novel.
Boy Ganchion: Reference to a character in *The House of Breath*.

To Mary Inez Goyen
TLS

Taos, N.M.
June 2, 1948

My dearest Mother:
    Your letter came this afternoon and I have just read it for the fourth time—I think I never want to read it again.
    I had feared you would be hurt by the piece in *Accent*, and for that reason I hadn't said much about it to you. But now you have read it and I have your opinion. I am always happy to have opinions (and Lord knows I've had my share since I started trying to make my way according to my own convictions and choice—but I am used to most of those by now, although it still hurts when they come from close quarters) and I am terribly disappointed because you did not care for this piece of work, for I have always hoped and wanted to please you and Dad. But that's one matter. The other matter is your constant desire to implicate Walter in the affairs of my life of which you disapprove, and I have told you before that I am just about fed up with this kind of hypocrisy on your part and on Dad's part. It is dishonesty, nasty backhanded slander, unjust from the beginning. But that is up to you and your own conscience and you will have to settle it with yourself, alone, as all of us have to do.
    I am not losing my temper, as you did in the letter; for I have learned that we never get any kind of understanding between us, any of us, when we quarrel and get emotional. And I don't live by the principle that says hurt others when they hurt you—I was not taught to act in that way and,

too, I have learned for myself. You do as you like, but please try never to make me ashamed of you.

We are all mature human beings, you and Dad and Kat and Jim and I. We simply have to make our choices in life and try as best we may to live up to those choices and to be faithful to them and to ourselves. This has been my greatest and most valuable principle so far in my life—to take the responsibility for my choices and for my actions. If I could enlighten others at all, it would be to this end. Too many of us are cowards in this world; we are afraid to say what we mean, we compromise. Has it occurred to you that what *I* see in life and in people may not be *at all* what you see? I have the right to my own perceptions, and I am striving as honestly and as clearly and as unmercifully, when it is necessary, as I can to put those things down as writing and as art. I can do no other, and you would not, finally, have me do otherwise. Ask yourself this question, honestly.

It has never occurred to you, I suppose, that my conception of life as I have known it and seen it and experienced it might be unlike that of yours or many other people. I must write as I feel; honestly, I try not to tell lies—I don't believe I have in these pieces in *Accent*. Underlying all that I have written there I believe you will find a profound sympathy and love for the people presented there. Others think so, too. In Dallas, it was this little piece and this piece alone which got me many believers. One man there said he felt that if I continued this sort of work on such a theme, I would make a real and valuable contribution to American literature. Margo Jones (and she is an East Texan) said the same, and she has talked about this work all over New York, and I have had as many as five letters from publishers she has talked to about it. This may mean nothing to you. But when I tell you that what I have said about Aunty and the others is genuine, *for me*, you must believe me. I love these people and I feel I must make them known to the world some way—for otherwise they go forgotten and unknown. Don't you see this?

Now I am going to get a little rough, my beloved Mom, about this continual reference to Walter, to my "leadership" and my "influence." This makes me damned sore, but I try to understand why you say the things you do about Walt, and I think I do understand. I'd be a hell of a shortsighted human being if I didn't. But whatever the meaning is, I'm tired of it; and I think you should have more respect for me than this. We've talked it over ten times, but I never seem to get anywhere with you. The only influence in my life is the good and the honest and the beautiful and the wise—no other. You speak of my life as selfish out here, as morbid. It is certainly neither. You may think it selfish because I am not there to give my all to you—who seem certainly selfish to me in many ways. You don't think, you never have thought; you never would let me teach you how to think. Walter is fine and good and kind and out to do something in the world. He has nothing to do with my writing—in fact he never even saw the piece in *Accent* until the proofs *came for it a month or so ago*. He never knows what I am writing. His knowledge of the people I am writing about is so flimsy it is amusing. He has had little or no influence on my way of life, on my beliefs or convictions; indeed, it is I who have helped him try to change his way, in many instances. We are as different as night and day; and in our life we recognize this difference and try to tolerate each other (which is the way any group of people who are intelligent and honest try to live together). You will have to answer to all of this within yourself—deep down inside you know that you are unjust to Walter, and if I ever pray it is that you will see that what I do that is wrong in your eyes is *my own fault* and no other's. When you blame him you are blaming the wrong person. Blame me and I can take it and will try to understand; but when you blame him it is something like a sin and I am sorry for you.

About a year ago I had to write Dad a terrible terrible letter. But it was time and I had to do it. During the war I had a terrible terrible letter from Kat, one which I'll never forget. And now this one from you. That makes one from each of you. I thought Dad and Kat had seen where they were wrong, but perhaps they haven't.

As for my living with Walter, that is my choice. If I want to go and live with a bull, that will be my choice and I have the right to do so. I have committed no crime, I have done nothing evil or sinned against all of you or society. But I simply won't justify it to any of you again. And as for my writing, let me tell you that I shall go on putting down what I believe I must, and God help us all to bear it if it is not nice or sweet or any of that. In the end I think you will see that it has its beauty and wisdom and honesty—and that is all one can aspire to, I believe.

As for what you said about Taos and this little house which we love so much and have worked like dogs on and have wanted to share with you all so much, I am just sorry for you, that's all. The good Lord help you.

Good night and you know, Mother, that I love you as no one else in this whole wide world. Please let Jim and Kat and Dad read this letter, and promise me you will not destroy it but always keep it. I love you all more, I guess, than you really know or will ever understand.

Bill

Mary Inez Goyen: (b. 1896).

June 2, 1948: The holdings of Goyen's letters to his family at the Fondren Library at Rice University include none written between September 28, 1945, and May 12, 1948.

your letter: Mrs. Goyen's reaction to portions of *The House of Breath* published in *Accent* is quoted in the following letter to William Hart.

Kat: Goyen's sister, Kathryn.

Jim: Goyen's brother.

To William M. Hart
TLS-1

Taos, N.M.
June 3, 1948

My dear Bill:

I send this along to you so that you may know what has happened and so that you may see more clearly the meaning of the work I am doing and the directions I am taking. This is a deep and galling hurt, perhaps the unkindliest cut of all, but I do know, Billy, that I understand, and understanding is all we ask for. You see the difficult part is that most of what I have put down and am putting down has come rudely from her own mouth and many times she is talking through my people's mouth.

Can you, my beloved and staunch friend Billy, ever really go back to the Merrill Street of your deep cisterned memoried self? Only this way, I know—only in stern meditation of it, in the hard and agonizing resurrection of it into the clear and merciless light.

Love,
B.

". . . Bill, when we came back your magazine [*Accent*] was here, and Jim looked for it in Dallas so he could not wait of course to read it, and me too as for that, but am sorry to say am really disappointed in your work, and if that is the kind of literature you are going to write, I hope you never succeed (and you won't). I have all ways [*sic*] felt like you will write the highest and most cultured things and the good of the world, and be a help to mankind, instead of the nasty, vile and sinful part. You know who you want to be like and I do too, and have known it, but would not let myself believe it for one moment, but you have proven it now, so I can't be with you in that sort of work. No wonder you did not ever want to see any of your old friends, I don't blame you, I will never leave Taos if I were you, that is where you belong, where you can live your own morbid selfish life, and you haven't gotten like this alone, no, no, as I have told you before. You have had plenty of leadership. I have prayed and hoped so long, for you to be what you were intended to be, but as I have told you before, You were not. So my hopes are all gone, for I can see your type of writing now, so I think it best for you to have all your mail and magazines such as *Accent* sent there, for I don't want to ever read anything else you write. And as far as your Adobe melting away, I hope if you put on a brick it will fall through, and it will, it may not right now but you can't succeed where you are and what you are, now I am really hurt worse than I have ever been in my life, such hope and confidence in you, I hope I don't live to see you write a book like D. H. has written, and that looks like your type. I hope this hurts you as badly as it has me. May God bless you and help you to see the way you should. This is all for now.

Love,
Mom

Now add this to one of your books, it will be wonderful that your Mother has lost hope in her son."

I send this along: A portion of a letter from his mother, quoted above.

To Zoë Léger
TLS-2

Taos
June 9, 1948

Dear Zoë:
    Activity out here in El Prado has been furious for over a week now, and by the end of this week we should be able to see ahead. As I told you in my last letter, Walt's room has been finished and yesterday and today two Indian women have been plastering the new addition. It will be most attractive. The new room has a charming little *portale* (which means a little porch with two columns, in our case) which looks out on the uninhabited fields and the huge blue Sacred Mountain beyond. We plan a little patio there and, eventually, we'll plant fruit trees and a few blooming shrubs. In time this will be a lovely place. It is hard work, really slave labor—but the results are always gratifying.

You've no idea what a stink the "Portraits" aroused in Houston—although I see by yesterday's letter that you've smelt it a bit after talking with Mother. Zoë, she was outraged, to say the least; and there came a letter from her last week which I think I never want to read again. She just couldn't take what I said there, and, bless her, I understand why; but it hurts just the same. However, I go on with the work, nothing can stop me, it must be said. I'm glad you had what sounds like something of an intelligent conversation with her—her letter was certainly emotional and completely bitter. You see, these people are family and friends and she, being not one whit literary, could not understand at all what I was doing.

I am so glad you liked the work, and the telegram from you was very exciting to get and thank you, Zoë, for sending the good words. I really felt encouraged. I have had several good letters of praise for "Portraits," and I am hoping to get the whole work, of which "Portraits" is a portion, into Random House (from which I've had a good letter) before the summer is out—that means hard work, and, more than that, hard, clear thinking. God knows what Mother will think when she sees the *whole thing*.

And Zoë, about what you said in yesterday's letter—"it is surprising that one who can live away from people, as you can, can get them down on paper as you do." For me, I have found that one who observes and remembers, most of all, thinks and meditates and reasons and perceives, if he can, does work as art only when he withdraws a little from "people"—people devour one, they eat up his energies, force him into defenses and poses, and, finally, scum up all clear thought. One doesn't create in a crowd. Here I have Frieda, who, to me, is Life and Power and Beauty. I sometimes spend long hours with her talking and listening. Then, besides a few other friends, I have only myself and my memory and what might be called a Vision which I struggle with so that I may get it clear and right. It must not be confused with other images, other worlds. When that is all finished and done, then there will be a great open place in me to be filled up again with something else. The trouble with us all is that in our time we take too much on ourselves, let too much come in; the result is that we are flooded and crammed and confused. This, at least, is true for me, and I must live and work this way. Nothing must come in one's head and heart while he is creating something BUT THE LIFE OF THE WORK AT HAND. That's what I have found to be true for myself. You might disagree.

Anyway, I'll be eager to see what you think of the finished whole, when it is finished. It is temporarily called *The Wheel Broken at the Cistern*. A secondary title, which I might use, is simply *The Speckled Canna*; for, to me, the image of that little, homely canna is a symbol for all those lives I knew which mean something in the world. We'll see. [. . .]

"Portraits": "Four American Portraits as Elegy."

To Zoë Léger
TLS-1

Taos
Tues., June 15, 1948

My dear Zoë:

[. . .] We plan to leave the latter part of August (this is not to be told to Mother, for I've not let her know, yet) for Portland, Oregon where Walt will attend graduate school and I'll probably either teach part-time or crawl on with my writing. We hope to be able to rent the house for the winter, if we can eschew sentiment. Sometime in July I intend to drag Mother and Dad out here by the hair of their poor old gray heads and try to give them a good rest and change—if I can manage it. Add to all this the labor of trying to write steadily and to finish the book and you might ask, how in the hell will it be done? But it must and will be done—I want to have it all down by the end of summer. The building program has robbed me of much more time than I had planned or desired, but now it can't be helped. I must get back to my writing schedule and I'll do it come hell or high water.

As for your question about Granny Ganchion. She was my grand-mother, Teutonic, rumbling, wicked, beautiful and wretchedly poor but an aristocrat inside. She had a helter-skelter family of nine, one of which is my good father. The Tatzlwurm is what obscured the tale for you. Frieda (who is very much like my Granny) told me once the beautiful and terrifying legend of the Tatzlwurm—he was a warted serpent-monster that lived down in the cellar of an ancient Inn among the wine casks, where he drank all the wine and lay, hideous and terrible, like a glutton and a curse to the owner of the Inn. He was Greed, he was Gluttony, he was Evil; he devoured the life and energy and vitality of the owner of the Inn, hounded him and cursed him and was deathless. Now do you see how I used him? He, it seems to me, lives like a tapeworm in all of us, gnaws away at us, drains us, tries to suck us dry; he may be our conscious, or Adam's evil in us, or many things. Each of us has his Tatzlwurm, his secret Monster of Greed; and we never tell about him, never acknowledge him. But I have seen his work in many people, and sometimes I feel his work going on in me. [. . .]

Yours,
Billy

To Charles Provine Goyen
ALS-3

Taos, New Mexico
July 1948

My dearest Dad:

Thanks for your letter received yesterday. I certainly have been worried about not hearing from all of you, feared some of you were sick or in some trouble. I can't believe that Mom would still hold grudge against me over the writing.

You say you've been under the weather—what is the trouble, Dad? I wish you'd let me know when you're not well. At least you can tell *me*. Please take care of yourself, and see a doctor when you're not well. I hope Mother isn't half-sick, but I'm afraid she is. This is the longest she's ever gone without writing me. Is Kat peeved at me, too?

Jim sounds as if he's going strong in school, and I'm glad. Of course I worry about him and the draft, but what can we do? I thought of him and Sue on their birthdays and hoped all of you were together.

I am thinking hard about fall and winter plans, as I wrote you last week. Whatever I do I mean to go on with my work—that's still first. I'll let you know and keep you posted—and you know you are always in my thoughts when I make plans for the future. I hate to go so far away from all of you, and I worry so because I feel you need me there, but Dad you know there's not much there in Houston for me but all of you, and one or two old friends. As you know, I'd thought seriously about Dallas and Margo's theatre; but then I'm not wholeheartedly sure I want to work with a theatre—although I may feel differently. I haven't heard from Margo for some time—that's because she suddenly went to Italy—and that's why I didn't come to Dallas in June, as I had thought I might. But she may send me word any day and some work to do, too. I hope so, for I could use the money.

Then, of course, Reed College interests me and always has, as you know. And the fact that Walt and I could be there together, enhances the prospect of going there. But it's so damned far away, and I had hoped to be near you. Life gets more and more complicated as we go along, Dad, as you well know; and many times it's agony to try to make the right choices. All we can do is think hard and carefully, and hope we do the best and right thing. Let me try to think and feel this thing out, and you know you and Mom are always in my mind.

I wonder so often if you need me there. Whenever you have a crisis there, it seems I am not around to be of any help. But Dad, this is not a selfish life out here—to me, it's like studying for the [words lost]. I am giving my whole life to it. It's not fun or a lark or any escape. Many times I feel you understand me better than poor Mom.

Just keep me informed of what goes on there, and promise you'll ask for me if you need me.

Write me again, and I hope to see you one day soon. Mother makes it so hard on me when I come home—especially with Walt—that I find myself dreading to come.

Give all my love, and remember I hold no hard feelings, my dear Dad, and that I love you two with all my heart. Thanks for your faith and confidence. And thanks for the stamps—and the mail you forward. Be sure to watch out for all *Navy* mail.

I love you, Dad,
Bill

Margo: Margo Jones.

To Allen Maxwell
TLS-1

Taos, New Mexico
Aug. 29, 1948

Dear Allen Maxwell:
Many thanks for your letter yesterday and thanks for returning the manuscripts. I quite agree with your attitude towards the stories I sent and appreciate, indeed, your feeling that, for the good of both of us, you should not print anything that might seem below the standard of writing of my present work.

The little stories you read were written during the war, when I was struggling with the compulsion to put down what I know and feel about the lives and worlds of some wonderful and beautiful and gone people. I feel I have come pretty close to what must be said in the last year; and I've been working intensively out here on a group of pieces that should be finished by Christmas. Certainly "At the Graveyard" and "Year of the Grasshoppers" feel inferior in intensity, in directness—and in clarity. Yet I shall try to get them printed somewhere, for I want them recorded, publicly—and I hope it can be done.

I'm sorry I quite forgot the *Southwest Review* during my absence from the Southwest last year. In California I had talked to Katherine Anne Porter about magazines that may print my current work and she had suggested *Accent*—and *Accent* right away took my "Portraits." Too, in a way, I may have unconsciously avoided Texas publication, since I did not want to exploit the work *first* as "regional" material, but as an exploitation of and approach to (in a kind of experimental way) personal and, in its largest themes, universal experience. And, as I told my good friend Mr. Lon Tinkle this spring, I probably felt that it might be foolish—and bad taste—to fling out into Texas some rather honest and certainly biographical material about my family. (God knows I have got myself into enough trouble with the publication of the *Accent* pieces—my good people, anything but "literary," read them quite by accident—an accident of the mails that sent copies of *Accent* to my home address by mistake—saw nothing there but a kind of ruthless exposé and, worst of all, a snobbish condemnation of my inheritance. This was the unkindliest cut of all, as you can imagine.) But this experience has, ironically, *freed* me; and now I may go on, with a kind of anonymity that we all struggle for, and say what I must.

I should like very much to know what you and others there feel about other pieces from my present long work. I enclose a few; and if you want to see more, or, finally, the whole finished piece, I'd be delighted to send it along and to have your help, if you might wish to give it. I've had several encouraging letters from Random House, who not only read the *Accent* work but were talked to (probably in Margo's compelling way) by Margo Jones, who had read fragments of the Texas work and wanted to help. We shall see what comes of their interest when it is time.

Thanks again for the very kind letter and the careful and sympathetic reading of the manuscripts. I hope we may arrange to get some of this work in print *in Texas*, now—if the work merits that. My best wishes to you, and please let me hear. I'll be here in Taos, as I wrote you earlier, until September 8. If you mail anything to me after Sept. 6, please use my

Houston address: 614 Merrill Avenue, Houston 9—and it will be forwarded to Portland.

Sincerely,
William Goyen

About Reed College—I've made Taos Valley a Gethsemane this summer,
worrying and fretting over having to teach again, fearing such public
activity might take too much writing energy away. But Reed people are
most sympathetic, want me to go on writing there, and I'll teach only
enough courses to keep me eating until I finish my present project. It
sounds an ideal arrangement, but we'll see.

---

it can be done: Those three stories were not published.
enclose a few: Goyen submitted excerpts from *The House of Breath:* "The Wind in the
Shutter," "The Fallen, Splendid House," and "Well-Cry for Swimma." Maxwell
accepted the first two.

To Margo Jones
TLS-2

3017 S.E. Claybourne
Portland 2, Oregon
September 21, 1948

My dearest Margo:
     [. . .] Since I know you are working terribly hard I don't expect to
hear anything from you. I do want to say that I have been in correspondence with Frank Taylor at Random House, thanks to you, and that I
expect to send my manuscript in to him within a few months. In the
meantime I hope to get funds through a fellowship which some friends
are trying to help me with. It is a scramble, Margo, and I have the added
struggle with my health and strength; but I don't complain, except when I
am taken away from my work. As we said, one has to be enormously
strong, keep pounding away at it, preserve and conserve his strength
however he can, save it from waste and put it out only in the direction of
what he has to say in the world. There is so much beauty in the world, so
much beauty that it must be told about powerfully, that one must save his
power for it. The natural world has such a secret power for me, it is such

a source of strength and affirmation, that in Taos I lived many days on end like a sleepwalker and Oh I miss it so! But then there are human beings, too, and they, too, are beautiful and treacherous and full of such mystery. God knows we need someone to tell us the human is beautiful these days, and we need to hear over and over again that even in our ugliness we must be loved into something more than ourselves and more than ugliness. My side is on the side of the human being, and the human being moving in nature, which is spirit; and nothing else seems important to me, and if I thought I could not spend my life laboring to perceive and to understand and to clarify what happens to us in the world, then I would want to die.

Often I think of your wonderful friendship and of your understanding and faith and I am unspeakably grateful for you, wherever you are. You know that I believe in you and in your work, we are really together in our work (how wonderful to know that we are joined in that). My biggest hope right now is that the play will be beautiful and moving and in the theatre and that when it is finally done you will feel that marvelous excitement and elation that come with the certainty that something wonderful has been achieved.

When the minute comes, do let me know what you are feeling and what the play is like. And please take care of yourself and remember that I don't forget you. I send my love and you have my prayers for a real achievement there. Walter sends his very best wishes, too.

Yours,
Billy

Portland: Goyen had followed Walter Berns to Reed College, where Berns would study political science. Goyen anticipated teaching English part-time, but enrollment dropped. He was writing full-time.
Frank Taylor: (b. 1917). Taylor actually left Random House before Goyen's novel was accepted. Decades later he would be Goyen's superior at McGraw-Hill.

3017 S.E. Claybourne St.
Portland 2, Oregon
October 14, 1948

Dear Mr. Maxwell:

Thank you for your cordial letter and all the information and suggestions it contains; it's certainly kind of you to go to this trouble to help me.

I have perused the list of available fellowships you sent, given a lot of
thought to it, and decided to ask immediately for further information on
some of them. However, as you say, the formalities involved and the
delays of the mails, etc., prolong the period of waiting—and in the end,
after all this, one may not be successful: it's like waiting for manuscripts
which, after three or four months, are casually returned unbought.
Certainly the Texas grant you mention would be a godsend, as an interim
stabilizer, and I'd be so grateful for it if it could be obtained.

You ask me to estimate a minimum requirement per month to permit
my going ahead with the book. At present I am living shockingly humbly,
considering the cost of soapflakes and hamburger, probably $50 to $60 a
month—so far. But then I've been here only a month so it's difficult to
judge fairly, yet. Anything would help, we know that; and in order to live
within a constricted budget that maintains a valuable purpose one finds
himself washing and ironing his own clothes, for example, with a kind of
ferocious glee, despite the suspicious looks on the faces of city neighbors.
Therefore, however modest the grant you mention, if it can be secured I
really ought to take it, or at least apply for it, don't you think?

Since we are discussing all these details, I might add that the problem
of health, since the war, has been annoying; it is related to strength and
energy, which I have to fight to preserve for their right and best uses. For
this reason, since the end of the war, I have hoped not to have to teach
school, despite my joy in teaching, because teaching is one of the best-
known robbers of energy—at least for me—and an excellent source of
Migraine, which has been my plague. Later I am sure I'll be able to keep
two balls in the air at the same time, but so far I've had to be very careful.

Please ask for any other information you desire and I'll be happy to
supply it. I am convinced that I must go on to finish this book. I had
hoped to do it quietly and singly, without assistance, for I have a kind of
stubborn pride; but that way seems impossible, now. We must be sure, of
course, that if I receive this grant it will not prevent my applying for or

receiving any other grant. I add that one horror I have is that of suddenly feeling the work die in my hands after having presumptuously taken help for it. But I suppose this is the risk one takes in such cases.

Thank you very very much for your interest and kindness, and thank you for offering to send the check before publication. Please let me hear from you—and many thanks.

Best wishes,
William Goyen

To Charles Provine Goyen
and Mary Inez Goyen
TLS-2

3017 S.E. Claybourne St.
Portland 2, Oregon
Oct. 22, 1948

Dear dearest Mom and Dad:
Very tired tonight, but want to get off a note to you two before bath and bed. Thanks for your letter yesterday, Mom: I'm sorry I waited so long to write last time—the time just slipped by, that's all. Will try to get a letter to you at least once a week from now, I promise. Don't worry, I am fine, no headaches since I've been here, and do believe the sea-level climate agrees well with me. Maybe the vitamins too—who knows? [. . .]

I haven't told you that a few weeks ago I had a letter from the editor of *Southwest Review* who has been very much interested in my present work, since it has a Texas background, and he wants to publish more of the book serially in *Southwest Review*. I wrote him that I would send him some material, did send it, and within a week I had a glowing letter from him, which I enclose for you to see—*please return it right away*—and he will publish quite a large portion of my manuscript late this year. Now he has suggested that I apply for a "modest grant" for young Texas writers to help me finish the book with. I immediately applied and am waiting for an answer. The editor suggests that I take this small grant of money as a stopgap until I can get word on the big fellowship I am applying for. He says he feels reasonably certain that a book of the quality of mine should not have much trouble getting help with which to finish it. This is terribly encouraging, and we must all pray that I am successful. If so I can quit this part-time work here and devote all my time and energy towards finishing this book.

Now I hope you will see this time what it is I am trying to do in the book, and not have your feelings hurt. Surely you realize by now that a writer writes out of his own peculiar background and uses the material he knows best, but what he writes is rarely true *completely*; he always creates something unreal out of what is real. Do you see this? Therefore, the Aunty in those Portraits is not Aunty at all, but somebody somewhat like her that I just made up out of my imagination to represent a person like that in East Texas or any simple country little place. This time I want to send you the material that *Southwest Review* will publish so that you won't be hurt by suddenly seeing it in print. Just remember that it is *fiction*, some of it based on real happenings, but not necessarily *true*. It is very hard to go on with this work if I feel you are against it and that you will be hurt by it. I am simply writing about something I know and think beautiful and sad and worth making permanent in print. Please tell me that you understand. I want to talk with you about this when I come home.

Mademoiselle has had a story of mine under consideration for over four months, and I hope this means they might take it. This is something else you must say a prayer for. For if they buy this story, that means I can come home for sure at Christmas. But I try to learn not to count too much on this darned market, just to take what comes. I also have money coming to me for stories sold to *Accent* and *New Directions*. *Southwest Review* promises to send a check soon, but alas they pay very little. It's the book that might make a bit of money, and I must finish it. Anyway, I am selling stories right along, and that is encouraging. And of course if I get one or both of these grants, that would be wonderful. But please don't get excited over the prospects, let's be realistic; for I don't want you to be disappointed. [. . .]

Hurray for the collards and I hope there are some when I come home. Makes my mouth water. [. . .]

My best to all, and love,

Bill
[P.S. unclear]

---

serially in Southwest Review: The magazine published four sections of the novel: "The River's Procession," 32 (Summer 1947): 316–317; "The Fallen Splendid House," 33 (Spring 1949): 131–134; "The Wind in the Shutter," 34 (Summer 1949): 241–253; and "Christy," 35 (Winter 1950): 7–16. The last was reprinted in the 50th Anniversary Issue, 109 (Autumn 1974): 432–444.
the big fellowship: He had applied for, and was to be denied, a Eugene Saxton Fellowship.
Mademoiselle has had a story: Over the years, this magazine published five Goyen stories:

"Pore Perrie," "The White Rooster," "The Ghost of Raymon Emmons" (which he later retitled "Ghost and Flesh, Water and Dirt"), "The Geranium," and "The House and the Day Moth."

To Allen Maxwell
TLS-1

3017 S.E. Claybourne St.
Portland 2, Oregon
October 25, 1948

My dear Allen Maxwell:

I cannot tell you how elated I was to find in Saturday's mail not only the check for the two stories but word that I have been awarded the *Southwest Review* Fellowship. The wonderful spirit with which all this was done for me and my work is so encouraging and gives me so much new confidence with which to go on writing that I want to thank you for that first. If there are others there to thank I should like to thank them, too; this is like a kind of Salvation.

The "modest grant" does not seem modest at all but, at such a time as this, rather huge; four months' secure time in which to work. Really it is very difficult to thank you for this help and kindness, and I just hope that you and the others can understand how wonderfully grateful I am.

Today I am assembling material with which to make application for the Saxton Fellowship, and I hope you will allow me to put your name down as a reference. The Saxton Fellowship sounds like it might be just what I want and need, and thank you for putting me on to it. We'll just keep our fingers crossed and hope that it materializes. I'll let you know immediately what happens.

When I am a little farther along and have some finished drafts of present revisions, I'll send them to you. In the meantime, please know that I am working very hard and with a new exuberance which comes from you and your help. My deepest gratitude for everything you have done, and my best wishes to you and to the others—

Gratefully yours,
William Goyen

Southwest Review Fellowship: Maxwell seems to have invented the "*Southwest Review* Fellowship," with its purpose being "the encouragement of excellence in creative writing

which concerns itself particularly with the people and life of Texas," purely for Goyen's benefit. The amount was $300. (Letter from A.M. to W.G., October 21, 1948.)
the Saxton Fellowship: On December 31, Goyen received a letter from Elizabeth Lawrence, an editor at Harper and Brothers, rejecting his application. The committee of readers for the Eugene Saxton Memorial Trust felt his style was "mannered," his mood "unvarying," and that such a "poetical, highly introspective treatment" was better suited to short pieces than to the novel (E.L. to W.G., December 31, 1948).

To Dorothy Brett
TLS-2

3017 S.E. Claybourne St.
Portland 2, Oregon
Oct. 25, 1948

My dearest Brett:

I am sorry to have waited so long to send a word; the time here flies faster than anywhere else, I am sure—and too I have been in one of those dreadful restless states in which I could do nothing but walk—for one solid week I was *aux pieds* in the city of Portland, in the dreary rain, going where God knows, but moving, all day. Really at the moment it seemed a waste and loss of time, but now that it has passed I know that I was writing very hard in my head and now I feel the results. One day I should like to write something about the curious relationship between wandering and sex, for there is surely a very strong one there.

Stephen has arrived and we are terribly happy with him. It seemed we waited ages. It seemed even at the last hour that he would not get here, for we were at the airport looking at his plane in the air over us when someone announced to us on the loudspeaker that Stephen's plane would not land, because of poor visibility, and would proceed on to Seattle; and then his plane disappeared! You can imagine our fury, with him so near. But he did finally come down, five hours later, after having been taken all the way to Seattle and back again. Now he is quite comfortable here with us and we are having wonderful talks. On Thursday he and I will go to Seattle where he will lecture, then we hope to go on either to the coast or up to Victoria, British Columbia, for a few days' tour and visit together. Won't that be wonderful? I have quite a mass of material on which I have been intensely writing, to show to him and discuss. It is a sort of divine gift to have at last someone with whom I can feel free and share distur-bances and experiences in writing and thinking. You have had him for that there in Taos and now I get him. Both of us are extremely fortunate, and I agree that we should be enormously grateful.

We have had a fortnight's duration of stunningly beautiful weather, sparkling autumn days with the trees golden on the hills along the river and the four white mountains squatting glittering in the background. This is a beautiful place, so moist and gentle and soft, with great green firs and spruces and beautiful misty rivers. I'd like to move all about in it—but that takes money and time, neither of which I have. Yet, my dear Brett, a glimmer of hope appears: as you know I have sold two stories from my book to *Southwest Review* and I already have the check in hand! The editors want to print my book serially and to help in any way to get it published—this is the first *concrete* encouragement I've had—and the check came when I was biting my nails for fear of going broke within a few months. The writing does go well, despite the lost week I mentioned, and surely it will go on and we will see this thing in print before too long. For a while I feared all of us would be dead and buried in Taos cemetery before a book of mine ever got published, and I did want to have something to put in your hands before we're all with the worms. Now, who knows, that may happen. But let's keep our fingers crossed.

But doors do open, dear Brett, just as you taught me; and I do believe that, now. It takes courage and a lot of risks, but if one goes on hacking away and believing, something *does* happen.

What is your life like there, now? Have you had snow yet? God knows I'd like to be there in the snow, to be able to peek out our kitchen windows and see your red light glowing! But it will glow again before long, never fear. Indeed, this is curious, but you know I have so far rather enjoyed the anonymity of a strange city, where I can go about unidentified and unknown and just blend in with the crowds. This gets terribly lonely, and I have been as lonely here as I've been in my life, but loneliness does pass, doesn't it—and out of a kind of solitariness one learns something marvelous and valuable. That is what I believe, the way I seem destined to live, and it is up to me to make that kind of life possible.

Stephen is terribly distraught by his debts in Taos and how kind it is of you to take care of them for him and sort of save his neck. He talks of it constantly and I tell him not to worry, that you will smooth the backs of all his little debtors there. He tells us of your gay lunches together and of your escapades here and there; and I believe he really longs to return to Taos and work there again. He would be a wonderful addition to our community.

Well, never fear, Brett, we'll make it somehow. It just requires a tremendous mental and emotional life that goes on always, day and night, and a constant working at what one feels compelled to do. Do keep sending your letters—remember what a large part they played in getting me through last year's horrid time of it; and I sort of depend on them. This year will be a better one, I must make it that way; and as long as one has his work and it is alive, that is about all he can ask for, isn't it? Remember we think of you and love you and we do miss you. Stephen is upstairs writing you and we'll send our letters together. Walt is studying furiously, but shouts out his love to you. Send all the news, and take good care of yourself. A cheerio to Polimar, and love again—

Yours,
Bill

Love to Frieda and Angie—I'll write them soon. The clay figures arrived and we have them—but they make us homesick.

———————————————

Dorothy Brett: The Humanities Research Center has 133 letters from Goyen to Brett, some cosigned by Joseph Glasco (b. 1925). Glasco, a painter and sculptor, was educated at the University of Texas, the Art Center School (Los Angeles), and the Jeppson Art Institute. In 1948 he enrolled in the School of Painting and Sculpture in Mexico. The Goyen-Brett letters began after Goyen left Taos in 1948 and continued until 1959.
Stephen: Sir Stephen Spender (b. 1909), who gained recognition with the publication of *Poems* in 1933. He is also the author of books of criticism, reportage, autobiography, and fiction. He first came to America in 1947 at the invitation of Sarah Lawrence College. At the end of the academic year, in the summer of 1948, he took a tour of the American West and Southwest, beginning with Seattle and Portland, then Taos, where he stayed with Goyen, then returning to Portland. See Spender's *Journals 1939–1983,* ed. John Goldsmith (New York: Random House, 1986), p. 94.
sold two stories: "The River's Procession" and "The Fallen Splendid House."
work there again: Spender worked on *World within World* at Taos for six weeks in 1948.
Polimar: Dorothy Brett's dog.

To Zoë Léger
TLS-4

3017 S.E. Claybourne St.
Portland 2, Oregon
Dec. 5, 1948

My dearest Zoë:

   I was so happy to have your letter, the first I've had from you since I've been up here.

   Of course my good family think I am teaching here, as most people do, but that's a fabrication that I reveal only to you, *so please don't betray me—* it's best to have them and other curious people think I am harmlessly in some groove; in this way they can dispose of me—as the curious always have to dispose of people they know stories about—and allow me to go on about my own business safely and with joy! You understand this, dear Zoë, I am sure.

I am living by the seat of my pants, as always, but no grumbling. I love my work, I live within it like some womb, there is for me, marvelous and beautiful joy within this work and in it exists the only reality, for me. Why complain, then, that I can't afford concerts or food I'd like or a new pair of pants, which I need badly, etc.? To regard the lack of these things as sacrifice would be a kind of dishonor to one's work, I believe. This little book is near the finish, although it has given me a hard time, and God knows it may not be a book when it is finished, but I think so. Perhaps the less said about it the better; I do know that it will probably cause a lot of grief, and this worries me so that I can't sleep sometimes, but then I am convinced that it has to be and also I know that it was written only out of love and a kind of vision I have had. One day they will see this.

I long to come home for Christmas, to be with my family, to see you and one or two others (no more); but this is impossible so I must forget it. It will be terribly lonely here. Yet I must drive on with this work and if I leave it I may suffer. This work is the most important thing in the world for me right now, I live it. Yet I know that I don't stand to make a hundred dollars out of the damned thing, so they can't say that I am working out of self-interest to make myself rich.

Portland and the vicinity, the magnificent Northwest, are very beautiful. We sit in our house upon which tons and tons of rain have been falling since we arrived three months ago. But when the sun comes and the skies clear for an hour, one sees stunning pearl-white mountains sitting all around and the river gleams under the three bridges. I made a short trip to Puget Sound when Spender was here and ah! there is unspeakable beauty, little green islands, snowy mountain ranges running along the Sound, marvelous mists and fogs and firs and spruce. I do love it here, it has a mysterious, Sibelius quality which makes me feel a kind of passion and yearning. This is a perfect contrast to the desert and mountains of the Southwest. I wish I could show the Northwest to you.

Last month the *Southwest Review*, hearing that I was rather destitute up here, sent word that they were going to award me their *Southwest Review* Fellowship—an award I'd never heard of—on the basis of two stories, excerpts from the book, which they will print January or February. The fellowship is modest, but comes in monthly installments for the next four months and is enough to barely scrape by on. God knows how grateful I am to those people; they have written me wonderful letters of encouragement, seem to believe completely in the book and want to do all they can to see it published. This kind of encouragement, backed up with real help, means everything in the world—and you can imagine my joy when their letter came, for I was on the verge of taking a job in a ski-boot factory here, and utterly despondent. There is a way opens up, Zoë dear, I swear to God it happens if one's got the guts to stick his neck out and keep it there long enough.

Walt is in Reed College here—where I had thought I'd get a part-time job teaching (but enrollment dropped, fortunately! And now I see that all this was in the cards, for I believe in the "cards")—he is studying political science. He has a new plan and he is exploring it; I agreed to come along, for I know several ex-Rice people who are on the Reed faculty, and I want to help Walter all I can. He is making rapid strides, loves his work, and now plans to study at the University of London next fall, if possible. If I can make it, I shall go to London with him—at an invitation from Spender who is our very good friend—and try to eke out some kind of life there and in Europe for a year or so. The book will be finished by then and who knows, maybe a bit of money. Anyway, this is the way we plan, now.

[. . .] Zoë my dear, you can understand when I say that I really want to work and live quietly, it doesn't really matter where one is, so long he is at his work. I hate talk about work and achievements, all that nauseating literary game; and you do too. This is why I rarely say anything even to my family. [. . .]

Dec. 5, 1948: This letter was incorrectly dated 1949 in *Delta;* in December 1949, Goyen was hospitalized in London.
book will be finished: See his letter of November 25, 1949, to Margaret Hartley.

To W. H. Auden
TLS-1

3017 S.E. Claybourne St.
Portland 2, Oregon
January 3, 1949

Dear Mr. Auden:
 I am sending you the enclosed fragment from the long prose work on which I am working, in the hope that you might find in it enough merit

to warrant securing some help for me with which I can go on working on it. Stephen Spender wrote me that you might be able to secure some financial assistance for me in the event the request for Saxton help fell through. That request was yesterday denied me on the grounds that the work is not a novel and that it is too "highly poetical and introspective" to be successful in such a form. I am sure now that I made a mistake in asking for help with which to finish a projected novel—and I suppose I must simply call the work a long prose piece, composed of related short pieces. I had a very nice letter from *Harper's*, which I enclose.

The first fourteen pages of the manuscript which I send to you will be published in *Partisan Review* shortly, and Mr. Philip Rahv of that magazine has written me some very encouraging things about three sections of the ms. which I sent him. If I can just manage to go on writing, I am certain that the work will have some worth; and if you can help it will be just like salvation.

Please let me hear from you if there is time, and whatever you say or do will be so immensely appreciated. If you want to see more of the work, I shall of course be happy to send it to you. Best wishes and thank you so much for your interest.

William Goyen

W. H. Auden: (1907–1973). Noted English poet and critic.
January 3, 1949: The original of this letter has the appearance of a draft.
letter from Harper's: The magazine accepted "Her Breath upon the Windowpane." It appeared in *Harper's* 201 (July 1950): 79–81, and was reprinted in the 1951 *Best American Short Stories*, ed. Martha Foley (Boston: Houghton Mifflin, 1951), pp. 139–143. Three years later, *Harper's* would publish "The Armadillo Basket" in issue 207 (December 1953): 61–65.
first fourteen pages: "A Bridge of Breath," *Partisan Review* 16 (June 1949): 567–577.
Philip Rahv: (1908–1973). Cofounder and editor of *Partisan Review*.

To Dorothy Brett
TLS-2

3017 S.E. Claybourne St.
Portland 2, Oregon
January 18, 1949

Dearest Brett:
Thanks immensely for the *very* elegant sweater which arrived here, it is

lovely indeed, so warm (I have it on now) and such a bright color which lends some indication of life to my pale face! I was most thrilled to get this and I hope you didn't spend all your sheckles [*sic*] on me. Actually my poor ribs are in need of much covering—some fat would be preferable, but fat costs money and anyway what is more to the point and nearer the truth, nervousness and worry eat fat, so my ribs are *my* fault—and you have sent a swanky bit of rib-cover. Thank you so much, dearest Brett. [. . .]

Alex Böker has been here in Portland. He gave a lecture to a Committee on Foreign Relations here last Friday night, then stayed on until Sunday when he departed for Seattle. We spent a lot of time with him, Walt and I went to dinner with him Friday night, then I went alone with him on Saturday since Walt was out with his floozy. [. . .]

We have had two weeks of snow, light but lovely. Now it has melted. Quite icy, frozen weather, down to 14 and 15; my sweater comes in handy—and the landlady presented me with the good overcoat of her ex-husband. Since he ran away with a young girl of 23, I feel like this coat is filled with desires and when I put it on I am quite transformed. Alex was much concerned because I have no interesting female friends and he was on the point of introducing me to a young lady friend of his here when he said she was "no longer young nor beautiful" and then I agreed that since the same description applied to me, he'd better not match the two of us. Never, mind, I'll just do as you say, stay warm in my pants and climb into bed with the electric pad which the landlady has lent me.

Dear Brett, don't be too harsh with me about my solitary life there in Taos—I was learning so much when I was there, the fruits of which we'll see later, let's hope—and, too, you were aware of the problem I was struggling with; often I felt I might be doing a kind of penance; that is over—and really if ever I were to come back to live there for some time I think all of it might be different. We free ourselves of certain fears and regrets that have previously bound us to ourselves as we go along—in fact growth seems a perpetual kind of bondage and freedom; and I know that for me the only kind of liberation is through my work. Once that is learned, all one has to do is scratch away at his work, hard and really with joy. The great troublemaker is one's great senses, with which he really works and through which he perceives, even has visions; yet those senses which can direct him into greater and deeper and more productive spirituality can, too, confuse him and torture him and even ruin him if he is not careful of what he is trying to do with himself. I have, being extremely sensuous, too often strapped myself in to myself too tightly. But it is an exceedingly difficult task to learn how to live with and through one's sensuality without being betrayed by it. I believe I am learning, dear Brett. One day we can talk about this, it is very important for all of us. What often looks like prejudice and snootiness is no more than fear—and this fear is of oneself.

Partisan Review has paid me in advance for the story they will print, and today Laughlin of New Directions sent me a small check (he's a tightwad) to keep me from fussing because he had to hold a piece of mine for the next issue of his anthology. He had promised to bring it out in this present issue. He wrote a most sympathetic letter. So if I am careful, I may be able to dart off to Seattle or some place myself and have a binge, which I need dreadfully. Just to ride along in a bus with my pajamas in a bag and see new faces for a few days would be a great refreshment. [. . .]

Alex Böker: Unidentified.
his floozy: Berns had met the woman who was to become his fiancée.
they will print: "A Bridge of Breath."

To William M. Hart
TLS-1

3017 S.E. Claybourne St.
Portland 2, Oregon
January 31, 1949

My dearest Billy:

Thank you so much for your wonderful letter—I cannot read it again for it terrifies me so, that I am believed in, that the faith of those few who have always had faith continues. Lately I have had the most tortured and agonized time of my life; it is bound up with this work; it seems I am compelled to go over again, very carefully, all my life up to now; and now I know that this book is only a reduplication of my life. For this reason it is an exceedingly dangerous book. But once it is finished, regardless of what happens to it, it will be there; and then I can go on.

The title of the book is *The House of Breath*.

I am in constant correspondence with an editor at Random House who is extremely intelligent and of enormous help and stimulation. It is refreshing to know that one can communicate with editors of publishing houses directly and that these men are men of integrity and great sympathy. I believe something will come of my relations with Random House, and if, in the end, the book is not published, it will be because I have chosen against it. But oh Billy, everything is in it, it is all there, and it has been written in the midst of great suffering, greater than any of you know. This does not mean that it is a great book, only that it is the best and most honest and most compelling work I could do, now.

I just thank you from the bottom of my heart for your marvelous letter. We are in a tradition, you and I; and often I think that despite my few beautiful friends in the world—Walter and Frieda and Stephen—the book is written for you and only you can really know the roots and the blossoms of all that I shall ever do, "successful" or not. We are in a destiny, you and I, and now we see that probably our lives have been conditioned by all that went on between us so long ago, all that was so dark and difficult and chaotic and absurd. [. . .]

---

an editor at Random House: Robert Linscott (b. 1896).
written for you: Goyen did not dedicate the book to Hart; rather it was "For Frieda and Walter."

To Zoë Léger
TLS-4

3017 S.E. Claybourne St.
Portland 2, Oregon
Feb. 4, 1949

Zoë my dear:
    Please don't be offended at my not writing for so long—I actually had you on my mind and on my list; and when your letter came last week I was in the midst of an illness I've been fighting for several weeks and have just recovered from it. The family doesn't know this, so don't divulge it. I've just worked and worried too hard and it's begun to tell off on me, that's all. Yet I can't see any letup in sight. Until the damned headaches come I can make it, but when they knock me out then I am done for, and it's so hard to pull out of them . . . and then the work is interrupted and I *am* in a state.

Mother wrote that you had called, and how she loves to talk to you! Your telephone conversations through the years are so amusing. Think that you have never laid eyes on each other! Mother says to hear you laugh is like a shot in the arm for her; and I do thank you so much for keeping in touch with her.

Good news has come during the past two months and it is this you no doubt heard rumors of. Zoë, dear, I just didn't want to say a lot about it to everybody for fear of seeming puffed-up and self-important; and, too, it was all just too good to be true and I wanted to keep it a secret for awhile. It's just that Spender took a lot of my work to Auden and together they said some wonderful things about my talent and want to do all they can to help me get along. Both have been exceedingly kind and encouraging and I am so grateful to them.

Then in December, I sent up some sections from the novel to Philip Rahv at *Partisan Review*, and he wrote a glowing letter back saying that he would publish one section, probably in the March issue of *P.R.*, and that he would like to publish other parts of the book. He in turn talked to Mr. Linscott at Random House, with whom I have been corresponding, and together they are trying to keep me going with the book. But Zoë dear, we must be careful about talking too much of all this, since I am so afraid of failing and then I will be a fool. All this just means that I have got some first-rate recognition and some offers of help *if* I continue the kind of work I have been doing for the past year. Yet it is so hazardous and I have to fight worrying and health, etc. so often—and there are those agonizing, barren days when nothing comes and I felt lost and cheated. This book has been *so* difficult, I can't tell you what a struggle it is and has been. This is because I am writing right out of my insides. And when it is finished, I will have examined as honestly and clearly as I can my life up to this time. The trouble has been that the writing constantly crystallizes into pure poetry; and this pleases Auden and Spender, who think I am meant to be a poet, but it displeases the editors, who feel I must keep "structure" (meaning plot) and realism in my work. But I am getting good criticism from these editors and writers, and that is a rare and valuable experience.

A great frustration and constant suffering derives from the family who are still hurt by what they have seen in print; and God knows what will happen to them if ever they see the whole work in print. So I turn from a feeling of guilt to a feeling of pity for them, and this keeps tearing me to bits. Yet the work must be done, and will be, although it may never be printed.

The title of the book is *The House of Breath*, and besides those sections of its early form printed in last Spring's *Accent*, there are to be sections in *Poetry* (when I can't be sure—probably March or April), *Accent* again (probably summer—these quarterlies are so slow), *Southwest Review* (the first section appears in the next issue—I don't know whether it comes out in March or April but do find out for I want you to see this section and the other section which will appear in the following issue); and, as I said, in *Partisan Review*. All this speaks well for the book and should make us feel that the book will be published without a doubt. Yet as a whole the work is not strictly a novel, it is rather, now, like the long dream of an amnesiac. Actually, it is in the form of one long monologue which breaks down into dialogues and into other monologues as the book progresses. Therefore, independent parts look good, but put together as a whole these parts present a very difficult problem, one which I hope I am capable of resolving at this point, although I don't know. This remains to be seen.

And our good friend, "The White Rooster," is appearing in its original and unedited form in *Horizon* in March. Isn't that exciting? It's a kind of vengeance of *Mademoiselle*, who cut it up so badly, you remember. While in New York, Stephen retrieved the rights to the story and gave it to Cyril Connolly, who said some awfully good things about it. I did think it was a wonderful story in its original form, and naturally I am elated to know that it finally will be given a chance in print as it was originally written.

So now it only remains for me to work as hard as I can, and as well as I can; for certainly I have the interest and encouragement of fine people. This terrifies me and thrills me at the same time. It is long and hard and slow, but I can do nothing else, I know that. I just hope my work justifies all that has come to me; and more than this, I hope and pray I can continue to work and produce. [. . .]

Poetry: "Three Artifices: 'Greets the Sea,' 'Discovers the Webs,' and 'Walks the Beach at Morning,'" *Poetry* 124 (May 1949): 84–85. These three poems were reprinted in the final section of Goyen's *Nine Poems* (New York: Albondocani Press, 1976), pp. 26–31.
Accent again: No further sections of the book appear in *Accent*.
Horizon: "The White Rooster," *Horizon* 19, no. 111 (March 1949): 180–193. A version which Goyen said had been "bowdlerized" appeared in *Mademoiselle* 24 (April 1947): 170–171 and 286–290. Spender used the unauthorized editing of the story as an example of the way American editors turn literature into the language of "news stories." See "Situation of the American Writer," in his *The Making of a Poem* (New York: W. W. Norton, 1955), pp. 174–192.
Cyril Connolly: (1903–1980). Founder of the literary review *Horizon*, which lasted ten years under his editorship.

3017 S.E. Claybourne St.
Portland 2, Oregon
February 13, 1949

Dearest Brett:

Valentine greetings! and last night I dreamt of you, you were very slim and young and lovely and we kissed on some road where I came upon you in a kind of stage coach à la Western Movie style! Isn't this curious? Anyway, this means I have been thinking of you and smarting under my silence. I haven't written, dear Brett, because those damned headaches have been at me again, for two solid weeks, and I am now a pale rag. But I am better. The only rub is that I have had to have a doctor, and it's expensive to go under the sheet, as you know, but worth it, I guess. He gave me a complete feeling-over under an enormous sheet, with a very pretty nurse, all eyes, feeling around too! and his decision was that I am working too hard, that I need a holiday, etc. He is now gorging me with hideous green pills and maybe they—or he—will help. At any rate, I'm better now, and no more worry. Just too much intense concentration, too much gray miserable rain, and an excess of worry over money.

Your Annunciation painting sounds exciting and I wish I could see it. What you say about those rare good days when one gets up under a kind of destiny and goes straight to his work like a blacksmith to his anvil and pounds directly away at *exactly* what he wants to shape, is just what I have experienced. It is one of those marvelous experiences that just make up for all the wretched sterile days when one strikes around feeling like an idiot and a cheat, with nothing to say, no thoughts, no blood. I truly believe these rare days are the result of some force working in one that has finally broken through one's resistances and lethargies and has its way. How much preparation one has had to go through, *inside*, for this miraculous moment, one can never know. The point is to believe that everything one does or sees or feels or thinks is *preparation* for some marvelous moment of execution and illumination that is surely coming if he will be patient and suffer in a kind of spiritual endurance. I firmly believe this, dear Brett, I live by it; otherwise one might surely get destroyed by himself. Slowly slowly one builds his life around this kind of creative faith, he lives for it and within it and because of it—I know this, I know this; and this is why I am prepared to live on and on like this, refusing to compromise, constantly readying myself for the time when I shall need every bit of my strength and clearheadedness to *execute*. This kind of life really is the most wonderful thing in the world; for although it is lonely and anxious and all that, one has the assurance that he is living for and within an Idea, an Idea of all beauty and all truth and all purpose. Isn't it marvelous to have dedicated oneself to something beyond himself, towards which he strives and strains and struggles? The story of your dream and how you woke screaming your annunciation to the hound and pussies is wonderful and beautiful; I have thought many times about it. This kind of experience makes one feel that he is *claimed* by some power, some force that wants to use him, and whether he belongs to no one else in the world he knows that he belongs to this force, and that is enough. It only remains to work and to prepare oneself and to keep oneself ready. [. . .]

The Cock story appears in March issue of *Horizon*, and two chapters of the book appear in March *Southwest Review* and March or April *Partisan Review*. As I see it now, the book should be finished by June, and I am in constant correspondence with Random House publishers, who will probably take it. I think I might get some money out of them soon.

Unspeakable weather here, a solid month of snow, very beautiful on all the fir trees but miserable for moving about. This is the worst climate I have ever lived in, I despise it; it depresses me day in and day out. Oh for a little sun! [. . .]

Thanks so much for keeping an eye on the house and thanks to the Worm Brigade for taking the snow off the roof. We'll reward them when we return in June. Take care of yourself and My God don't get the hot foot in that Electric blanket. That is, however, a way of dying in one's own shroud! Yet I don't expect you to see your end this way; I have your End envisioned as one coming on the bank of some river where you have just caught an enormous Trout who, in the name of all the wretched fishes you have caught and we have eaten, finally wreaks his vengeance on you and carries you off, like the corpse of Queen Elizabeth, down the river to a Purgatory of Fishes and Worms. Be careful, dear Brett, thanks for your letters, and remember we love you.

Yours,
Bill

3017 S.E. Claybourne St.
Portland 2, Oregon
March 8, 1949

My dearest Brett:

This is just the briefest of notes to say first, that I have at last signed a contract with Random House publisher for the publication of my book *The House of Breath*, and that I have until September to finish it. I have got a small advance payment out of them, which saves my life at this most difficult point, and when the finished manuscript is sent in I shall get more money. I know you will rejoice with me and Walt, and I wish we were there to celebrate this with a naked bunny or a splurge at Sagebrush or at Frenchy's. I am quite relieved and now hope to bang away at it until I finish the book.

Spring has come with a great shock here, no one was expecting it. Within three days trees actually shot out little leaves; and now, in this soft and sweet air, daffodils and crocuses and primroses are blooming! I am wild with it. The winter was awful to remember.

I am quite recovered, am taking very expensive injections from my doctor for the headache and they might help. I am hoping for good results. The point now is to regain my lost strength and time and then plow into work again. The sunshine and new air help immeasurably.

How is your winter and are you painting hard as ever? I'd love to come down there for a few weeks. Could I bring a marvelous and beautiful and delicate little Russian girl with me and would people talk? I have known her for only two weeks and am completely smitten with her. She is brilliant, charming and finishing Reed College this June. What in hell will I do with her? I can't stay away from her. I'd love to run down to the little house with her and show her to you and the desert and mountain to her. Would—or does—this shock you? Christ, I don't know what to do. Maybe this will pass. The sap is rising. Keep this under your hat and don't tell Frieda or anyone. But if I talk to you about it, it helps. I've never found a girl like this one—a gamin, picaresque, elusive, an artist to her bones; oh, for Christ's sake!

All is for now. At least I am feeling blood in me, and now to get back into work and back to health and spirit. I think of you, and wish I could talk with you. Work hard and write to me, and remember I love you. Wish I could see you—

As ever,
Bill

Russian girl: Dorothy Robinson, a senior at Reed College.

To Spud Johnson
TLS-2

6625 S.E. 31st St.
Portland 2, Oregon
May 31, 1949

Spud my dearest:

  I am sorry to've waited so long to answer your very sweet and at long last letter, but then Stephen arrived practically in the middle of your letter and then everything got chaotic. Now his first week is past and we are all three settling down to our own work and our final week here in Portland. In the interim Stephen's plans have quite crystallized and it now appears that since he'll have only a few days in Taos he'll just stay with us in our little house. You are so kind to offer your room, as I knew you would, and now we don't have to worry.

  Reading your letter made us awfully homesick to see you and it is wonderful to know that in about three weeks we actually shall. Our winters have been long and difficult, but then our spring and summer are here; and it is right that we'll all be rejoined in them. Your winter sounded full of hard work, and cats, and yet some serenity. Ours was awful, because I was sick in it and Walter worked like a dog and we had about three crises. But we came through, and we are both as well as we've ever been—really I have sort of bloomed, suddenly, in my old age! This may be because I have found a beautiful and sensitive girl that I don't know what to do anything with! The entrance of a beautiful and talented and sensitive girl has always threatened Wally and me as a kind of awful inevitability—as you know—but what a blow to find her entering on *my* side of the stage. I suppose I really ought to talk to you about all this, and if it's not too late when I get to you I'll do this. At any rate you'll meet her, for she's coming to visit us in July. As you know, beloved Spud, in relationships like Walter's and mine the most perilous things keep developing, and we have to keep constantly battling. But Wally and I love each other so much that we just can't afford to complain about the struggle. [. . .]

---

sensitive girl: Dorothy Robinson.

To Margo Jones
ALS-3

Taos, N.M.
July 7, 1949

Sweet Margo:

Thanks for your letter yesterday and for your constant support and belief, as always. You know, dear Margo, that I understand so well how life goes up and down, producing a bit of money and then snatching it away. I know you weren't embarrassed at Stephen's having written you, for we can always feel safe and free to ask each other for help (of all kinds)—since we really work *together* in this world. I hope some day to be able to help, really *help*, those I love and believe in, as they have helped me. Please know that I thoroughly understand, as you do, when no help—i.e. *money* help—can be given. There really is much more important help—and that I always get and am thankful for. You know.

The Europe plan seems just right for everything now—this is my time for it—life seems used up here in Taos and most other places—and I have friends and believers in England. You know the time comes when we widen and stretch out, take in more life and more difficult life, expand the material of ourselves—and to deny this is wrong, is crippling, is really a kind of cowardice. It's part of our *search*, dearest Margo. My going to Europe would be no holiday. I think I've *never* had a holiday, everything seems to be a part of one's work, some contribution, some new vision into it. To live in London would be to work and grow in London. And since I have published there already, and since my book will be brought out there—I am not moving away from my own area, but into a wider one.

Just be assured of my belief in you—as you say, we share the same dream, isn't it wonderful?—and God I wish I could help *you* in the bad times. But remember me then, anyway.

Do your work, hard, as you always do—and don't worry about this. I *know* I'll get to England some way. And once the book is out (Jan.), then perhaps the picture will change. I want to go in late September. If you are in New York, then, I'll certainly see you. In the meantime let me know of your work and life when you can, and always remember that we are joined in the same good life. Bless you and thank you, dearest Margo.

Love,
Billy

Walter sends his respects and good wishes.

Stephen's having written you: Stephen Spender urged Goyen to move to London for a while. He appears to have written Margo in search of funds to send Goyen abroad. See Goyen's *Paris Review* interview, pp. 70–72.

published there already: John Lehmann (1907–1987) had accepted a portion of the novel ("The Worlds of Charity") for U.K. publication in his quarterly, *Penguin New Writing,* no. 40 (1950): 64–73. It proved to be the last issue of the magazine. See Lehmann's *The Ample Proposition* (London: Eyre and Spottiswoode, 1966), p. 72.

To James Laughlin
TLS-1

Taos, New Mexico
July 13, 1949

Dear Jim:

I hope you aren't mad at me for waiting so long to send you the sample pages of the translation. However, I knew you were in Aspen and that you probably wouldn't have time to look at it before now, anyway. Besides this, my life since I arrived back in Taos three weeks ago has been one continuous muddle: Sickness, hard labor on the house to make it habitable, the arrival of a girl I'm probably going to marry pretty soon, last minute work on my novel which goes to Random House by September 1—not to mention countless visitors who pop in on me.

But I am now cleaning up chapter 13 and promise to have it to you within a week. I do hope you'll accept it, for I enjoy doing the translation and I need the money. I've got my hands full, though, and I hope you won't want the complete job too soon. After September 1, I'll be comparatively free. Anyway, we'll see what you think.

Frieda and all of us rather expected to see you here in Taos before this—we thought you might come through from Aspen. If so, do let us know and we'd all love to see you.

Thanks for the patience and I'll send the chapter within a week, then. Hope Aspen was a good change and an exciting one for you.

Regards,
Bill

---

the translation: Goyen had stopped work on his translation of Cossery's *The House of Certain Death* in 1947. Laughlin then sent him Cossery's second novel, *The Lazy Ones*, to translate. *The House of Certain Death*, in Stuart Kayser's translation, was published by New Directions in 1949.
a girl: Dorothy Robinson. They never married. In his *Paris Review* interview, Goyen recounted how she had been discouraged by his editor about leading the uncertain life of the artist's wife: "this blessed girl has passed on among the leaves of autumn" (p. 71).

To Ernst Robert Curtius
TLS-2

Taos, N.M.
August 22, 1949

My dear Dr. Curtius:
    Please excuse this typewritten letter for I have much to say to you and I fear my own handwriting might be difficult for you.
    I have thought of you so often and of our very warm and, for me, rare meeting together in Taos. This meeting has become for me one of the most impressive experiences of my life, although we certainly had a rather quiet and simple conversation. Yet I was in such distressing straits at that time; and the power and directness and sympathy of your insight into my life and my work that has to be done helped to crystallize my distress into a firm and positive basis for action where it seemed I could not act or choose. I took all you said very sternly and meditated on it for days and days; and then I finally knew that you were right and that you spoke objectively and detachedly, for the sake of my work and for the sake of poetry—or the struggle for poetry—in the world, to which I am uncompromisingly dedicated. I am so grateful to you; and now we have a friendship based on that meeting and grounded in the world of which we spoke that afternoon.
    I have frequent letters from Stephen and I believe his life with Natasha is quite a happy one, now, and that this happiness might last for a while. I no longer have any fears of living near him and his wife for a while, for it is clear that I must keep myself removed from the several sources of

sometimes almost overpowering love that pours onto me. I am grateful for this love and I need it; but one must learn to direct love, through himself, into his poetry and into his truth to make his works contain it. In this way, it seems to me, one uses love and transforms it, nourished by it himself, and returns it to all nature and back into the world; and so is not devoured by it or bound by it. This, I believe, I have learned, is the kind of "liberality" or "freedom" (of which we spoke in Taos) which contains within it all sensuality as well as all purity, does not deny love and does not perish within love. For it is necessary for me to feel myself, really in a religious or spiritual kind of way, as an agent of some force or of some mission or some purpose working its way through me. It is when I lose this feeling that I feel betraying and betrayed, that I feel cut off and isolated, and so evil. In this light, within this kind of morality, one does not really ask for such things as "success" or reputation; one is really only asking for his right to do a daily work, a slow, steady, flowing daily labor with his material and using his gifts; to keep his connection with his source, and to be free and ready to change and melt into everything and to take everything into himself. This *must* be my way—yet, in America, one feels he must *plead* for the right to this way of life, beg a kind of clemency, a kind of *permission*—and I am determined to make choices always in favor of this way of life. Yet my tradition here in America makes me feel that I must constantly apologize for myself, that I must *explain* that because there is this compulsion within me I make the choices to make and live as I live. This creates the tension which surely you feel here. There is surely very little freedom within which one can accomplish a creative life; and so one has to fight to create within himself this world of inner freedom where he can do his work slowly and with meditation and in his connection with the poetry of the world. I am quite sure this might be true anywhere; but right now I feel so powerful, and even deadly, a resistance to this inner world of which I speak that I almost despair. I have no intention of running away from such a situation, for I feel that one must try to do his work *within* his situation and not, by escaping, outside it. That has been my criticism of Stephen's life and work, if I can criticize these. [. . .]

Ernst Robert Curtius: (1886–1956). Scholar and translator of *The House of Breath*. He put into German many American masterpieces, including *The Waste Land*. Goyen's correspondence with Curtius includes items in the Universitätsbibliothek, Bonn, Germany, and in the HRC.

Natasha: Stephen Spender's wife, the former Natasha Latvin, the concert pianist, whom he married on April 9, 1941.

THREE

London

New York

Dallas

Chicago

Saratoga Springs

Houston

1949–1951

15 Loudon Road
St. John's Wood
London N.W. 8
October 13, 1949

My dear Jim:

Thank you very much for the check for October which was forwarded here to me yesterday. You are probably astounded that I am in England— I meant to find you when I was in New York for a few days waiting for the ship, but then I got terribly sick with New York Hayfever and had to be put to bed in misery, and scarcely got aboard the ship because of it. Anyway, Taos got miserable for me during August, for reasons I'll someday tell you, and I was able to come to England with the help of some friends in Taos who wanted to help me come along with Dorothy, my fiancée. Dorothy is studying in Paris this winter and I just decided to be with her at any cost. But when I got to Paris last week I couldn't take it—somehow I knew immediately I couldn't work there, and I have an immense amount of work to do immediately—so I came on here with Walter, who is in school at the London School of Economics. I have found a little room in Blenheim Mews and will stay here and work intensely for two or three months, as long as my money lasts. I'll be near Dorothy and with Walter, and so far I really am as happy as I've been in a long time and feel very well. I am revising the last 100 pages of my book for Random House, and if all goes well it will be published in late Spring 1950.

The Cossery is going very well and I have already finished about half of it. I certainly shall have it for you by January, so I believe you can count on that. Cossery is in Paris, I understand, and if I get over there again, and I shall have to—to see after Dorothy—I'd like to meet him. Could you let me know how to find him? I'd appreciate a note from you. And you can continue to send the checks to my home address in Houston or on here to the above address if you will. I am counting on the checks each month and Heaven knows they will help. I really do feel that I can work here without the strain and pressure of so much nonsense and superficiality that I felt in Taos—and here I can live and work quietly until my scheduled work is finished by the end of the year. If it's all right with you, I'll just wait until I have finished the translation before I send it on to you, unless you'd prefer to see it chapter by chapter. Please let me know what you'd like and I'll be glad to conform. Once again, thanks ever so much for the prompt payments, they really do mean so much to me. I find living quite cheap here now, and I go on living the way I always have. Please have confidence in me there.

My very best wishes, then, and I'd like to hear from you.

Faithfully,
Bill Goyen

England: Goyen had traveled with Dorothy Robinson and Walter Berns. The former proceeded to Paris, where she studied art. A number of letters to his friends give the impression that he was alone. In the preface to his *Collected Stories*, Goyen wrote, "When I was two-thirds through my first novel, *The House of Breath*, I announced to my editor, Robert Linscott, that I was going to live in Europe for a while. He was astonished that I would make such a radical move and seriously concerned that the book would lose focus and vitality. I went, and the immense experience disturbed my concentration not at all: what I saw in Europe I put right into my novel: it fit very well—ancient frescoes, grand avenues, plazas, noble ruins—into the little town of 'Charity' that I was creating out of my own home town of Trinity, Texas."
Blenheim Mews: Goyen rented a room for writing while he lived at Stephen Spender's house.
late Spring 1950: The House of Breath would be published on August 9, 1950.

To Margaret L. Hartley
TLS-2

15 Loudon Road
St. John's Wood
London N.W. 8
England
23 October 1949

My dear Margaret:
Many thanks for your letter and the galleys for "Christy" which arrived this morning in three days—as quickly as I got mail from you in Portland! I have corrected the proofs and here they are, with many thanks. I am very pleased with your edited version, I think you did a masterful job at retaining the essence of Christy, a sort of distillation of him—and I feel you worked very carefully at it. For this I thank you so very much, it really is a joy to be able to work with such good people as

you at the *SoWest*. I'll be eager to hear what people will say about Christy, so please let me know what you hear.

Incidentally I am now planning to work on, with some of the ideas developed in *House of Breath*, dealing mainly with an enlargement of "Christy," and for this I have asked Guggenheim assistance. Heaven knows what my chances will be, but I've tried. Won't know until March, and by then I'll be at work on this second book. I submitted *SoWest* as a reference, and thanks for whatever help you can give. The Grant really would be a blessing and a kind of vote to go ahead with this work. I am so tired of being poor, there have been so many years of this, it seems; but I am not complaining and if to do my work means to be poor, there is no choice, as you know.

London has got very cold and clammy, but there is so far a kind of romance in these gray days for me. I work inside all day, take off for several hours, then go to it again at night and work until one or two a.m. I did go yesterday to the wonderful medieval town of Canterbury, spent hours in the ancient cathedral. An unforgettable day.

I spent an evening with Edith Sitwell last week. She is something magnificent out of the fifteenth century; but I felt an immediate connection with her and went away loving her. She is a museum piece, one of the last of England. She loves America, oddly enough, and will return there next spring.

I am trying to live completely alone for a while, to build my life around my work, to absorb myself completely in the life of my work. In this way, I believe, one is purified with a kind of clarity which makes him a better human being in the relationships with those he loves and serves; and, too, for me in this way, a basis or foundation is created on which I can then work out in other directions, but always in terms of my work. This may, I hope, explain a lot to you who have been so kind and so genuinely interested in what happens to me; and I hope you will see this as another of countless attempts, not without pain, to hold to one's vision, not to cheat the vision, nor to simplify it, but to nourish it, illuminate it and refuse to compromise it.

For it seems to me, again, that the world, which one so loves and so wants, can be had by the artist only—in its greatest magnitude—through and within his work (as, surely one's "work" comes to him through the world, obversely); one's language must become the world speaking, the speech of life wherever human beings have lived or live it. Or dream of living it . . . but the struggle, and the suffering, is to find one's speech. In this way one sees his whole life as a search for his own speech, like the slow, difficult learning of a foreign language, even, in order to become a citizen of a country and speak for it in its own tongue.

Well, anyway, I think of all these things here, as everywhere else, and nothing has been interrupted by my great move across the ocean. The main thing is really not to change by being moved, but to go on producing the same kind of fruit or flower, or whatever, like the transplanted plant.

Thanks more than I can say, once more, for your faithful careful interest and help, and for your loyalty. I wait to see "Christy" in print, and let me know if I can help in any way. My very best to Allen, hope he didn't get as seasick as I did (and after five years at sea in the Navy!), and just whisper a hello over beloved Texas as you go around in it. Not Buckingham Palace, not the Thames, nor the Place de la Concorde can corrupt my love for the cottonfields, the liveoaks, and pines and the rivers I saw at dusk in East Texas as I drove out of Texas towards the ship in New York last September. My affectionate greetings to you, and let me hear often.

Faithfully,
Bill

---

the galleys for "Christy": "Christy" appeared in *Southwest Review* 35, no. 1 (Winter 1950): 1–16.
Edith Sitwell: (1887–1964). English poet known as much for her formidable personality, eccentric dress, and outspoken opinions as for her poetry.
Allen: Allen Maxwell.
as seasick: Maxwell had been on naval maneuvers for several weeks.
five years at sea: Goyen was in fact at sea from January 1943 until August 1945.

To Spud Johnson
TLS-2

15 Loudon Road
St. John's Wood
London N.W. 8, England
October 29, 1949

Beloved Spud:
I am just now getting to where I can write articulate letters, but even now not very decent ones. I have been trying to get to you, as it were,

through London and work and new personalities for over two weeks now; and until now it has seemed that all this London fog was between us. In a way, too, I have been afraid to allow myself to love all of you away from me too much, for fear I might feel a homesickness that would hurt too much. I do spend a lot of my time, as always in a new place to come to, just sitting and biting my fingers and remembering all the places I have been in and bitten my fingers in thinking of all the places I longed to be in. This is a kind of tormenting analysis I get snared in, but it is really inevitable for me because I am forever trying to understand what I was in the places I lived in: Taos, Napa, Portland—all of them sad, and tinged with a kind of failure.

But I am working very intensely here in Stephen's house, I have a nice large room to myself with an enormous desk; and here I work day and night, except for a few trips on Sundays out into the English countryside. Of course you know of my ten days in Paris before I settled down here in London: how I was quite disillusioned with Paris (for me now, anyway) because of a lot of things I'll tell you later about. This may be, in part, because Dorothy got terribly sick and we were alone, and I could only just glance at Notre Dame, for instance, as I raced past it in search of a doctor. The cafés seemed filled with bearded things like the worst of our summer art students in Taos; but the Louvre and the Tuileries were so exquisite that I didn't care. And the streets were dirty and reeking with loud and vulgar taxidrivers; but the Seine was lovely with autumn leaves in it and the lights of the beautiful old bridges. I spent a day at Chartres and Versailles—too magnificent even to remember: one just has to see them again and again. I had an afternoon with Sylvia Beach, who first published Joyce, and found her a charming and simple American woman who has migraine (I left her some Histamine); a few hours with Truman Capote who a few days before on his birthday had driven down the Boulevard San Michel in his jeep flinging roses into the crowds. Life in Paris seemed absolutely berserk to me—and now I know what Paris "gaiety" means. The Champs Élysées is thrilling and chic and full of fashion and class, the restaurants full of good food; and the city, in general, full of millions of gay people who just refuse to take life seriously, it seemed. One should just come to Paris with some money and a carefree mind and let go—then it would be amusing and scintillating.

London, on the other hand, is gentle and gray and sometimes full of terror, for me—I am sure it is the war that hasn't left the city. Yet I have felt such peace here. Life goes along at a moderate pace, trying to be comfortable under perverse circumstances, reading, writing books, drinking oceans of tea, looking like scenes on a shaving-mug or a teapot.

To walk down Regent Street and turn into Oxford Street is a great thrill
for me, although the shops are just beginning to sell things of fashion
again. But despite the austerity, the feeling is of elegance and dignity and
taste.

I spent one afternoon at a tea at Lady Cybil Colfax's—the last of the
salonkeepers—and there I met old Lord Escher, looking like Brett with a
beard, and his American wife, Lady Escher. Walt and I go to tea with
them this week. That evening I had dinner with Edith Sitwell, who was
magnificently Gothic, great figure in floor-length red velvet cape, long
pale hands whose forefingers had huge amber rings on them, the most
delicate, frail temples, fluted nose and eyes like half-opened shells. She
plays out her Gothic role to the last line, God knows what she really is
like; but I loved her from the first moment, really fell for her. She is
absurd, unreal, exquisite and treacherous. She spoke poisonously of her
enemies and suspiciously of her friends. I hope to see her again.

The rest has been work—I have really been stimulated to work here in
London; so far there is none of that outside tension, pressure which I felt
at home. I am working mainly on the last 100 pages, which I had hoped
to get done in Taos this summer, and the trouble now is that what
happens in these pages threatens to devour the other 200, so that I find
myself trying to rewrite the first two-thirds of the book *through* the last
third—I regard this as a kind of wonderful illumination into the deeper
meaning of this work, and I am tremendously excited by it. But it is
extremely difficult for me, and I'd like to spend many more months on
it—the danger of this kind of thing is that I might very well spend the rest
of my life on this first book, and get no farther! But this can't be, because
I have absolutely promised to get the complete thing in to Random
House by January 1 at the latest. So I'll have to do it. Anyway, a kind of
continuation or further development of the character Christy might be a
second book, and through him I can say more about what I've learned
since I started this first one. Incidentally a very much-cut version of
"Christy" will appear in December's *Southwest Review*, and I'd like very
much to have you see this. This is about the third draft on the present
Christy and, because a lot of the material is quite frank, it has been cut
out of the *SoWest* version. But I'll be interested in hearing what you think
of this. [. . .]

Sylvia Beach: (1887–1962). Proprietor of the bookshop Shakespeare and Company in
Paris, who published James Joyce's *Ulysses* in 1922 after it had been turned down by
several publishers because of its explicit sexual content.

To James Laughlin
TLS-2

15 Loudon Road
St. John's Wood
London N.W. 8, England
5 November 1949

My dear Jim:
    This is to acknowledge the receipt of your check for the translation for
November, and to thank you so very much.
    Idlers in a Fertile Valley is going along nicely, and I think we'll all be
pleased with the result—I hope so.
    My life here is very little more than work, both day and night, the way
I like it. I expect to be finished with everything by Christmas, then I'll
come home around the first of the year. So many difficult things are
happening within my own life—which I will tell you about one day—but
I am trying to keep all that outside the life of my work, until it is finished.
It is possible, more so than anywhere I've been so far, to live a quiet and
workday life here in London; and for that I love being here. It was such a
gamble to come, particularly at the moment of my highest work—if we
had talked of this in New York, where I was in a devil of a spot, unsure,
indecisive, etc., I'm sure you'd have advised me to stay at home. But I
took the chance and thank Heaven it was right. I suppose one should be
able to carry his work anywhere so long as it is securely inside him, but I
know myself so well, that I am so hypersensitive to environment and
atmosphere, that I always go through hell trying to decide whether I
should move or not. Anyway, this move was a good one and a justified
one, I see now, and was only a move from work to work. [. . .]

Idlers in a Fertile Valley: Alternative title for *The Lazy Ones.*

15 Loudon Road
St. John's Wood
London N.W. 8, England
9 Nov. 1949

Margo my dearest:

I am all right, adore being here, am working terrifically night and day, do little else until I am through. Finish book in a month, then I'll be freer.

Did spend 10 days in Paris—magnificent, inexpressible, beautiful—but couldn't work there. Here it is sad and a bit grim, but I am with good people, comfortable, and do my work. The atmosphere of London is very conducive to work, I find—and I'm as content as I've been for years. The problems we discussed that day in Gramercy Park seem less insoluble now—so often have I thought of your wisdom that day—and I believe I have made the right choice. I am alone, live only to work and under-stand—and I feel *alive*.

Saw Old Vic Theatre do *Love's Labour's Lost* last week—kept telling my friends the Spenders that they just ought to see a Margo Jones Shakespeare—I was disappointed until the last act—then what a produc-tion! Lavish, stunning costumes, *real* Elizabethan spirit and feeling. Lots of Elizabethan music and dances—all done as kind of dance-panto-mime—too *much* to suit me. Michael Redgrave a little *too* dancy and *cutish*—but last act was real rich theatre. These British *do* catch and project the genuine Elizabethan tone and flavor—guess they have it over us there. Also saw a Restoration play, *The Beau Stratagem*—superb, real stuff—Kay Hammond in it. Also *The Heiress* with Peggy Ashcroft—whom I met after the play—we spoke of you—she had seen *Summer and Smoke* in N.Y. and thought it best of anything running, praised it unreservedly!

The rest is work until I finish. Then I hope I have money enough for Xmas abroad in Italy or Austria—then home early in January. Think of you, dearest Margo—and hope this season in Dallas is great success. Remember I don't forget you—Take care—Let's keep in touch—As ever,

Billy Goyen

What a fuss over *Streetcar* here! The British don't know what in hell to think. They seem awfully against American theatre right now.

I am alone: Goyen made no mention of his fiancée, Dorothy, in any letters to Margo Jones.

The Beau Stratagem: Goyen means *The Beaux' Stratagem,* a comedy by George Farquhar, first produced in 1707.

The Heiress: By Ruth and Augustus Gortz, a 1947 adaptation of Henry James's novel *Washington Square.*

Streetcar: Tennessee Williams's *A Streetcar Named Desire.*

**To Margaret Hartley
and Allen Maxwell
TLS-2**

*15 Loudon Road
St. John's Wood
London N.W. 8, England
25 November 1949*

My dear Margaret and Allen:

I'm a bit disturbed at not hearing from you since my letter of some weeks ago—and the proofs—but I presume it is because you are very busy with the December issue and other things.

I have *finished* my book at last, the revisions are all incorporated and the manuscript is typed up and shortly to be in the mails to Mr. Linscott. This last bit of work on the manuscript almost wrecked me, for I got going on a spurt of energy, worked about fifteen hours a day, usually without food, and now I am looking up out of the ruins around here to see what is left of the world and the people I left behind. I find that my friend Spender is in America, irony of all ironies, since I am a guest in his home; that it is virtually Christmas in America so far as we here are concerned: since all packages home must be in the mails by *tomorrow;* that I have lost about five pounds and look like a scarecrow in the mirror. At the last I did find I couldn't sleep during my few hours in bed, so with the help of Mrs. Spender's doctor and the Welfare State Nationalized Medical Program, I got a bottle of stuff that has put me right out of the world again! But it is all over with, and I am so relieved and so glad.

Because my money is low and because I really *choose* it, I am returning to America on January 20—which is not far off. If I can get on a January 4th sailing, I'll take it, but I shan't know until after Christmas. Anyway, I have felt such a terrific conflict and tension between my feeling for America—and what I feel a compulsion to express about America in literature—and what is becoming increasingly a forceful influence on my, what shall I say—*sensuous* outlook (the paintings in the museums, the castles, the cathedrals, etc., all of which I saw very early in my career abroad), that I have been quite unsettled within. The point is, I expected this; but I find now that I am just not ready to surrender to this foreign influence; that is, I am not ready to give up my feeling for what I already know—that feeling out of which I want to write for a while longer. For sometimes, now, I feel that I want to go completely Sixteenth Century Florentine and write prose that would be like embroidered tapestries of orchards and birds and beasts since I feel so strongly that our literature in America must become lyrical, sensuous and positive again. But this implies a new kind of language, really; and I have just discovered my own language and it is American and it is southern. Can you understand my conflict? A synthesis would be magnificent—but then I am not even ready for a synthesis. So I want to come home and hear my language and continue to use it.

Knowing this, then, I quite boldly want to sort of run in to Italy in December for about three weeks if I can—but that seems quite improbable now, since I am anxiously holding on to my remaining dollars until I get safely on that ship. I've sold the River Sequence from the book to Mr. John Lehmann's *New Writing and Daylight*, but I don't believe that will get me very close to Italy, since the poor British can pay very little. Anyway, we'll see how things go as time passes.

I do hope all is well with you there, and don't think I forget you here. For the past month I've done little else but work, in one of the most terrifically intense sieges of work I've ever known. Now we'll see shortly whether anything comes of it.

Warmest greetings to you there, I'll be waiting to see the December issue with "Christy" in it; and remember my gratitude to you both. More news as it happens. Do let me hear from you.

Faithfully,
Bill

---

the River Sequence: Chapter 4 of *The House of Breath*, pp. 21–33. It was not published in Lehmann's *New Writing and Daylight*, but rather in Lehmann's *Penguin New Writing* (New York: Penguin Books, 1950).

To Spud Johnson
TLS-2

15 Loudon Road
St. John's Wood
London N.W. 8, England
January 5, 1950

My dearest Spud:

I am back in London after what seems incredible centuries in old worlds, and now I find you are on the road. But by this time you are surely in Mexico, despite Mabel's hatred of motoring, and I hope you are in sun and happy.

My three weeks in Italy were so overwhelmingly beautiful I cannot write about them yet, only say that it was Rome that really got me, got into my blood. I was eight days there, three in Venice and five in Florence. Venice was all golden and marble-white, with mauve and pink-white Renaissance palaces brooding over the mysterious canals—and the most beautiful people in the world were gliding about in gondolas or strolling in the lovely piazzas: the young men, so ravishing, seemed to have just come right down from the ceiling of the Sistine Chapel in Rome and were walking about the streets—so Michelangelo was right, they *are* like that, they *are* a race of lovely graceful sensual people right out of the frescoes and the sculptures. But nothing can match the sensuousness, the undercurrent of pure sensuality mixed with a haughtiness, a mysteriousness that exists in the worlds of Rome. Imagine, in December, days like our Indian Summer, though more tropical, hot, languid, with flowers blooming, vines and lizards crawling over the ruins of centuries, here the white torso of a sculpture brought from Greece by the Romans in the third century, there the fallen capital of a column once erected to Venus or Apollo, over all the odor of eternal Roman brick and Roman Umbrella Pines, everywhere the gentle, faint sound of plashing fountains, and birds singing. How they loved the bodies of their beautiful people, this race! To walk about the streets in Venice or Florence or Rome is like walking in a hall of voluptuous nude bodies, they are in the air on columns, along the edges of buildings on arches, fountains, in gardens, everywhere. It was a liberation to escape the Middle Ages which had got so oppressive in France and in England. And the paintings which one has dreamt all his life of seeing were the greatest thrill of all—there they are, those wonders that had before existed for one only on pages of books, on the walls of little chapels, on domes, ceilings, hanging in the palaces of the Medici,

the Farnesi, the Uffizi, the Pitti, and in the Vatican. Suddenly, on behold-
ing all these, one feels a living continuity with all history, that was the
most buoyant emotion of all.

I feel raped, now; and I just want to lie quietly for a long time, and
remember. My eyes feel worn out, and I want only to look at something I
have known for a long time and that is familiar—like a Safeway Market or
a Ligget's Drugstore.

Most absurd of all—I fell down about sixty magnificent marble stairs
designed by Michelangelo in Rome—the famous "Spanish Steps" and
very badly injured my right knee. I tore loose the cartilage and now
nothing but an operation will mend it—I can scarcely walk and then only
by going stiff-legged. So I am quite depressed but keep trying to tell
myself that Italy and Michelangelo were worth it. Yet this presents a
serious problem, for I am planning to sail for New York on the 20th of
this month and now I don't know what to do—whether to stay here and
have the operation or wait, or just decide to be stiff-legged the rest of my
life and buy a cane with a golden head on it. Surely you will laugh with
me at this—but what to do?

But at least the book is done and taken as is; I had a cable from
Random House saying they would publish it "with pride," and I guess it
will appear on the Spring list, probably in April. Can you believe it?

Two days ago came a little casual postcard to Wally *Beins* and *W. C.
Goyen* from the Tax Office in Taos, saying that our property in Taos
would be sold at public auction on the third Monday in this month unless
we paid immediately back taxes amounting to $5.10! We are in a rage.
This is the only notice we have ever had concerning taxes, we were
informed that our property was exempt because of our being Veterans.
We got terribly nervous, what with all of you gone and no one to investi-
gate and help in Taos; then we found that Brett hadn't left Taos so we
wired her. We've had no answer yet. Can you do anything? What a
nightmare—the house and land being auctioned off and we thousands of
miles away and defenseless. Would they really do this, do you think? Send
advice and suggestions at once.

It will be heartbreakingly sad to have to leave everyone here in London and Paris, but it seems the best; and I want to be in N.Y. for a little
while. I am praying for a Guggenheim Fellowship in March, but you
know what luck I have with that sort of thing. Anyway my money is
practically gone, and with what's left I feel I'd best get back home where I
can better scramble for myself if need be. They watch me like a hawk
here because they think I am here to make money off England, being a
writer.

Dearest Spoodle I am still in a funk, crippled, tired, enchanted—but I do think of you with the same old love; and it is an elation to think that we shall probably see each other before too many months now. Please give my love and Walter's, too, to Mabel—I want you both to know, again, that all this could never have happened if it hadn't been for your help and loyalty, and I thank you from the bottom of my heart. Take care of yourselves, relax and think in Mexico, and remember my love. [. . .]

To James Laughlin
TLS-1

15 Loudon Road
St. John's Wood
London N.W. 8, England
January 15, 1950

Dear Jim:
   Sorry to have been silent for so long, particularly about the translation. It is finished and I'll get it to you shortly, as I promised. There has been an agonizing and upsetting interruption in all my plans—I was to sail for New York on next Thursday, Jan. 20; but several days ago I had a fall and busted the hell out of my right knee. I have not been able to walk at all; and two days ago the doctors told me I must have an operation at once; something is torn loose inside the joint. This means three weeks in hospital and three weeks reconditioning of the leg; so my journey home is now postponed for six weeks. This has put me in great distress, since, of course, I had planned things otherwise; but at least my work is all finished, the novel is in and the translation done. Naturally, there is so much else I want to do and I resent the loss of these weeks; but it can't be helped now and I'll just have to go through with all this.
   At any rate, Jim, you will have a chance to look over the Cossery, and when I arrive we can discuss it, if you wish, and I can be on the spot to do alterations, etc., if you desire. So I believe the book won't suffer because of this delay. But am I due any more money? As I said, I had counted on $250; I've received $200 so far. You can understand how badly I need this $50 now. Do please let me know at once, if possible. Just continue to use the above address. I count just short of 50,000 English words—doesn't this entitle me to $250?
   Hope all is well with you and your works. Eager to see you, and I

count on it in about six weeks. I'll be waiting to hear from you, and sincerest wishes for accomplishment, etc., in 1950.

As ever,
Bill

---

three weeks in hospital: Goyen was later to make use of this experience in his next novel, *Half a Look of Cain* (1994), in which a character named Chris—a young American—is delivered to a London hospital by two companions—a young man and a woman. Chris has severe damage to his right leg from a fall and has to be operated on. See the chapters "The Enchanted Nurse" and "The Rescue," published in *The Collected Stories of William Goyen* (New York: Doubleday, 1975), pp. 240–254 and 255–267.

To John Lehmann
ALS-2

58 Wellington Road (basement)
St. John's Wood
London N.W. 8
February 5, 1950

Dear John:
    I have completed my second wretched week here in this hospital at St. Alban's, and after another week (which at this point seems unbearable—I am in a ward filled with screaming children and where there have already been three deaths), I hope to be free, if still in a plaster.
    As you know, I shall not be returning to the Spenders, and this means added expense until I can take my ship—for this reason, a source of great worry to me now, I ask if you can possibly pay me now for the story to appear in *New Writing*. If you can find it possible to do this, it would help immeasurably. My greatest thanks for this. Please use the above address.
[…]

235 E. 22nd Street
New York 10, N.Y.
c/o A. S. Menke
March 17, 1950

Dearest Mom and Dad:

I'm already just about fed up with this place and wish I could leave tonight; but I keep hanging on here until I hear about the results of the Guggenheim Fellowship and to help with work on the book. I have worked very hard with the manuscript, correcting it, etc., and yesterday it went to the press for the printing of the proof sheets. My next job will be to correct those, then the book will go to be finally printed. It is now due out in August, which still seems a long time off.

This city is so expensive and so noisy, and it is doubly difficult for me because I have to live with friends who keep planning things for me and places to go, which doesn't leave me a free minute. I work all day at the publishers and when I go back to the Menke apartment, dead tired, they are ready to go some place. You know how long I can stand this kind of pace. I so want to get out of this city and settle down in a quiet place and go to work; but there is no question of its being right to stay around here a little longer for the sake of my book and my work. I am meeting a lot of people, and all this will help the success of the book. I met Mr. Cerf just after he had returned from Houston and he told me many people asked about me and my book. He said they gave him a great party and that they were planning to do the same for me in August. I said no thanks. He said he stayed one night at the Shamrock and it broke him. I still don't feel that I am fully home and won't until I see all of you. Seems like home is always so far from where I am. I know you are impatient to see me, and I wish I could just run on down there right now, but I just can't until my business is finished here. So please be patient, as I am trying to be. [. . .]

A. S. Menke: Friends with whom Goyen was staying upon his return from London.
Mr. Cerf: Bennett Cerf (1898–1971). Cofounder of Random House and publisher.
the Shamrock: Houston hotel known for its extravagant size and expensiveness (later demolished).

c/o Random House, Inc.
475 Madison Avenue
New York, N.Y.
April 2 [1950]

Dear dear Margo:

When I had your letter, or where, I can't even remember—I am dead from the throat down, I'm just managing to swallow without breaking something, as Mama says—I came home from England as bright as a fish and thinking Home again, U.S., my country, my language, the ones I love, etc. . . . and as soon as I put my foot on that dock a kind of mildew began to cover everything. That has been three weeks ago, and I hate this city, and I am the loneliest I think I have ever been in my life; but I can't move, I can't move . . . because where would I move to? Random House are very kind to me and they want me to stay here, if I can, until June when they will publish some advance paper-bound copies of *House of Breath* as a feeler to see what critics and some authors will think of it; then if it goes off well, they might advance me more money for this second book I am writing. So June may prove me.

The people here excite me—but it's a morbid excitement, wrong, the kind I want to run away from. These people here are like a wind and I am a kite, and they just keep blowing me up higher, higher—and farther and farther away from them and everything that is on the ground where I want my feet to be, just on the solid *ground*.

Remember our talk that autumn afternoon in your Gramercy Park apt. before I left last year? Did you do what we talked about? Because I did. The point is, beloved Margo, I don't want to be like all those people, sick and so nervous and scared to death. Honey, I need to talk to you, I need to touch you because you're solid and real. . . . and I'm melting, and unreal. Write to me, and when will I see you? Do good work, I believe in you, I count on your belief in me. You'll get a copy of the book in June, and I'm waiting to hear what you think. My love, as always, dearest Margo . . .

Billy

---

second book: Ghost and Flesh, Goyen's second book of fiction.

To Katherine Anne Porter
ALS-1

[No address]
April 2, 1950

I've just got to tell you how much courage you give me, Katherine
Anne—and I don't mean that we ever have to speak of it again, seriously
or with vino—but I must say that every time I've touched you I get
courage and not fear, or sickness, or lamentation—and thank God for
you—

Respects,
Bill Goyen

Katherine Anne Porter: The novelist had moved to 108 East 65th Street, New York
City, the previous November, and Goyen was seeing her during his stay in Manhattan.

To William M. Hart
TLS-2

26 West 85th St.
New York 24, N.Y.
April 25, 1950

Dear dear Billy:

Your birthday gift arrived yesterday and it moved me so that you
would want to send me money who need it so badly yourself. How shall I
use it, as something so hard-won and so needed by both of us? At first I
thought I'd just buy food to eat to keep me working—but then I thought
I must find something that will be more permanent than food eaten,
something that will remind me of you when I look at it. Since I need
music so desperately, and have none, and since I need it to work with, I
have decided to buy from a Third Avenue Pawn Shop where I saw it in
the window an old, sad looking manual phonograph with its handle to
crank it up. Will you accept this, dear Billy? My wants revolve only
around my work, and my life in my work, and I ask only to keep fed, keep
well and keep alive to what is going on inside and around me. You must
tell me if you think the phonograph is a wise and worthy purchase with

your wonderful gift. I have found, as you have found, that certain records hold a world in their music, and that if I play those worlds over and over they are suddenly rendered to me, like an account which I have to pay; I simply cannot live without music, all kinds. I despise the radio and I have spent some of the most lonely times of my life in a room with a radio.

It is unspeakably lonely here—that kind of loneliness that has some kind of unknown terror in it. I am not afraid, but I am full of fears. This is a time in my life when I must, once again, organize all my lonelinesses— for they *mean* something, they hold something within them that must be *told*—and we are tellers, we tell everything; there is a time for telling. This glittering city is full of strange and beautiful and worthless people, and it seems I have met all of them in about three different large exquisite rooms. With one hand one draws these people to him and with the other he pushes them away.

But I am working, in one of the most fertile times I have ever known. Everything is going on inside me, lives, worlds, memories, prophecies—I say this with my sincerest heart, and I must stay alone with all these and get them clear and right. [. . .]

God bless you for coming to me when I need you, you always know; and I thank you from the bottom of my heart. One day, my dear, shall we wear rings on our bony fingers and plumes of feathers and lace around our skulls of shell and bone? for we grow old, dear Billy, we grow old . . .

I love you,
Billy

To Katherine Anne Porter
ALS-4

26 West 85th Street
New York, N.Y.
May 3, 1950

My dear Katherine Anne:
    If I may, I'd like to send you a copy of the galleys of my book—is it asking too much of you to read only galleys? I do it with trembling because I respect and *fear* you so much! But I won't be happy until I do, so if you'll let me know whether there is a good time for you to read— and if you'll send me an address—I'll pass the proofs to you. If you'd rather wait until you've had your rest and returned to the city, please let me know. I'll wait for word, and an address, before I send these.

I sent a copy to Glenway Wescott, because he had called in Random House to ask for one—it may be that he can help me get a grant through the American Institute if the work merits it. This was his suggestion, since I had been suggested by somebody for a grant offered annually—a thing I didn't know about but would be so happy, and relieved, to have if I should be worthy of it.

Anyway, it would be such an honor to have you lay eyes on the book—although I'm running a risk of getting pounced upon by you—because, as I've told you, you've been for a long long time a guiding principle to me in my work, and it seems right to return a thing home once it is finished.

I guess I got lost once or twice and maybe more times in this book—but give us the right to get lost and stumble around in our big old rubber boots—so long as we are trying to *get out* of the thicket or the swamp and are not just wallowing and tramping around for the mere easy agony of it or the sound of our own lost feet—you know what I mean. I mean I want *out* of all this mess and mire and that a book, or something, is a way of getting out—into light and air and sight.

Anyway, again, I've put down all about the swamp and the thicket and the boots, and it's *there*, put down for always, for me. Now I look at all these other things that have got to be put down, this finished.

I want to *talk* to you—about all these things that we have to do, and I want to laugh with you about it all—and above all just praise you for what you've done—in your work and for mine.

It's not for this reason alone, though, that I want you to recover your full strength; and I sincerely hope this change will give you rest and refreshment and that you return in full blast.

Let me know, then, what you'd like me to do about the galleys, and I'll follow.

Take good care—I think of you.

Greetings and respects,
Bill Goyen

May 3, 1950: No correspondence from Goyen to Porter (the short note of April 2, 1950, excluded) between January 29, 1948, and this date seems to have survived.
the galleys: Porter reviewed the novel in the *New York Times Book Review*, August 20, 1950, pp. 5, 17.
Glenway Wescott: (1901–1987). American novelist and diarist.
a grant: Wescott and Christopher Isherwood (1904–1986, British fiction writer) both put Goyen's name on the list of candidates for a grant from the American Academy Institute of Arts and Letters; he never received one. See Wescott's *Continual Lessons. The Journals 1937–1955,* ed. Robert Phelps (Farrar, Straus, Giroux, 1990), p. 267.

26 West 85th Street
New York, N.Y.
May 25, 1950

Dearest Spud:

Bless you for all that hateful struggle with the Frigidaire—I don't know what we'd do without you. And for everything else you've done. I don't know how to thank you enough. When I am rich I'll just support you for the rest of your long life—and don't laugh at the word *rich*—my dear, I had the scare of my life last week when Random House called and said the Book-of-the-Month Club had selected my book with three others for the final reading! Out of the final reading comes the Book-of-the-Month (for Sept.) and I'm, at this moment, *that* close to something like $40,000—I'll know by May 26—it's incredible, crazy, and impossible. My book—though I wish it could—couldn't satisfy 300,000 readers. Anyway, it'll be recommended for "further reading" by the B-O-M-Club and reviewed by them in their news sheet. At least it means a few more sales, maybe.

It's all exciting and quite beyond me—and I tell you because I want to excite *you*, too and to remind you to keep me beholden to you cause I might one day pay off!

Yes, there are *somebodies* here I care about, but I feel so alien and unyielding—just one of my enclosed, lonely cycles—don't know how to break it. I am working well, however, and have sold two stories to *Harper's Magazine* and got a bit more money out of Random House. I have material out of which I hope a second novel will be wrested, but all I can do now is play around with it. I can't work intensely until I get away from here. [. . .]

---

the Frigidaire: Johnson was looking after Goyen's house, which had been rented to Claude Anderson, a wealthy Philadelphian, while Goyen was in New York.
Book-of-the-Month Club: The House of Breath did not become the September selection.
two stories: "Her Breath upon the Windowpane" and "The Armadillo Basket."

223 East 75th St.
New York City, N.Y.
July 10, 1950

My dearest Billy:

Thank you for your lovely letter, I send a reply tonight before beloved Walter arrives in the morning—at 8 a.m. in Hoboken. I shall rise at seven to get there to see his incredible ship touch this island. How right that we two should meet again on a dock and one of us coming over the water to the other: our whole life together has been watery, we met upon water, loved and suffered there, parted at a dock in Honolulu, again at a dock in Southampton, England. Now I meet him at the edge of water with a bottle of bourbon and *The House of Breath* in my hands—and who standing on that dock will know what a life is rejoining there, what lives embrace what lives, tomorrow. My God, our lives, all our lives, are legend, and one sees himself living out the legend, watches it like a story read aloud or told by some freed, disembodied Narrator. Over and over we find each other on the shore and lose each other there; I am haunted, haunted by Glaucus and the bitter weed. Say this for me if ever I go before you do, and Walter too, for only you two know it.

New York is like cigarettes or any drug, one hates it, curses, makes resolutions against it, but the eyes, lips, lungs, organs want it, and it taints them. I despise it one morning, walk about loving it in the afternoon. In this summer it is nice, the people hanging out their windows, sitting on the sidewalks, casual, quieter, gayer, prettier. In one evening one can go into an apartment and meet there the most devastating people, elegant, wicked, brilliant, beautiful, gifted. The avenues seem to take the whole world into them, and the buildings seem delicate and frail in the late blue hot afternoons. Last week one night I walked down Park Avenue toward the apartment of one Alice Astor, where I was invited to dinner, with the voices of Granny and Malley and of Charity, of my room and my lonely haunted youth in it, calling in my brain; and I thought Oh New York City, you are my oyster, they are wineing and dining me because they hear I have written down a book that might be something. And with my hair perfectly combed, and untouchable, I went shyly in to meet Miz Astor and shook her hand of diamonds and rubies. There were people who were talking and had been talking about *The House of Breath*, and I remembered that most magnificent of Balzac novels which I have taken to my bosom as my own, called *Lost Illusions*, and knew that I should have to write one like it, and I will. I have arrived, my darling, I have arrived in New York City, O I am here and they have met me with my suitcase in my hand. But when they think I'll be here, as I told you, I just won't, for I'll be gone where they can't reach me, and then we'll see. But right now this boy's gonna see what there is in all this and he's gonna put it all down.

And now I think how strong I feel, with such a new power, and it terrifies me, my face fat and handsome, my hair shining and my new suit so pretty; and I know that it is because I am gay now, being liberated of that gigantic and sapping burden of *The House of Breath*. Yet that life on those pages is my truth and my doom and it is after me, I can hear it following me down the streets of New York City—and one day it's going to catch me and take me back again, and then I'll be sick and sallow and gray, abusing myself, passed by, like Christy, on the streets, face lined like a dead man's; and I shall have my reality again, such a hard, suffering reality. Cauze honey this ain't right, all this laughter and gayety and impressive running up and down, I know that, they don't, but I do.

The truth, dear Billy, is that I have put my life's truth down, done it in isolation from the world, in vision and near-madness, in sickness; I have—and no one really knows this but I—brought myself up from the well into light and among the voices, and here I am. Now I am in my time and in the world, and I must serve these and be of those, find them out, clarify them and speak of them.

Oh they are all coming by to see what I am, the young ones are bringing their manuscripts of poems and stories, they call on the telephone, send me letters and knock on my door. I let them all in. I give them a good look. Some kind of bandwagon, they don't know just what, is passing by and they all want to get on. There are interviews, there are radio programs, even television; there are huge parties where the editors of magazines come to shake my hand and to introduce me round. I say all this to you because it is a kind of recording of it, as though I were writing it in my notebook. But I ask myself, Where is *The House of Breath?*

How strange it all is, how dangerously strange.

Random House apparently will not pay my transportation home in August; they rather scorn my being in Texas after publication. I may not be able to afford the trip, yet do not commit me either way, we'll see. Anyway, I am working out the play and I am thinking hard on the novel which I see quite clearly now. But who knows when these things will be ready—years, perhaps. [...]

Sit with your ghost, dearest Billy, he will treat you right. Some flesh

just wants to be ghost, that's all, and ghosts have their worth and meaning. Remember, as you sit, that I'm sittin, too, dear one, and so we are
settin together, in our rooms or in crowds, inviting ghosts to have us
ghostly if we can't be had fleshly, for we *are* both. Remember I love ya,
settin there . . . and that ghosts may be the longest-lasting. And that no
one can take from us the right to go mad.

I love you,
Billy

Glaucus: In Greek mythology, a god of the sea who was once a mortal man. In his
mortal life he spent his time on the sea. The figure is important in a number of
Goyen's works and seems to be associated with Walter Berns.
Granny and Malley: Characters in *The House of Breath.*
like Christy: Character in *The House of Breath.*
Sit with your ghost: Goyen was rehearsing the themes of his next work, *Ghost and Flesh.*

To Katherine Anne Porter
ALS-3

[No address]
Oct. 10, 1950

Dear Katherine Anne:
 Here these are, and thank you so much for inscribing them.
 Here, also, are a few newspaper clippings I thought you'd like to see.
 I have never fully or "properly" (as the British say) thanked you for
Yaddo and all your support—how to do it except by keeping my mouth
shut? I am *so* grateful, Katherine Anne.
 William Humphrey worries me—some kind of rancour simmers inside
him. Was it me, do you think? Anyway, I'll tell you what I think—I
believe he is fighting himself. Once he said to me, "I hate all Southerners;
I never want to see the 'South' again." And I said, "even Faulkner and
Katherine Anne Porter?" What I know for myself, and maybe Humphrey
will know, is that until one writes from *himself,* from that tiny center of
light in him, he goes a bit wrong and shadowy. As long as one writes (and
lives, is what we really mean) from those darker areas of bitterness and
hatred in him, what comes from him will not come from *him,* but from
outside.
 Oh well, I felt this so strongly. We'll see.

Thank you, too, for the photograph. I'll stroll by the hollow of the tree
on Friday afternoon again and look for books and clippings and photographs. Funny—that photograph is something I feel I've *got* to have.
Thanks for all, and take care—

Yours,
Bill

"Daily circumstances" are hard; but last night I found this in Yeats (about
William Morris): "His mind constantly escaped out of daily circumstance,
as a bough that has been held down by a weak hand suddenly straightens
itself out."

---

for Yaddo: Porter had recommended Goyen for a fellowship at Yaddo, the artists' and
writers' colony in Saratoga Springs, New York.
William Humphrey: (b. 1924). Novelist, most of whose fiction takes place in or around
Clarksville, Texas, where he lived as a youth.

To David McDowell
TLS-1

5017 Drexel Boulevard
Chicago 15, Ill.
Dec. 5, 1950

Hello Dave:
    To greet you and to say that I'm in my work here, spite of hell and
high water. I think it's a pretty good place, here—neutral territory,
anonymous ground. I really have gone underground, for I inhabit a little
dingy basement box of rooms from which I rarely emerge, and then
looking like an aphid. Did emerge to go down to Dallas, as you know;
and that proved to be very nice. But I made the mistake of trying to
casually stop by home in Houston, where my mother is ill, only to be
there when my father had a heart attack. Now the whole damned works is
falling to pieces. But back here—what could I do there but fall with
them—and to work.
    When you can, and if you don't mind, could I see the Paul Bowles, the
W. C. Williams, as you once suggested? Would like to hear from you.
Hope all is well there. Give my greetings to your wife, I hope she is fine,

and good luck to both of you. Hello to Albert Erskine, too. I'll keep you posted.

Cordially,
Bill

David McDowell: An editor at Random House who later became one of Goyen's editors.
Chicago: Goyen had moved to Chicago with Walter Berns, who was studying for his doctorate in political science at the University of Chicago.
the Paul Bowles: The novel *The Sheltering Sky* (Norfolk, Conn.: New Directions, 1949).
the W. C. Williams: The story collection *Make Light of It* (New York: Random House, 1950).
Albert Erskine: (1911–1993). Formerly editor at Louisiana State University Press and of *The Southern Review*, and Goyen's future editor at Random House. He was Katherine Anne Porter's husband from 1938 until 1942.

To Robert Linscott
TLS-2

5017 Drexel Blvd.
Chicago 15, Ill.
December 12, 1950

My dear Bob:
  I am up now and rarin', can breathe without the girdle they had around my chest; so all is well. Back to the worktable. In bed I got a lot done, read a lot and thought a lot. I thank you very much for the Bowles, but I just can't stand it. That book has pleurisy, too, can't breathe, no air, no *scope*—or just enough breath to blow that wind instrument that makes a cobra dance, and that's inevitably, in Mr. Bowles's mind, a phallic symbol; the eternal gesture of hand-on-fly. But thank you for sending it. I hate it. So much that I got *two* copies—one came today from David McDowell, along with the brighter W. C. Williams—I had earlier asked to see both these. Shall I send one back? There's not a friend I'd give them to. Don't despise me, but there's so little I like or can read very much of.
  I worry about dear little Truman. I had had letters from him and Pearl Kazin, who is there with him now, and answered right back. Then to my horror I read that Mt. Etna is erupting again, right, apparently, into

Truman's backyard. Poor thing. I can see him fleeing in absolute panic
and havoc, his novel ms. and Vesalius, which he has been reading, under
his arms, his Bronzini scarf flying in the wind. Have you heard? Do let
me know when you hear he is all right.

Pardon the harangue about advertising. I rather liked fussing that way
since it made me feel like all the rest of the writers I hear about. It was a
kind of gesture, but there was a tincture of seriousness and sincerity in it,
too, because recently there had been some good things said about *The
House of Breath*, here and there, and I thought you might say something.
But enough of this. What matters, and really matters, is that the new
volume grows daily in my mind and I am enormously restless with it.

My troubles aren't any more prolific than anyone else's, I am sure—
and at least I'm thankful they come when I can cope with them: witness
my good father's going on a drunken spree when I was at home, demol-
ishing a perfectly good car that *belonged to somebody else*. I had to pay for it,
as much as I could give him, since he could not, obviously. The psychology of the whole affair mushroomed overnight and I found, to my
unspeakable surprise, that the poor fellow had been eating out his heart
because of me and my doings and a lot of other things I hadn't been
aware of. How selfish of me, but I got out of there as fast as I could. Such
things (and cold weather) can give one pleurisy in a minute.

I miss you. And I thank you for your tender letter. I'll see you when I
go up to Yaddo, but send me news, and take care. [. . .]

---

up now: Goyen had had an attack of pleurisy.
Truman: Truman Capote (1924–1984), who was spending time in Taormina, a
picturesque hill town near Mount Etna. At the time of his stay, André Gide, Eugene
O'Neill, Jean Cocteau, Christian Dior, Emlyn Williams, Orson Welles, Donald
Windham, and Gaylord Hauser were also in residence there (Gerald Clarke, *Capote: A
Biography* [New York: Simon and Schuster, 1988], p. 212).
Pearl Kazin: Young writer.
about advertising: Goyen had written Linscott protesting the absence of ads for *The
House of Breath*—specifically its absence from the Random House Christmas advertise-
ments. Linscott replied that the book had been well advertised at the time of publication and that the firm now had more recent publications to advertise.
the new volume: Ghost and Flesh.

To Margo Jones
TLS-2

5017 Drexel Blvd.
Chicago 15, Ill.
December 18, 1950

My dearest Margo:

I had started a note on a Christmas card to you, but it got too long so changed it into this. This is my Christmas Wish to you, dearest one, and you already know what it is, for it is the same as always, has never changed, and *will not*. It is full of long long love, solid faith and belief in your life and in your work, and another expression of loyalty to these. Bless you, dearest Margo.

But Margo I will have to say a little more, Christmas or no, and that is that I am goddamned fierce right now. You expect me to be, I am no poetic worm, I am in a fight, have always been, for art is a fight as well as a dream and an ecstasy. I don't need to say this to you who are an old fighter and one of the fiercest and most inspired I have ever known; but I say it to define my present state of battle. Who ever thought that to write as I try and must would be a bed of violets; I never expected it to be. I am out to cause trouble, serious trouble in the intestines, groins, hearts and brains of men; I have prepared myself for this and now I am ready, and at any cost, to wield my weapons. I say weapons, for that's what you fight with, in art or in anything. And in art the weapons are love, faith belief, toughness and a stubborn-headed stand for the truth and the beautiful.

All right; I have wanted so much to come down there, you know it well enough, we have spoken of it enough. So far I have not done much more on the play because I have been working night and day, and I mean night and day, me and this room and this typewriter, since I got back from Houston and Dallas. But I have ideas, the play is alive and rarin', and I hope to see what I can do, after Christmas. Yet, Margo my dearest Margo, right now I feel that I wouldn't come to Texas if they gave me the Adolphus Hotel. I will have nothing to do with the bickering over books, the literary jealousies, the catfights and backbites that go on wherever there are three "writers" and "critics." If those people believe in me, as they so thunderingly professed, almost killing me with love, then let them not change their minds. I will have no part of these overnight love affairs where in the morning you are kicked out and forgotten. Honey for me love goes on and on, the kind of love I'm in, I mean. And Literature is no sex-affair, no two-hour ecstasy. For me it lasts my lifetime.

I refuse to be involved with second-rate squishy people, and you know who I mean down there. I've always run a hundred miles when they come near. Now I may be second-rate, I'm not evaluating myself; but the best I can do is give myself to first-rate people when I can.

So for the time being, I'm awfully ferocious and prefer to be alone and away from it all, all that stuff. I know that if you attach yourself quickly to those who bray about your greatness, your genius, your this and that, you will find yourself, a little later, abandoned and betrayed by these too-ready praisers and babblers. Until some of those people down there, and any-where, can make up their minds about *The House of Breath*, I'm not going near any of them. I know what I think about it, I know what I tried to make it; it is not up to me to come down there, or go anywhere, to help settle their minds. Either they take it or leave it, believe in me or don't.

This has nothing to do with you, dearest Margo, you certainly know that; I don't even have to assure you. For I love you and stand by you and count on you. Work is the thing, it must be stayed with, it must be done.

We'll see how it all goes. But I want it known widely and roundly, how I feel and where I stand. I will fight. I have written something of this same to Lon today.

God bless you, and drink an egg nog for me as I will for you.

My faithful love,
Billy

The play: Goyen had begun the first dramatization of *The House of Breath*.
take it or leave it: Reaction to *The House of Breath* was heated when it appeared in 1950—especially in Houston: "I fell out of favor with many people in the town, let's put it that way, and just about disinherited by my own family. I had nasty letters, bad letters from home and heart-broken letters from my mother and my father. Generally the attitude was one of hurt and shock" (*Paris Review* interview, p. 74).
Lon: Lon Tinkle, Texas journalist and critic.

To Allen Maxwell
ALS-5

5017 Drexel Blvd.
Chicago 15, Ill.
December 31, 1950

My dear Allen:
It's New Year's Eve and I send my love and make all kinds of wishes for

you and yours, for your projects, works, health and peace of mind. It is like a warm fire to sit before, to think of your faith and friendship and to know that I carry it on with me out of passed years into a new one.

I thank you so much for your letter that came on Christmas Eve. I was alone and pretty far underground, *both* ways—for I live in a basement—and your letter's arrival was like you knocking on my door. Bless you for calling on me at such a time, Allen.

The point is this, Allen—to keep naming over all things live and dead, to keep taking inventory of it all; and to pray to God and good friends that you can stand up under the strain. Not to let anything that has happened pass by without trying to get hands on it. There is this necessity to *touch* everything—to try to give it a name—or at least to leave one's touch on things. I think children feel this when they go into a new room—how they have to go around, upon pain of being thrashed or fussed at, and put their fingers on all the things.

I am sorry your family have been ill. Lon wrote that he was sick, too. Do hope you are all recovered.

Will we be called back to uniform, Allen? Or will you, rather, for I resigned my commission two years ago. This means I might be a private.

This is an ungodly place to live—like Berlin, winter 1900. Filthy snow turned the color of fudge by smoke and cinders, bleak stone apartment houses, no light, dirt, and strangers huddled in street corners waiting for buses. Yet I have *chosen* it, of my own will, it is my own responsibility. Until I can feel sure that I am not needed here, by Walter, I will not leave. One day I hope you will let me talk to you about all this, for I have needed a friend to talk to—and that quite desperately when I was last in Dallas.

I think, in this terrible state of mind I've been in, of all the places to be or go to—but the real blood-life is here—the most difficult place to be, it is true. But it is true, I believe (for I have found it out, before) that the most difficult places—where there are pain and suffering—prove later to have been where *life was,* had chosen to be at that time; and that something was *yielded* by the painful experience of that difficult place and time which could never have been given to one in any other place. The hard problem of one's life, if he is like me, is to know where to be, where his *reality* is, whether he is imagining, deluding himself, escaping, or what. It is the question, then, of pursuing one's own *reality,* of chasing oneself incessantly in order to keep trying to discover the *truth* of oneself.

It is easy, and simple, to go to the easiest, simplest areas—but then one has sacrificed the very uses of his life—and then what good is a life?

You see how I am thinking and struggling, Allen. I don't mean to exaggerate or dramatize it, but it is a bitter struggle. Because you know all this, without my ever having to tell a word of it to you, because you are and have been a companion to me along this road, I love you and thank God for your faithfulness. We know this, too; so what more is there to say? What we do, and what we ought to do more often—and I hope we can—is get a bottle of beer and laugh together. Bless you all—and Happy New Year!

Ever,
Bill

---

called back to uniform: It was the time of the Korean War.

To Ernst Robert Curtius
ALS-3

c/o Random House
457 Madison Ave.
New York 21, N.Y. U.S.A.
December 31, 1950

My dear friend:

I have wondered if you have ever received *The House of Breath*, which the publishers were to have sent to you some months ago. And if you have received it, I pray so sincerely that you have liked my attempt to show the lonely, fragmentary existence of a group of people who grieve over the loss of a *community* of human souls but who piece together *within themselves* a whole and see it whole, and with wonder and a kind of spiritual fervor.

It is done, then, this first work; and with its faults and weaknesses, it is precisely the way I should choose to make my beginning if I had it to do again. For me, I say humbly, this first book is a foundation for all my future work—and, indeed, a basis for my own life, for my own emotional and spiritual and intellectual problems. For one sees his life as *oeuvre*, as a construction; life and work lend hands to each other.

That wonderful, warm, affirmative meeting we had in Taos that summer is a memory that marks the beginning of something great and significant in my life and work. There was such a connection between us, such a *union*—it serves me in my difficult hours. I pray we do not lose our connection—and I pray that you will find evidence of it in my work.

So I am in my work, hands and flesh and soul, deeper and deeper; the problems of life press harder and harder upon me—I am alone, I have abandoned and have been abandoned; the flesh cried for flesh and the spirit for spirit—and *il faut avoir le courage de tendresse*. Moreover, it is a perilous time in which to be alive, in which to dedicate oneself to the life of his sensuality, the breath of his vision—yet it is all one gets—his *time* in the world, and one so loves it all, the world, and men, and the beauty of first things. Give me courage, dear friend, and do not forget me as I never forget you. [. . .] [rest of letter lost]

To Katherine Anne Porter
TLS-3

5017 Drexel Blvd.
Chicago 15, Ill.
January 14, 1951

My dearest Katherine Anne:

It seems wrong that our love letters should be in type; yet with one's fingers most of the days on the keys, it is quite natural, and in the flow of things, to go off from revisions, etc., into variations, like a pianist modulating out of his scales or compositions into his own little measures and bars. Anyway, it seems right, again, because, for most of us, letters rise out of our work at hand or present images in the mind. Still I do hate typewriters . . .

Bless you for your letter this morning; I write right back, like a conversation. I have needed conversations badly, this family I've been staying with are nice, good Chicago sides-of-beef; liberal-minded, practical-minded, with nothing, it seems to me, ever *left over* from their daily lives except scraps of the same dough of their daily biscuit, which they just roll and pat into more biscuits—you know what I mean. But I have had, nevertheless, a very good work period and I believe I've accomplished a bit. Now I'm ready to hike out of here, into different air, and try intensely to shape up this second little book—this I hope and pray I can do at Yaddo. One interruption—a nasty attack of *pleurisy!* It lasted two and a half weeks, but it is going, now. What an agony that can be; I thought of you, but I didn't want to tell you.

I am glad you liked your "pink azalea." But I had sent a *white cyclamen*— it was just like you, to my mind, when I saw it in the florist's window. I asked them to wire Kay Florists on Lexington Ave. to send you this delicate, pert, pure little flower—Kay's had sent you the other flowers last year; and you get this pink azalea! Never mind, it brought love, pink or white, dearest Katherine Anne; and I know you will make it bloom again.

Incidentally, the Russian gal I put some acreage between (me and her, I mean), is now a wide-eyed employee of the *Sat. Review of Literature*.

As for the ugly medal I would have got if I would have been awarded the National whatever-it-is, it is a small reward, grant you. And what you say about allying oneself with those committees, fronts, etc. I agree with wholeheartedly; that was the thing that helped most to try to destroy me in New York—the plans and projects of publishers and editors. It was hard for an innocent, beginning writer who had rather based his actions on the word as spoken. Yet, too, the presence and power of such as you on these committees is one's only hope; for when you step out they replace you with Irita Van Doren or Taylor Caldwell, and then the jig is up. I remember reading how Pound made his choices and then stung the committee. If that young racehorse Buechner won the award, it would just mean we would get more books next year like his; for publishers know a good thing. So—it's not that "I want you to vote for my book" etc.—you know that—I choose not to think about competitions for the best this and that, for it roils my work, and worst of all, makes me feel as if I were engaged in Intramural Sports, a tennis match or something, out to win—win what? The only thing, of course, to win is that Grace that will make us write more powerfully, more honestly. You know. You have helped *me* know. Yet it *is* that, wherever I am, whatever I am doing, if I know you are involved in the game then I know there's going to be hell to pay before the others get away with anything. I've said this to you before. And if you resign yourself out of these activities, then the chances for their ever improving into anything of honesty and merit are less. For this reason, dearest Katherine Anne, please stay on these committees; even if you cast *no vote* at all, *that's* a vote.

I so look forward to seeing you—it will be, probably, the last week in this month. I'm afraid to stay too long in New York (besides not being able to afford it) for fear I'll break the march of this present work. Better stay longer in that city after it is all done. Anyway, I'll get in touch with you. Keep well—and *stay* light on your feet; because you are the brightest thing I know. Bless you and love you; see you soon.

Faithfully,
Bill

---

the Russian gal: Dorothy Robinson, who was no longer Goyen's fiancée after they returned to New York on the *Queen Mary* in 1950.

the National whatever-it-is: Porter was vice president of the National Institute of Arts and Letters from 1950 until 1952. As such she was able to promote Goyen for one of its annual awards.

an innocent, beginning writer: But Porter's perception of Goyen at this point was skeptical. In a letter to Eudora Welty written on November 8 of this same year, Porter says, "Bill Goyen flew up on some kind of an errand, saw more people and got more gossip in three days than I do in a year, living as I do in almost the exact center of this island . . ." (*Letters of Katherine Anne Porter*, ed. Isabel Bayley [New York: Atlantic Monthly Press, 1990], p. 407).

Irita Van Doren: (1891–1966). Editor of the *New York Herald Tribune Books.*

Taylor Caldwell: (1900–1985). Pen name of Janet Taylor Caldwell, prolific author of popular melodramatic novels set in the past.

Buechner: Frederick Buechner (b. 1926). American author whose first novel, *A Long Day's Dying* (Knopf, 1950) was published the same season as Goyen's *The House of Breath*. Buechner's book was hailed by Malcolm Lowry, Carl Van Vechten, Leonard Bernstein, and Christopher Isherwood.

To Ernst Robert Curtius
TLS-2

c/o Random House
457 Madison Ave.
New York 22, N.Y. U.S.A.
January 18, 1951

My beloved friend:

Your letter has meant so much to me. I cannot tell you how much your faith in me helps me; and I am grateful to you from the bottom of my heart. What you say about *The House of Breath* and about my life-work gives me that kind of spiritual help that I so need in this world of flesh. For, as you remark, I am intensely in both worlds, flesh and spirit, as all artists are, and that is the greatest problem of the artist, the source of greatest suffering. The bridge between the two worlds is there, it is sometimes the body of the artist, then a bridge of flesh; it is sometimes the soul of him, and then a ghostly bridge—but, as we have said, breath bridges the worlds.

I want to answer your questions: you ask about my actual way of life. I am alone, restless, shifting; I have such an overpowering feeling of anonymity, of un-belonging, of homelessness. Herein lies the potential power of objectivity which the artist must have, I know; but herein lies, too, my suffering and my often almost unbearable loneliness. My greatest suffering comes from unused tenderness, from unused sensual energy.

True, one directs these onto his work and struggles to make his work absorb both tenderness and sensuality. But there is the world, too; there are these people. The world is so beautiful, the human figure, face, spirit are so beautiful; one belongs to these, too. Yet I know I must have the courage of my tenderness—though when I have used it upon people, such suffering and such near-destruction of all of us has resulted that a kind of fear has risen in me. Sincerely, dear friend, I have always felt myself to be claimed by some force that wants to use me for itself, for its own aim in the world. This has rendered me unclaimed by any other thing; I can only belong to that force, that power that wants to use me in the world. But I am young, I am an animal as well as a spirit. These are my daily problems—and I do not complain of them, for I know they are the problems of the human artist's situation in his world. I would not remove my suffering any more than I would invite it—I only ask the courage and the strength to *understand* my suffering and the right to go on exploring its causes and its uses in my time.

So I live alone and not in any one place for very long; yet by nature I long for a place to root myself—but where? I do not like cities, I am not meant to live in them—I need to sit and think, to look, to feel the soil in my hands, to touch the simple, *first* things—do you understand? I live as a writer; my whole day, my night, is spent within my work; it has devoured me and I belong to it; if I cannot work I will die, like any laborer. I know, I know this is my destiny; and I accept it. What you told me in Taos and what you have told me in this letter makes me know again, for the hundredth time, that I would die for my life as artist in the world. By now, you know these things of me.

If one is dedicated, surrendered to his vision, then, dearest friend, he can only follow where it will lead him, do what it requires him to do. That is my life. I am poor, I am alone, I am full of suffering. But I am full of faith, too, and I know joy, and I love life and the world. [. . .]

To William M. Hart
TLS-2

Yaddo
Saratoga Springs, N.Y.
Feb. 4, 1951

Billy:
   Forgive me for being so long silent—I have been in one of my Hells and in a desperate way, ending it, at last and at the final hour, it seemed,

by rushing up here, where I had an invitation to spend two months working. That's all right, dear Billy, it's all passed now, and I am settled in here, with every comfort imaginable, and with complete privacy and seclusion, to try to finish *Ghost and Flesh* by April.

The records came, Billy, and I thank you so much. I played them at once, then put them away for a long long time. [. . .] Forgive me for not letting you know about the receipt of the records, but understand that I was very ill. Do not worry, for it has passed.

Dear Billy, it is so lovely here, quite white, so quiet, so pure of air, the coldest air in the world right down from Heaven. There are a few very nice folks here, most of whom I have known before—we all work in our rooms and meet only at dinner and afterwards, when we wish. Eleanor Clark is here, a dear friend; Elizabeth Bishop, a strange and marvelously curious woman, hurt and knocked awry someway, by something—already I am extremely fond of her; Wallace Fowlie, gentle, intelligent, good; Alexei Haieff, a composer—and three little chicks of writers one never heard of. I am so far very happy here.

Write me here, dearest one, and remember I don't forget you, love you.

Billy

Eleanor Clark . . . a dear friend: (b. 1913). American novelist and essayist, wife of Robert Penn Warren (1905–1989), Pulitzer prize–winning novelist and poet.
Elizabeth Bishop: (1911–1979). American poet.
Wallace Fowlie: (b. 1908). American literary critic.
Alexei Haieff: American composer.

To Peggy Bennett
TLS-2

Yaddo
Feb. 12, 1951

Boo back to you, Miss Lucy Locket!
A delight to hear from you, you seem in better spirits, bless your hide; I pray you stay thataway for a little spell; pray the same for me, Peggy. Yaddo heals, it is so pure and untouched, now; all the scars and blights of those before us are hidden under these blue snows; the trees out my window (did you know I live in your room in East House?) are blooming,

like an orchard, with snow blossoms; nothing but the delicate designs left by God knows what kinds of little animals that rush at night over the snow. I walk some, breathe down this cold air from Heaven, chat now and then with the other guests, keep to myself and hover over my work. It is a blessing to know that a long free stretch of worktime lies ahead; I am so grateful to Yaddo for this. So I have really settled in, quite peaceful, my ghosts haven't found me yet—but never mind, Peggy, they will (I wonder if those tracks on the snow . . .). But the point is, and you know it and I know it, we've got to love our ghosts and try to reason with them, our Old Ancestors, and old First Men, Old Adams and Old Liliths, they're all in us, tormenting us, hovering over us: *we are more than "people in our time."* We are joined in dust—I ponder and brood over dust and light, the poverty of dirt, the little speck of light the dust draws to and hovers around; I think of Edgar in *Lear*, wild in his skins, the traveler lost in the hill, his old kinsman blind on the road, the joining, oh so beautiful, of father and son. I am full of this kind of thought and God help me to shape dust and light and "poor, houseless poverty" into some little form, shaped itself out of dust but held together for a little while by the light I beg for. This is what we are about, Peggy, you and I and, it seems, so few others; this is what we are holding out for, this is why we are, as you said to me on your postcard to Chicago, like the driven snow; we are on the road, roadrunners, the dust at our feet, we will not stay for long and let our dust settle. It is in our minds and hearts that we must settle the dust, and I must tell you I join you in that incessant, suffering and marvelous settling of dust, and you join me.

Stay with it all, Peggy, we've got a long way to go. Let's keep in touch, please, and pat the babies for me and say hello to Bill. Send a word—

Ever,
Billy

Peggy Bennett: (b. 1925). American author and wife of poet William Rossa Cole (b. 1919).
Miss Lucy Locket: Goyen's nickname for the petite Bennett. It was inspired by the nursery rhyme about Lucy Locket losing her pocket.
My ghosts: In the stories he was currently writing.

To Margaret L. Hartley
and Allen Maxwell
TLS-1

Yaddo
Saratoga Springs, N.Y.
March 8, 1951

Dearest Margaret and Allen:

Here is a piece of *Ghost and Flesh*, and I wonder what you will think of it and whether you will want to print it. It is related to the other parts and pieces of this strange little book, yet, as I think you can see, it stands on its own feet and is meant to. I am sorry it comes so late, but not too late, I hope, should you wish to use it for the summer issue. If you can't have it, I will understand, but I do beg you to give me your impression of it, tell me how it hits you. I need your opinion.

Now I see that this book will be, again, not so much *about* anything as it will just *be* something—I want it to be a figure of light and dust, an *object*, bound together by the lives of people in it—this is the substantial sinew of the book; but in the hands I should like the book to be, as it were, a shape of dust and light, of ghost and flesh. Do you see; am I insane?

So let me hear, and don't be afraid to say your mind.

Yaddo goes appallingly strange and mysterious at times—the isolation, the beauty of the woods, the haunting overtones, in the air, of the lives of people here. But when I leave I think I shall have battled something out for myself; and I hope to have this little book as a relic of the battle. I think of you two, day in and day out; stay with me; I love you dearly. Send me a word.

Faithfully,
Bill

---

a piece of Ghost and Flesh: He sent them the story, "A Shape of Light." They did not publish it. It later appeared in *Botteghe Oscure* 8 (1951): 249–276.

Yaddo
Saratoga Springs, N.Y.
March 14, 1951

My dear Bob:

Thank you and the girl in the office for the subject for meditation—
the title *Ghost and Flesh*. I think I will stick to it, after examining it
thoroughly and tearing myself and the book to pieces for the twentieth
time. I do not mean to be stubborn-headed and I sincerely thank the girl
for putting me to the test; she helped me enormously. I'm not out to
convince her, or anybody, only myself—which is the only way to honestly
do one's work, you will agree. However, if after thinking about what I am
going to say, you and others still think the title a serious mistake, then let
me know and I'll go over it all again. Anyway, listen to what I have
thought and am thinking, and see what you think, Bob.

Ghost and Flesh is to be a "book"—by that I mean a unified, integrated
whole, a *single* gesture although complex and varied in its meaning and
meanings. The predominant gesture in *The House of Breath* was a turning
inward towards a whole, within one's self: the attraction of (searching for)
parts or fragments towards a central whole or wholeness. The conclusion
of this gesture, this inner action, was an *outgoing* one—the Narrator in the
end is "on the road," going where he has to go in order to "be what he
has to be," towards building, towards connecting, towards giving out
(after this intense taking in). The Narrator is you and me and every man
who would find the image of himself and use it to rebuild the world of
human experience and to honor it. *Ghost and Flesh* has as its predominant
gesture, then, this outgoingness—towards a whole (again). I test the
validity and honesty of this by feeling within myself this gesture; for I am
working toward a more vigorous, a wider, clearer objectivity towards
experience, and it is this objectivity which I hope to fully achieve in the
novel to follow *Ghost and Flesh*.

To experience the predominant "gesture," then, or the "idea" of *Ghost
and Flesh:* the people of the world of this book are driven by the need to
communicate *beyond* themselves to something greater, more permanent
than the everyday gestures of life, more stable, to be members of a whole:
a "household," a lost family, a community of pilgrims, a cause, the
physical world of first things. They reach ("The Kite") into the air; they
go down (the buried message in the grave of Son's mother); they salvage
and lift up (the drowned pilgrim from the sea); they follow what is

popularly presumed to be supernatural phenomena but is, in reality, the simple reality, the substantial truth—"Bailey's Light." They are after "first things"—the simple beginning things: light, air, dust—to re-name them, to re-claim them—in a world where all things seem fouled and abused by overuse and wronguse. The people, then, shuttle, hover, swarm, disperse, vanish, appear; there are faces at windows, fingers at panes, knocks on doors, feet on floors. There is bound up with this kind of ghostly action the idea of always returning to the place of experience (as "ghost" [idea] or flesh [physical body]) to better understand it, to "get it straight," and so make their accounting. (For must we not make our own accounting, and not rest until we do?) For these people are after the truth, the bloodtruth of themselves, the reality of themselves—and in looking for it they feel themselves a part of some mysterious tradition, some continuity, originating somewhere (in their deep and dark depths of consciousness) moving into them in their time and through them on to their followers— they quite literally, in most cases, try to reach this by messages, letters, records, knocks on doors, or just by *touching* with their fingers. Yet they seem outcasts of their society, of their time, because they are people of unrest, refusing to be fragmented, longing for the whole—their time, which is fragmented, seems to reject them back into fragment; but they are joiners, connectors, agents, instruments. And what they leave behind them as "ghost," letters, messages, graves, dust, a light traveling over the ground, a lantern in the trees, the skeleton of a fallen kite, tales which have grown into legends about them, remain as the recorded shape of their experience, is itself the very link, the very connection with what went on before them which they have communicated to their followers: in the book the Narrator himself, who is a disembodied voice, a tale-teller, a recorder, passing it all on, keeping it alive, keeping it "straight."

It is the portrait of the artist, too, on another level—for surely this gesture contains hidden within it the meaning of the artist's shaping spirit and activity in his time; he is a kind of magnet that attracts and carries about, seeks for, heavily loaded with it, the enormous burden of humanity's ghosts—and that in this sense he exists in a kind of twilit graveyard world surrounded by the ghostly part of everything that ever had flesh or blood or light in its face and upon its limbs—he is laboring to make the epitaphs for all things dead and so keep them alive, to return life to them. It is, then, a divine project that he is about, and a very human one, too; for with one hand he is handling and caressing life and with the other he is warming death. For what can the artist belong to except what he must, despite *himself*, abandon (as ghost *or* flesh), destroy, turn away from so as to build it again. He will have his experience and he will have his *idea* of it—he is both ghost and flesh . . . a platitude. This seems to me the moral struggle of his life and the source of his suffering; and which his life, got into his own hands as often as he can take it, must show to him the means and the ways and the courage to endure it and give form to it.

So, simply, we are all part-ghost, part-flesh; the ghost in us we pass on to others, by dwelling in them or round them, haunting, tormenting, giving hope, giving belief. All flesh—the ghost in us destroyed, ignored or betrayed—we are no more than fragments blown a little by the wind, like scraps of a torn-up letter. There is the connection, the pattern, the whole—here is our hope, here lies the root of our belief in the dignity and beauty of the cruel, constantly failing human race. There is this *spiritual continuum* and the individual carrier of it, like a message, as he goes on "the road." The artist tries to shape the message, give it its difficult clear meaning, keep it straight, keep it from dust and the grasshopper and pass it on before he, dust and victim of the grasshopper, passes on, too.

The book will *be*, as a whole, as an entity, what I have here delineated—it will not just *tell about it*. In this sense it is closest, again, to poetry; yet it is *not* "poetic prose." The book will *be* light, growth, darkness, searching, shaping. It is *about* fragments and shapes of stories and tales, told by this one and that—narrative fragments bringing into concrete reality, substantial and precise, this pervading poetic *is-ness* of the whole. It is, in this sense, a further exploration of the responsibility of the artist (on the highest level) and of the living human being (on the most basic level) to life, as moral struggle to find wholeness in one's time.

The book will be a world, pointedly contemporary but of all time, and *absolutely and most distinctly not* the "decaying and decadent South," loathed tag, in which all expression is welded into an image—and this image to convey the life of a figure, or a tale-telling wanderer, moving in a world where the natural rhythms of life have broken off into fragments. Its reverberating and unifying theme of contact, touch, communication between permanent and passing, eternal and ephemeral, precise and mysterious. . . . with the tone of a wanderer's song, of varying long stanzas. He is alive and stirred alive, and brightly, by the elements, the seed, dirt, air, light; to project some greatness of spirit, growth, dignity, nobility. For I will combat the modish fictive conception, so false and so sensational, of man as lurid, bestial and glitteringly smart, moralless, that does all it can to portray the indignity of the human soul; I will combat it with simple, powerful, compassionate lives, I will do this as best and as powerfully as I can.

The people of the book are, I hope, raised into a realm of legend, they seem eternal people exerting their living influence and effect on other people. My aim is to try to lift them into this realm, as figures of dust and figures of light. *Ghost and Flesh* is not just a "collection of stories," then; nor are the stories "tales of the supernatural." It is a book of shapes, gestures, objects, integrated and drawn into unity by the lives of people creating them; concretely and directly set down, yet rising and expanding into a mysterious complexity off the page or in the mind of the reader. What, though, is left is what was begun with: objects, gestures, permanent recurring shapes and images which hold within themselves, tight and complex and so seldom yielding, their own meaning. Yet stories are told. But if they are "charming" stories they are more than that, too. And I think their form, which the stories have chosen for themselves or discovered for *me*, is new and unique.

The style tries to create the folk, a speech-style which, I hope, will subtly and delicately, suggest the personality of the character it tells about—direct, unadorned, matter-of-fact, precise, moving into a more and more complex framework and network of detail (both inner and outer landscapes fused and sometimes symbolized in a concrete object— the kite, the stick of Old Somebody with which he knocked on houses, the letter, the ball of light) which becomes symbolic and mysterious and ends up having told more than is on the page, revealing an intricate and involved mess of lives and meanings. The style will attempt to achieve a complex simplicity. The scene will have a size out of all proportion to its length and should expand beyond the page. If the scene in one story, for instance, originates in "Creecy, Texas," it ends everywhere. The scene radiates from the narrating character—at the center, generally—yet who is somewhere outside what is narrated, though mysteriously involved and implicated.

Now, this is so long-winded I must beg your pardon for it. Yet it is a little essay on the substance of *Ghost and Flesh*, and I hope the meaning of the title and the book. The book is no more about Southern people or about the decay and decadence of the South than *The House of Breath* was. Turgenev's stories and novels about Russia are about Charity, Texas as well. I had not been aware that so many reviewers, so many readers of the "general public," had so disliked *The House of Breath*. I beg you not to publicize *Ghost and Flesh* as a book of tales about the South. It is a book about the world and men and women in it. Please let's try to softpedal this "Southern writer" business. I am looking for a language and a country to give my work to, and I can only start with what I know and have in my ears and go on from there. I feel sure I am going through to another plane, another level, another country, and that we shall see in the novel to come. I am concerned with the total involvement of humanity, Bob, and not with the involvement of people in a single region of the United States; and, above all, and simply, the vision and the beholder, what the flesh does with the ghost.

So far as I can see, unless one of the stories melts into another to make a very long story, there will be eight stories, amounting to between 200 and 250 pages, maybe a bit more. I believe I can finish the whole lot by May 1. Could the book be brought out, say, in November? I'd like that if you could manage it and think it best. Why don't you look over this long harangue and see what you can boil out of it by way of a description of the book, then let me see what you've got and I'll help from there. I hope you will want to say that they are unique stories and in a new style.

I am so overwhelmed and intensely involved with this conception, this kind of vision of all passing things, Bob; I must wrest something permanent from it and shape it. What does it mean, that we are Old Somebody's Children, figures of dust but loving the dust and touching it for our moment? I want the enclosed piece, "Old Somebody's Children," to be the opening piece, and I enclose it to give you an idea of what it wants to do. This is not its final form, but only an indication of what it will be. I want to remove the "I" to a further distance, cut it further away from the "I" of me so that it will be an objective "I." When I showed it to Katherine Anne, she read it carefully for a couple of days, then brought it back saying it was to her mind the best work I had done, that it was better than the best parts of *House of Breath* and that it was her opinion that it showed great growth. She asked me to dedicate it to her. But see what you think—and I know you will howl a little, in your kind and helpful way, about some of the lyrical or, better, "insubstantial," parts. But it is not in final form. I do think it will cast a clearer light on the meaning of the whole book.

Have you seen Calvin Kentfield? Don't let him go easily, for I cannot tell you how much I was impressed with his book. I believe he will do wonders, a beautiful talent.

Forgive, again, this great sheaf of words, but I think them all to the point, and thanks with all my heart for putting your mind to them. And thank my good girl friend for her help and interest. Let me know how she responds. May come in to the city for a day or so soon to see about some business. Will see you, of course, if I do.

Faithfully,
Bill

the novel to follow: He was writing *Half a Look of Cain,* but *In a Farther Country* (1955) would be published next.

"The Kite": This was retitled "A Shape of Light" in the book.

The grave of Son's mother: In "Pore Perrie."

drowned pilgrim: In "Ghost and Flesh, Water and Dirt."

supernatural phenomena: In "A Shape of Light."

eight stories: That remained the number in the published book.

boil out of it . . . a description of the book: The jacket copy simply read: "For his second book, Mr. Goyen has written a group of eight extraordinary stories, integrated by a common theme and a unique style, and dealing with simple, compassionate men and women, driven by a desperate need to reach beyond themselves and find in life a kind of absolute truth."

"Old Somebody's Children," to be the opening piece: Retitled "Children of Old Somebody," it appeared sixth in the collection; "The White Rooster" was first.

Calvin Kentfield: (b. 1924). Fiction writer whose stay at Yaddo overlapped Goyen's.

To Katherine Anne Porter
TLS-3

Yaddo
Saratoga Springs, N.Y.
Easter Sunday, March 25, 1951

Sweetheart:

I have just finished talking with you, all the kitchen women listening, perhaps, but no matter (as Jim Still says). They are all my friends and they know I am bound to love somebody, I am sure it even makes them happy that I do—my best friend, fat Rose, knew that I wanted to have a private conversation, so she made it a point to drop a barrel full of pots and pans on the floor so that I might talk in peace. I am glad we had an Easter conversation.

As I said, it is a disturbed and disturbing day. Since I am part weather, I feel it as though I were participating in it. Winter, I think, really wants to go, but acts as though it doesn't know where to go; and spring is trying to get in, where it certainly belongs—they meet, kind of wrestle and fuss, a big handful of absurd and futile snow falls down, then the sun comes, then a fit of rain. I love this kind of battle, the Equinox is like that, too; and at sea it was the most exciting thing the War had to offer, weather. So it is Easter Day. I had found a big cardboard Rabbit in a showwindow downtown, went in to ask if it could be bought, the nice man said no but did I want it for my little boy? I said yes, and he gave it to me. I brought it home and put it on our dining table as an Easter centerpiece. The women loved it. Also left a little Easter card for Rose and Mrs. Haynor and they were as pleased as if they had a new hat. They are kind and they feed me and look after me, after all of us; and I have seen how the slightest gesture of gratitude rewards them. Besides, they are good, kitchen women, the old kind that I love and fear the world will lose.

The days are trancelike, as I said . . . where do they go? All I know is that my mind is possessed with something that is using it. I have all kinds of insights into books or stories I will want to write; and at the moment my present work, like you that time in Saratoga Hospital, has flown high up in a tree. It has removed itself a great distance from me and I cannot reach it. Don't you think, my dear love, that the life of work sometimes, like ourselves, has to withdraw to purify and strengthen itself before it can let itself be had again? I will not force it to come to me, nor will I ride these pages to death, like a horse; I will wait; I will take my time. Anyway, something is always going on, is it not? There is never *nothing* happening within me.

About Albert and Linscott. This is an extremely delicate situation, as you know, my darling; and I suggest we take it very slowly. I ask you to wait to talk to Albert until you and I can sit down and talk, ourselves, about it. I do know that the two men dislike each other intensely, Linscott is jealous, backbiting. On the other hand, he is completely loyal to his writers. I do not complain of lack of belief from him, I only tire of—but I'd better not even write this; I'll wait until we can talk face to face about it. So my advice is to wait until we can talk before you talk with Albert. Too, my darling, you must fight *your* battles, do *your* work, save your strength for this. You know by now that I can do my fighting when a fight is necessary and for the good things. I am not afraid. I have never thought of it all as anything but a good fight most of the time. I wish you hadn't said on the phone this morning, referring to my not being afraid, and to Calvin's remark—"I hope we haven't got you wrong!" Calvin might ask himself that question, but not you, dearest love, for you know—I *know* you know.

As I told you before, I shall not take any more money from Random House as advance, for to my mind this only further restricts my freedom and I will have at least that. When they pay me they push me, and I don't want to be pushed. When I signed a contract last autumn for two more books, they offered to pay me outright a lump sum. Yet the two books were to be delivered to them over a three-year period. I refused to take a lump sum and Linscott then said I could have a monthly sum whenever I needed it. I have needed it several times and have taken bits of $200 now and then; but I will not take any more. For when I take this money from them I feel as if they are buying *me* and not the work, and indeed that is their (Linscott's) attitude; I don't like the feelings of being bought—so early. If I were farther along, if I had a reputation, more than one book published, my situation would be different. But I firmly believe, my darling, and you have helped teach me this, that a beginner must be free and unentangled. Whatever work he does, then, will be his *own* and it will come from *him*, not from contracts (which write a lot of books) or promises or liens. Let the Capotes and all the others take their fat advances, and live in foreign villas; I want my work to stay free. You can see, then, why a Guggenheim Fellowship, awarded on merit, would keep me free and on my own feet. If that fails, I'll just pull myself together and take some kind of job somewhere until I can earn enough to quit and live as a daily laborer at writing. You do agree with me, don't you darling? Of course, because we have talked of this so often. And your life, at my stage of the game, was precisely the same. I loved your freedom, your fights, your steadfastness. These have brought you to where you are, "right up there on top," as we once put it; and now publishers can jolly well look after you and take care of you or they'll lose something very precious.

I think you and I are here and together to, among so many other things, help each other keep his freedom, hold to himself, not betray himself; this is what we ask of each other and of all those we love and believe in. All else follows, in its time and place; but we must begin by possessing our *selves*. Indeed, we have based our love for each other on just that.

Now what are you to do about your New York life, dearest Katherine Anne? I wish I could help you. You are loved by all, and they love you for your work as well as for yourself. But will they not let you do your work? Surely you will settle into it, darling, once you are completely well again. Regard this as a part of the general recuperation period.

Please take care, remembering how I have you in my mind, loving you as I do. I wait for your letters and I wait for our meeting again. Bless you and love you.

Bill

P.S. One more thing, to get it off my chest, darling—I had a squabble with Linscott this last time in N.Y. because I found the "readers" at Random House who caused such a fuss about my title, etc., were little college girls just out (I know one of them quite well), who know no more about writing than Rose. It is to these people that Linscott takes my work and it is the flippish opinions of these gals which he passes on to me to take seriously. I am still in a rage.

kitchen women listening: The pay phone available to Yaddo fellows was in the hallway just outside the kitchen.

Jim Still: (b. 1906). Kentucky fiction writer and poet.

good, kitchen women: Porter took umbrage at this remark. In a letter to her brother, Paul Porter (1887–1955), she remarked: "I remember something Bill Goyen wrote me once from Yaddo about the 'Good kitchen women' there (the cooks and waitresses) of the kind he loved and 'feared was vanishing from the earth.' Jesus! Oh, if ONLY the females would keep their place, knitting and having babies and cooking, and let the great gorgeous male ego spread its tail and strut before them, they only lifting from time to time their dazzled eyes, how pleasant life might be. No criticism—no needs or wants of their own to disturb the masculine self-absorption, no demands, no nothing: just a bag of humble instincts too rudimentary to require any attention—well, how bloody selfish and stupid can even a man get, I do sometimes wonder?" (January 15, 1952, in *Letters of Katherine Anne Porter,* p. 415).

Calvin: Calvin Kentfield.

To Katherine Anne Porter
TLS-2

Yaddo
Saratoga Springs, N.Y.
April 3, 1951

Sweet Katherine Anne:

Snow all morning, turning to rain at noon—a bronzey air, melancholy; I have worked until now (3 p.m.), am dazed and fuzzy, shall halt and get out in the rain. What I really want to do, if I can get up enough courage, is to mill and loll around in the rain, eat a sandwich somewhere and be absent from that lonely board where only Polly and I have sat for three nights running. The Negress, Leonora, is here, Rose is on holiday for a week—I need a change of fare and faces and placemat. I am very tired, sleep very little at night, if you could look through these windows any night after midnight you'd see a most absurd sight: me pulling bedclothes off one bed, dragging them behind me to another of these three beds, making up a second bed in quick and touselly fashion, tossing upon it, repeating the same dumbshow, on and on through the night. Nothing serious; trouble with work is that it won't let one alone—I am at that stage.

I think of asking Elizabeth to allow me to stay until May 15. I am scheduled, now, to leave on May 1—but to where? Darling I cannot bear New York for very long, even with you in it! You understand—it suffocates me, riles me, embitters me, falsifies me. Please understand. Too, I am not at all sure I shall have finished *Ghost and Flesh* by May 1, and I am wary of leaving here with work unfinished—you know that fight to get back to unfinished work. So, if Elizabeth can put me up, I think I might ask this—but I am not sure, yet. I want to think about it in the rain this afternoon.

At any rate, plans are difficult to make, there are so many places to be and yet no place, really. All we *know* is that we two shall be together somewhere, so that's that . . . sea or desert. Yes, I hope and want to come to you on April 23 and 24—then we can talk out plans, exchange suggestions, etc. I do think we must try to hold out, wait until then . . . I fear Elizabeth would not be impressed with too many goings and comings; too, I feel hard and unhappy as it is, that we might better do our work if left alone for a few more weeks. Can we, darling? I want you to show me *work accomplished* when I come, you heah me?

But more of plans, later . . . give me a few more days. My head is so full of work, plans, desires. If Walter and his blessed bride are to be in the house in Taos from June 15, I'd want to give them a decent and uninterfered-with Honeymoon, so I shy away from the desert until I know what they want and will do. Too, there's this craving for the sea. Maybe we can combine the two—that's a lot of running around, takes time and money . . . and I mean to go right into work this summer, as soon as I finish this present book. So we must *talk* it all out, and the time will come. In the meantime we sit tight, work, brood and surmise.

Yesterday I had a physical examination by Dr. Rockwell for the Guggenheims. He found me in "good health"—everything fine and in good working order, only a little nervous. I plan to begin my tenure on May 1. The Foundation has been wonderfully kind and welcoming— letters of praise and commendation, etc. I feel so honored, so humble, so proud . . . and so *relieved*.

Do you go to the Committee meeting on April 6? It's that stuffy, embittered, meddling Tate . . . the farther I am from him, the better I feel. When shall we young ones haul off all that driftwood from the beach—the Tates, Trillings, innumerable and omnipresent Van Dorens— all second-rate, parasitic compensators and backbiters?

Work, my darling, sleep under the rain, see your friends and help them, rest from your weariness and rise up out of this last nasty sickness. I will steal a little Crocus from a Saratoga lawn, or send you some green new shoot from Yaddo soil. Wait, and keep the trust. I miss you and love you.

Bill

Polly: Polly Hanson, resident secretary to the director of Yaddo.
Elizabeth: Elizabeth Ames, director of Yaddo.
Guggenheims: Goyen received the first of two Guggenheim Fellowships in 1952.
the Committee meeting: The Awards Committee of the American Institute of Arts and Letters.
Tate: Allen Tate (1899–1979). American critic, fiction writer, poet, and teacher.
Trillings: Lionel Trilling (1905–1975), and his wife, Diana Trilling (b. 1905). Both literary critics.
Van Dorens: Carl Van Doren (1885–1980), critic; Mark Van Doren (1894–1972), poet and critic; Irita Van Doren, editor.

To Ernst Robert Curtius
TL-2

Yaddo
Saratoga Springs, N.Y.
April 9, 1951

Beloved friend:

You so honor me with the translation! I am so proud, and it is the closest way for us to touch each other—let me help you in any way I can—we can work together, even over this distance which is so great one cannot imagine it. What a gift from you to me, my words into yours and into your beautiful language. I thank you with all my heart.

First let me tell you that I am living as a guest on a large and wealthy estate up here in this great and beautiful wood, some two hundred miles from New York City. I may live here for a few months, by invitation, there is no expense; and I may work to my heart's content. Yet I am inexpressibly lonely, I am terribly lonely, only with my work and with the torment of my imagination—but, in the end, one must rest content with these, for they are the most permanent, the longest-lasting things. But I torment myself by asking can the spirit foster itself and the flesh go untouched, unfostered? For I am flesh, proud yearning rankling flesh; and I am spirit that knows the uses and the truths of the flesh. Thus my grief, thus my torture. You know me well enough to understand what more I do not say.

I work daily, like a laborer; and that is the way I like to think of myself, as a daily worker. I see ahead of me a lifetime of daily work, day after day, trying to catch and hold and record the meanings of human experience which hover over one, vanish, appear, proclaim themselves, possess one. There is no question of any other kind of life for me, I am claimed by my nature, I am committed to it, I will give my life to my work and my vision of it. I have many friends who love me and whom I love, but none to come all the way; I love passionately one or two but I cannot have them; I shall never attempt marriage again in my life.

Soon I hope to finish *Ghost and Flesh* and I will send the manuscript to you and ask you to talk to me about it. Then I plan to leap immediately into a third book, this one about a subject that haunts me and one which I must try—it is about Glaucus, the Greek boy who ate of the strange weed of the sea and changed his life. He left a friend on the shore who, until this day, continues to watch the sea and the shore for his friend who might one day return; and he thinks himself to find, perhaps, the weed, the thought, the magic, the mystery which took his beloved friend from him and into a world which he cannot enter.

Now, my dearest friend, to the questions you ask—concerning the translation:

1. breezeway—a long, screened porch where people sit in the summertime
2. *Ola*—a woman's name
3. blackland farm—yes, a farm whose soil is black earth
4. Feed and cartons of Pet's milk—"feed" is food for horses and cows; Pet's milk: the little tins of evaporated milk which country folk buy in large quantities, and in cartons
5. Commissary—This is simply the store or market serving little communities and where their supplies are purchased
6. hunching in the dark—that is, couples embracing and squirming, moving their bodies against each other in the dark
7. grinding in her own glitter's ashes—yes, grinding in the ashes of her glitter. I mean that her "glitter," her fleshly glow, has burnt her down to ash
8. an old charred drummer—a "drummer" is a kind of traveling salesman, one who goes about selling goods from town to town
9. priss—a "priss" is someone, usually a flirtatious girl, who flaunts herself about, putting on airs coquettishly, so a man who is "prissy" is an effeminate man who tries to show off in order to gain amorous attention. It is used derogatorily
10. hotcha—just a slang term which a "priss" would use
[rest of letter lost]

---

the translation: Curtius's translation of *The House of Breath*, titled *Haus aus Hauch*.
Glaucus: For an earlier reference to Glaucus, see letter of July 10, 1950, to William Hart.

Yaddo
Saratoga Springs, N.Y.
April 18, 1951

My dearest one:

Cold, strange days of shuttering light and darkness, sudden wild storms followed by pacific periods of pure sunlight—almost as if the days were possessed. I work and wait to work, do little else, don't even read. Now I am walking a bit again, the leg is much relieved and the bad period is all over.

My life is so spare now, my darling (most exactly the way I like it), almost like a Monk's, that I cannot fill my letters with news of people or events; and I find it difficult to speak of the work at hand—you must forgive my pinched kind of messages these days, dearest Katherine Anne. Yet pinched, spare, or expanded—they are messages of love, our old loveletters; we've never had any other kind.

Darling it is not a right or good thing to dread coming into the battlefield to join you—which is the way, forgive me (or rather give me your understanding), I feel about the City. I find myself feeling as a Knight must have felt, knowing he had to ride into the briars where the serpents lurked in order to see his princess. Too, I may leave Yaddo on May 1. This is not an impulsive statement, yet it is a rather emotional one; so do not put it down as a conclusion or use it as a basis for any thinking. If I do decide to leave then, however, I'll just wait until that time to come to New York. If I decide, you see, to expand the present work, to plant a few more rows, then that will mean more months instead of more weeks—and in that event I shall want to leave Yaddo. I am really hoe-in-hand at this writing, yet rather leaning on the hoe and gazing over toward Vermont.

Let me wait, let me see, let me find out. In the meantime my love I love you. Bless your heart.

Bill

---

the leg: Goyen's knee injury, for which he had been operated on previously in England. At Yaddo the leg was giving him excruciating pain and causing him to lose sleep. He consulted a surgeon, Dr. Rockwell, who said that Goyen's early morning sprints at

Yaddo, for the sake of fitness, had caused the adhesions and ligaments to tear (Letter to
K.A.P., April 12, 1951).
Let me wait: Porter was demanding to know when he would return to New York City.
In fact, he made arrangements to return to Texas. See note to letter to Margo Jones,
May 25, 1951.

To Robert Linscott
TLS-1

Yaddo
Saratoga Springs, N.Y.
April 22, 1951

My dear Bob:
   Thank you kindly for the birthday present of books that arrived several
days ago. I don't know what to say to you about the delivery date of *Ghost
and Flesh*, only wait awhile. I am not going to rush it, of course; and, too,
I have planted a few more rows and will wait to see what comes up. I'm
sure I've about used up Yaddo, something has gone dead here, so I am in
the midst of new plans, to where, in God's name?
   Word from Malcolm Cowley, Glenway Wescott, *et al.*, the "judges"
who read the partial mss. of *Ghost and Flesh* for the National Institute
Award which I spoke to you about. Tate, my enemy, won out for his
candidate, a young poet named Anthony Hecht, 22 or so some such, or
so Wescott writes. Anyway, I find the award was a year's residence in
Rome—I certainly wouldn't want that; so all this went on behind my
back and quite unbeknownst to me. But these Cowleys, Wescotts, Van
Dorens praised the ms. (four stories from it, *including* "A Figure of
Dust") highly and said it showed great growth and development.
Opinion, pro and con, seems, finally, as you know, to contribute very
little—I simply must do what I must and as well as I can, and the Devil
take the rest. Opinions of "judges" is one thing, of college-girl "readers"
in publishing houses another—but it all amounts to the same thing in
the end, only a double check on the writer: he analyzes, ponders, eats
his own flesh, then goes his own way. You've got a risk in me, you've
always had a risk in me, but then this ought to make it a little more
exciting to say the least; since most of the rest is so cozy and sure and
self-protecting. I know you're with me or I just wouldn't be there with
you, that's all. You know what tremendous emotional problems, as well
as aesthetic ones, I suffer in my work—but something will come of it.

So stay with me and shoot straight with me, Bob. I think of you. Let me hear—

Faithfully,
Bill

Malcolm Cowley: (1898–1989). American critic, editor, teacher, and literary historian. *Award:* Goyen had been proposed as a Fellow of the American Academy in Rome. *Tate:* Allen Tate.
22 or so some such: Hecht (b. 1923), an American poet, was twenty-eight at the time.
"A Figure of Dust": Early title for "Children of Old Somebody." In *Ghost and Flesh* the phrase appears as the story's subtitle.

To Margo Jones
TLS-2

San Marcos, Texas
May 25, 1951

Margo dearest:
   I've just called home and Mother read me your sweet letter. Darling I haven't written because I've been in such a quandary, with nothing specific or particular to say—and, I am so tired, so tired of being in a quandary. Most of it is my own fault, if fault it is—but dear Margo, for the record, I have tried all these things because I had to; and if they have all led me to this terrible, terrible pass, then I must face it and endure it. It is, as I know you know, surely the most critical time of my life. I must work it out alone, leave it to me and keep your faith in me.
   It is an evil time when something so large and so long a foundation under me has washed away. Now, it seems, that everything I step on slides away, as though I cannot cross this river, everything flows on, slips out from under me. I went through my own Hell to make the decision to stay out of Taos this summer; that decision made, and the arrangements to come to your apartment in Dallas, I felt quiet for the first time in months. Then your telegram knocked me flat again—it was uncanny, sinister, evil, the way every plan made seemed to crumble as soon as it was formed. I came up here to spend the intervening time between Houston and Dallas; now this seems pointless, for I am not *here*, that's all; I must leave at once—it was wrong to get so far away, so alone at such a wild time in my

life. The dear Doc has been the marvelous, faithful friend she has always been, saying little, giving everything. God bless her warm soul.

Now darling please don't feel guilty or responsible for this disappointment—it was quite beyond your own doing and we must take it and re-make plans. I thought it the simplest and most expedient thing to come to Dallas when I found I could come right into your apartment, which I know and where I would be at home and at ease immediately. But to look for apartments in Dallas, to move, stock and barrel, into an apartment I don't know at all would be too difficult and quite beside the point. I won't do that, and please understand why. Thank you with all my heart for offering to help with the other apartments. We'll let it all go and try something else, someplace else. You have too much to do to shop for apartments for me—I never asked you to do that nor meant for you to. Bless your good heart for wanting to help.

Leave me to myself for a while, let me collect myself and clear my head. I must get to my work soon or I will simply die, that's all. I cannot whirl around like this. I will, believe me; you know that. Keep your faith and your trust in me, and you know I keep mine in you. I'll be at Merrill Street until I advise you further. I return there tomorrow.

Give my love to Liz Ann and my other friends. Please use your discretion about speaking of my state of mind at the moment, Margo—the less said, the better. I love you and need your love. More later.

Faithfully,
Bill

Honey you know I won't touch that check, but bless you for offering it. Now how could I! I'll return it from Houston when I get there.

San Marcos, Texas: While finishing *Ghost and Flesh*, Goyen lived in various parts of Texas and New Mexico.

your apartment: Goyen had agreed to live in her apartment until September 15. Then on May 18, Jones had wired him, "completely unforeseen theatre business problems necessitate using apartment for theatre office this summer. Desperately sorry."

The dear Doc: Dr. Jean Ranch-Barraco, a Houston patron of the arts and an oral surgeon.

Merrill Street: His parents' home in Houston.

Liz Ann: Elizabeth Ann McMurray.

To Katherine Anne Porter
TLS-2

3164 1/2 Pickwick Lane
Houston 21, Texas
June 6, 1951

Darling Katherine Anne:

I lag so, right now; forgive me. So I send you this quickly as possible, via Special Delivery. Now we have said *pace pace*, found our peace again, and wonder why we had to find it again or why we ever lost it, if we did. I guess it is right, dearest one, that there is a time in love when love becomes a curious kind of battling . . . a kind of stamping and tossing of manes—who will ever understand it?

So we are stiller, both of us—I am removed to a place of work and my work strewn all around me, solitude all day and all night, the kind of brooding and mulling over it all that we spoke of together so often.

I am proud of Glenway's little document, delighted it is done and on its way to do its work; I have always loved his good, clear, tough mind— but I think, still, that his language is somewhere, somehow, precious, not quite his own (do you feel this, ever?), a kind of borrowed elegance to it, a slight kind of affectation. Forgive me, but I can smell out this kind of thing most acutely, and at once. Bless him for his intrepidity, his real championing of what he believes and holds to. I shall write him a note at once and thank him, for myself, for his fine new cause. Surely you will get the medal!

I am pleased with your new assignments of work—money at least and at last—and overjoyed that you will slip into daily work again. Keep your health and your strength, darling, and hold your love and faith and patience. It has seemed, since we've been apart this time, that we are the only two people in this world who can talk to each other—for we have found our language, our *own* utterance. We are unique, darling; our love *is* unique, yes, of course I know it, I know it—it has to make all its own language and its own laws, hew out its own clearings and break its own wilderness and make its own roads. No wonder we have sweated and wept and struggled so—what else could we have ever expected? It will not end, no matter that things in it end or come to finish; it has no end, it only begins again—so there, take it, let us take it and do what we can.

Bless your heart, calm yourself, I work to still myself—to do that thinking which you teach me and without which it can all become a low wailing on the floor. God love you, I love you. Of course we cannot kill good Adam and Eve . . . but doggone their souls, sometimes!

Bill

Do please tell me what you are writing in the way of essays, articles, etc., and if you will and can, do please send me carbons of them. They are speaking from you, will help keep me alive and answering you.

Pickwick Lane: Goyen had now moved to Houston to finish *Ghost and Flesh*.
Glenway's little document: Apparently Wescott had supported Porter for a medal from the American Institute of Arts and Letters. If so, she had to wait a long time. It was not until 1967 that she received the Gold Medal for Fiction.

To Katherine Anne Porter
ALS-1

3164 1/2 Pickwick Lane
Houston 21, Texas
June 11, 1951

Darling—
   I am in a plague and fury of work—at last. Now, after two weeks, I feel like a sound and good Guggenheimer—I am really *at* it.
   It helps me to know you are at it, too: so let us work together, through the distance between us, yoke it with work and love, my dear one.
   I bring my head up to send this love-note and this faith-note—stay at your work and help me keep at mine. Take care, darling. I miss you and I love you—send just *notes* until you get your work done.

Bill

---

you are at it, too: Porter was again working on her short story "A Vision of Heaven by Fra Angelico," which she had begun twenty years before. It was never completed to her satisfaction and remains unpublished.

614 Merrill Avenue
Houston 9, Texas
June 13, 1951

My dear Ernst:
  Thank you for your letters; I send the answers to the queries—

p. 35—"for all good things in the world"—that is, "we joined in the name
of all good things in the world . . . our joining was dedicated to all good
things in the world."
p. 42—"quarry of ants"—Steinbruch

Dear Ernst, it *is* all very wonderful—our meeting each other in this work,
our joining there. For me, it really is a joining in the greatest reality of us
both, there where the spirit is, and the flesh, too.
  Your Summer program seems busy and full enough, and very interesting, too. Tell me what you will say of Vergil on the BBC; do tell me what
your life and your work are like, for I should like to have an idea of you,
too.
  As for me, I am calmer, stiller; although I must go very carefully for
some time. I am fast at work, it is my only life. I shall stay here in Texas
for another month or two, then I am not sure where I shall go—but it will
be some place where I can work. I shall keep writing to you, and I hope
you will let me hear from you when there is time. Send the continuation
and I shall hasten to answer your queries and to help you in any way I
can. I so hope and pray the Zurich publishers give us a good answer. I
think of you and wish you good work and joy and good health; and I send
my love.

Faithfully,
Bill

Steinbruch: Reference unknown.
the Zurich publishers: Die Arche, run by Peter Schifferli, would publish Curtius's
translation of *The House of Breath* in 1952.

614 Merrill Avenue
Houston 9, Texas
June 15, 1951

My dear Ernst:

 Joy and Hooray! It is the most wonderful thing that could happen, our working together; and congratulations to us both! Now we *are* joined, even over this distance, in this work; and I am so proud I can scarcely speak. I agree with what you say about not leaving too many of the idiomatic words and phrases in the original, and I approve of the idea of an index or vocabulary in the back of the book. All this gives me such joy and such pride, in such a cold time. Dear Ernst, I shall do everything I can to help you and I promise to answer your queries at once so as not to delay your progress. I suggest you send your letters to me directly at the Houston, Texas address so that they will not have to be forwarded from New York—this will save time. I hope you may publish some parts of the translation in German magazines, for this will let many know what we are doing. Bless you for all this. I hasten to send the following answers to your latest queries:

Love—
Bill

p. 3—"saw annunciations": saw figures and drawings and scribblings (phallic, sexual, erotic) on the walls like terrible and thrilling announce-ments of the joys of the world—also the fertility symbol in these which the Narrator observes in a sterile time of his life when nothing will come alive.
p. 18—"Bulls"—Taurus, in the constellation.
p. 19—"blooded lights"—"lights": the organs of dissected fowl (lungs, heart, liver, etc.); "blooded"—filled with blood.
p. 20—No, the seeds are not to be smoked, but the "fronds"—i.e., leaves of plants (tobacco, etc.).
p. 21—"snap-turtle"—i.e., a "snapping turtle," a certain kind of turtle with a beak-like mouth that snaps or bites.
p. 21—"jeweled perch"—that is, little perch (fish) that dazzle and glitter like jewels—the spots and flecks on them—in the sunlit water.
p. 22—"fungus flowers"—fungus (a parasitic growth) grows on old logs

and tree trunks in little flower-shapes and bud-shapes.

p. 24—"brambled, locked"—"brambled" means rough and thorny; "locked" means the brambled berry bushes were entwined and locked together so that it is impossible to separate or untwine them.

p. 24—"mayhaw"—a kind of berry that grows on a vine, and from which good jelly is made.

p. 27—"wooden cattle"—i.e. drowned and swollen cattle that look like wooden carved figures of cattle as they float along on the river or lie in the bottomlands after a flood.

p. 75—"Bell's Palsey"—a dreadful kind of nervous disease which paralyzes one side of the face and draws the mouth to one side of the face.

p. 76—"excrement upon the floor"—literally. In public toilets, filth of what men leave behind.

p. 76—"shells pouring"—any kind of seashells; I mean the (to me) exciting and mysterious sound of shells falling upon plate—I mean only to evoke this sound.

p. 77—"louver"—louvers are the little wooden strips in a shutter which let in or close out the light when manipulated.

P. 78—"thickern"—a contraction of "thicker than"—the way these people say it.

p. 78—"slues"—(sloughs, slews)—marshy, swampy lands.

p. 82—"Holy Rollers"—a kind of popular and vulgar religious sect in the South. They are roused to such a pitch of religious fervor and emotion that they fall to the ground and roll about.

p. 87—"take spells"—yes, moods or states of mind—here a yearning, a longing.

p. 87—"curlimakews"—"curlicues"—curls or twists, ornate and embellished; in this instance (l. 16), the mother has "worked" or fashioned (sewn) these twisted and curled designs in her daughter's blouse.

p. 88—Epaminondas' butter—relates to a fable told to Southern children about a little Negro boy named Epaminondas who stole a pound of butter and hid it under his cap; the butter melted in the sun as he ran away with it, and so he was apprehended.

p. 88—"catbrush"—i.e. the little children, Berryben and Jessy, brushed against the legs of their mother as cats do, as she stood at the kitchen stove . . . a gesture of affection and a begging for attention, as cats do.

p. 89—"bugle in the woodstove"—i.e. the sound of the wind in the iron woodstove was like that of a soft bugle blowing. I have heard it.

p. 90—"falseface"—a mask which children wore at Hallowe'en, etc. Hence, literally, a false face.

p. 90—"Dennison paper"—a particular kind of colored paper used for decoration, for paper costumes and trimmings. "Dennison" is the name of the firm that manufactures this paper, and so the paper has come to be designated by this name.

p. 92—"havers"—means "halves." That is, children force each other to divide into half whatever they are eating and so share it. The first one to shout "halvers" gets half the other child's treasure. Literally: "divide!"

p. 93—"croakersack"—a "towsack" or sack made of tow (flax or hemp); rather like burlap; called "croakersack" because these sacks were once used by fishermen to carry fish called "croakers" (because they make a croaking sound); in this case "croaker" meant frog, again because of the croaking sound.

p. 98—"expression lessons"—i.e. instruction in "expression" or dramatic recitation. Children studied expression and then performed in public, in school or church or at home—they recited or "expressed" such poems as Longfellow's or Wordsworth's or country ballads, or sang songs, etc.

p. 100—"bind us"—i.e. bind us together—or "join us together in love, etc."

p. 103—"we pumped in the swing"—children "pump" each other in a swing by standing together, facing each other, while first one then the other bends his knees and pushes the swing forward . . . I hint at a kind of sexual movement.

p. 105—"a painted bead"—a cheap, brightly painted bead lost from a necklace of beads.

p. 114—"Epworth league"—In the Southern Methodist Church, a league or organization of young people—named after the founder.

p. 117—"sheet"—i.e. bed linen, a sheet from a bed—the Ku Klux Klan dressed in sheets, with only their eyes showing through openings in the sheet, so that they looked like ghosts or fiends.

p. 120—"lavalier"—lavaliere: a necklace or pendant worn by women.

p. 121—"carline voice"—a witch-voice; a hag-voice; an old woman's voice.

p. 121—"What kin are we"—specifically, what relation are we to each other, how are we related, how are we relatives?

p. 123—"crepemyrtle"—a little flowering tree common to Texas and the South.

p. 123—"gizzard-like . . . moon"—an organ in fowls, rather like the liver . . . it is eaten in the South. In this sentence I mean that strange shape seen on the temple (the region on either side of the forehead) of the moon's head which resembles in shape and figure the gizzard of a fowl.

p. 125—doilies—a small ornamental napkin or mat, used at table and usually embroidered by the hands of country women.

p. 125—"dirtdobber domes"—dirtdobbers are a kind of wasp, and their houses are made of little domes or knobs of mud.

p. 125—"cilia-built"—i.e. built by the cilia or little hairs of whiskers of insects, antennae, etc.

p. 126—"grain"—I mean the designs are in the shape of grain (like wheat, maize, oats, etc.).

p. 126—"lacunae"—cavities (lacuna).

p. 126—"hummocks"—a knoll or ridge or little hill.

p. 126—"phalliforms"—yes, designs resembling the phallus.

p. 126—"felted with fuzz"—"felt" is a fabric of wool or fur used most often in the making of hats—here I mean that this old cowboy hat appears as if it had been made of "fuzz," and so "felted" with it. "Fuzz" is the vulgar or common word meaning the bits of dust, wispy particles of dust and dirt.

p. 126—mason jars—glass jars used for preserves, jams, etc., also for other foods and even milk. These jars have a special top or lid, and they are a very common household article in the South particularly. Named after the man (Mason) who fashioned them.

p. 126—"tapshoes"—that is, shoes with metal "taps" or pieces on the toes, used for "tap-dancing." Theatrical shoes.

p. 126—"blueing bottles"—little bottles which hold the fluid called "Blueing." Blueing is used in the laundering of clothes to make them fresh and clean, in the country. The bottles are blue because the fluid is blue—hence its name.

p. 126—"gentian light"—I mean light of a gentian color; blue-violet colored.

p. 129—"love in the cotton gin"—The cotton gin is a large warehouse or building where cotton is processed or purified of its seed. The "gin" was a favorite secret place for lovemaking, because of the many soft beds of cotton lying on the floors in the dark. There were many amorous and exciting meetings here.

p. 129—"shellbarge"—I mean a barge filled with shell or gravel. These barges transported shell up and down a bayou called "Green's Bayou"; and often they were moored to landings and therefore afforded a trysting place for lovers, at night.

p. 130—"the sons of grief at cricket"—this is a quotation from an A. E. Housman poem. The lines:
"See the sons of grief at cricket
Trying to be glad . . ."
So . . . I mean this boy is "playing the game," trying to be glad, although his heart is breaking.

p. 32—"riggings"—no, not sails. A "rigging" is the apparatus erected in the oil fields for the drilling of oil wells. Riggings are tall steel or wooden tower-like structures erected over the spot where the oil is to be drilled for. From these riggings hang many lines and ropes, and the machinery for seeking oil is suspended from the center of these mysterious-looking towers, which can be seen rising abruptly out of the flat lands of the East Texas oil fields—really a surrealistic landscape.

p. 44—"lidded stock tub"—the great wooden receptacle filled with water from which the cattle, or "stock," drink. It is covered with a large lid or cover when the cattle are not drinking from it, so that children will not fall into it.

p. 119—"desire faileth; it is the burden of the grasshoppers"—an allusion to the book of Ecclesiastes—where the grasshopper is used as a symbol of senility and the loss of desire.

p. 121—"a wart for lechery"—in the country, a wart on the nose or face is taken as a sign of sensuality or lustfulness. Yet once it was considered a "beauty mark"!

p. 121—"Joy's sister"—Not "brother," because the inference is that a woman is speaking . . . the reference, too, is to the Grandmother, within Folner's mind. [. . .]

p. 123—"A drooping eye"—an eye whose lid is drooping, half-closed; rather like a sleepy eye.

p. 123—"the devil was beating his wife"—folklore says that when it rains and the sun is shining, the Devil is beating his wife in Hell. Hence simultaneous rain and sunshine is an evil sign in the minds of Southern countryfolk.

p. 125—"sift over the strings . . . prism"—I mean the sifting sound of the feet of rats over the strings—it reminds one of the delicate yet sinister sound that little glass prism-shaped objects make when blown by the wind. For prism curtains were, in the South, lovely and delicate curtains made of strings of glass prism-shaped objects, and these curtains hung between rooms. The wind in them was heavenly and almost celestial music to hear. The rats' feet over the strings in this connection (p. 125) seemed to evoke the same sound—as if something of glass were being "sifted," like glass dust or glass sand.

p. 126—"rubbish onions"—I mean onions so long left untouched that they are now no more than rubbish; they lie like a pile of rubbish.

p. 127—"furred with raveling"—I mean the strings, so old and rotted, have raveled into strands and seem furry—the strings have fallen into a furry state.

p. 127—"a ragged peacock"—yes, a peacock whose feathers are ragged, torn.

p. 130—"Senior Night"—this is the night in American high schools when the "seniors" or graduating class perform. It is their farewell to their High School, and they "put on a show" for the rest of the school.

p. 131—"freaks"—the horrible deformed persons which carnivals and circuses exhibit. Usually they are kept in "stalls" or little pens and the crowd walks by to look in at these monsters sitting on floors covered with sawdust for the sake of cleanliness.

"Bitterweed"—I think this kind of weed grows only in America. Surely it is a vulgar form of the little yellow daisy—it is bitter to taste and is considered a tramp weed; but it grows profusely in Texas particularly. My dictionary says: "any of various plants containing a bitter principle, as the ragweed and the horseweed; and sneezeweed of genus *Helenium*, esp. *H. tenuifolium*." You know, of course, that I use it symbolically—and the early title of *The House of Breath* was *The House in the Bitterweeds*.

Faithfully,
Bill

N.B.: Ellipses in the letters to Curtius regarding translation of *The House of Breath* represent duplicate answers and queries.

index or vocabulary in the back: No such apparatus was appended to the published translation.

"See the sons of grief . . .": Goyen slightly misquotes Housman's Poem XVII in *A Shropshire Lad*. The actual line reads, "See the son of grief at cricket . . ."

the burden of the grasshoppers: Goyen paraphrases Ecclesiastes 12:5: "Also when they shall be afraid of that which is high, and fears shall be in the way, and the almond tree shall flourish, and the grasshopper shall be a burden, and desire shall fail: because man goeth to his long home, and the mourners go about the streets" (King James version). He titled one of the stories in *Ghost and Flesh* "The Grasshopper's Burden."

To Katherine Anne Porter
TLS-2

3164 1/2 Pickwick Lane
Houston 21, Texas
June 29, 1951

Darling:

I send my own unmontaged montage to show you the kind of town and world I'm settin in, trying to make something permanent and that will last—in the middle of people who insist on celebrating what vanishes. It's fun reading all this stuff—I think I enjoy most the *Houston Press*, it beats any tabloid I've ever seen, even that one in Paris. What a taste it gives the tongue, raw and wild and absurd and insane-tasting.

Sweetheart, forgive no longer letters, because I am at my task all day long and up until I drop to bed around nine or ten, tired and fuzzy-headed. Surely I am driving to the end, now, and I must stay with it.

I thank you, my darling, for your help with the agent problem. I'll bide a few more days until I hear from MCA, then I'll consider all. I suppose there really is very little that can be done at this point, since I am already contracted for another book beyond *Ghost and Flesh*—the mistake, I think, was to sign the contracts without the aid of agent. Now everything seems in such a mess, Linscott is cagey and cunning, never answers my questions, I don't know what in hell is going on. But it's all in his hands, since I allowed myself to sign the contracts under his aegis. (*Houston Press* verbiage). When this second contract is fulfilled, I'll do something. In meantime, I wait to hear from Ned Brown as well, for I am interested in writing for a film or two, I sincerely think it will teach me something I want and need to know about telling stories. You let me know what you hear and let's work on this Hollywood thing together, for we might be together there soon—hooray!

So leave me labor on with this manuscript and get it to where the dogs can't touch it, honey. I won't be hale and whole again until I get this done—I am again in the world of *Ghost and Flesh*—and sweetheart, I see again, now, the more I consider and meditate on that world I am trying to tell about as well as I can that it is speaking about households lost or never found, and families ruined or betrayed or never fully formed—of children and mothers, children and fathers, homeless poverties, poverties of dirt, and a moiling, restless search for households and family, for child and kith . . . and all this kind of thing. I think the book might exist with integrity as a whole world, but not so well as fragment of a world—thus it is or will be a *book* and not a bunch of stories. I must know what you think, my sweet mistress and master. Strange how we are both thinking of children . . . how my mind keeps returning to those mothers-and-child in little quiet glens, on logs in woods. I must get it down, because it speaks of my time as much as of any time, of the union of men and lost father-hood, the orphaning of unfostered children and the grieving of childless women . . . a fiendish, vile and longing society of ghosts with only flesh to hang to. So much more.

Darling, I speak to you daylong and in the nighttime; we *do* speak to each other so fully, so wholly, as though no one else could understand or tell or listen. I love you in this world. Take care, dearest Katherine Anne.

Your
Bill

The feeling of this town, in a sentence, is that it has just been a smash-hit Broadway show and the producers are going to make a lot of money, enlarge their guts and just have a lot of good sex, liquor and T-bone steaks during a long long run, no more to worry about, it's a hit!

MCA: Music Corporation of America, which has a literary department.
Ned Brown: Hollywood producer.
logs in woods: Allusion to Goyen's "Children of Old Somebody," the tale of a child disowned by elderly parents and left to grow up in a log.

To Katherine Anne Porter
TLS-2

3164 1/2 Pickwick Lane
Houston 21, Texas
July 3, 1951

My darling:
   Now everything is here—today came the little sample of Essence de Bain, smelling so beautiful, also the Celestial Portrait, which I agree with in part but not wholly! Thank you with all my heart, dearest Katherine Anne, for these Divine and Fleshly gifts. For a minute I thought the large envelope carried "A Vision of Heaven" and I opened it trembling. Yet I know it will come when it is ready.
   Sweetheart I have been in my rounds, rising at six, moving about in the flow, no interruptions, the world of *Ghost and Flesh* in this room. I wear myself out, working sometimes six to seven hours at *one* stretch, then I go to sleep for an hour, rise again and continue. This is the way I must work and the way I must live to work, I know it, have known it. It has been so hard, this time, to commit myself to the loneliness of this task—you know about this loneliness and this commitment; how one fights it, this stern and loveless commitment, until it is no use. Now I am wholly committed, given over, ghost and flesh, and I shall stay that way until I go through to

the end. Still, it is difficult to judge, as you well know, it is all so deceptive, there are elations that peter out, unwarranted, and all that.

I see now, all alone and to myself, how each of these stories is a
creation, not so much like a firmament or a universe as like just a humble
bird's nest, woven and knitted together with claw and beak, the stuff for it
found in the commonest places, bits of string and twig and straw from the
fields. At least they are my *own* nests, though many will cry that they are
too much my own; but let them cry; it is compulsory, it has been urgent
and passionate and the best I know how to do at this time and with what
materials I possess and have discovered for myself and have tried to
control. For me, it is all expansion, or rather deeper delving, and it is a
further attempt at *definition* and manipulation of definition. It will take a
lifetime, this whole long slow difficult exploration and shaping, but that is
what my lifetime is for, I would not change it, nor will I, "success" or
failure.

Anyway, honey, I'm tarred, and I love you, and I wish some stillness for
you, some steadfastness, do please steady yourself and help me steady
mine. I cannot see beyond this work, but surely beyond it lies something
more to go to, to give to, to make and take; and all this will come in its
time.

God bless you, and I bless you; and I do wonder and worry how you
are now—maybe you count too much on me, my dearest one, maybe this
is breaking you—I never wanted to break you or weaken you. You do this
for me, always have; but I beg you do not let me destroy your heart and
mind and work. I pray for you and think of you and love you, my beloved
Katherine Anne.

Goodnight, and a Glorious Fourth, with watermelons and firecrackers.

Bill

To Ernst Robert Curtius
TLS-1

614 Merrill Avenue
Houston 9, Texas U.S.A.
July 10, 1951

My dearest Ernst:
So you are home again by now, and I thank you so much for the first
pages of *The House of Breath* in translation. I find them thrilling and

exciting indeed, and the translation seems to me splendid as I expected. Thank you with all my heart for the loving care with which you do this, dear Ernst. I think the title in translation fascinating and beautiful to speak, and your taste and judgment and feeling for the language are always superb; thank you again.

I am finishing the second book, a book of tales and stories, and by the end of July I shall send the finished manuscript to my publishers. I am eager to get to other work, yet I am so tired and so hungry for friends and talk and amusement; I have worked very very hard, and so alone. For a while I have thought of trying to come to Europe for a few months, on the Guggenheim Fellowship; yet I must go on working. Still, I might be able to continue my work there, in Paris or in Rome. If I should come, and it is still only a thought, might I come to visit you? It would be late autumn, in November probably. We might think about this.

Let me continue to help you where I can. I am so proud of your work and I think of you with love and with gratitude. Let me hear from you. Bless you.

Love,
Bill

---

the title in translation: Curtius translated the title as the alliterative *Haus aus Hauch*.

To Ernst Robert Curtius
TLS-9

[July 1951]

Dearest Ernst—Since I began this work, word has come from my editor at Random House, Mr. Robert N. Linscott, that *The House of Breath* has been sold to the Zurich publishing firm of Verlag Der Arche [*sic*] for publication in October of 1952. I had nothing to do with this and it upsets me enormously, for I had so wanted your translation to be the one published in Germany. Can you do anything about this, at once? You see, these American publishers, once they own one's book, simply go about trying to sell it to foreign publishing houses for the highest sum they can get, they care nothing about the literary standards or reputation of the house, only the highest bid. Please, dearest Ernst, can't you write to Verlag Der Arche and get them to use your translation? I have today

written to Mr. Linscott asking him to help your translation—I had long
ago informed him that you were at work on the book. I believe something
can be arranged between you and Mr. Linscott. Do try your best. It will
break my heart if you do not succeed. If I had known of this earlier, I'd
have stopped it—but publishers treat their authors only as chattel or
merchandise, and all their business goes on behind one's back. I am so
honored by your working on my book and, more important, we understand each other, you *know* what I have attempted to do in *The House of
Breath*—and I am afraid some run-of-the-mill translator will do a bad job
for this Zurich firm. This worries me awfully and I am dreadfully upset.
Do please let me hear what you think at once, and let me continue to help
you with your translation.

I am now in Texas, at the home of my mother and father. I have been
in a critical mental state, dearest friend, ill and tormented. *I need your
friendship and love at this time.* I cannot work, I am very lonely and ill.
Please send me a warm word at once to my home address:

614 Merrill Avenue
Houston 9, Texas
U.S.A.

I wait to hear from you and I need your words.

Love, faithfully,
Bill

I send you these two photographs for the moment—until I can find a
better one for you which I will inscribe.

p. 16—"A piney-woods rooter"—this is a kind of pig, a common animal of
the East Texas region. His snout is long and ugly, hence the comparison.
p. 16—"little feist"—(adj. "feisty" meaning nervous, meddlesome,
restless) there is a kind of quick, meddlesome little dog called a "feist";
and frequently any mischievous, nosey, capricious person is called a
"feist."
p. 16—"what was this man who made it?"—that is, *who* was he, what kind
of man was he, what was his secret nature?
p. 20—"hairy carriers"—specifically, I mean the hairy legs of bees and
such insects which carry pollen.
p. 21—Methodist women in the South sit in the hot churches in the
summertime and fan themselves.

p. 22—"creatures"—yes, horses or any creatures or animal that comes to a river to drink.

p. 22—"fording wagon"—when a wagon crosses a river that has no bridge, it "fords" the river by going through the shallowest part of it.

p. 22—"snag"—a tree stump or the jagged end of some branch of a tree or bush which protrudes from the water or is below the surface of the water. Hence, anything drifting along may catch or be "snagged" on it.

p. 23—"they rolled her over a log"—a method, used literally, to force the water out of the lungs of a drowned person. Country folk use this method.

p. 23—"Katydids"—a "tree frog" or little insect which inhabits trees and sings, much like a cicada.

p. 23—"drank his homebrew"—yes, drank beer. "Homebrew" is home-made beer.

p. 24—"niggershooter"—an instrument made by country boys for shooting birds and often used as a means of mischievously tormenting Negroes. It is a kind of slingshot made of two rubber bands tied to a forked stick. I suggest you keep the term in its original rather than try to translate it.

p. 24—"potlikker"—a regional term for the juice or soup resulting from the boiling of any green-leafed vegetable. It is often drunk as a delicious beverage. I suggest you keep this term, as many other dialect terms, in its original; since it and they are virtually untranslatable and, too, ought to be kept in their original, it seems to me. Do you agree?

p. 25—"shotgun houses"—a little house of the East Texas region, a box-like little house with an open space straight through it and rooms on both sides of this space.

p. 25—"clappety"—East Texas dialect—means loosely-constructed, ramshackle.

p. 25—"dirty yard"—a grassless yard. Characteristic of many of these little shotgun houses.

p. 26—"crapshooters"—dice-players. To "shoot craps" means, therefore, to throw dice.

p. 27—"rushnests"—nests made of rushes or grasses that grow by and in streams.

p. 27—"left my sand in bars"—I refer to sandbars—bars of sand formed in rivers.

p. 27—"mulch"—yes, manure; or the rich substance formed of rotted grass and leaves mixed with soil. A fertilizing agent.

p. 28—"Red Rover"—the name of a mythical person in a children's game called "Red Rover." In the game, the children, who have chosen sides or teams, call out to each other, "Red Rover, Red Rover, Come over, come over . . ."

p. 28—"Dios"—should be *Diós*.

p. 30—"ruby beads"—beads the color of ruby-red beads worn around the neck.

p. 32—"broken yellow swords"—when palmettos, which are tall sword-shaped plants, are broken, they resemble broken swords. They are yellow-colored.

p. 34—"Blues"—purely American. Means "sad one." Derives from the Negro songs, sad and mournful, which are called "Blues Songs." Suggest you keep the original.

p. 34—"lyin in cotton"—that is, planted with cotton. Fields lying in cotton are fields full of ready cotton, white and ready to be picked.

p. 36—"our names were broken"—here I mean that our very identity was broken, destroyed—we became therefore anonymous.

p. 36—"Glaucus and magician grass." Dear Ernst, this whole passage is a subtle and abstract play on the legend of Glaucus and that legend is indeed the framework or structure for so much of the novel. Glaucus, as you know, ate of the magic grass or seaweed which delivered him from the shoreworld to the strange and mysteriously beautiful world of the sea. The "I" of this passage, then, is Glaucus, and the other one is the grass which, eaten, delivered Glaucus to the sea-world.

p. 38—"set in the bus stations"—"set" is the colloquial for "sat." Christy sat in the depots or stations where buses left with passengers for various towns and cities. He longed to have someplace to go, as did all the people who boarded the busses and left.

p. 40—"stickerburrs"—the thorny burrs on plants that grew among the grass in the South. They stuck into children's feet and caused great discomfort. Not a nettle, but quite like one.

p. 42—"and a good ride"—that is, Boy often rode the little calf as a horse is ridden. He therefore had a good ride on Roma the cow when she was a calf.

p. 43—"MKT"—the actual name of a railway line, or train, in the South. Means "Missouri, Kansas and Texas."

p. 44—"canna"—yes, the flower; so beautiful and so common in the South.

p. 44—"Piney"—yes, smelling of pines—or made up of pines, so that "piney woods" simply means a wood full of pine trees.

p. 45—"broilers"—a particular size of chicken. When it grows to this size it is often broiled, and so gets its name this way. Hence, a "frier" is a chicken of a certain size and age, best when it is fried. Strange how these creatures get their names from their edibility!

p. 46—"flyswatter"—an object used for killing, or "swatting," flies. Old folks sit all day with this object in their hands, so as to keep the flies away.

p. 48—"game of Statue"—another children's game. In this game, the largest child takes the hands of the other children, one by one, and whirls them around, then flings them away. The flung child must freeze into and hold the pose or attitude into which he falls—thus resembling a statue.

p. 48—"cheat a pose . . . ransom his face." What I mean here is that when Folner was flung into his statue, he would not keep it if it were tragic or dramatic, but "cheat" and change his pose into something gay or sophisticated (blasé); but even his disguise could not "ransom" or buy off his real face. So he could not, even then, betray his reality or disguise what he really was—even in a children's game. He could not even cheat children.

p. 48—"roundhouse"—literally a round house, immense, in railroad yards, where locomotives turn around—or used to.

p. 48—"squash"—a regional vegetable. Also called yellow squash or summer squash.

p. 51—"boll weevils"—insidious insects, weevils, which eat and destroy cotton.

p. 51—"hoppers"—abbreviation for grasshoppers.

p. 51—"rawsin bellies"—regional slang for men who work in lumbermills. They get stained with the rawsin [resin] from freshly cut lumber. Suggest you keep the original.

p. 51—"jew's harp"—a peculiar backwoods musical instrument, very small, shaped like a tiny lyre and held against the teeth while the single wire prong is plucked. The teeth resonate the sound of the plucked prong and the movement of the lips varies the timbre from low register to high.

p. 52—"across the tracks"—That is, Fred Suggs lived on one side of the railroad tracks and the Ganchions on the other. Often the residential sections of a little town were demarcated or divided by the railroad tracks. One side was considered the "right" or preferred side, the other the "wrong" or undesirable side. A questionable man was one who "came from the wrong side of the tracks."

p. 53—"firewagons"—that is, fireengines—or, in the early days, wagons which carried the apparatus with which to fight fires in the town.

p. 53—"duplex"—a double house, one made up of two flats or apartments, with a family living in each.

p. 55—"shale"—the sloughed-off flint or shell of rock. In this case, sloughed particles, resembling the scales of fish. [. . .]

p. 55—"whiskery"—yes, whiskered.

p. 55- "Sienese"—that is, delicate and fine as the line in Sienese drawing and painting (Sienna).

p. 56—"paa-ahs"—this is a phonetic spelling of "pears." The old man sold pears from his wagon; and I remember his calling out this word to sound like "paa-ahs."

p. 58—"cute shape"—she had an attractive and diminutive shape to her body. If one has a "good shape," this means he or she has attractive bodily proportions. "Cute" does not mean beautiful or lovely, but engaging or charming.

p. 58—"kewpie"—A "kewpie doll" is a pretty, starry-eyed, painted-up doll, flirtatious and coquettish. Long gone out of fashion in the South, but one time given as a prize at Carnivals, etc.

p. 58—"to the sticks"—that is, to the backwoods. A dialect slang term.

p. 58—"cinch"—this word means "for certain," "for sure," "without question."

p. 58—lava soap—a common soap used in the country, of very low quality and very harsh. Also of an ugly color.

p. 60—"whiskers"—that is, she had to have *men* around her.

p. 61—"nope"—dialect slang for "no"—intense and emphatic use of "no."

p. 62—"frogboy"—In Carnivals, in the freak shows, there often was this hideous deformity, resembling a frog in feet and hands, and so-called frogboy. His voice croaked, and he had warts on his scaly body. I remember seeing one when I was a child.

p. 63—"drawn up and spiney"—means withered, drawn and shrunken, almost to a spine and nothing more.

p. 63—"banty"—abbreviation and slang for bantam.

p. 64—"make me tarred"—phonetic spelling of "tired." "You make me tired" means, in this dialect, "you bore me," "you make me sick," etc.

p. 65—"balling the jack"—in a hurried fashion, speeding away. This derives from the old children's game of Jacks, in which a dozen little steel, star-like objects are picked up from the floor with a bouncing ball. To "ball the jack" is to play the game very rapidly.

p. 65—"Texis far's Borger"—yes, "Texis as far as Borger."

p. 65—"Miss Perfecto"—A slang term meaning "Miss Perfect"—one who considered herself perfect. Derogatory.

p. 66—"to hound you all"—to annoy, torment, bedevil you all.

p. 67—"cousins into statues"—refers, again, to the game of Statue. The children who played the game were cousins.

p. 68—"S.P."—another abbreviation for the name of a Southern railway or train. Means "Southern Pacific"—this railway runs from the Southern states to the Pacific Coast states and back.

p. 69—"C.C.C."—means "Civilian Conservation Corps." One of the measures, some ten years or more ago, the U.S. Government used to alleviate the problem of unemployment. The "CCC Camps" were literally camps of men and boys, set up in the wooded areas of various states to combat plagues of insects that destroyed trees, to engage in reforestation, etc.

p. 69—"tireswing"—a swing hung in the trees and made of an old rubber tire.

p. 69—"pussimons"—phonetic for persimmons.

"goobers"—dialect for large peanuts.

"possum"—yes, means opossum.

"croakersack of roastinears"—a croakersack is a sack made of burlap or hemp; roastinears is phonetic for "roasting ears"—i.e. ears of corn good for roasting.

p. 70—"Chatauqua"—a kind of touring carnival and medicine show which in the old days visited the little towns.

p. 70—"to beat the band"—not so much "giggling louder than" as giggling full force or in the extreme or as loud as possible.

p. 71—"priss-like"—here I suggest you keep the original. It is purely a dialect term meaning something like "one who puts on airs," a derivative of "prissy," but well-nigh untranslatable.

p. 71—"ruckus"—dialect. Means a stir or a fuss—to cause a ruckus is to "make a fuss" or stir up disorder—rather like *"faire tapage,"* but not as serious.

p. 72—"punch the time clock"—In large factories and offices there is a clock whose handle is pulled by employees when they go to work and when they leave work. The handle causes time on the clock to be punched on a card (a "timecard"), and this is the official record of hours worked, and by which the employee is paid.

p. 73—"hayrides"—joy rides on a wagon filled with hay. [. . .]

p. 74—"sissy"—the word commonly applied to an effeminate boy: a vulgarization of "sister."

p. 74—"I'll swan"—a dialect slang phrase, really untranslatable, meaning something like "I declare" or "for goodness sake."

---

use your translation: The matter was resolved by Curtius's translation being accepted by the firm to which Random House had sold the rights, Die Archer Verlag.

To Katherine Anne Porter
TLS-2

3164 1/2 Pickwick Lane
Houston 21, Texas
July 17, 1951

Darling Katherine Anne:
    The great cool jar of Jean Naté arrived yesterday and I love it and thank you for it; also the Gorky, exciting indeed. I had not seen the Gorky correspondence at all, and last night I read in it until after midnight—another world. This is the kind of thing I need right now, what with a longing to read but a reluctance to get into fiction; it came at a perfect time, darling, and I thank you again.
    But we are in an absolute swelter here and my little workshop hangs in a white glare of heat all day, beginning in the early morning—and I sweating and stultified in it but working right through, somehow, finishing with headache, no appetite, stiff back, addled brains. Yet not much longer, I feel sure. The stories in *Ghost and Flesh* are varied—an idea, as Pound said, held at different depths in the mind—where the idea goes deepest it is most difficult, of course, and it is the stories at the deepest depth that I want you to see, to dive down to with me. I shall be criticized for these latter, for they will say, again, that I am obscure and mannered, that I have put too much of a distance between me and the reader and all that—but it will be, it is my own thing, my own vision of my experience and let it stand as that.
    I see that M. Capote is getting all the screams these days again, little articles written by total unknowns in magazines single him out as the "most promising young writer of this generation," etc. Princess Caetani sent me her second letter yesterday urging me to hurry and send her a story for the fall issue of *Botteghe Oscure*, but please to send the very best I have—for she published the first chapter of T. Capote's new novel in her last issue and she thought it quite the best thing he had ever done, it was very beautiful, etc. *Why* do they keep measuring me against him or even thinking of me and him in the same breath? It is Mr. Cerf's doings, I know that and have known it. Never mind, I'll destroy that. I can see easily that *The Grass Harp* (Capote's new novel) is obviously influenced by *The House of Breath*, and Truman has written me to as much as tell me so: the poison is reaching for the antidote! But enough of this.
    Sweetheart I sent two stories to Cyrilly by airmail special delivery last Monday, (that is, she received them yesterday)—I do hope she takes one

or maybe both. I think they are very good, at least *I* like them—and one ("A Covenant of Ghosts") I had a delicious time writing. The other has been in the making since 1946, although it may not show it, and at last I brought it off, I think, a few weeks ago. Whatever the story sale brings in will be of a great help, for honey, it's awful hard to live within the Guggenheim grant in a city—and my royalty statement from Random House shows me a couple hundred dollars in the *red*. Never mind, let them sell Schulberg and the rest, but they will not influence my books, red or no red.

I really see no one but my family, whom I visit every Sunday. Occasionally a friend comes by in a car and takes me to buy my food, otherwise I walk and tote it back. I work hard hard and am most constantly alone. Soon, when this is over, I shall take some kind of rest, if even for a week—someplace where I can sleep, eat correctly, swim or walk or take the sun, for I have had little rest for years, really since the end of the war in 1945, it has been one constant grind of work and tension and worry; I want to be strong and have health and live and write a long long time, I must take care of myself. I say this now my darling because I feel so flimsy and so fagged, ahm jes tarred, thas all.

Love and adore you, I pray for you so tenderly and I have you like a little blue, pale blue egg in the nest of my mind. Bless your heart and soul, I love you.

Your,
Bill

---

the Gorky correspondence: The complete works, including correspondence, of Maxim Gorky (1868–1936) were published in thirty volumes between 1949 and 1955.
Mr. Cerf: Bennett Cerf, at Random House.
Cyrilly: Cyrilly Abels, the fiction editor of *Mademoiselle*.
"A Covenant of Ghosts": This may be an earlier title for one of the stories in *Ghost and Flesh;* Goyen published nothing under the title, nor is there a manuscript at the Harry Ransom Humanities Research Center by that name.
Schulberg: Budd Schulberg (b. 1914). American novelist and screenwriter.

3164 1/2 Pickwick Lane
Houston 21, Texas
July 20, 1951

My darling:

Thank you for your long to-be-read-in-bed letter that came just a moment ago. And forgive me for not "answering" your questions—I thought I generally did, but I am in a fuzzy state, mind all in my typewriter and in these manuscript pages. Sweetheart, those lines, "*Her nis non home . . .*" are from a beautiful little minor poem of Chaucer's called "Trouthe" . . . and thank you for the lines of Thoreau's.

And dearest one—by now we both know to listen to talk about each other with tongue in cheek or up our sleeve or somewheres—you know that strange, tingling sensation that comes from hearing about one's beloved from other mouths . . . I get a kind of wicked glee out of it, and go away knowing what I already knew, which is generally to the contrary of what has been said. The friend is a good friend, a very gifted one, Samuel Barber, with whom I hope one day to write an American opera, etc. We have exchanged letters all along, Sam and I; and in no way could he deduce that I have had a "severe nervous breakdown"—yet what if I had? One has a right to have his own nervous breakdowns, I should think; or should one consult with his friends aforehand? The nonsense and pure passing triviality of New York conversation, all those clacking tongues, yet nothing is ever said, pure cocktail chatter and gossip, another form of Yaddo conversation. Some very good people have had "nervous breakdowns" and for very good reasons . . . I have not lately been able to manage one, although before I was sixteen, I had a couple, being what I was. Do not think I "keep anything from you," my dearest darling Katherine Anne; I am safe and going along, I have had a black, hard time, as you, but I do my work and I go along, as you do. We know each other, what kills the heart, what grieves the mind, what puts us to bed with sleeping tablets; the others do *not*. Anyways, I am all right, be assured; I am talked about a lot, to be sure, but all I have to do is appear in New York and the talk changes. Talk is wind, coming from all four corners, turning the weathercocks' beaks from one corner to another, round they go on their little steeples, we inside at that old pipe organ, at our instrument, the tune is heard, never mind. If I were to get upset at all the things said or written to me about you, about some of my other friends, I'd live in a constant hopping and worrying—but I think we must still make the *donkey carry us* as we go along the road, not listen to the bystanders who suggest we do everything another way, carry the poor animal on our backs, etc. Let it go, darling.

Sweetheart! If'n you give that magnificent Raveau to someone, please put it into *my* trust, I long for it. Yet you ought to keep it yourself; but for Heaven's sake let me have it if you give it up, keep it in the family. And, too, the same for the Muzio. I have a little portable three-speed machine here, my own, it plays all speeds and kinds of recordings; El Prado, no. That is somebody else's house now and, too, a kind of monument, a repository; but I want the treasures I love and require to live with and near me.

This poor Schmucker—never take me for one of these! Or a McCullers. I am an artist, was always one, I do my work, it is here and will be here to show; I need no influences, no models, no "help," I fail by my own hand or succeed by it; that is the way I feel and I am very very bull headed about it, stubborn and fierce about it, indeed. I know of no other life, no other packet of bones and blood, like my own; my work emanates from these, my life and my bones and my blood—now, then, can I depend on other bones and blood? What I live by is the *spirit* of great people in this world, in my time and before my time—the great Russians, the great French, the *very* few Americans: Porter, Faulkner, Whitman, Thoreau; *not* Hemingway, *not* Fitzgerald (ha!), *not* Hawthorne, *not*, *absolutely not* that old fussy, tidy spinster Henry James . . . and *not* a lot of other people.

My love, you *did* sound ill-tempered on the telephone and I loved your voice, which is why I called, to hear it; but I must admit I was cast down all day and all night by it, by your ill fortune, by your loneliness . . . mine seemed so much to bear. Still I'd do it again, and will . . . I need you in this world; and we have joined, we have *joined*, that's all there is to it.

Darling, as for destroying myself on this book, that is nonsense. It seems to me we destroy ourselves in *every* book and mend ourselves by finishing it or cutting it adrift . . . for to me, beginner indeed, it has seemed that creation is destruction towards building again, towards reconstruction. Never mind, we mend quickly, we repair ourselves, just as women who bear children do . . . that is the miracle. You used the word "punish" on the telephone . . . you said, "I don't see why you have to 'punish' yourself so . . ." Honey, it is no more punishment than most things . . . who ever thought creation (and I think of my stories as creations, whatever they are) was a game of croquet? I cannot believe, either, that creation is a bottle of whiskey, à la Hart Crane, or a Dostoievskian paroxysm, or a Rimbaudian convulsion . . . yet neither can I see creation as something down alongside of a blue-watered swimming pool with avocadoes waiting on a sunporch at lunch, etc. Never fear, I will not destroy myself. I lurch and lunge into it, then withdraw and say to hell with it, go away about my business and sleep, eat, fool around, then pounce upon it again.

Darling, please sleep better . . . think of that star of Yaddo, I want you to be like that, I want to be like that. Yet stars rise and fall, too, they sink down below that dark rind of Heaven and drop into the darkness; yet they rise again in the glowing east, remember that.

Sweetheart—I am *so* tired of hearing from all these people who are enjoying, regardless of the consequences, their sweet second-childhood— these Cowleys, Tates, *et al.*, who keep trying to make us of this generation feel that we are having such a dismal damned dull time of it when they had so much *fun*—back in the Twenties—they keep telling us how much *fun* they had. Yet what has their "fun" come to but a not-even eloquent telling about it in their fifties, what work came out of all that gayety, what have they to show? Thank God *you* were not on that hill in New Jersey with those people having so much fun on Sunday afternoons, the Tates, Cowleys, Crane, the Josephsons, etc. etc. I feel a little bored with it all— as if they kept saying to us, "*You're* not having any fun, your poor wretches!" etc. etc. If *they* were exiles, My God what are *we*?

Sweetheart, *adieu*, lift up your spirit, help me lift up mine. Life is long, and so much in it; we just have to have it all twice, that's the pain of it. But who could better have it *double*? I love your sweet soul, heart and face, I need you in this world . . . *coraggio!*

Your Bill

Samuel Barber: (1910–1981). American composer of lyric and romantic music. Goyen wrote an unpublished work for chorus and orchestra, "For Samuel Barber," based on a portion of *The House of Breath*.
somebody else's house now: The house was rented to a tenant. Goyen did not sell it until 1958.
Schmucker: Perhaps a pun on the name of artist Charles Schucker, one of the Yaddo board members.
these Cowleys: Goyen is railing against Cowley's *Exile's Return: A Literary Saga of the Nineteen-Twenties* (New York: W. W. Norton, 1934).
the Josephsons: Matthew Josephson (1899–1978). Expatriate American critic and biographer, who with Gorham B. Munson edited the little magazine *Secession*.

To Katherine Anne Porter
TLS-2

3164 1/2 Pickwick Lane
Houston 21, Texas
July 27, 1951

Darling Katherine Anne:
   Here at last is this long, strange piece that took more from me than anything, I believe, I have ever given myself to . . . and oh, I wonder what it is, even yet. It is mysterious how one's work or the product of one's self speaks to him and tells him how to look at his life . . . I had sometimes thought it the other way round; but not so here . . . surely this voice that speaks to me in this long piece is one outside my own voice, engaged in a dialogue with me . . . my feeling, now, is that "A Shape of Light" is a long letter written to me by somebody out there somewhere whom I never knew . . . and on these pages I mean, more than anything else, to try to create a stillness, a moment of listening silence filled with the speaking tongue of this distant Teller. Oh if I could only achieve what I define to you here . . . that, like Boney Benson's, is all my craving. I go on further, anyway, to try again, to do what I may have failed to do here: it is a lifetime, this trying, as you know, my dearest one.
   But—even if the reader says, in the end, "obscure!", "you are trying to confuse me, trick me!", surely he can see that, at least, I keep trying to *extend* the meaning and meanings, widening them out, letting them rise up and expand, sink down to concrete definition, then soar again, lifted up and away. I want it to go spiraling around and around, taking hold and letting the hold go, as if the substance were a bird from the hand, as if the piece itself were, finally, the "message" and had a life of its own—the point, I think, is to leave it free, to watch where it will go and where it will lead one, like the message itself. In the end it ought only to go, wafted on away, into invisibility, into the region where no words are; and then reader, like narrator, must take it from there in the sky of his own brain's firmament and make his *own* accounting and meaning out of it all; it is all left in the mind of the reader; and the narrator, too, vanishes.
   I am for clarity . . . but I do not want to tell too much, for that, again, it seems to me, is a muddying.
   The piece which precedes this long piece, called "Hotel Easter," I shall send to you shortly; it contributed to this whole—it was my Easter, beginning one year in the Chelsea Hotel in New York, continuing the next at Yaddo—and out of that composite Easter rose this whole huge

meaning for me—and I mean to show a mind and a spirit laboring and struggling *through* all this to find its honest and passionate record and accounting of what happened to it.

Enough for now, my sweetheart. I am near through—at least I have stepped up to the next step and there I wait and rest a little while to see if there is another step or that wide, bottomless abyss that means no more possible steps can be taken in *this* direction: "abandonment" in Flaubert's conception of it.

I love you and miss you and I pray that you are hushed and still and over your work. Bless you, I love you so.

Your,
Bill

"*Hotel Easter*": Retitled "Nests in a Stone Image" when it appeared in *Ghost and Flesh*. *Flaubert's conception:* Goyen perhaps confused Flaubert with Paul Valéry, who stated, "A poem is never finished, merely abandoned."

To Ernst Robert Curtius
TLS-4

614 Merrill Avenue
Houston 9, Texas
July 27, 1951

My dear Ernst:

Forgive this delay, I have been working tremendously hard in order to finish this book by August 15. Its title is *Ghost and Flesh*, and it is a group of tales and stories, all related and based on a common theme. I have tried to achieve a kind of legendary poetry, as you saw in "Children of Old Somebody." It pleases me enormously and gratifies me to know that you like Old Somebody, and thank you for what you say. *Ghost and Flesh* will be published early in 1951 [1952], probably January or February.

You ask, dear friend, about the influence of American writers . . . I want to say to you that I feel so very much alone among American writers and that it has always been my purpose to make a new kind of American literature, all my very own, and out of my experience as an American in the world. I respect two writers above all in America and they are Katherine Anne Porter and William Faulkner, but neither has been a model for me or has acted as an influence on my own work—except in the influence of the spirit. I cannot read most American writing; and feel that it is either imitative of certain expatriates (Pound, Eliot, Hemingway, Henry James) or simply artificial and not deriving from the writer's own world and experience. I am therefore, to my mind, very much alone and choose to be that way, stumbling along in my own discovered direction. It is my purpose, above all, to restore to American literature particularly, but to contemporary universal literature, the lyric, the passionate, the compassionate. My enemies are those who write out of bitterness, sophistication, cleverness, perversity, "modernity," toughness.

Of non-American writers, I indeed feel a special obligation to the beloved Joyce, to Flaubert, to Balzac, to Proust, and especially to Yeats who, if I may say so, sometimes seems too close to me in vision and attitude to life.

Please read, if you can find them, two stories of Faulkner's: "Old Man" and "The Bear"—these, to my mind, are his masterpieces. If you cannot find them, please let me know and I shall send them to you. As for Hemingway, I hold little interest in his work, for his world is not mine and his language, for me, unreal and temporary and often affected. Yet he was a great and dedicated artist and I love his life for that.

I do not know *Origin*, the magazine of which you speak, I have heard several times of Charles Olson, but I know nothing of his work.

I hope, dear Ernst, that you can meet the editor in Switzerland; and, again, it has been one of the greatest joys of my life to work with you and to have your mind at my work. Below are the answers to your queries: p. 15—"hotcha"—this term means something like "Oh boy" or "hot dog" and was usually uttered along with a gesture to mean how good or exciting something was. It really has no meaning beyond the gesture itself, is one of those words that express only a gesture. For this reason, I suggest you use it in its original.

p. 53—"squash and yellow-legged chicken": "Squash" is a common Southern vegetable; "yellow-legged chicken"—a favorite Southern frying chicken—these two dishes, fried chicken and squash are favorite summertime foods in the South.

p. 69—"comtometer"—phonetic spelling for "comptometer," a business machine used for computing—it makes additions, subtractions, multiplications, etc.

p. 69—"C.O.D. Cafe"—Cafes in America have amusing and absurd names, often. "C.O.D." means "Cash on Delivery." In America, parcels which may be paid for upon delivery are marked "C.O.D."—hence the cafe borrowed this term!

p. 69—"roughnecks"—in the oilfields of the Southwest, laborers who work with tools and riggings are labeled "roughnecks"—they are commonly tough and rough men.

p. 50—"worst suit a hair"—means "worst head or growth of hair." Country people say "suit of hair" as if the hair were worn like a suit of clothes!

p. 55—"The little pure white puffs"—puffs are little *poufs* (Fr.), that is, little wispy, soft balls. Rather like fragile cocoons—certain insects build these as their dwellings.

p. 55—"mocked hand"—that is, the hand that set the trap is mocked by Fate that took the hand away and the trap remains, outlasting the hand that laid it.

p. 56—"glassy picture"—the picture had a glassy finish to it; shining, glossy, or as if made of glass.

p. 73—"wienerroasts"—In the country, on picnics in the woods, folks roast "wieners" or frankfurters over open fires. The frankfurters are impaled on long sticks or wires and held over the flames or coals. These picnics are called "wienerroasts."

p. 77—"frenchharp"—the common name for "harmonica." Often called "mouth organ," too.

p. 133—"Dressing shiplap"—"shiplap" is the name of certain pieces of lumber used for building houses: wide strips which overlap each other. To "dress" shiplap is to refine it or smoothen it. Certain lumber mills have it as their principal business to "dress" lumber, prepare it for building purposes. The "dressing" machines make an unearthly whining kind of noise.

p. 134—"a Haint"—dialect for "haunt" or ghost or spirit.

p. 114—"plaster ruby"—that is, an artificial ruby (gem) made of some cheap substance such as plaster of Paris.

p, 136—"chowchow"—that's right: mixed pickles; a kind of relish which Southerners adore.

p. 141—"whirlimagig"—commonly used for any object that whirls or turns wheellike. Here, specifically, it means the "Ferris Wheel" at the Carnival.

p. 144—"prismcurtain"—a curtain, usually dividing rooms, made of little glass prisms, transparent, strung on strings; very lovely, perhaps you have seen them; they were very common in the old days in the South. The breeze tinkled them and the changing light of night and day was enchanting in these bits of glass.

p. 147—"raveled strips of fingers"—that is, his fingers were thin and ragged-looking, as if they were raveled cloth—the image here is the scarecrow, a dummy figure dressed in rags with long raveled strips of arms and set in the fields to scare away the crows from the crops.

p. 147—"bladed torso"—his torso, particularly his back and shoulders, seemed made of blades of flesh and muscle—they appeared through his clothes like blades. Cf. "shoulderblades."

p. 119—"Old Mother Lode"—no anybody. I mean she is the "mother lode"—in mines of silver or ore, etc. The mother lode is the core, the center, the source of all the ramifying veins of ore. Hence, "ore of what dark cursed vein?" Folner is therefore called the "precious shard" (fragment, splinter) of the Old Mother Lode . . .

Bless you, dear Ernst, and once again, my love and my great esteem. Let me help you where I can.

Yours faithfully,
Billy

Origin: Magazine edited and published in Ashland, Massachusetts, by Cid Corman. It flourished from 1951 to 1957 and was later published again.
Charles Olson: (1910–1970). American poet.

To Katherine Anne Porter
TLS-2

3164 1/2 Pickwick Lane
Houston 21, Texas
August 5, 1951

Darling Katherine Anne:
    Sweetheart, I am perishing in this incredible, insufferable heat of 102 and 103 degrees, my workshop is a sweatshop and I can scarcely bear it. My work so near finished, I have had a kind of awful letdown, both physical and spiritual: physically, my back has that sword in it again that I get once in a while, I cannot straighten up or lie comfortably in bed; I am really dead dead tired and what I need is a little rest and laughter and good sleep; yet I cannot afford it, and that depresses me and traps me.
    This week ahead will see the end of the manuscript and then it goes into the mail. I want to mull over the book as a whole for this week, then oh how I wish I could go to some cool riverside and hang my feet in it, bathe in the sun, sleep and give in.

Darling, I know why you couldn't write me about "A Shape of Light" and I agree and I understand; we shall *talk*, not write about it. But do not please be too severe with me for those little venomous letters that answered some of your allegations—for they were rather severe themselves, you remember. Do not please regard me as hostile to criticism—I cannot see how you can or could and I am sure you know that my spirit yearns after yours and asks yours questions; still, my spirit must stand up whole in itself, too, if it can. Let my mind enter into your mind, dearest beloved, and yours into mine, wander into it like a cat into the shade, that quietly and peaceably. Between us, you and me, is this Shape of Light, and though I do not mean to put it onto you as a burden, I do know that it speaks out of a wholeness and a terror and a hope that we both have known, separately and together, and lately; it is a record of so many things, but certainly of this. I do brush against you like the cat again, waiting for your hand to come down through my fur. I am a good cat, a good artist (if I am) for many reasons and because of many beings in this world, now and before; but surely because of your hand, cat-stroker, and your art, artist. Please do not be too stern with me about my defending, sometimes, my little work from hopelessness and bitterness; for I have none of these in me, you know that; nor you: most times you seem to me the only hopeful one in my world; you *hold out*, and I know what for, I know what you are holding out for, I join you, did before I *joined* you.

We do learn that the art or craft of writing what one knows and learns becomes more and more enormously complex—for a mind like mine, anyway—there is a tremendous splicing and division of shoots of sentences—into roots, tendrils, little leaves, more seeds—to isolate even one tendril is to find, again, the whole parent growth again, all in the single little separated tendril—it is this enormous *multiplication* in the mind, this breeding breeding that does not rest; how, oh God, to tell it, how to tell the story of it like Boney Benson the shape, yet it goes on, or doubles back, or takes another track, looping and lapping over itself into layer after layer, thick then thin, transparent then opaque—but let me run on behind it, to follow it right to its source, to lose it again; my God, it has been this kind of time for me, my Katherine Anne, and what I have learned I can only speak about and when speech goes or when I am away from words, then there is the gesture, like the working mouth of a mute, the sign language of the fingers and brow, to use. Darling, never think I do not know that this is the kind of task and work and vision that can kill but must not be betrayed; for there is what beyond it but the grave and the dirt and even then the shape rising from it, going on?

God bless your soul, you have kept me in my work and in my life these horrible months; and I know where you have been, too; do not fear it, do not try to give up anything; it is all inescapable, here we are in it; I love you, bless you, pray for you.

Your Bill

Thank you for sending the photographs to Linscott—be strong and work—*do do.*

Boney Benson: Protagonist of "A Shape of Light."
the photographs: Pictures of Goyen to be considered for use on the jacket and as publicity for *Ghost and Flesh.* The photograph used on the dust jacket bears no credit line.

To Katherine Anne Porter
TLS-2

614 Merrill Ave.
Houston 9, Tex.
August 14, 1951

Darling:
    Your long good letter just now, and thank you with all my heart for it, my sweetheart. I have always known that we both loved Icarus and knew what he meant; indeed, my first attempt at writing a long piece of fiction when I was eighteen was about that son, it was called "Fly High, Icarus!"—a not very flattering title, but I had it all done, and I see that I have forever since been trying to tell that story over and over again. I know, I am sure that my whole life is bound up with the legends of Icarus and Glaucus, and I find myself telling about them in everything I write. "A Shape of Light," which I have been trying to write for so very long and which finally crystallized around that strange and mysterious little legend I read last summer in a Texas Folk Lore pamphlet, really tells the story of Icarus, for the message itself, cut adrift from the kite made of good stuff "off the place," soars and hovers and falls, and all search seems to be for it or to find a meaning for it . . . Yes, I remember our conversation about the Brueghel painting whose reproduction hangs in your drawing room, and I told you then how much I loved the story of the father and his artifice and you told me that you would one day write about it. I am so delighted that the line in "A Shape of Light" unraveled it

all for you, and I wait with what joy you well know to see your story; it begins beautifully and with great sweep, my darling. Finish it and do please send it to me.

It is now near midnight, my last night in this room where I have spent this unforgettable summer (2 1/2 months) writing *Ghost and Flesh*, unspeakably lonely, receiving your beautiful and steadying, tormenting and upheaving letters, speaking to you on the telephone, so much alone— but indeed I myself made it all that, chose it; my work is done. Tomorrow I move my things to the room on Austin Street, stay the night on Merrill St., then continue to get my possessions in order until I decide where to take a week's rest. Then to immediate work on the play.

I finish this, then, in extreme fatigue, for it has been a painful day of pulling up little roots, putting things back into boxes and trunks, remembering so many other days like this one.

I'll write again from Merrill St., my beloved Katherine Anne, and you please write to me there; do your work and pick up your steps, go on, with my love and steadfast faith and unswerving adoration. My dear dear sweetheart, good night.

Bill

---

legends of Icarus and Glaucus: See especially Goyen's "Bridge of Music, River of Sand" (*Collected Stories*, pp. 280–284).
the Brueghel painting: "*Paysage avec le Vol d'Icare.*"
your story: Porter apparently never completed it, although as late as December 1972, in a talk with students, she yoked her experience as a witness of a moon shot at Cape Canaveral with the story of the flight of Icarus (Joan Givner, *Katherine Anne Porter: A Life* (New York: Simon and Schuster, 1982), pp. 494–495).
the play: First of two dramatizations of *The House of Breath*.

To Katherine Anne Porter
TLS-1

3804 Austin St.
Houston, Texas
August 27, 1951

Dearest Katherine Anne:

Back from Galveston, and into my *pied à terre* yesterday—and on my feet, I feel. These rooms are large and vacant (I had thought there'd be only one—there are two, a kitchen and a little old bathroom) and old-fashioned—funny alcoves, huge, barny closets; and all in a very old and déclassé part of the city. But I think this can be a good workshop and storage place, and I am grateful for it.

I have had, as you well know, a blank, timeless period of no words: and I see that I have evoked that in you; something has held all words back. There . . . they stop again.

But they do come again to tell you that such literary discussion as to who said what, and whether first or second, whether borrowed or modified, does something chilling and strange to me. That I showed you and gave you the truth and the words for it when I said in that room in East House, "the flesh is the bridge to the spirit" seems very wonderful, to me, although you said you had always believed the contrary. You remember the very line is in "Children of Old Somebody," for I had been thinking so sternly of all this and had written "Children . . ." to speak about this. Briefly, that I might have helped you to your work again, to your words, is just the very crowning of my brief time as man and artist, dearest dearest Katherine Anne; and once I said to you that our working on each other was our immortality and that or this is what I meant.

So do your work, my sweetheart, and let me feel my way out of this forest of no-words; so much has been poured into my mind, so many words: hot, cruel, loving, accusatory, that it is like a jammed till in an old streetcar where not one nickel more will go in, nor any come out. Surely you are responsible for a strong portion of this—but it will not last, for you and I are meant for words between us. Now you have yours, let mine rest. I love you—

Bill

---

in East House: Porter visited Yaddo while Goyen was in residence, February–March 1951.

To Katherine Anne Porter
TLS-1

3804 Austin St.
Houston, Texas
Sept. 3, 1951

Lady:

Bless you and love you for your gentle letter, my first to this house. I love the dark big tree where our separate nests hang, the tree is there and we know where its roots go. I work hard again, this time on the play; and I know, again, how lost I feel when I lose connection with you. Yet nested birds leave their tree or sit very quietly and huddled in their own built place—and I remember Yeats said that beautiful bit about birds making their nests out of their own spittle and the artist spinning his web out of his own bowl—

I miss you and think of you and need your letters; work hard, and I am so happy for you.

My love—
Bill

---

the play: First dramatization of *The House of Breath*.
lose connection: Porter was breaking with Goyen at about this time. He had gone directly from writing *Ghost and Flesh* to writing his play, and she felt that his pleas about unfinished work were excuses not to be with her in New York. In December 1951, she wrote and requested the return of all her letters to him. See Givner, *Porter*, p. 381.

To Ernst Robert Curtius
TLS-2

614 Merrill Avenue
Houston 9, Texas
September 14, 1951

My dear Ernst:

Thank you for your letter and its enclosed article called "The American Scene." I am sorry to say that this article, so far as I am concerned, is no more about the "American Scene" than most others, for it praises our worst and less distinguished writers and shows, at a moment's glance, that the author of the essay has very little sense of evaluation of American writing. Yet the British have lately so tended to embrace the violent, the sensational, the perverse in our literature as to make me quite despairing of their once very acute and penetrating judgment. To speak of Gore Vidal as "one of the restrained, graceful, aware young novelists that America is producing" is enough to demonstrate to an informed reader that the author is merely skating across the frozen pond of contemporary American writing and quickly reading all the very conspicuous signs: Vidal is certainly one of our four worst writers, ill-equipped, misguided, weakly talented; the mouthpiece of and panderer to the Homosexual Cult; few of us can read him. I could go on, dear Ernst, but I shall not, it is not worth it—the great danger is to be misled by such facile assessments as this. I rarely read such articles, as I rarely go to see Hollywood movies . . . where the second-rate is glorified.

I have endured and worked through the hottest, most insufferable summer of my life, and the second book, *Ghost and Flesh*, is finished and at the publishers. I have rested a bit and am now at work on a play, which I want to finish by Christmas. All in all, I am well and working well.

You mention *Other Voices, Other Rooms*. I, too, found it thin and flashy and often disgusting—but it set a direction, established a fad and a cult, and the problem of serious, gifted, quietly-working writers in America is to break the back of this monster and get us back to literature. That is my purpose, as it has always been. To be of such purpose in such a country and in the company of such contemporaries is indeed a lonely predicament; the making of literature seems a poor calling in such a world and time as mine and in such a country. *Mosquitoes* I like less than other Faulkner novels, yet it is unmistakably Faulkner and has its moments of greatness.

Dear Ernst, I thank you for the very splendid pages of translation which you have sent and you make me so proud and I want with all my heart to be worthy of you. I hope you and your wife have rested well in Switzerland and that you are in good health and good work lies ahead. Bless you, dear friend, I send my faithful love. Let me hear from you.

Ever—
Bill

Gore Vidal: (b. 1925). American novelist.

Other Voices, Other Rooms: First novel by Truman Capote (New York: Random House, 1948).
Mosquitoes: Second novel by William Faulkner (1897–1962) (New York: Boni and Liveright, 1927).

**To Margaret L. Hartley
and Allen Maxwell
TLS-1**

*3804 Austin Street
Houston, Texas
Oct. 8, 1951*

My dearest Margaret and Allen:

Your most magnificent letter brought me home again to "A Shape of Light," God bless you; for I see now that I had opened such a territory of terror and truth for myself that ever since I have been fleeing it, betraying the light and betraying Boney Benson: I had opened such a grave and seen such sights as to believe I might be mad or hallucinated and that no one else could possibly see—this explains my terrible aloneness in this most dreadful summer of my life. But now, as always before, you join me, and I guess that is the only way really to call you to me, by sending you written pages, and by finding your most calm and beautiful and steadfast "aye" in the mailbox.

"A Shape of Light" will appear in an Italian magazine called *Botteghe Oscure* sometime in the winter, probably before your issue appears—but do not be dismayed, for this is not an American publication. It was sold to this distinguished magazine, which is edited by a princess named Marguerite Caetani, for $400, and I know you will not rue me that—it will also help my European reputation, if there is such a thing. She does not object to reprinting, if it can be called that, in this country; and in the past many American writers have had stories appear simultaneously in *Botteghe Oscure* and such American magazines as *Harper's Bazaar, Partisan Review*, etc. . . . a kind of simultaneous American and European printing. I know you do not object to this, since *Botteghe Oscure* is so special and so limited in reading audience—my main objection to it. That you will give a goodly part of your next issue to this story, which belongs so much here at home, in this region—and, indeed, which derived right here from the office of *Southwest Review*, where I first read the little tale or really just a paragraph called "Bailey's Light" and remembered that I had heard the tale often as a child and had even been shown the roving light by parents and elders—rewards me in just the way reward ought to come: by bringing the story *home again*, enlarged and illuminated, I hope, to leave it there.

Bless your hearts and souls for all this, you give me such a sense of accomplishment, of communication, of *being*, again. I love you both very dearly, and I need you so.

Let me hear.

Faithfully, and in love,
Bill

The only stipulation is that you acknowledge the first appearance in print of "A Shape of Light" in *Botteghe Oscure*, published in Rome, Italy.

Botteghe Oscure: Journal published and edited in Rome from 1948 to 1960 by Princess Caetani (Marguerite Chapin), an American, who was related to T. S. Eliot.

To Ernst Robert Curtius
TLS-4

614 Merrill Avenue
Houston 9, Texas
October 8, 1951

My dearest Ernst:
Thank you so very much for your wonderful letters and your continuing belief in me. I am working very hard, writing a play and correcting the proofs of *Ghost and Flesh*. I have read your translation carefully and find it so beautiful and so lovingly handled that I can only love you for it—it *is* an act of love, dear Ernst, and of faith.

Please, yes, I should like the title pages exactly reproduced—and yes, "What kin are we?" means "Howin are we all related to each other?" By "Under the Land lies all the Title" I mean that there we are joined, *below* this walking, talking, difficult life of ours, somewhere where we are still and side by side in a community of kin—*there* is your title.

On page 8, line 3, "napworn" means worn down as a rug is worn down by too much use—"nap" being the coat of a rug.

Do please, by all means, add the short notice of the book—this would give me the greatest honor and pleasure, dear Ernst; that, is, of course, if you really want to. For the book needs the signature of your great hand, and that will be forever, I shall most certainly supply you with some suggestions for this—and I should like to show you something written by Katherine Anne Porter about the significance of this book, its place in the development of the novel and of prose, etc. So please let me know when you decide to write this little notice—I hope you might give your opinion and evaluation of the book, too—and I'll send you any kind of help you need.

Yes, "phallic shapes" or "phallic designs" is a good substitute for "pricks," although I love the word.

p. 43—"the crooked mile that families walk"—i.e. the stumbling, suffering life of families.

p. 123—"Bloodgreen maple leaves"—the color of some blood has a greenish, copperish hue, and I meant this.

p. 142—"wild as storm moons"—comparison with the ravaged and wild-looking moons one sees in storms, when the clouds part for a moment.

p. 144—"A shambles of the nest"—"shambles" means the ruined remains; a wreck. The "moulty" old worm—"moulty" means falling into senility, decrepitude; "shale," the scales falling off something old and dry, almost as dandruff or scab.

p. 148—"crawdad hole"—a "crawdad" is a crayfish; they live in holes in the ground.

p. 148—"ba-abe"—variation of "baby"—this is phonetic and the word is drawn out as it is sung in the lyric . . .

p. 148—"Peeping Tom"—one who spies in windows, for erotic reasons.

p. 149—"thieves in the Pen"—"pen" is abbreviation for penitentiary or jail.

"to pee . . . boot"—"to squat to pee" is said to effeminate boys who "probably have to sit down to void as women do."

"Pour it out of a boot"—a common expression referring to the stupidity of certain people who "don't have enough sense to pour urine out of a boot . . ."

"Cicerian"—yes, phonetic for Caesarian.

"play show"—to make believe, to "put on a show," the way children do, dancing, singing, pantomime, etc.

p. 150—"fresh sheep"—i.e. sheep in heat, in their cycle of fertility.

"Cornish cocks"—a Cornish Rooster, very beautiful species of fighting cock . . . very male and daring and exciting.

"pale wet lips"—yes, they are weinercolored, but I had imagined them to be of that pale weiner color, and also to change in color: I am fascinated by the change in the color of lips under different circumstances, aren't you—how their color seems to register what is happening, emotionally, to their possessor.

p. 151—"Cups and Saucers"—common name for "Buttercups."

p. 151—"pore"—phonetic for "poor."

p. 151—"tarred"—phonetic for "tired."

p. 151—"crepey"—i.e. like crepe, the quality of the stuff or fabric.

p. 154—"asleep with [the light] still on"—i.e. he had fallen asleep with the light still burning, still "on" . . .

p. 154—"nippled and shafted"—"shafted" describes the shaft of the penis, as though it were an arrow—and, yes, erect, too. "Nippled" refers to his breasts, his nipples not his genitals. I mean to show him as a magnificent shape of flesh.

p. 155—"boy beholden to man"—i.e., the obligation of boy to man, of boy to become man, man of flesh and use of flesh: the secret yearning of body after man, boy as the seed, man as the fruit of that seed—this mysterious connection between boy and man—all *male*; do you see what I mean, dear Ernst? Boy's obligation or secret duty to man is to *become* man, in all his flowering, and to make "the world an orchard" . . .

p. 159—"like a piper"—refers to the Piper who led the rats to the river, an enchanter, etc.

p. 160—"tubafours"—phonetic spelling, precisely the way these people speak it, of "two-by-fours," pieces of lumber given that designation because they are two inches thick and four inches wide.

p. 161—"swim up . . . the river"—yes, I mean "down" the river to the mouth . . . I used up rather indiscriminately here!

p. 161—"blue face"—no, not "drowned" . . . refers to autoeroticism . . . Freud, I think, says autoeroticists are often detected by a kind of blueness of face; interesting, don't you think? Also, in the country, boys who play with themselves are often detected, in country fashion, by the strange hue of their face.

"dove"—yes, means "dived." Country folk say "dove."

p. 162—"this young brightness"—means Boy; Christy refers to Boy as "this young brightness."

p. 162—"clean-peckered"—that is, fresh, clean, untouched sexually. "Pecker" is slang for penis.

p. 162—"owal"—phonetic for "owl."

p. 173—"the little green fuzz"—refers to the green moss or lichen that grows on moist rocks by rivers . . . also an indirect reference to pubic hair, for it is like that. I wanted this whole chapter to be sensual and full of sexual undertones . . .

p. 174—"beebee shot"—the "shot" or little bullets fired from a rifle. In America these little rifles are called "B.B. guns," B.B. representing the name of the maker.

p. 177—"the shivering brethren horses"—the horses, huddled together in the cold at night, have seemed to me to be like a mysterious family of brothers or, in a larger sense, of kinfolk, a sad, shivering little family, lost in the freezing night.

p. 180—"O home me"—here I used "home" as a verb, though that is certainly not grammatically proper. But then one does "home" birds, as pigeons; and this is what I mean—"bring me home," "draw me home" . . .

Dear Ernst, take my love and my profound respect and my heart's deepest gratitude for the love you pour into this work; it joins us, like Christy and Otey, below the level where there are only whispers and sighs; and there we are joined, like them, forever, through this work and this love. Take care, I think of you; and I pray I might see you, somehow, this winter. Send me word and let me help you where I can. My greetings to your wife and my best wishes to your work.

Faithfully,
Billy

To Ernst Robert Curtius
TLS-2

614 Merrill Avenue
Houston 9, Texas
October 30, 1951

Dearest Ernst:
    Answers to your queries, and I beg you to forgive my delay—

p. 155—"As though it was smitten upon him, close as flesh"—i.e., as though it were branded upon him, like a stigmata, and close to his body as the very flesh.
"this vision must be meaning of boy beholden to man"—means that through this vision of Christy, Boy felt that mysterious connection between Man and Boy. [. . .]
p. 160—"like a thief of despair"—that is, like a thief who is full of despair,

like a desperate thief would be better. [. . .]

p. 162—"tell him by the stopping of a woodpecker's pecker"—that is, tell him by killing a woodpecker so that the pecking of his beak ("pecker") on the tree is stopped.

p. 166—"the very patch of Hell"—a "patch" is a small plot of ground, so that this means a small piece of Hell.

p. 168—"She was a rabbit in the house"—she was so meek and shy and elusive, like a rabbit in the house.

p. 172—"circumcised (is he?)"—that is, he is wondering if he is circumcised; first he thinks he is, then he conjectures it . . .

p. 172—"vauted" is "vaulted"—a misprint.

p. 181—"responding each to each"—or "responding each to the other"; but I liked the sound of each to each.

p. 175—"bottled news to be broken against the hands of the House that sealed the bottle" refers to the early custom of putting messages in sealed bottles and casting them into the sea from ships; so that the message, usually a desperate one, was found on some shore and help sent, etc. This means that the secret messages of people in the House, bottled up in themselves by their own hands or will, could only be discovered by themselves, by breaking open the sealed bottle with the same hand that had sealed it.

p. 176—"He is all our Sin"—"He" is Christy . . . and I mean to speak of Christy as a kind of Christ figure, a man of flesh and spirit, Man. This is a kind of final apotheosis of him.

p. 177—"tire-swing"—a swing hung from the branch of a tree made of abandoned automobile tires—the child sat in the tire.

p. 178—"lily pads of chickens"—that is, floating or swimming chickens, spread-out, looked like lily pads. "Lily pads" are simply the floating lily plants in rivers.

p. 179—"your garland of news"—that is, his garland, like the garland of birds round Christy's neck, is really a necklace or wreath of words bringing news and secrets . . .

p. 180—"we are involved"—means everybody, all mankind.

p. 144—"just a shambles of the nest where the moulty old worm sets": a "shambles" of the nest means the ruins of the nest, the ruined remains of the nest; "moulty" means falling into the ruin or a state of raggedness and fadedness, such as the moulty feathers of a bird. So that this sentence means: "that the house is now merely the ruin of the 'nest' where the ragged and ruined old worm (Tatzlwurm, Phoenix, etc.) sits." The house is falling away, and the people in it; but it is built again, recreated, by memory, by speaking of it, by breath.

p. 144—"this souring fruit"—Yes, the fruit in the jars . . .
p. 144—"shale"—yes, slate, or pieces or sloughs of slate.
p. 145—"I touch the beads for Christy"—I refer to the rosary, although
of course Granny Ganchion means her string of ruby beads; for each
bead she touches she calls up the name and memory and celebration of
those she thinks of. This time it is Christy. So she sits in the cellar
touching her beads (necklace) as though they were a rosary, remembering
and calling to life her kin. [. . .]

Bless you, I send my love and gratitude again; and dear Ernst, please
take care of yourself. Do please let me know how you are—we have had
so little time to speak to each other and our lives. I pray you are all right.
Goodnight.

Bill

To Ernst Robert Curtius
TLS-2

614 Merrill Avenue
Houston 9, Texas
October 31, 1951

My dearest Ernst:
Bless you with all my heart and love for the most wonderful essay—
how could I possibly change it? It is more than I ever dreamed of, and
please do let it go as it stands. These are your words and your opinions,
and, for me, the very greatest I could ask for and from a very great man of
letters, dear Ernst—for me, this is a kind of crown upon my long and
lonely work on *The House of Breath*. Concerning the Katherine Anne
Porter essay—it is still, I find, in preparation, and may be very slow in
forthcoming—and, moreover, I find that you have touched on many of
the points her essay will set down: that my work in this first novel carries
to its extreme length the explorations made by Joyce, Flaubert, and
Proust. So let us keep this yours, dear Ernst, and wait to see what Miss
Porter will say—
Dear Ernst, though they all speak in America of "influences" on my
book, I do know that it came from deep within me, that it flowed out of
me, and that in America when I wrote *The House of Breath* I was a completely isolated young writer trying to find his own voice and his own
language, as well as his own landscape, for I would have no other. I do

feel, and I hope you might say in your Nachwort, that I *have* after very long and lonely and arduous meditation and work, found my own language and my own landscape, and that these are not at all a regional language and landscape, for upon the language and landscape, for instance, of East Texas, has been superimposed the language of men, of human beings "alive in the world and involved in each other," and the landscape is one through which living men and women walk. My relation to the other young writers of my time, my contemporaries, is again very much an isolated one, since I am a poet and a lyricist, among other things, and I speak of the deepest simplicities that bind men and women together or sunder them apart, and I speak of tenderness and love; my contemporaries choose to speak of brutes or of contemporary monsters, freaks, psychotics, etc. It is my purpose to continue to try to show a *continuity* in the world of men, through men, a "chain," one to another, to return us to the first things, as Genesis, as any beginning; but mainly to speak of love, to sing of love, and not to let love die. Many critics and readers say that I am the Faulkner of the next generation, that I shall add something to his world; I have been compared to Thomas Wolfe, but it is stated that my art is more disciplined and my skill greater. Yet, I am simply myself, and you know it and I know it, and thank Heaven enough critics know it to have raised me to a rather solitary position in American Literature as . . . "William Goyen." What more to say, dearest and beloved friend? I am opposed to and the enemy of the sensation in modern American literature, to the simplification of modern life, I want to make *literature* that will speak for my time and out of my time and stand for all time.

For as you know the people who inhabit *The House of Breath* are the people of my time, isolated, separate, lonely, but bound to each other beneath and below themselves; and they exist through thinking of their lives and trying to find a meaning out of their lives and out of human life, among so many other things. The point is to keep one's *selfness*, one's personal identity in a world that will try to make us anything but ourselves; for only as ourselves can we be the good instrument, the faithful and honest instrument for what happens in our world and in our hearts.

Incidentally, it might be interesting to you to know that it has been said that my work marks the end of the Hemingway influence on young American writers and a return to the lyrical, narrative and dramatic.

And, bless friend, I am asking Random House in New York to send you a copy of Faulkner's Nobel Prize Address; it is very fine.

I have been working very very hard, exhausting myself, sleeping little, for I am trying to finish a play by Christmas. My second book, *Ghost and*

Flesh, is now in proof, and when there is a copy available, you shall have one at once. So please forgive me for delaying this answer a little; I have been trying to make a bit of money by writing some book reviews, and there have been other complications, too, in my life—as all of us have. Just please do not speak of our not ever meeting in the flesh again, for that breaks my heart a little; I am so sure that we shall be able to meet before too very long, beloved Ernst; believe in that, be patient for that, for we shall have so much to say to each other. Despite our meeting or not meeting in the flesh, we have our union you and I, we have our joining, and it is a magnificent and beautiful and permanent one, and I do thank God for that joining with you, I cannot tell you how much I thank God for that.

One other thing—do you think you might send the excellent essay to either the *Partisan Review* or the *Kenyon Review* here in America? I feel sure either of them would welcome it most warmly—and your essay will be the first serious critical appraisal of the first magnitude that my work will have had in America. Do please think of this and let me know what you think.

Dear dear Ernst, we do have our bridge of breath and our marvelous friendship does now exist within the life and warm flesh of speech, and between our minds there fly, like birds from tree to tree, our thoughts of human love and human understanding; and wonderful friend and great man, these thoughts, we know now, will never die. Your beautiful and moving letter has made me weep tonight, and I love you, Ernst, for it.

Goodnight,
Bill

---

wonderful essay: "Zum Erstlingswerk eines jungen Amerikaners," *Neue Schweizer Rundschau,* Heft 11 (1952): 669–675. Slightly revised, the essay appears as "Nachwort des Übersetzers" in the Curtius translation of *The House of Breath* published in 1952, pp. 188–196.
Porter essay: The only piece on Goyen published by Porter was her review of *The House of Breath,* "This Strange Old World," *New York Times Book Review,* August 20, 1950, pp. 5, 17.
Nobel Prize Address: In 1949 Faulkner was awarded the Nobel Prize for Literature, and his publisher, Random House, issued his acceptance speech as a pamphlet.

FOUR

1952–1954

55 Morton Street
Apt. 3K
New York City 14, NY
March 11, 1952

My dearest Dad:

At last time to write you, though not much. I am so busy and so many things to do. But I really am well and much stronger, the doctor is giving me Vitamin shots three times a week and this gives me a huge appetite. Last week he weighed me and I had gained 2 1/2 pounds in that week, so I am coming up. Too much work and worry, Dad, but I can meet it now. I hadn't realized how down I was until I got weak and dizzy and overly nervous; then I called the doctor and he came out and took me right to the hospital where I had a good rest and good food for a week, then came out much better. Of course the hospital and doctor bill threw me, but I'll just have to manage that somehow—it took all I had made thus far on the second book. Random House are wonderful to me, they won't let me starve; but I hate to owe them money. I'll manage, dad. That's why I thought maybe we ought to sell the car, for if I could make $300 to $400 on that, then that would take care of the hospital bills and doctor bills. But wouldn't advise selling for less. Just see what you can do, Dad, and let me know; for I feel we might be living beyond ourselves. Too, I have been getting offers to read from my work around here and that might pay pretty good money. I have read on two radio programs here and have been a tremendous success. That means I ought to stay around here, from the point of view of making money if from no other; and, too, I am very happy here this time. After all, my friends, my publishers and my work are here, and I think it is wise to stay around here for as long as possible. [. . .]

And please don't be disturbed by nasty reviews of my books here and there—it will take them some time to see and understand what I am doing—and in the meantime they fight me and attack me and say ugly things. It has *always* been like that for somebody who has something new and painfully true to say in the world. Just wait and you'll see.

B.

---

55 Morton Street: Goyen had left Houston and moved to Manhattan.

55 Morton St.
New York City 14, N.Y.
April 9, 1952

Billy dear—

Where are you—are you there, and all right? It is very real here, in this room which I have made my own, having put work and loneliness and sickness and love into it. Outside, most time, it is an unreal world—yet one realizes when he goes out that the store and mass never existed until he looked up and saw them. Some mornings when I go out I look down Morton Street and see the funnels and masts of a great ship at the foot of the street, two blocks away: for I am on the river's (Hudson) side. I hear the boats' and ships' whistles in the night and during the day. It is quiet and like a European village—and so I am quite content.

I work on the novel, on some stories (which I *must* sell) and on some pieces which I eventually plan to make a book of. Could you please send me the *fact* of the amusing and fantastical situation you once described to me: the burnt house with the couple living on in it. The *fact*—was it that they lived on the grounds in order to claim the insurance? It is the ground, solid and real, that fantasy is based upon which one must have and upon which one must build. Otherwise, as in most of these campy writers, it is all sensation and prissiness. [. . .]

[P.S.] Oh Billy—that little girl who was murdered in Houston recently—I suddenly read a notice of it in the *New York Times* and had a chill—I am still under the pall of it. For, dear Billy, that little girl was my model for the grave children in "A Shape of Light": "cat sucked hair . . . country child garments" etc.—the ones in the graveyard. She lived next door to me at Pickwick. And often came in to me with her mother who used my phone—remember? She was a mistreated, lonely, and unhappy little thing—with such pale, hollow, deathly eyes. So much was so close to death, then, all around me.

---

the couple living on in it: A similar situation is incorporated into the plot of *Half a Look of Cain.*
at Pickwick: Pickwick Lane in Houston.

To Katherine Anne Porter
ALS-2

130 W. 23rd St.
New York, N.Y.
[Undated (May 1952)]

Dear Katherine Anne:
   Thank you very kindly for the beautiful book which came yesterday. I treasure it and love it and wish it well in the world. I know you will be praised for these splendid pieces.
   I am deep in my work and there is where I will live for these several months: for, for me there is that time when all life seems to be drawn into what I am ordering and shaping; and I think one faces his life and the world that holds it by sitting in a corner, over it. But we all have our ways and our perceptions, and the less talk the better. Do wish me well, for you know what your well-wishes mean to me, and God knows how well I wish you, beloved Katherine Anne.
   God love and keep you—

Bill

I hope you are "set-down," as you said your furniture did, there in your charming quarters. Take care and be well.

---

the beautiful book: Porter's first book in eight years, *The Days Before* (New York: Harcourt Brace, 1952), had just been published. The jacket drawing was by Paul Cadmus (b. 1904), American representational artist.
deep in my work: Half a Look of Cain.
wish me well: While relations between the two had cooled considerably, in a letter of July 11, 1952, Porter reported to Goyen that, in a visit to France she had visited the River Goyen in Brittany and brought him back some of its water (Givner, *Porter,* p. 381).
your charming quarters: Porter had moved to 117 East 17th Street, New York City.

55 Morton St.
New York City 14, N.Y.
June 22, 1952

Hello dear friends—

Forgive the silence since I left you—it's been like an air-raid in this city ever since I returned: one has to spend most of his most valuable time in one of two kinds of shelters (or both), a safe, good bar or a locked and barred room. Work and people and doings take all my days away; but be assured I am here.

When I left Texas I packed a great trunk with promises from my family that it would be sent on immediately. In it I put "Suddenly a Thief," and lots of my own manuscripts. The trunk *just* arrived two days ago! Forgive me—and my family—and be patient a little longer. I had read about 1/3 of the ms. before I left. I'm eager to go on with it. So can you wait a little longer, and forgive me?

I hope your summer is not so bad as it *really* is—the heat, I mean. So far it's all right here—but the noise! All my neighbors, whom I never saw all winter long, have suddenly come to life and have begun hauling out lines of shabby washing across my only two windows so that my only view is family wash, the buildings around me have spewed out scores of yelling and cursing children, husbands bring their wives out onto the fire escapes to try and murder them *there*, where it's cooler; and there seems to be a fire every ten minutes, because a little fire engine that was so warm and quiet all winter in a kind of pen on my street (which I had never even been aware of) scampers out and hoots around and around—and the *Baseball Games* on the radios! I find myself sitting here keeping a scorecard and rooting for the Dodgers (who *are* they?), sitting on *my* fire escape drinking a bottle of beer, the wash flapping in my face, work hanging, soot in my eyes—New York, New York! I've got to get out! I hope to get to England in July. So think of me reading the play in this gay and insane surround.

Do your work, nourish the young, be sweet to the bright little dog, and remember I think of you. Give my greetings to that sensitive and pretty girl I met at your house—tell her to write about it, to *do* it, give my love to Florence—and take, again, my sincerest wishes for your happiness and good work and good life. [. . .]

Camille and Frank Rosengren: Proprietors of Rosengren's Books in San Antonio. They moved to New York City in 1952.

"Suddenly a Thief": Play manuscript by Frank Rosengren, who wrote under the name Frank Duane.

Florence: Florence Rosengren, Frank's mother.

To John Igo
TLS-2

Shelter Island, L.I., N.Y.
July 27, 1952

Dear John:

I must write this note to you at once this morning before I begin my day's work, for I have just had your note forwarded up here to me. And I want to tell you that I did not *at all* find or feel your very wonderful letter of so long ago to be "impertinent." Your letter stirred my thinking quite, and the reason I have been so long in responding has been my own inner turmoil and fight with present work which has been going slowly and badly because of summer, the city in summer, and my own inner problems. A kind of immobility, paralysis almost, had set in—and I have not been able to write letters for many weeks. At last it has been broken, for an old friend suddenly appeared out of the blue, one I hadn't seen since the New Mexico days, and brought me right up to his heavenly farm on this benevolent little island. I have been here two weeks, now, and yesterday I made the decision to remain up here through September, for I have got good workdays back for myself, the work is going well again, I am healthier and free of that City for awhile. After next week, I shall be occupying a charming little Gate House on a large estate in East Hampton, Long Island. There is where, God helping, I shall finish this third book, this novel (called *Half a Look of Cain*). But you must continue to write me at 55 Morton St. and my mail will be forwarded at once.

I shall be in the company of several painters at East Hampton, some of them very very good painters, perhaps you know their work and hate or love it—anyway, they are dedicated artists and working very hard. Motherwell is there, Jackson Pollock is there, both the Brookses (James and Alexander), and a marvelously gifted young Texan (Dallas) and a good friend of mine, Joseph Glasco. So it will be good company, no?

I have lived around painters and musicians most of my life, but I particularly like the association of painters. I am not much for communities of artists, having had a bit of my share in the past ten years: New Mexico, San Francisco, Yaddo, etc. And I must live and work alone, however hard that is. My little house is standing alone in some rather savage-looking woods, removed and silent. But I shall have other artists close by, and that will help.

There is, actually, so much I want to say to you—in reply to your good letter and in general—but that will take time and I hope you will give me it. What you say about your sensibility is very important to me; my great aim, really, is to return literature to what is called "sensibility" (but I would do that anyway, being made as I am, good or bad)—to combat sophistication, dishonesty, misrepresentation, etc.—to help us return ourselves to a way of *feeling*, a way of looking and responding to our own human experience. And so much more. Your letter was so full of things to talk about, maybe we can one day talk for a long time, or slowly talk in small letters. I ask you to write me as often as you wish, need to, are able to—and I promise to keep that touch with you as I am able. Do promise me this, John. I am glad you want to devote yourself to an art, and I say get to it, stay to it and hold to it. And let your devotion come from your own insides, as slowly as it wishes or as rapidly, but at its own pace and in its own skin, breathing its own breath and no other. So courage to you, you have my support and very best of wishes; talk to me about it; give your best to it. We shall say more to each other—I do not for a moment think you are unreal: but do please bring along the pretzels and apples because we both seem to like them. So thank you again—for both letters, for what you say in them, and for your belief in my work. Do your work, find your *own* eye and keep it watching and gazing; and anchor your *own* heart deep in the depths and ride it from there, like a buoy. Bless you, and let me hear.

Cordially,
Bill Goyen

John Igo: (b. 1927). San Antonio–based teacher and writer.
"impertinent": Upon publication of *Ghost and Flesh*, Igo had written Goyen a letter praising both his books.
large estate: Belonging to the painter Alphonse Ossario, on Georgica Pond in East Hampton.
Motherwell: Robert Motherwell (1915–1991).

P.O. Box 1526
East Hampton, L.I., N.Y.
Tuesday, Aug. 19, 1952

My dearest Dad:

It was so good to talk to you last night even if we did have trouble with the connection. I hope you had a pleasant Birthday, and you know that I thought of you and thanked God for you, you dearest Dad. You know how much I love you and depend on you, as I always have. Just take care of yourself and trust me and try to be with us for a very long time, for a good time lies ahead and we will all be together for a long time, I know. I hope I can make you very happy one day, and you know I work for that. So Happy Birthday again, and god bless you.

I am very happy here and I believe I am going to do some good work. I have been in rather bad straits financially again, for I have not finished anything to sell and I have had a fight with my publishers, so have only the Guggenheim money to live on. As I have a few little debts still from the hospital and all, I have to go along very carefully. But I will make it, never worry. I am about to finish a couple of stories which I think I can sell at once, and that will solve everything. Everybody asks for my work, but I will not give it up until I feel it is the very best I can do, money or no. I live simply here and it doesn't cost much. The car would be a great help, though an added expense. Too, I cannot yet make the payments on it, and I hope it does not strain you too much. When I begin to sell again I'll repay you, never fear. The novel is coming along, the play will be ready one day, and I am writing stories. Too, when I get a new publisher I'll probably get a little money there. So stick with me and believe in me—I only want to be a good and honest artist, nothing else. My health is good and I am in good spirits. Do, then, see if you can find someone to drive the car to New York. Then I could have it to maybe come home in October—maybe even go on to Taos for a few months. It would give me a lot of freedom, Dad. [. . .]

I love you always,
Bill

---

the hospital: For surgery on his knee.

To Margaret L. Hartley
and Allen Maxwell
TLS-2

130 West 23rd St.
New York City, N.Y.
September 24, 1952

My dear Margaret and Allen:

I was on the verge of sending you a telegram last night because you have been very much on my mind lately, but I decided to save the money—forgive—and send you a letter this morning. I have been on Long Island for the past two months, working very hard on the novel (*Half a Look of Cain*) and I returned to this noisy and disturbing city only a week ago. I have moved again, this time on West 23rd St., as you see above, and in the company of a very marvelously gifted painter, Joe Glasco, who is from Dallas and a friend of mine. We share a long wide loft at the top of a kind of little factory building, and all around us are small workshops and little factories where hundreds of people are standing or sitting at small machines, making something, I don't know what. At night, all the buildings are dark and empty and we are the only residents in this strange block. But our loft is very nice and Joe works in one end, I in the other. A small, very old and croupy bird, a canary we bought in Kresses for a dollar and a half, lives with us, and that is all. I think it will be a very fine arrangement, for we both do little else but work and we enjoy each other's company. You must know Joe.

I hope to finish the novel by the first of January, but that means intense work and staying in good health. I mean to do it. I just skimp by on the Guggenheim, but thank Heaven for that, for that allows me to work my best.

I miss hearing from you, and when long silences go by I get worried. I want to assure you that I am all right and that it is a very very happy time for me. Do please send me word that you two are all right. You are through your summer, Margaret is home from the mountains (though I know she wishes she weren't); and I hope your little brood of family are all well and marching along, dear Allen. Send me news about yourselves, and remember how I love you and hold you faithfully in my heart always. I always have a little sickening revulsion towards and fear of this city when I first come back to it after having been away, but that will get under control with time. I wish I could see you, *how* I wish that. I have been missing you very poignantly these last several days. So say hello to me and take my love, again. Please take care and I am with you in your work, dearest Margaret and Allen.

Always,
Bill

---

a canary we bought in Kresses: The bird was later transmogrified into a macaw, "The Roadrunner from Woolworth's," in *In a Farther Country.*
home from the mountains: Hartley had a place on Devil's Gulch Road in Estes Park, Colorado.

To Ernst Robert Curtius
TLS-1

130 West 23rd Street
New York City, N.Y.
September 26, 1952

My Very Dear Ernst:

I am back in New York City and at a new address. I am very much better, much stronger, and I am hard, very hard at work on the novel to be called *Half a Look of Cain.* The two months on Long Island were a balm to me, though I worked very hard towards the end; but the fresh air, sunshine and ocean did very much towards mending me. It was mostly overwork and nerves, but that can be very bad. So I am back here for the winter and I hope to have the novel completed by early 1953. I am still so disappointed that my voyage to you had to be postponed, but we both know that it was best; and now we still have that to look forward to.

I have so much to tell you, to talk to you about. I have lived so much alone and with such a death-grip on my work, in such torment and with such obcessions [*sic*] that I could not much longer go on. There is a point where an artist must, it seems to me, relate his work and his vision to another human being, to a *beloved;* and I had to come to that. I had come to where I could not bear my own vision, simply, and I could not face what I had learned through the suffering of loneliness. A larger growth was necessary, yet I was filled with fears. In the last month I have made a decision which I shall hold to with all my heart and life, and that is to join another and to try to make my life with that one. For I have found a base, an island in love where I had been adrift in a torrent before. Already I see my work so much more clearly, I see it *through* the beloved. I feel I can die, now, where before I could not. I have so much work to do, so much to tell and to discover; I love human life and I love my own human life, and I must shape and order these, or die, die *within* life, I mean—and that is not even Death.

So I am stronger and deep in my work. I have always been strengthened by your faith in me and by your love for me and my work, and I thank God for these, dear dear Ernst. I pray for your health and well-being, for your great, permanent and beautiful work, and I am so grateful that you have touched and illuminated my own little work. My life is, as it always has been, very simple and full of days' work. It is very hard, for I have very little money, but whoever thought to have any? That I might keep my health and strength and keep to my task is all I ask; and that I may be a good and steadfast and loyal Lover is what I pray and work towards, for an artist is a lover and all art a lovemaking. I send you my loyal love and I ask you to send me yours and to send me word of yourself as often as you can. And still we wait for our meeting. Bless you my wonderful friend Ernst.

In love,
Bill

P.S. You ask if I know Spanish. Yes, indeed. I'd love to have your translation. Please?

To Charles Provine Goyen
and Mary Inez Goyen
TLS-2

130 West 23rd St.
New York City, N.Y.
September 30, 1952

My dearest Mother and Dad:
   Surely enjoyed the talk with you both last Friday night, and I was glad to find you safely home and that you had enjoyed the trip. Too, I'm so glad you have a new bathroom and kitchen. I know you will enjoy these. I am comfortably settled in my new place, now, working doubly hard. I am trying not to get upset or disturbed by this noisy, crazy, city; and if I do again I'll just leave. For I just work hard to finish this novel by the first of

the year, and I believe I can. So I'll lie low and do my work for another month or so, then I wish I could come on down, pick up the car and go to the little house in Taos for a few months and finish up the book. Joe would like to go, and that's fine, for I'd never go alone, as you know. We are very good together, for he's quiet and works very hard and I do, too. We share the rent and cook our meals together, so that solves my big problem. I'll let you know how things develop regarding the trip down. The main thing is to work, now. [. . .]

---

this novel: Half a Look of Cain.

To William M. Hart
TLS-1

130 West 23rd Street
New York City, N.Y.
October 8, 1952

Dearest Billy:
   A word, and a word only, forgive me, to say that I am moved here to this new place and that I am all right and doing nothing but work, being completely absorbed in it. I can manage to finish the novel, *Half a Look of Cain*, by the end of the year if I can manage to keep fed and in health, which I certainly count on. [. . .] Think of me way up high with a flagpole sitter, and we join there, beloved Billy. [. . .]

---

a flagpole sitter: Reference to a section of *Half a Look of Cain*, later published as the story "Figure over the Town," which first appeared in *Botteghe Oscure* 21 (1953): 223–238, was reprinted in the *Saturday Evening Post*, no. 236 (April 27, 1963), pp. 48–53, and was selected for *Best American Short Stories of 1964*, ed. Martha Foley and David Burnett (Boston: Houghton Mifflin, 1964), pp. 125-135.

130 West 23rd St.
New York City, New York
October 19, 1952

My dear Billy:

[. . .] I am working very intensely, in a strange life hoisted like a flag *above* the landscape, yet looking down into it. I am not in New York City, but anywhere. I am living with a most marvelous beautiful human being, a painter, a magically gifted painter and I wonder if you have ever seen his work—he is Joseph Glasco, Dallas is his home but he was born and lived for three years in Oklahoma. I have known Joe for some time, we were together on Long Island this summer where we shared a cottage and worked very well together. We have joined, then, having rescued each other from a kind of death which you know well, and I write here only to bless the rescue and honor it and to say that I pray to God to keep us both forever grateful for it. You will one day meet magnificent Joe, green-eyed and fair, gentle and supreme artist. Wish our life well, for we have embarked upon it with every belief held back for life together, with every trust and faith the choice was made for, and honoring the Walters in the world who made such union possible and who gave it such meaning.

I long, sometimes bitterly, for New Mexico—perhaps that is because the autumn is here, because I am embarked on a very serious and obcessive [*sic*] work, and because El Prado is the place for treasures. But there is so little, so very little money, and we both have work to do that is dangerous to move at this moment. Too, we are installed here, where we have those things we love; a little golden bed I bought in East Hampton (Long Island) at a second-hand shop for $11.50 and I shall keep it all my life; a golden lamp, with beaded golden fringe, a sweet and loving canary, already irrevocably beholden to Joe and me, which we bought at Kresses for $1.50, my iceblue glass lamp which I finally, as you remember, fetched from home, and my little shadow-box mirror. (Do not tremble at the fear that I might in the next sentence ask for the Piranesis, dear Billy!) And, above all, in the enchantment, the strangeness of a world created half out of fear, both of us being so vulnerable to the other, as lovers are, and half out of great and deep human love and respect for each other's silences and loneliness; we are in a fortress in the midst of this hellish, tearing city that seems to have been built for all the wrong things and purposes; we are in a fortress; at night, when the three floors below us are empty, for the factory-workers (they make purses, hats, candlestick holders and the like) go home at six, we pull an iron gate across the stairway and snap the padlock on it—we are locked away up here. It is the first time I have felt secure in this dangerous city. [. . .]

Faithfully,
Billy

To Charles Provine Goyen
and Mary Inez Goyen
TLS-1

c/o General Delivery
Taos, N.M.
Feb. 27, 1953

My dearest Mother and Dad:
   A short note to say I have finished the book and have sent it in to Random House. I am very tired and feel lost, but am resting and sitting in the sun. Wish me good luck with it.
   All is well, the weather is beautiful and springlike again, and Joe is finishing up his work. We hope, if we can manage, both of us, to leave for New York around March 8 for two weeks. May not go, but I have promised Princeton to speak there on March 26, and, too, I want to see the movie of "The White Rooster" which will be shown at Princeton on March 27. I really want just to stay here, but don't know. Will let you know.
   Am anxious for spring, to get some chickens, plant a garden, fix up the house. It's been a long winter. Right now I just want to forget all that work and relax for a little while. Just wanted to tell you that it's over and that I am all right. Hope you are all well. Please take care of yourselves, and let me hear from you. More later. Too tired now. Joe sends hello. Give my love to all, and I love you with all my heart.

Bill

---

the book: Goyen had submitted a version of *Half a Look of Cain.*
the movie: The film version of "The White Rooster" premiered at Theater Intime, Murray Theater, Princeton, on March 25, 1953. It was directed by Robert S. Macfarlane.

To Maurice Edgar Coindreau
TLS-2

130 West 23rd St.
New York City
March 11, 1953

Hello Maurice!

We are here, since yesterday, but not really here, yet. The trip was a rough one and left us both shaky and goofy—I am done in. Add to that the affairs with *Half a Look of Cain* which are boiling right now—and I am involved with editor, agent, etc. But we're here, and safely.

Now to make our arrangements and plans for work on *The House of Breath*—will you let me know when you want me to come, when you have the most and freest time, and I'll get there. Next week, any time from Monday on, would be most desirable for me, what with this fatigue and these tensions over the new book—but, again, you make the plan according to *your* time and schedule and I'll try to comply. I have a set-to with my editor this weekend, over the manuscript. Do please send word, or you can call, if you wish, Algonquin 5-0485. I'm so eager to see you, how nice it will be! We'll work and talk. [. . .]

The letters to Maurice Coindreau are taken from *Delta* 9 (November 1979).
Maurice Edgar Coindreau: (b. 1892). French translator who was completing his translation of *The House of Breath*.
we're here: Goyen and Glasco had just traveled from Taos to Manhattan. Glasco was having an exhibition at the Viviano Gallery in New York from March 24 to April 18. Goyen had an appointment with his Random House editor, Robert Linscott, regarding the revised *Half a Look of Cain*.
when you want me to come: Goyen planned to visit Coindreau in Princeton.

To Margaret Hartley
TLS-2

P.O. Box 17
El Prado, New Mexico
April 27, 1953

My dearest Margo:

Your beautiful letter—please don't be anxious about me—I am through it all, for that's a part of it, too, the coming through bitter disappointment; the work stands, right here in my house, there it is, it is mine, from *me*, the best I could do. It will have to wait. It cannot be destroyed. I love it. Now I go on to the play and some stories. I have quit Random House, in a great battle: I told them, as I had a year ago, that I was in the wrong country, that they are deserters, traitors and scoundrels; they will see, or I will. But I am free, and that is the way I not only want to be but *had* to be. After criticizing the weaknesses of *The House of Breath* up to now, they *now* turn on me and ask why *Half a Look of Cain* was not like *The House of Breath?* They would make me insane, I cannot live in such a relationship. New York, its art, its publishing, its personalities, is a madness, and I am out of it, free. I shall live here, simply and quietly and do my honest work. I have no money, I do not know where any might come from; but I must face that and see to that, too; for that, too, is an honest manifestation of my work. It all came up like trees or springs, from the nature of what *is:* it is my life and I take it as that.

Joe and I are strong and fine and happy and we have our peace that comes out of joining together for what is best in us and in our work. What else?

Now—we speak, as easily and as unselfconsciously and as unguiltily as the wind rises and blows away, what we feel and think to each other. We could not be such friends, love each other as we do, if we spoke otherwise. Nothing of you as I respect and love you is affected by what happens in your work on the magazine. Now you rest in this, my beloved Margaret. It will never change. Bless you.

But the Spring issue of *SWR* I find poor and revoltingly academic and intellectual; I flee that, as you know. After our discussions, from the point of view of the *magazine,* on the use of paintings on the cover, this abominable, derivative horror on the cover of the current issue sickens and appalls me. Most of the issue I find pretentiously intellectual, in the jargon of the New York avant-garde intellectuals, the Village throw-offs, the Vernon Young—whoever *he* is—Santa Fe sham and artiness; I loathe the tone and feeling of it, dearest Margaret—and Allen—and I must tell you. It is in the wrong—whatever wrong is—direction, I feel; and I am disappointed in it. I am glad I am not in it, all the wrong company.

Dearest Margaret, who is behind all this?

If I cannot go on telling you what I feel, we are dishonest together, that is all. There is something we must hold to, more and more we must sacrifice, name the cheaters, the false and the treacherous; we are so few; I tell you I have been in the battle, I have seen it and fought it; I know our enemies. I haven't withdrawn, I have emerged, that's all. We *must* talk.

Under it all, through it all, is my love and belief for you and in you; I
know you are only one there on the magazine; but I must tell you what I
think.

It will be all right, because I know where I stand and what I believe and
what I can do. If I fail, I must study my failure and see where it takes me
and what it came out of and where it leads. Trust me to that. More later. I
am going to finish the dramatization of *The House of Breath* this summer,
if I can manage. I want you to know I have not changed, nor will I ever, in
what I feel for you. God love you and bless you, always. [. . .]

---

disappointment: Random House had rejected the revised *Half a Look of Cain.*
the play: The dramatization of *The House of Breath.*
Spring issue of SWR: A special issue guest-edited by Vernon Young.

To Maurice Edgar Coindreau
TLS-2

P.O. Box 17
El Prado, New Mexico
May 10, 1953

My dear Maurice:

Thank you for your good long letter; I had been anxious to hear from
you. It all sounds good, and congratulations to you, heartily, at the
mailing of the manuscript, and my deep gratitude to you for loving it and
giving your best to it. I am extremely fortunate and proud, dear Maurice.
Now we shall see what comes of it.

Our Spring has been wild and cold, with blizzard and dust-storm
alternating, then a golden little span of two days sunshine and faintest
green. This spring has been a hard one, the hardest in most old-timers'
memory; but surely it will change soon. I have had to hold off planting
my garden because of the freezing nights and the sleet and snow; but I
planted one flower bed and one flower box—God help the flower bed
outside. Joe and I do our best with the flower box, which we heave into
the house at sundown and out again at noon. The little Nasturtiums and
Forgetmenots and Bachelor Buttons struggle, but they are an inch high,
despite the weather. In the midst of this spring violence, Joe is building a
spacious studio annexed to this little house. It will be very large and very
high, with an enormous glass window giving upon the Indian fields and

the mountains just beyond—not a house or human being in sight from
that direction. Yesterday we found a most magnificent pair of very old
oaken doors some eight feet high for the studio entrance. Two Indians are
laying the adobes, and by early June, Joe will be able to paint in his new
studio. It is very exciting. I am trying to keep to my desk a few hours a
day, I have a little story going and the play is active again—I plan to have
it away from me by middle August.

Half a Look of Cain is here again, I asked for it back, and I'll think about
it a while before letting it go again. I want very much to show it to you;
maybe you could publish parts of it in France, or perhaps you might see it
the way I do and want to translate the whole for French publishers. I
think maybe Curtius will do that for the German publishers. The two
American publishers who have seen parts of it have for some curious
reason beyond me been "shocked" by it! This has me bewildered. They
all praise the writing, the form, etc., but they profess not to understand
what I am talking about! Let me know if and when you'll have the time or
interest to see the manuscript and I'll send it to you. A long section of it
will appear in June in *Southwest Review*, and I have just heard that another
long section will be printed in that magazine printed in Italy—called
Botteghe Oscure.

Also, a small story, written some five years ago here in New Mexico,
will appear in *Mademoiselle* in summer. It is called "The Geranium." A
playwright named Greer Johnson is making a play from "The Letter in
the Cedarchest," and I think he might do a good job. Ought to make an
amusing play, don't you think?

The reviews coming from Germany, I must say humbly, are most
wonderful. Curtius sent me two very long critiques last week which are
very flattering. [...]

---

your best to it: Coindreau had recently turned in his translation of *The House of Breath* to
the French publisher Gallimard, which published it as *La Maison d'haleine* (1954). It
won the Halperin-Kaminsky Prize. His preface to that book is available in his *The
Time of William Faulkner* (Columbia: University of South Carolina Press, 1971), pp.
132–140.
A long section of it: "The Enchanted Nurse," *Southwest Review* 38, no. 3 (Summer 1953):
185–195.
another long section: "Figure over the Town."
"The Geranium": *Mademoiselle* 38 (April 1954): 108–109. Illustrated by Joe Glasco.
a play from "The Letter in the Cedarchest": Greer Johnson's (1920–1974) play, *Whisper to
Me*, was produced by Margo Jones in 1955.

To Maurice Edgar Coindreau
TLS-1

P.O. Box 17
El Prado, New Mexico (Taos County)
May 19, 1953

My dear Maurice:
Here comes the ms. of *Half a Look of Cain*, and I don't think you'll be "shocked" at all by it and I certainly don't think you'll be bewildered. You might well be disinterested, etc. but nothing else. Anyway, I believe you will see what I am talking about—and *not* talking about; what my idea is, why there is a "ghostliness" about the world of the book, and what I mean by flagpole sitting, rising and falling, love, the wound, murder and healing. It is, above all, a very urgent and necessary statement, for me.

If you care for the book, if you think it of value within the body of my work, then you will unequivocally have my permission to put it into print in France, either as a whole with Gallimard or someone else, or in parts in magazines. Use your judgment, which I trust without question. We should, of course, have to speak to Jim Brown about it—but that would come later. [. . .]

Jim Brown: Goyen's agent at the time.

To Maurice Edgar Coindreau
TLS-1

P.O. Box 17
El Prado (Taos County), New Mexico
June 29, 1953

My dear Maurice:
Forgive me for waiting so long to answer your fine letter about *Half a Look of Cain*. The manuscript came back to me a few days ago. Joe and I have been so insane with the building of his studio that neither of us has had much mind for anything after work but food and bed. The work is at its end and a magnificent building stands in these green fields to attest it.

Your comments on and your point of view towards the novel pleased me very much—and more than that, they are the first *I* have been able to

understand! I agree with what you feel and say, Maurice, and now that
I've had your (and John's) opinion, I can see the whole a little more
clearly. We shall wait, as you suggest. I want to say more later, but right
now I want to thank you deeply for reading the work so carefully and
with such heart and honesty—I needed that so badly. Give my deepest
thanks to John, too, for his help and his good interest. We'll see how it all
turns out. In the meantime I am working with the play, and I'll send the
manuscript to you this early fall, I hope. [. . .]

John's: John Rust also read the manuscript.
We shall wait: Coindreau had suggested that the subject matter of *Half a Look of Cain*
was "ahead of its time," and publication should be delayed (according to later
conversations between Goyen and Robert Phillips).
working with the play: He was making the stage adaptation of *The House of Breath*,
produced off-Broadway in 1954.

To Margo Jones
TLS-1

P.O. Box 17
El Prado, New Mexico
July 20, 1953

Margo dearest:
   Now you've got me worried about you! I never *really* worry about you,
but I get concerned. Because I want you, very specially, to be all right and
to be going along the way you have to and must; if not, something's
wrong in the world. Still, dearest Margo, what the hell, we are not
crippled or crackbrained, we can make our way, nobody owes us a living
and all that. But we are people who've got an idea in our heads that's got
to—and is going to—work and show itself. We call on each other when
we could use a little pushing and little help, and we push always, give if
we can. How I wish *I* were rich and could bail you through a few months!
   People like us always live ahead of themselves in every way, in the
bankbooks, in the mind and heart; that's the very natural basis of our life
and it can't be changed without something very good and very worth-
while being lost. So we hobble on. There are the times when we *run*, and
those are the bright wonderful times. I've watched and seen you run and
you've seen me. That's our life story, Margo dearest.

So you put me to rest about you and I'll try to do the same about me. I am writing a play that will be as beautiful and real and right as I can make it, and I will stay with it for years if necessary. The rest? It comes and goes, but the work is the reality and it goes on. Now I know the same is true for you, but *tell* me, and right away. God bless you.

The same love,
Billy

---

a play: Theatrical version of *The House of Breath*.

To Maurice Edgar Coindreau
ALS-1

P.O. Box 17
El Prado (Taos County), N.M.
Oct. 7, 1953

Dear Maurice:

Thank you for your letter and for its news. Mine is the same—very hard work on the play, which is nearing its finish. I am very much pleased with it, though it has cost me agony and sweat, I can tell you. I have written the songs for it, too and they haunt me. We shall see what people think of it when I finally let it go. I'll let you know when I have finished.

Our days are golden dreams of silver wheat and corn in the fields, the mountains are burnished and a cold wind blowing. We freeze shortly. Our house is ready, we hope, for winter—and we now have gas stoves installed. Joe's studio is truly like a temple, so grand and majestic in its proportion and grace. My garden has gone to seed—seed is sad, somehow, after the bloom—and our sunflowers have big dried faces like clocks—big as heads. The sheep are driven down our road, daily, the cattle and horses, too, all down from the high country around us, to this valley. Magpies are back, meadow larks too, and a hundred other kinds of birds are passing over us every day. This is an enchanted time, the great turning of the season. I live like a root in dirt—that simple, with that kind of connection. I am free of the literary world I could not endure, that is not for me.

I pray that you are well and not too lonely. Courage, once again. Bless you for all you do, and let's keep in touch, Maurice, dear friend.

A playwright has just sent me his script of a dramatization of "The Letter in the Cedarchest." I'm going to read it tonight. [. . .]

To Ernst Robert Curtius
TLS-1

P.O. Box 17
El Prado, New Mexico
December 13, 1953

My very dear friend Ernst:

I thank you from my heart for your thought and time and energy put into the manuscript I sent you, and for the good and so-much-respected letter which came several days ago. I know how you are limited, now, and I do not ask great portion of that energy which you must keep for the things of your life. One of the precious things I have lost during your illness has been your letters to me written in your own hand—but they will, I know, come again. It is your mind I need with me, I *do* feel it with me, whispering into my days of work and doubt—and I remind you that mine whispers and breathes into your days, and blesses you and wishes to heal you. That is our connection, beloved friend!

I sit in my little house, buried as it is in deep, pure snow, watch through the windows the cattle huddled together and steaming in the cold white air; and I see the shining Magpies feeding in the white fields: this is the imaginary Christmas card I send to you, with deep love and with wishes for growing strength, for peace within yourself, and for the happiness of your wife and those you love.

It is purity of mind one strives and wishes for—an area of purity and simplicity where one pulls up, as from a shore, out of the mud and the swamp some whole, clean shape—a rescue. For me, I know that the work of the artist is a salvaging and a purification. Knowing this, what else can I do but what I do, how else can I be but what I am? *Half a Look of Cain* lies in such a buried world—I have lifted the life of it a little; now I let it lie at its own depth—what else? We *do* have to know what to take, what to turn away from and leave. The life of the work haunts me still, like A Shape of Light that rises from its buried place and goes over the land for a while, bewitching me, then vanishes. But all this says only how I feel about something I have had the audacity to shape among some kind of life, nothing more; only a comment. Your comments came sound and strong and clear to me, and I thank you heartily for them. I stow away the manuscript and go on to new work. I plan a group of stories called *Crossings*, and I have written a few of them. And I struggle to finish the play.

What I pray for is your increasing strength and for your wife's strength and courage—and for word of you when you can send it. I am well and strong and at my work. I send my love and my thoughts.

Bill

---

the manuscript: Half a Look of Cain.
you are limited: Curtius had had a stroke.
your wife: Ilse Curtius.
A Shape of Light: Allusion to Goyen's short story of that title.
stow away: Curtius had advised Goyen to put *Half a Look of Cain* aside for the time being.
Crossings: Early title for *In a Farther Country* (New York: Random House, 1955).

To Maurice Edgar Coindreau
TLS-1

P.O. Box 17
El Prado (Taos County), New Mexico
January 11, 1954

Dearest Maurice:

Just a note to say the second copy of *N.R.F.* arrived and how proud I am of it, how thrilled. It is so beautifully, carefully, delicately handled, your work; and I love the title. I am exceedingly fortunate and bless you for your loving care in the work.

We are stunned by the most radiant weather, loveliest in history for January: clear, sparkling air and golden fields, for the snow has melted, and pink mountains. A kind of strange trance has fallen over everything. Joe works ten to twelve hours a day on a magnificent blue canvas, and I labor through the play, still shaping and clarifying it. I am also trying to shape a book of stories to be called, so far, *Crossings*. "Zamour" is one of the stories. They are about people who very subtly depend upon each other for their life, and when the relationship is broken, there is collapse. I mean people who need each other to keep each other's fancy and fantasy alive and real, who create for each other another territory, who make delicate, swinging bridges for each other to cross over. There are stories about birds in Woolworth's, one called "Spain"—a woman creates Spain in another room of her house and thinks herself Queen of it; her husband has hired a young man to watch her all day while he is away—he is a woodcarver and has created Spain for her, even to the carven birdcage, though she thinks she loathes him and that he is the enemy of her Spain, etc. This will be a major work and will go slowly, carefully—all the "stories" will be about the same thing so that, I hope, the end result will be a "book," not a collection of stories, not a novel—a world. But first the play must be brought off, and that will be soon, I pray. [. . .]

N.R.F.: Nouvelle revue française, which serialized Coindreau's translation of *The House of Breath*.
one called "Spain": This story was the basis for his second published novel, *In a Farther Country* (New York: Random House, 1955). "Zamour" did not become a part of this book. Instead, it was gathered in *The Faces of Blood Kindred* (New York: Random House, 1960).

To Dorothy Brett
TLS-2

El Prado, N.M.
January 20, 1954

My dear Brett:
    I will tell you something I know and have learned bitterly—there are people in the world who are *disturbers:* they make that their kind of profession; often it is subconscious. But one comes, finally and through much pain, to know them upon sight, to *sense* them—and then one can only flee them, protect himself against them, withdraw further. There are others who are plainly *destroyers*. It is the duty of the artist to know these people, and to evade them.
    But more: an artist is a disturbed, distressed, obsessed human being. Joe and I are haunted and obsessed [*sic*] with our work. One spends half one's youth trying to escape his obsession and his torment, the rest of his life he spends struggling to find some way to live with it, as he has now learned that this is the very condition of his life—remove it and his life is violated and betrayed.
    Art, of course, is a way of life. We are finding it, you, Joe, I, others. The search for it is the basis of our life. To explain this to others, to

justify it or clarify it is not our business—we must never allow ourselves to be brought to this.

You know that Joe and I are very happy people, but we live together in a kind of isolation, too, as artists must—neither of us can enter the world of the other, either to help him or "save" him.

Every artist I have ever known or read about has had about him, by nature, a *reserve*—as I told, or tried to tell Mabel that drunken (Cognac) evening when she was stroking my leg until it was raw. Those people who try—as Iris did not—to break this reserve or to force themselves into it by whatever means, excuses (which they themselves believe to be honest), subterfuges, etc., are in reality the enemy of the artist. For what they really want to do is to interrupt, interfere, block, bring to question the work of the artist. The world is full of sorrow and loneliness, Brett, and is not our business and our work the speaking of that sorrow and loneliness, the comforting of it, the *pacifying* of life? Therefore, where one's *art* serves, or strives to serve, what can one *himself* do better?

As for me (and the very same is true for Joe—that is why we have miraculously come together, and it is a marvel in our lives), I live in the world of my work, having been willing, long ago, to risk giving up the other world, to take that change. Every day I create it again, and I must live in it with the people I am making in it; it is a world of regularity, so often of immobility (as Flaubert said); and when it seems I am least working I am often working the hardest. No one need know this but I, and it will not be justified to anyone, explained, etc. Something in my freedom, my right as an artist is violated when outsiders push themselves into my reserve, beat at my door, criticize me for being inhuman, un-friendly, unneighborly. And there is something false in this attitude of the outsider, something which makes me both afraid of him and wish to defend myself against him. I do not wish to be involved, as you know and so beautifully understand, and thank God. Otherwise we couldn't be the loving neighbors and deep friends we are. I do not wish to be involved, involved as I feel I am with the whole world, trying to be honest towards it, trying to see it clear and whole in my task as an artist. Therefore, dear Brett, I feel that you involve me even when you tell me of the secrets of other people—I am involved at once; and I do not wish to be. You see this, and you understand. If I wished or felt compelled to be involved with the world and the people in it on *that other level*, then I should at once become a nurse or missionary, as I have often thought of becoming. But no, I live with the world at that other depth, difficult and dangerous as it is, and there I must stay. Find me there, but find me there in my work, and judge me there.

I love writing to each other once in a while; for we can speak there where we cannot face to face—for some human reason. Maybe lovers ought to part once in a while, so that they might write beautiful letters to one another!

I believe in your "Crucifixion" and count on it—I feel you are putting everything you have learned and kept silent about into it. It will be your great work, I'll bet on that.

Love,
Bill

Mabel: Mabel Dodge Luhan.
beat at my door: Goyen was furious that a Taos neighbor kept dropping by unannounced at any time of the day or night.

To Maurice Edgar Coindreau
ALS-2

P.O. Box 17
El Prado (Taos County), New Mexico
Feb. 3, 1954

My dear Maurice:
Yes, your letter was full of good bright news, bolstering me in a period lately of desperately agonizing work—and thank you for everything that is happening. But, dear Maurice, the Preface—I wept on it, I'm afraid—it is so *tender* and so loving—it is beautifully done. I value it above anything that has been said—it is so honest, simple, so at the elements of it all—I cried—why? it is just *right* for me, that is all I can say. You know, and I know you know—and how I am blessed by having someone like you to know. I feel *crowned*, quietly and lovingly and secretly—I wear the little crown around here, where I am strangely restless and disturbed, not in my head but in my loins, in my veins—it is the work, so hard to face at times, as though I don't want to see what it shows—yet it is all glorification, even of the terrifying—work, I mean; and there is so much to catch and tell, so much, all out there, all in one's pockets, in one's sleeves to pull out like a magician—but it fights me now, and I don't want to fight. It is some battle in the veins and I must let it pacify itself. The preface has stirred and moved me so deeply—I feel strange and say strange things to you.

A lovely letter from the infirm Curtius about *Cain*. He advises me, as
you, to put it away for awhile—as I have, long ago. He writes: "I have
read your new work three times and my impression is that you wrote it
with your heart—even, if I may say so, with your blood . . . I am struck
with its religious character (not in the sense of the Church of England,
bien entendu). It is Folner's story and therefore the reader of *The House of
Breath* won't be surprised. But what will surprise him is the absence of
everything belonging to the outer world. It is an amazing phenomenon of
a purely introverted attitude towards life . . . The reader has the feeling of
being slowly involved in a dream, in which all the problems of your
present life appear and center around Marvello . . . *Half a Look of Cain* has
deeply moved me and there are other points I want to discuss with you
but again I implore your indulgence. My advice would be to keep the
manuscript and stow it away, read it after a year or two but continue your
work as you are."

I haven't mentioned the play to you lately—I am still working slowly
and carefully on it. It will come; it takes patience. "Spain" has grown into
what may be a strange little *nouvelle*—who can tell? I adore it and I think
the people in it like me.

Soon—the baby. It is all too wonderful and exciting a realization.
What can I say to you to convey my love for you, for what you are and
what you have done?

The sight of a family of 18 Quail, all running together in early mornings and at twilight, over these fields, innocent, guileless, trembling in
beauty—a vision that carries me through these days. See it, too, dear
Maurice. And I am so—proud.

Love from me—
and Joe, too
Bill

---

the Preface: Coindreau's preface to *La Maison d'haleine* (Paris: Gallimard, 1954),
pp. 7–18.
Cain: Half a Look of Cain.

Via Margutta No. 53-B
c/o Boromeo
Rome, Italy
April 14, 1954

My dearest Brett:

Such a dazzlement and dash, so much new and old, so much vivacity and beauty here, I have not been able, quite yet, to collect my mind. I have wanted, and Joe too, to send a long letter about what has happened to us and how we are living; but until now both Joe and I have been trembling with excitement and rather dazed by strangeness of this new life we have taken upon ourselves. I cannot even remember what I have written to you from Rome, but I do think I have told you that we were enormously fortunate to find this charming and beautiful studio here in the old Via Margutta, and that we have taken it for six months, hoping to God that we can manage that long. The rent is high—$100 a month—but between us we might manage. Food is expensive, everything is expensive. But we struggle at the little lovely markets, coming back with artichokes, spaghettis, a bunch of anemones, a few eggs, slices of meat. Joe already cooks a luscious Italian meal, and the wine is so good. We have an Anna who sort of came with the place, and she comes twice a week to clean and help us get into shape. She will help our Italian, as she knows no English except "Okay." I am, incidentally, studying Italian again, this time hoping to master it enough to use it intelligently here.

As there is a Congress of Modern Music going on here in Rome, and a gathering of many modern composers whose music is being played for the first time, including Milhaud, Stravinsky, Poulenc, etc., Joe and I have been busy at nights going to concerts. Some have been very exciting, others dull. I have already begun to set up a work schedule for myself, and I hope to finish the novel called *Spain* here. Also work on the play. Joe is not yet working, he runs out to see pictures and churches, but soon he will begin.

We spent Sunday at the Villa d'Este, an indescribably beautiful place of fountains and blooming wisteria, anemone, fruit trees, lilies, acacia, and great wide groves of olive trees and fig trees. Spring is so heavenly here, such scents, and the warm Roman sunshine. We went down into the mysterious cascade around which the Romans built a Temple of Vesta with ten of the Corinthian columns still standing, and a thunderstorm caught us; we hid in a beautiful and terrifying Grotto where water fell thousands of feet into a kind of Dante crevice. How strange.

Next Sunday, Easter, we go to St. Peter's to see the Pope appear at his window and bless the millions in the great plaza.

Yesterday to the Borghese Villa and the Museum of pictures and sculpture—there we saw a room full of masterpieces which Göring had bought from Mussolini and had just been returned. The old scoundrel had chosen the very finest pieces for himself—but they have come back.

We have two canaries who sing all day in the sunshine. The mama laid two eggs but ate them one night, only to lay two more; and now she sits cozily on them day and night. We have a little balcony overhung with blooming fragrant vines and surrounded with brilliant flowers. Standing there one can see most of Rome below. Our floors are covered with purple and yellow 18th-century tiles. Oh how lovely it is. So we'll stay in it six months and maybe have to sell our suits to pay the rent—but it will be worth it. [. . .]

Rome is so noisy! The Italians seem always involved in argument or passion—but how kind they are to us. The French were haughty and deceitful, I felt. I did not like Paris at all this time and do not care to go there again, for a while. Americans have raped and changed it. Venice—a dream not to be spoken of, yet. Now I want to go to Greece! So close, imagine.

Thank you for your letters. They help and they are good to receive. Just keep your stride and follow your own path, beloved Brett, and remember you have what I can be and do for you, always. So stick to your guns and walk your way and hold to what you hear and the other passes away. I send my faithful love and thank you for everything you are and have done, in all these years. [. . .]

Love,
Bill

Rome, Italy: Goyen had won a second Guggenheim Fellowship, and he used it to live in Italy for a year.
Göring: Hermann Wilhelm Göring (1893–1946). German National Socialist leader and commander of the German air force.
Mussolini: Benito Mussolini (1883–1945). Fascist Italian dictator.

Via Margutta 53-B (c/o Borromeo)
Rome
May 5, 1954

My dear Maurice:

Are you all right—and I am fine, somewhat settled and working every morning from 6 to noon. I have not felt so alive in my work for a very long time—is it Italy, is it removal from my own country, what, and who knows? I am alive again, deep and thrilling to feel, and my work feels true and my own. I have had a very violent reaction to Rome, out of which I could not write to you—but now I can, for it is passed through—and out of it have come some things for me to know. The sensuality, the spirituality, all wound together—the bitterness of these—and so much to feel, to question, to ponder: I went away, for awhile, and I thought I couldn't bear it; too much was brought to bear on me; I lost my equilibrium. But I have bounced back, now, and all is steadying. Joe has been my good support, and we suffered a lot together. Thank God for him.

Rome is expensive, Rome is noisy and fashionable and living on appetites; it is frightening and difficult and crazy, filled with beautiful, lively people, lovely flowers, fountains, marble and gold. Nowhere have I ever felt the sensual and the spiritual so warring with each other, and within myself. I am keeping my notebook carefully and honestly, trying to record for myself what is happening to me. The novel called *Spain* and whose title I think might change to *Surely the People is Grass* is alive and going along like a dance—at least *I* am happy with it and there are some stories progressing. It is a very good time from the point of view of my work.

The reviews of *La Maison d'haleine* are being sent to me by Gallimard and surely you have seen them by now. They seem very good and I am deeply pleased with them. Always they pay you highest tribute, as they should, and this makes me very happy. So we have, I believe, made a success in France, and all because of you, my dear friend Maurice. How exciting it was to receive the first review and how I wished we could have read it together. Somehow it seemed for *you* and not for me. I feel, again, so proud and honored, and it is to you I owe it all. Do tell me what you feel about the reviews and whether you are pleased and satisfied.

I got worried about money and wrote to Gallimard to ask if there was anything for me there. They answered that there was $100 in my account but that problems of exchange and, above all, the eccentricities of Random House's agent, that Russian woman, in Paris, prevented their sending it to me. So I suppose I can't have it. Never mind, I'll manage. But I do have to sell something soon!

I do want to enjoy Italy, to move about in it, but I know, again, that only my work matters—and it is for that, certainly, that I am here or anywhere. I know I need a rest, fun, etc.—but if the work is not alive I am miserable and sleepless; and if it is alive, then what else is there to see or do?

Anyway—Joe and I stroll at sunset through the streets, see all the beautiful young lying on the Spanish Steps and pressing against each other in the parks; we take bus trips into the country on Sundays, and sometimes have spent whole sunny days meandering through the city. Joe is completely happy and vivacious, though I have given him some anxiety—but he understands and is with me—he is slow to come to his work, but he will. We have a project that delights—I am writing a very private story about something beautiful and secret and he will make drawings for it—it will be in a lovely little cloth-covered book I am having made. It is called *At the Baths of Hadrian*, and I think you might one day like to see it. [. . .]

[P.S.] Little Pigeon is going full speed ahead towards a Fall production, so they write me.

Surely the People is Grass: Another tentative title for the later novel published as *In a Farther Country*.
that Russian woman: Mme. Strassova.
At the Baths of Hadrian: Uncompleted project.
Little Pigeon: Character in Greer Johnson's adaptation of "The Letter in the Cedarchest," *Whisper to Me*.

To Ernst Robert Curtius
TLS-1

c/o American Express
Rome
May 28, 1954

My dear Ernst:
Yesterday I met Mr. Dohrn from Switzerland with the money, and I am so very grateful and need it badly. I am anxious to know where it came

from, whether my publishers in Switzerland or from you, do please tell me. Mr. Dohrn did not know. Wherever it came from, I am deeply thankful for it—but I do need to know its source, and I know you will tell me. My deepest gratitude to you for this help, dearest Ernst.

Rome has been almost a disaster for me and for my friend, Joe. As you have heard by now, we are leaving the city on June 1, and we shall go to the island of Ischia, hoping to find that place, which we do not know at all, cheaper and a better place for work. As I do not know where I shall be, I can give you no address until I find one there, or wherever; but I shall send you word as soon as I am settled and tell you where you can reach me. Joe and I shall remain either on Ischia or somewhere in that region for two or three weeks, I shall try to get some work done, and then we shall come to Switzerland so that I can have a week's visit with you. So, if you have not already written to me, please do not do so until you hear further from me.

I am sorry to seem so vague and disturbed, and please do not think me a problem—it is just that I made a mistake in thinking I could live here in Rome for several months. Before I knew it, the simple living expenses were more than I could support, and everything went wrong. It is my hope, and my dear friend's too, that we can make up for this bad time by finding a place to work in and live quietly and cheaply; if not, we shall have to return to America soon. But this must not, and will not, mar our meeting, and soon, now, that will happen. And that you, beloved friend, who have meant so much to me in my life and work, should help me again, is more than I can thank you for. What a friend *you* are, indeed!

I think I told you that I sent a letter to Mr. Schifferli in Switzerland about *Half a Look of Cain,* to tell him that my publishers in New York have no claim on it and that it can be arranged, modified, etc. between the two of us, and with your word and help if you wish to give it. I asked him please to write to you about it, or to me. You and I can discuss this when we meet. You don't know what this means to me, to have the book, which I love and which represents, for me, a great step forward in my work, printed. [. . .]

----

where it came from: Curtius had sent Goyen money out of his own pocket.
Mr. Schifferli: Peter Schifferli, a Swiss publisher. This publisher did not issue *Half a Look of Cain,* but he did publish *In a Farther Country,* under his imprint Die Arche, in 1957.

Forio D'Ischia
Provincia Di Napoli
Italia
June 4, 1954

My dear Maurice:

Your long warm and glad letter came to me in Rome only a few days before Joe and I left. We discovered this heavenly beautiful island and moved here a week ago. It is so cheap! We have taken a little house of two floors, two large rooms upstairs, large kitchen (Joe's studio) and bathroom and foyer downstairs, a window on the sea, a well full of rainwater to drink, Gabinetta, too, all for a little less than $40 per month! We've taken the house for the month of June, and if we like it and if our money lasts, we might stay on through July. At last, quiet and peace one can manage to pay for, sun and sea, vineyards and groves of lemons, oranges, olives and figs. We are very happy here and we shall both have good long uninterrupted workdays. We are 2 hrs. from Naples, 4 1/2 hrs. from Rome.

Wonderful news came to me out of the blue last week—my German publishers have written that they will publish *Half a Look of Cain* shortly. I have written back, asking for permission to make some changes and additions, and they agree. Of course I am delighted; and for some time I have been enlarging and clarifying parts of the novel. So—on July 1 I go to Zürich to meet my Zürich editor, Peter Schifferli, and talk with him about the publication. After Zürich, I'll go to the Oberland of Switzerland to see Prof. Curtius for a few days. His doctors will not allow him to come to Rome, he is too frail. I feel he is very ill. Whether Joe and I can return to Ischia after that, we are not sure. We may have to come back to Naples—or to Genoa—the end of July and take a ship home. Rome was disastrously costly and took so much of our funds—but at any rate we both want so badly to stay in Europe through the summer, and of course I would love to be with you in Paris in September—what a wonderful thing to happen to us, together in Paris! I assure you, dear Maurice, that we'll do our best to stay over here. My work has not come so clearly to me in two long years as it has since I've been in Europe. Suddenly I know all the words, I see all the depths—for that blessed vision into the core of one's deep work he would do anything, almost. So it has come to me, and one day it will make me very happy to lay it before you to see how you will receive it, my wonderful friend.

"The Grasshopper's Burden" comes from a passage in the Bible and I
wonder if we couldn't use it, some way, in that sense so as to convey its
Biblical meaning? "The grasshopper shall be a burden"—that is, the curse
of sterile desire. Perhaps, in this connection, simply "The Burden of the
Grasshopper"—the insect that devours, with its appetite, all fresh and
lovely things—and because this image is used throughout the story. You
decide, and let me know what you feel is right.

Sunday, June 6

Dear Maurice—the picture is changing. Now I may have to go to
Zürich sooner, and, perhaps home sooner. We think now to go on to
Zürich on June 15, stopping in Florence for a few days. I may have to go
earlier in order to meet Curtius, whose plans keep changing. He is so ill,
and lives by Doctor's orders. At any rate—could you wait to write until I
send further word. I am very excited about *Half a Look of Cain* and I'm
eager to show you the new shape of it—

------

about the publication: As late as 1971, Goyen was uncertain whether a German translation had been published. He asked Robert Phillips to look for copies when he lived in
Düsseldorf. According to Patrice Repusseau, the book was not translated into German
(Note to letter 11 of "Letters to Maurice Edgar Coindreau," *Delta* 9 [November
1979]: 98).
"The Grasshopper's Burden": One of the stories in *Ghost and Flesh*, which Coindreau was
translating.
to meet Curtius: When Goyen finally achieved his anticipated meeting with Curtius, he
found that a stroke had left the man speechless.

To Dorothy Brett
TLS-2

Zürich, Switzerland
June 30, 1954

My dearest Brett:

Sorry so long a silence—we have been here about ten days and love it
very much—and I have been constantly with my publishers and with
Prof. and Mrs. Curtius. The book *Half a Look of Cain* is under terrific
negotiation, they are trying to swindle me, to be as cunning as all publishers, and I am holding out; but it looks as though it will come through as *I*
want it. I am tired to death of the wiles and tricks of publishers, and, alas,
I have not found them any different here from those in America.

Both Joe and I have been very happy in Switzerland, and after Italy it has been such a relief, such peace and order and cleanliness. We are in an inn on the side of a hill overlooking the Lake, the Alps in the background, and the old-world town of Zürich below. The coffee, the chocolate, the food, the beer are all delicious; and such comfort—the beds, the baths, the rooms. We have made a very fine friend in a lovely woman named Elisabeth Schnack, who is the translator with my publishers here. She has lived in China and Manchuria for many years, her husband was killed by the Nazis in Norway; she is German, and has translated the stories of Lawrence, among many other books. She has taken us about the city to many charming old restaurants where there is good food. [. . .]

The Swiss are not the warmest creatures in the world, nor the most beautiful; but they do let one alone, and that's a relief after the nudging and yelling of the Italians. Their countryside, as you know, is beautiful, all the flowers, never such roses. Joyce is buried on the hill just behind us. Joe went last night to see the Old Vic Players in *Hamlet*. Also a huge exhibition of Picasso here at the Kunshaus, all the drawings. My publisher is a little squeaking mouse. [. . .]

Joyce: James Joyce (1882–1941). Irish novelist, buried in the Fluntern cemetery on a hill in Zürich.
my publisher: Peter Schifferli.

FIVE

Taos

New York

1954–1957

To Robert Linscott
TLS-2

P.O. Box 17
El Prado, New Mexico
August 16, 1954

Dear Bob:

[. . .] All well here. Wide, enormous, lucent skies and this light shows up everything as it really *is*, the truth is in the light and one cannot escape it. This makes it hard enough to bear, to survive, but what else is there to survive by except the light of the truth? It was good to see you, but I was so deeply depressed by it—I cannot tell you; something is so dead, somewhere, what has laid such a pall over life in this wonderful country, over that desperate corpse of a city where the population has taken a wrong turning, all enterprise, all endeavor in New York shows a wrong choice, a false one, a kind of doom that waits at the end of Fifth Avenue where every parade ends. I came to Texas to find my mother very ill again and the life of that family seeming to collapse. Where is America? I kept asking myself, and I had ached and longed to come back to it after a month in Europe. Where is America? Some of us must try to keep it alive, in the tradition of our old ancestors who broke wilderness and built their little houses out of wood and brought up their families to this. I am an exile, but at home, where every exile should be; and I do my work, there is so much to be done, I have not enough time nor peace; but I will not change. You do not hear me, you do not care, you do not care whether I survive or not, whether my truth survives, you have heard too much of the lies, read too many lies; that is a tragedy; it is a question of money, and in the end the death of money will have the whole company; but something else lives and breathes, as simple and ancient as grass; but who will hear that? [. . .]

---

the whole company: Random House.

P.O. Box 17
El Prado, New Mexico
September 22, 1954

My very dear Ilse and Ernst:

I received your two letters yesterday, at last, and now I know where you are and what has been happening to you. I need your letters, if just sketches of what your life is like, for already I feel isolated. We are in the midst of our Indian Summer, a sad golden time with the trees turning their colors and the grasses burning yellow. The air is smokey and filled with lazy wasps and there is an autumnal sadness over all the world out here. I have been working through long, killing days, falling exhausted to bed early at night, but rising very early, before sunrise, into a crystal, fresh morning to begin again. It goes on like this, into an endless golden timelessness. There are those terrible dark days when one does not believe what he is writing, for what he has to tell sinks deep in his breast; and then it takes great faith to go on.

Ernst, you ask me about how I am reacting to New York—I must tell you that when I passed through that city enroute to Texas and New Mexico I had a meeting again with my so-called editor at Random House. There was such a pall of death over him, he had no life; that city was dreadful, it paralyzed me. My editor kept pleading with me to show him my work, which he hasn't seen for two years—but I ask you how can I show my work to a dead man and one whom I have no faith or belief in? He kept saying to me, "Only tell the truth, Bill, that is all you can do; just tell the truth in your work." This annoyed me and finally I said, will you please refrain from using the word truth upon me, for I feel you have read lies, heard lies, spoken lies so long that you no longer know the truth. How, then, can you judge or assess truth? I am afraid we had a difficult time together, he and I; and I cannot bring myself, who care about the simple truth, to attach my work to him and his publishing house again. I must find another publisher. But where? How? I must trust my work to an agent, I suppose; but where to find an agent in America who is not in a dishonest alliance with some publishing house? You see what they publish here. If it will not make several thousand dollars, they will not publish it. They do not care about literature; they must sell and please. I want to sell and please, too; but I must speak my truth, and I believe truth sells and pleases. They do not know this, for they do not know the truth. I can see you smiling, dear Ernst, and I can watch your lovely face, Ilse, as it grows dark and angry when I say such things.

I go on working. *Spain* will soon come to you—I do hope I am not burdening you with stuff to read, but I write for you, with you in my mind and my heart, and it is natural to send away to you what I have done. I think it will take three more months to properly finish, as I must, this little *Spain*. In the meantime I struggle every day against the worry of money, of debts. Sometimes I despair and think what a terrible battle and exhausting task, this daily daily work, alone and believing in it, with so little to come in from it to keep me existing. But, then, that is the daily struggle and anxiety of every artist, is it not, and one we settled for a long time ago.

How I wish we could talk! Alas, we shall have only letters, and so few, for some time to come. Do you go to Rome? All that is a dream. I do not believe, beloved Ernst, that my trip to Europe was under an unlucky star, as you wrote. It was under my own star, and I had my own buried struggle I carried, like my luggage, with me. The haunting, tragic and beautiful world of Europe was also my own; I had to come to some terms with it in my breast and that was like a struggle to live. I came there out of loneliness and utter fatigue from fighting away day after day at my work that was so difficult; I came knowing I had not one cent in the world that was my own, but money borrowed from someone else which I would have to repay. I had come to a maturity in my work, I felt I had risen to a *man* in it; and I came, as I had been living, under a darkness of sadness that seems to be my own very inheritance, American, peasant, a mixture, as the woman in *Spain* lives under, a longing to bring to some fulfillment the small haunting vision that is my own, by very God. *That* was the star I traveled under, dearest Ernst.

Frau Schnack is now translating the stories in *Ghost and Flesh* and I believe she will do a good job. But I mourn your loss, for working with you was a rare joy in my life. Next year, when you are fully well and strong, perhaps we can do some work together. Incidentally, I have heard from Fischer again, and they are most enthusiastic about my work and want to have it. I must find a way to give *Spain* to them, and I think I can. Do you ever see them or correspond with them?

Ilse! the wonderful coffee pot as a Christmas present! Good—I long to have it. You must ask me for what you might want in America, and I'll manage to send it to you. Joe is blooming, painting a lovely picture. Europe's pictures influenced him enormously, and he is beginning a new phase of work. It is a joy to see him work. He seems very happy here, now. But somehow for me it is so *sad* here. [. . .]

so-called editor: Robert Linscott.
Spain: In a Farther Country.
Frau Schnack: Elisabeth Schnack (b. 1899). She became Goyen's German translator because of Curtius's incapacitation.
Fischer: Fischer Bücherei, a publishing firm in Frankfurt and Hamburg. It published *In a Farther Country* under the title *Im fernsten Land* (1957).

To Maurice Edgar Coindreau
TLS-2

P.O. Box 17
El Prado (Taos County), New Mexico
September 27, 1954

My dear Maurice:

Autumn is out here and all the wasps are singing about it, lazy in this smokey landscape where the mountaintops are golden; always the wind blows, too, and the season is gently turning. Sad, again, some gentle sorrow over this landscape and over me; but what joy, for me, in *Spain* that is rapidly coming to its end. I long to show it to you, and I hope that will happen within the next two months. Also, I have finished the two stories written during my stay abroad and I am sending them both to you *herewith*.

You are home again, where your own garden is suffering autumn, and already you are back at your classes. I want you to have a good beginning again, and all my wishes are for further and further fulfillment for you, dearest Maurice.

After a series of letters to Random House, I finally, and to my regret, after having falsely accused her, absolved Mme. Strassova. It was Random House, who dug around, while writing me that there were no funds for me there, and found the money. Then they wrote that they had been holding it—since May—in order to find out what it was for! It amounted to a little over $60, but was a fortune to me. Dear Maurice, I am determined to find another publisher. I have no contract with Random House, owe them not one cent. Can you help me find a good publisher, one who will respect and trust my work and stay with me until I am an old, gray man? I don't know where to turn or whom to ask to help; maybe you can. If I were to sell *Half a Look of Cain* to another American publisher, then I should have to, by Random House's stipulation, refund to them the advance they paid to me. But when I do sell *Half a Look of Cain* to an American publisher, it will be somewhat of a different book. That will be done after *Spain* is finished. I have no agent and fear them. They always, in the past, just got me into a lot of trouble and seemed only to complicate my literary affairs, taking great pieces of money meanwhile. What you suggest about getting rid of Strassova I wholeheartedly agree with, and your help in getting shed of her I'll appreciate enormously. But the important thing, now, is to find a right and good publisher, and you just might be able to help me. My relations with Mr. Linscott at R.H. have been so strained and he is so negative, I must be free and start again. Thank you for any help or advice, Maurice. [. . .]

---

two stories: "Old Wildwood" and "A People of Grass."

To William M. Hart
ALS-2

P.O. Box 17
El Prado, New Mexico
October 10, 1954

My dear Billy:

I want to say something to you—without having to write it—I can only speak with you, letters are nothing. It is so beautiful here now, somehow so sad. I walked this morning through those mysterious fields that lie out beyond this house and which I rarely go into because I keep them a secret and very personal—and there *are* frightening things in them, I am a little afraid of them. They are love-fields where often at night I see the dark shadows of cars parked there. Everything there, now, is going to seed . . . but I believe, from my window, that at one time or another I have seen *everything* there in the fields.

No one knows the despair of work but the worker—and one must not speak too much of it. To work after the secrets and terrors of nature, to repeat nature, to be involved in it, is a tragic involvement, much as the glorious involvement in human nature: that is the unalterable condition of one's life. I have been lately in a profound anguish, but when this work is finished I shall have forgotten it, so one must not speak too much of it. I hope by Christmastime I shall have put it safe in that place—like a high shelf—one is half-content, half [words missing] when one, alas, leaves the instrument that has dealt him such a bitter blow at the heart. [. . .]

But this is far away. In the meantime, Joe is having—tomorrow—a little cement-block workroom built for me. If it becomes a reality, it will be a blessing for me. I need a little dark place so badly. [. . .]

---

when this work is finished: In a Farther Country.

To David McDowell
TLS-2

P.O. Box 17
El Prado, New Mexico
November 8, 1954

Dear Friend Dave:
Greetings and I hope everything is well and progressing with you. I write to you to ask your advice, if you can give it, and your help if you won't cause complications or embarrassments. I've finished a fourth book, a novel called *Artifices of Spain,* and I don't know where in hell to send it or even how to go about showing it. After these two years of silence and hard work, with peace and daily work far away from the mill, I've got the disputed novel *Half a Look of Cain* into, or nearly so, shape, and have it to offer along with the new novel. With these two books I'd like to find an editor who looks one in the face, who is not so uncertain of himself as to be relied upon in the way of opinion. I cannot, in all honesty, continue my old relationship, you know—for it was and still is negative, too complicated for simple work, has some pall of death over it; I have to reject that, Dave.

But how to move or where to go is beyond me—I have no agent, am alone (and like it), need some friendly advice. Perhaps it is not very ethical to draw you in this, I don't mean to do that at all: if that is the case, you must of course simply write to me and tell me so. But if you can freely speak to me about the situation—i.e., some publishing house to submit my work to, to make a fresh and strong beginning—and there to stay, I hope, for the rest of my writing time—you'd help me more than I can tell you. I don't want to run hastily into a bad situation somewhere else; but as I am so far from it all, I don't know about houses and editors anymore—nor agents.

Thank you sincerely for what you can say to me—and if you find it unfeasible to involve yourself in this (What *is* it? I still don't know precisely what happened, except that there was such an orneriness about—something—that I figured it best to pull away and clean out my own brains and go on working, which is the simple point, anyway)—just tell me so. I wish you well, and my best to your family.

Ever—
Bill Goyen

David McDowell: Editor at Random House.
Artifices of Spain: Working title of *In a Farther Country*.

To Ilse and Ernst Robert Curtius
TLS-1

P.O. Box 17
El Prado, New Mexico
November 14, 1954

Beloved Ilse and Ernst:
   There you are in Rome! I am so happy for you, that you will have a sunny winter of fountains and beautiful people. I had your little letters yesterday and it means very much to me to hear from you. [. . .]
   Dearest Ernst, you said so many beautiful things to me! I hadn't the slightest feeling that you were silent—so there; there are many ways of talking and often the least communicative is that one that uses words. The wonderful conversations we had; I am forever grateful for them. And bright smiling Ilse—a memory. I love you both so dearly and want you to be safe and merry and faithful.
   Ernst—do you think it possible that I might get some translator's commission from Bollingen; I am apt at French and might translate some poet or poet's journal or little novel, or the like; I must have some way of earning money; I have none; in that way I should not have to take a job but could go on with my own work and the other, too. What do you think of this? Do you think Mr. Wolf would help? When you told me you were working on Valéry, that pleased me, for he is a very great mind and needs your mind. [. . .]

---

you were silent: Reference to Curtius's muteness during Goyen's visit in Flimsdorf, Switzerland.

Bollingen: The Bollingen Foundation, established in 1948, administers a prize in both poetry and translation.
Mr. Wolf: Kurt Wolf (1887–1963). He and his wife, Helen Wolf, were American publishers of European authors.

To David McDowell
TLS-2

P.O. Box 17
El Prado, New Mexico
Nov. 16, 1954

Dear Dave:

Your letter yesterday and many thanks for what you've done there; this may change the whole unhappy situation and simplify it to what it ought always to have been: a matter of a writer working in confidence. It would make me happy, indeed, to work along with you—there is so much ahead—and I believe many worthy things will happen.

So I send along, under this letter, the manuscript of *Artifices of Spain* to begin with. I think it better to have you have a look at this one first, then follow with *Half a Look of Cain*. The latter is a big work and one which I am eager to show you; the little novel enclosed is of a different caliber, but a big one, too, I believe. Anyway, less said at this point the better, for I dislike talking too much about what is written before it is read. We can talk together after you've read *Artifices of Spain*, for I hope I can manage to come to New York shortly for a few weeks—I need to clear up a lot of sort of backwash, talk to you about a number of affairs of business and just generally take a fresh foot with you and Random House. It's been a long solitary time in which I've battled for the kind of freedom every writer must have—inside—but in the meantime business things (France, particularly) have tangled up, and I'm no good at any of that. If I can borrow the money around here, I'll come shortly and to stay a few weeks. By then, perhaps, you can have found time to read *Artifices of Spain* and we can discuss it, *Half a Look of Cain* which I'll bring along, and other affairs. It would be a fine pleasure to see you and talk again, Dave.

Thank you, again, heartily, for your good help and I feel genuinely that this will be a strong and profitable beginning. I wish you well, as always, and thank you for your confidence.

Yours,
Bill

P.S. Dave, I forgot to mention above that last week, after many letters of interest in my work from Little, Brown, about whom I know nothing except that an Associate Editor there named Seymour Lawrence has shown through the past year a gratifying enthusiasm for my work, I sent a copy of *Artifices of Spain* to same. I've in no way committed myself—how could I—but I was free and broke and wanted to see what they'd think. This shouldn't interfere with anything, I believe. I can either recall the manuscript, or just let it go, whatever you think. Let me know if you feel I should make some move . . .

---

what you've done there: McDowell had arranged to take Robert Linscott's place as Goyen's editor at Random House.

To Ernst Robert Curtius
TLS-1

172 East 96th St.
New York 28, N.Y.
March 10, 1955

My dearest Ernst:

How are you and Ilse? I think of you all the time and love you dearly. I hope and pray you are well and warm and happy there. I am all right, it is a struggle hand-to-hand, like a war; but when has it not been so? My head is above water, just barely, but I am *here* and loving you there.

I am making application for a Rockefeller Grant which would enable me to go on writing for another year—a novel. I need a letter from you speaking of my work and recommending me. These letters are embarrassing, but alas one must have them. Do you think you could write such a letter to Mr. Paul Engle, State University of Iowa, Iowa City, Iowa, right away? I hope this won't put a hardship on you, dear Ernst. And let's hope and pray I get this—though I am skeptical. Still, one must try.

Soon I shall send you and Ilse the little Romance which Random House will publish in July or August. It is called *In a Farther Country*. It is both merry and sad, I believe; and I do hope you take to it. I have re-worked *Half a Look of Cain* and think to show it to a publishing house here called Criterion Books—they are new and have written to me about this book. I must wait, however, and go along slowly. It is all so slow, but that is the right way, I believe.

Do you work much? Tell me about yourselves, please; for I miss hearing from you. I am all right, so long as I can do my work. [. . .]

---

172 East 96th St.: Goyen had left Taos to reside in Manhattan once again.
a Rockefeller Grant: His application was denied.

To Margo Jones and Greer Johnson
ALS-2

172 East 96th St.
New York, New York
June 15, 1955

Dearest Margo, Dear Greer:
   It makes me sad not to be with you from the moment it all began there—to see it come alive and grow—but I hope I haven't put a burden of concern on you by bringing my poor problems into a beautiful and excited time. Forgive me if I have. Forget my worries and do your fine work and I'll try to come when I can make it. I had hoped it would be otherwise—but it isn't, so let's go on from here. You know my mind and heart are with you. From two such fine and talented people something lovely and worthy will come—and I only hope I can be there to see it alive and before my eyes. This is a thrilling and challenging time for you, Greer, and I know of no better one in the world to share such a time with, to *participate* in such a time with, than beloved Margo. Together you will make us all very happy and move us and charm us. Bless you both. I'm with you and believe in you. This good thing that is happening makes everything all right, the worry over work that does not come alive, the long waiting to come, within one's self, to what is one's own. There is no living to be got from poetry, but the fullest life, and the loveliest, is there.
   I am sad not to be there—but I will not be downhearted as one might be. Under any other conditions, I would borrow money to get there, but I have borrowed myself into such debt that I cannot do it again. *Something will happen soon!* I know it and I count on it. Relieve yourselves of this problem of mine and give everything to the beautiful work at hand; and forgive me for not being there with you now. I'm with you in every other way. Be happy—and believing! Soon—someway—

Love to you,
Bill

and hello to Little Pigeon, Sister Sammye, and Old Mrs. Woman.

---

come alive and grow: Whisper to Me had opened in Dallas in May 1955, directed by
Margo Jones, and at the Players Theatre in Manhattan November 21 of the same year.
The Manhattan version was directed by Marvella Cisney and starred Ruth White,
Dorothy Sands, and Mary Finney.
Little Pigeon, Sister Sammye, and Old Mrs. Woman: Characters in the play.

To Mr. and Mrs. Ramsey Burch
Telegram-1

WESTERN UNION
NEW YORK, NEW YORK
JULY 25, 1955

DEAR VI AND RAMSEY MY HEART IS BROKEN THAT I AM NOT THERE WITH YOU
ALL BUT MY THOUGHTS AND MY PRAYERS ARE WITH YOU AND WE KNOW THAT
MARGO HAS JOINED THE LAST HOUSEHOLD AND THE LONGEST LASTING SHE
LIVES ON IN US SAY GOODBY TO HER FOR ME GOD BLESS YOU+ BILLY.

Mr. and Mrs. Ramsey Burch: Ramsey Burch was an associate director and actor in
Jones's theatre, and Violet Burch was Jones's personal assistant.
My heart is broken: Margo Jones died on July 24, 1955, of accidental carbon tetrachlo-
ride poisoning, the result of chemicals used by a professional cleaning service in her
apartment. See Helen Sheehy's *Margo: The Life and Theatre of Margo Jones* (Dallas:
Southern Methodist University Press, 1989), p. 299.

To Robert Ernst Curtius
ALS-1

172 East 96th St.
New York, New York
December 5, 1955

My dearest Ernst:
  I am happy you like Elisabeth Schnack's translation of *Ghost and
Flesh*—I've not seen it. She is a sensitive woman and she has worked hard
on this book. She is now gathering eight stories of mine to make a small

volume for Suhrkamp—to be published in Spring. I do desperately want
to be free of Schifferli; have tried all these months. But he kept fighting
to keep my work, and my American publishers gave *In a Farther Country*
to him. But that is the last. I now hope Suhrkamp will take over my work.

Nothing happens to my work in America. How could it, where there is
nothing but television and millionaire best-selling authors who write
quickly and stupidly? There is no writing life in America now—no serious
writers—a few with some talent, but they are not read. Nevertheless, I do
my work, and wait, and endure. I am teaching one class at a university
here—I do not care for teaching, but it helps. Do please send your book
of essays to me. Are you well? At peace? Is Ilse, dear Ilse, well? I love you
both—I wish I could be near you. I think of you in my heart. Joe sends
love to you. Think of me as struggling to work and to endure. Please send
me news of yourselves.

Love as always,
Bill

---

a small volume for Suhrkamp: It was *Zamour und andere Erzählungen*, published by
Bibliothek Suhrkamp (1956).
teaching one class: At the New School for Social Research.
your book of essays: Kritische Essays zur Europäische Literatur (A. Francke, 1960).

To Charles Provine Goyen
TLS-1

172 East 96th Street
New York N.Y.
Jan. 8, 1956

My dearest Dad:

Well, we're in the New Year and I hope it's a good one for us all. I
intend to make it one and I think the prospects are good. I am in pretty
good shape except for one thing that's worrying the hell out of me and
that's the damned dentist bill which is just about a year old and I can't
manage to whittle it down much, although I pay him a few dollars when I
can. The original bill was $225 and I've got it down to a little more than
$100 and now he is getting impatient. I've got to get that thing paid off
and don't see how I can in the near future. It would take a great load off

me if I can get him paid, or a good portion of it, anyway. Naturally he wants his money and has been patient all these months. I wonder if you could help me get this thing out of the way, either by borrowing some for me or lending me some until I could repay you? I hate asking you when you have doctor and dentist bills of your own. I can manage with what the New School pays me for teaching, but I can't find much left over after rent and food to pay back such a big bill; there is just nothing left. I keep hoping I can sell a story and that would take care of it, but so far nothing has broken. If you could help me a little towards this damned thing, then I could repay you and satisfy the dentist. Don't be upset if you can't, please Dad, it wouldn't put any more hardship on me than I've had; but it would relieve me so much if I could get this bill paid and then get a kind of clean start. Surely I'll make more money this year, and I must, somehow. The Random House payments are over—the advance on my new book—they stopped with the last one as of Jan. 1. But my salary from the New School will cover that, so I won't be without some income, just enough to pay for food and rent bills. I'm trying to associate myself with a new agent and she has three stories, but so far she hasn't sold anything. Still, I know something will break, and I am working hard towards that. I do some book reviewing for $20 here and $50 there, but that's not steady; when it comes there's always a bill to pay with it. I am well and happy and not going to worry over things, let come what will and do my best. If this worries you or puts you in a spot, just tell me and that's all there is to it. God knows it would relieve me if I could get this man paid and forget him.

I want you to be well and take care of yourself and Mom. I hope I can see you all in the Spring, somehow. Keep writing and take care of yourself and don't worry over me. Thank God I have you and I love you dearly. Let me know about this and please don't get upset with it. Nothing is going to happen if it doesn't work out. God bless you Dad, for everything. Give my love to all.

Bill

---

a new agent: Phyllis Jackson.
some book reviewing: In 1955 Goyen published five book reviews in the *New York Times Book Review*. But in 1956, the year of this letter, he published only one.

To John A. S. Cushman
TLS-1

645 West End Avenue
New York, New York
March 10, 1956

Dear John:

I'm in trouble with so many old women this morning. Yesterday's mail brought me two unhappy letters from a furious Elisabeth Schnack (Zürich) about the Suhrkamp situation. Never mind, we are on the right track and are doing what has to be done. She will see this, in the end. (She is the translator, you remember, of the book of stories at Suhrkamp. She doesn't like Mohwrenwitz, but this is confidential, please.)

The other letter is an outraged one from Princess Caetani, enclosing a check for $200 as payment for "A People of Grass" which, she says in trembling handwriting, will appear in the April issue. She loathes agents, rebukes me for putting one after her, says she thought we were friends, that she had never had any mention of fee for the story from me; goes on to say I am a scoundrel for wanting money for my stories, etc. Well, I am now in disrepute in both Paris and Zürich, not to mention Rome. Never mind, again, the payment, though less than what I had specifically asked by letter many months ago (by $50), is here; and now I want to surrender my fee to your agent in Rome as soon as possible. Will you, then, please, tell me at once what it amounts to and I'll get it to you. Thank you for this prompt help. This curious feeling of literary editors about paying authors has always stumped me, ended by upsetting me. I hope I'm not going to get the reputation of being a money-minded author. It certainly has all been in the *mind*, so far as I am concerned, so far. Thank you for helping to bring it down to a more tangible area where one can get hold of it.

I hope the Virus didn't get you—but then if it didn't, the Law did, alas. I'm off to the University of North Carolina where I've been invited to sit at some Writers-Students Conference this Friday, Saturday. I'll hear from you before then. Again, my sincere thanks for this and all other help.

Cordially,
Bill Goyen

David McDowell will speak to Donald Klopfer at Random House about the reversion of rights to *The House of Breath*. I hope we can find someone interested in reprinting with certain abridgements—or without. I'll speak soon to you about this. He suggested I talk with Frank Taylor at Dell about this; but then I'm no good at that and I need your help. Frank is an old friend.

John A. S. Cushman: Of the Translation Rights Department of Curtis Brown, Ltd., which was briefly Goyen's agent.
Mohwrenwitz: unidentified.
Princess Caetani: Marguerite Chapin.
my fee to your agent: Curtis Brown took a $20 commission on the story.
the Law did: Cushman had been called for jury duty.
certain abridgements: Goyen's own leather-bound copy of *The House of Breath*, given to him in Rome on his birthday, April 24, 1954, by Joe Glasco, was later given by Goyen to Robert Phillips. This copy has many cuts and deletions made in Goyen's hand for public readings.

To John A. S. Cushman
TLS-2

645 West End Ave.
New York 25, N.Y.
March 18, 1956

Dear John:

Well, I'm back, and exhausted; but it was very rewarding. I'm lucky to have got back, what with this terrible weather—but we made it.

I found your two letters here, and I thank you for them. I had, some months ago, gone through the rigors of debate over Arche Verlag and Suhrkamp, and, having no literary representative, took the advice and suggestions of Prof. Curtius and Frau Schnack. I found Suhrkamp to be a distinguished firm. I have met and dealt with Schifferli at Arche and dislike him, distrust him: this is from personal experience. I believe it is known that Mohbrooks and the others favor Schifferli and work with him. I therefore, after your consideration and with your approval, think we ought to go on with Suhrkamp. I'd feel hesitant if you didn't agree with me. You do, don't you? I found that Arche had not "made very big efforts to introduce this author to German speaking public" as the agent's letter states; and I know that Prof. Curtius and I worked together on the translation of *The House of Breath* independently, without any use of agent or publisher. It was, indeed, Curtius who took the manuscript (in translation) to Schifferli. I, therefore, do not feel it a "matter of fairness to give the first opportunity to publish the stories to Schifferli" (Arche). Am I being unfair? Schifferli still has two books of mine to publish and the translation of them has not even begun. He would only shelve the stories and let them wait.

As for *Half a Look of Cain*, I don't understand how or on what grounds these gents "told Schifferli about the changes the author will make." I am not yet sure of them myself! The agreement on *Half a Look of Cain* was made between Schifferli and myself in his office; the novel belonged to no one but me. I am, as you know, making revisions on *Half a Look of Cain* and will submit the manuscript to you shortly.

Forgive it all for being so complicated; but I feel Schifferli's hand in this again, as I expected. Still, we had to go through this in order to confirm and clarify all this. Thank you sincerely for the help. Now, and *only* if you approve and are with me in it, we can go ahead at once and ask Suhrkamp for the contract and the advance, and let them proceed with publishing the stories—which they have, ready for galleys, in their hands. Mrs. Schnack is a wonderful woman and her anger was directed against agents, all agents, because, as our Princess feels, "they take money, they don't earn and are generally suspicious." Oh my.

I'm in the process of getting reversion rights on *The House of Breath*. McDowell says they are mine if I wish them. Should you talk with him, or what should I do? I plan to revise and abridge a bit, particularly the parentheticality and maybe some little rearrangement of the first thirty pages. McDowell agrees to this. Now I hear that *Ghost and Flesh* is about to go out of print. Maybe we can meet and talk about this—it seems so lengthy and complicated on paper. I hope I'm not taking too much of your mind and time. I know you're crowded with back work. Thanks for what you can do and whenever you can do it.

Cordially,
Bill Goyen

I'm back: From a writers' conference at the University of North Carolina.
the stories: Zamour und andere Erzählungen.
our Princess: Princess Caetani.
McDowell: David McDowell.

To Dorothy Brett
TLS-2

New York
Feb. 14, 1957

My dear Brett:

The long silence has meant a mean stretch of work that almost wrecked me—ended with a siege of what turned out to be muscle spasms in the back and chest, a little frightening but quickly over. But I finished the little play and it is going to be produced! What excitement. It will be called *A Ballad for the Theatre* and will be done in the Circle in the Square Theatre here, the very best off-Broadway theatre, all very gifted people. There are little songs which I have written—wrote a long time ago on that old piano out there—and I hope it will be magical and lovely. We begin casting and rehearsals next week and should get it on the boards a little after March 15. I'll let you know exactly when we decide on the date. Joe and I are very excited. There's very little money involved at the outset; but if it goes well, many things might happen. The point is to do a fine job and all other things will follow. I am exhausted, but ready to go on. I'll send particulars as they develop. Something nice might happen. It is my very first play and I'm very proud, for I've always wanted to write for the theatre, to hell with books for awhile.

Joe is finishing what must be a gigantic canvas which he won't let me see, yet. His studio has proved not too successful—all the gloomy trek on the subway in snow and filth. But he'll last it out until spring, then we'll see what to do. It's so tiresome having no money, squinching and pinching and worrying—in the country it's not so demoralizing; but in the city it's too depressing and too stark a struggle. Still, there is something I must get done here and I cannot leave it until I see that through. Then to hell with it. [. . .]

A Ballad of the Theatre: An early title for *The House of Breath* on stage.

To Dorothy Brett
TLS-2

New York
March 3, 1957

My dear Brett:

   The hectic life goes on, with promise of being even more so. Still, it is all very exciting and things are going well. We are interviewing actors and actresses and will go on this week, hoping to have cast the play by the end of the week, then go into rehearsal. The play will have its first performance either on April 1 or April 8, not sure yet. Will let you know. What a thrill! Just hope it is something beautiful and magical. It's a grueling thing to read the actors; poor things, they have a tough life, but they are, generally, very nice people and full of pep and ambition, if not always talent! The old ones are a little talkative and we have had some Loulous. One came in to read the part of an old woman, promptly took out her teeth, flung off her shoes and proceeded! Another man removed his hairpiece to show us he could play older parts. Poor things, they'll do anything to get their jobs. Joe is designing and building the most fragile and beautiful set and his sketches for the costumes have everyone ravished. So we should have something lovely—or who knows? Anyway, we are both full of excitement and working long hours, quite nervous and very hopeful. The theatre is the best little theatre in New York, by far the most distinguished one—the Circle in the Square. So keep your fingers crossed, for heaven's sakes. Don't know whether there'll be any money in it, but if it's good, then everything will follow. Anyway, it's a beginning in the theatre, what I've always wanted. [. . .]

   Our fat landlady comes in in the evenings to charm and delight us with long monologues, she is my next book without doubt. She's a dear thing, but a hellion, a real Fury, something of another world; she has had many lives and done terrible things in them, I feel, and this one is the one that will catch her. I wish I could save her, but who can? I must tell you all about her this summer. Soon we must make some kind of summer plan. Money *must* come, we have only pennies—and a stack of bills. But it will change, I know; keep holding out. [. . .]

---

fat landlady: Unidentified by name. Some years later, Goyen intended to make her one of his *Six Women* in the proposed book by that title. The others were Frieda Lawrence, Margo Jones, Katherine Anne Porter, Dorothy Brett, and Millicent Rogers. Rogers was a close friend of both Frieda Lawrence and Dorothy Brett and lived nearby in a large house at Ranchitos. The Millicent Rogers Museum in Taos today holds her extensive collection of Indian art, artifacts, and crafts. After Goyen dropped his former landlady from the projected book, he added Mabel Dodge Luhan.

To Alan Collins
TLS-1

224 Riverside Drive
New York 25, N.Y.
March 24, 1957

Dear Alan:

Many thanks to you for your solid help and support in all this theatre business. It is coming along, to my mind, astonishingly well and I feel, skeptical as I generally am about these things—and afraid, too—that it might be something pretty exciting, this play. Quintero is still charming and aloof and success-shocked, but I have a feeling he will come around, if only it's not too late. There's still no word in the papers of the opening date or anything else about this play, and it is two weeks before opening. Ted Mann comes back tomorrow from Puerto Rico so maybe we can put a hot poker to him.

It would make me happy if you'd get those New York film people you mentioned to see the play. Do please, Alan—I'll get them seats if you'll let me know. I want you to see one of the two previews on Saturday or Sunday afternoon, April 6 and 7—or, if you'd prefer, on opening night. Please let me know which and how many tickets, and I'll get them for you immediately. To my astonishment I learned yesterday that not many seats are left for opening night, and I want certain people there above all others.

Another thing I'm concerned about is getting the critics there—Atkinson, Kerr *et al.* Would hate to have the second string. What can I do about this? Quintero ought to help, but we have to hurry up. Can you help or advise? This is the time to do it, now.

Thanks for the note to Loomis at Random House. I'll send the manuscript of *Zamour* shortly.

We are working to make this a first-rate production and I believe it will be; and we've resigned ourselves to having to work without the real support of the producers there. I've written another scene, so that now the play runs just about full-length, with intermission, two-act-wise. I've also strengthened and pruned and tightened the whole thing, out of rehearsals, so that a lot of my fears are gone. I think the play is strange, beautiful—but what playwright doesn't? Please stay with me, for I have strong hunches, and I thank you with all my heart for your help, Alan. I'll keep in touch. I'm at the theatre most of the day—CH 3-5646.

Yours,
Bill

Alan Collins: An agent at Curtis Brown, Ltd.
Quintero: José Quintero (b. 1924). He had directed Geraldine Page (1924–1987) in *Summer and Smoke* in the Circle-in-the-Square production in 1952.
Ted Mann: (Né Goldmann, b. 1924). Brooklyn lawyer and producer who, with Quintero, founded in 1951 the Loft Players at Circle-in-the-Square, a small theatre at 5 Sheridan Square in Greenwich Village.
Atkinson: Brooks Atkinson (b. 1894). *New York Times* theatre critic.
Kerr: Walter Kerr (b. 1913). At this time, theatre critic for the *New York Herald-Tribune*. He was later to join the *New York Times*.
Zamour: German title for the book Random House would later publish as *The Faces of Blood Kindred*.

To Charles Provine Goyen
ALS-1

Wed., March 27, 1957

My dear Dad:

    I am all right but very very tired. I feel I am on the verge of something firm—and I hope to God that it comes off. In the meantime, I simply cannot go on like this, without a penny and depending on Joe to lend me money. You must try to help me, if you have to borrow it—I hope I can pay it back. I have nothing—and at a time when I need it badly, very badly. Please borrow $100 for me, Dad, and help me through these bad weeks. I wouldn't write this to you if I weren't desperate. I am so tired, to my bones, of being dependent and broke. How much longer will it last, I wonder? Help me now and I hope I can repay you soon—or let me pay back the loan a little a month. Maybe something wonderful will happen on April 8. Thank you with all my heart—it kills me to have to do this. God bless you, I love you all,

Bill

April 8: The opening night of Goyen's play *The House of Breath*.

To Anaïs Nin
ALS-1

*[224 Riverside Drive
New York 25, N.Y.]
April 1957*

Dear Anaïs:
    My play *House of Breath* (imagine!) opens at the Circle in the Square
April 8. Please come. I need you there. And call the theatre at once to
make reservations because to my astonishment there are only a few left. I
must have you there. If you have any difficulty ask for me at the theatre. I
am beside myself with anxiety and tension—it might be beautiful—if *only*.
I'd love Jim to come too—all of you. But your face I need. More later.
Where am I?

Bill

Anaïs Nin: French-born novelist (1903–1977), whose true lifework was an enormous
diary, edited in many volumes by Gunther Stuhlmann.
Jim: James Leo Herlihy (1927–1993). Detroit-born novelist and playwright, who
dedicated his first book of fiction, *The Sleep of Baby Filbertson* (1959), to Nin.
Where am I?: In her diary, Nin records having called Goyen after receiving this note,
and he was sick in bed. He told her, "I have been under such a great strain, the usual
strain of putting on a play, besides my other anxieties." But the play was a great
success. Nin called it "a bit of magic, poetry and subtle levels of feeling . . . It seeks a
free form for the theatre, an impressionism. Goyen calls it a ballad. A very moving
theme. Seeking escape from home, parents, and never quite making it, even though in
this case the home is death and stagnation . . . It was beautifully cast; because of the
young actors' respect for him, he obtained the best of them" (*The Diary of Anaïs Nin*,
vol. 6, 1955–1966, ed. and with a preface by Gunther Stuhlmann [New York: Harcourt
Brace Jovanovich, 1977], p. 80).

To Dorothy Brett
TLS-2

*New York
April 30, 1957*

My dear Brett:
    You must forgive us for not writing. Have been in a whirlwind around

the play, full of chicanery and deceit, etc. I have been and still am *exhausted*, ill and confused. I have had to try to stay quiet, although I've found that impossible. There is too much to be told now and, besides, I don't know the whole story yet. A lot is happening and many good things might come about; but I am stone broke and tired, trying to get through the last weeks of teaching, to make plans for summer, etc. A fine producer, no doubt the finest in New York theatre, has asked me to write a play for the fall, agents are involved and quibbling, I am waiting. If this goes through, then I must be near agent and producer this summer—but where? I cannot bear to stay in the city, it would kill me. There is no money and when it comes in it may not be very much. So I am in this quandary. Please be patient with me until I work it all out. Because I am so tired and beaten up, I can't make decisions very fast—too, any decision is dependent upon others. I'll be all right, but it will take a little time. The play is absolutely beautiful and astonishing; there is talk everywhere about it. The theatre closed it last Sunday; a furor is going on around it. Such a shock to work so long and hard, sacrificing everything, then lose it all so suddenly. We have all been stunned and a little crazy. So many mysteries and confusions. I am depressed and tired. Never mind, I did something and gave everything I had to it, so did Joe. I need a rest, and food, to collect myself and clear my mind. I made $57. on a play that should have made me ten times as much. Oh well, this is New York, and it is a nightmare where nobody knows what is true and what isn't. I am *not* embittered, just tired and confused, and that will pass. [. . .]

A fine producer: Unidentified.

SIX

*Erwinna, Pa.
September 30, 1957*

My dearest Mom and Dad:

Have just talked to you and want to tell you what I am doing. I was called out to Hollywood to write a long ballad for Burl Ives to sing at the beginning of a picture and at the end. The picture is called *The Left-Handed Gun* and is about Billy the Kid. I think I did a good job and they all liked it. I worked very hard on it and of course got there right in the middle of a big fight between the producer and the director of the film, as I generally do, and it wasn't very pleasant. But I did my work and it was successful. The picture was already finished and all the money was spent, so they paid me only $1000, but it was fifty thousand in experience. I met many film producers and made many contacts that will bring results, I know. My own producer was eager for me to work with him again and I am sure that I'll get some kind of picture assignment sooner or later. I was called out right in the middle of my play for Broadway, so had to interrupt it, but it was worth it. Now I am back at that and hope to finish it within another month or two. Then, I am working on the *Playhouse 90* play, too. These are keeping me busy every minute. I have such a good agent, a wonderful woman, and she is right behind me. I am sure this is all leading up to some fine work that will make me some good money, so don't be impatient, just have confidence. The work is slow and very hard, takes every minute, but it will be worth it. It was the moving that got me, because I came back right into the middle of moving. We are in a very nice old country house in a quiet little village and both Joe and I love it. I have to go to New York often on the train, but that isn't far. Thank goodness I'm not teaching, will try to make it without teaching. All my students are writing to me begging me to come back, but I am through with that. I am sure all this work will bring something good. In Hollywood I worked day and night in my hotel room and in the studio at Warner Brothers where the film was being cut. I really got to know all about the picture business and am fascinated with it, want to write a film. So I am at present working on television, movies, and plays, and something ought to develop. Just be patient and stay with me, for I know something fine is coming. [...]

Erwinna, Pa.: Goyen had just moved to Bucks County, Pennsylvania.
Playhouse 90 play: Unidentified.
a good agent: Audrey Wood (1905–1985), who handled Goyen's theatrical properties at International Famous Agency. She suffered a stroke in 1981 and remained in a coma until her death in 1985.
old country house: Goyen shared the house with Joe Glasco.

To Dorothy Brett
TLS-2

Erwinna, Pa.
October 27, 1957

My dearest Brett:

Such a whirl, again, that I am dizzy from it all, half the time in the city running and talking about all this business, and the other half working out here in the beautiful countryside. Things are shaping up, now, and soon I should be able to settle down on a full working schedule out here and not have to run to the city so often. The play is by no means "off," what a strange word people get about one's business so far away. The play has never been shown to the producers, as a matter of fact, and is still in the oven, cooking slowly. I have great hopes for it. In the meantime I have developed my first film and am about, I hope, to sign a contract for it in a few weeks. I shall then be working on the play and the screenplay by March or April. It's all very exciting, except as yet little money has come from it, but it will, in time. It is a slow pull, slowly uphill, but more and more promising.

We are very happy in this good old house, comfortable and clean. The autumn has been beautiful, but today it is very cold and we've had snow flurries. We both love this country and love living out here—it's a good solution to the New York problem. It's exhausting to go into that city and one comes back a wreck, but alas we both have to do it. I just might make a little money for the first time in my life, but I am going about it care- fully. I have found that those who make the most money in the entertain- ment world have the least of everything, including money—they are terrified; they are constantly talking poor mouths; I find most of them the most arrogant, tiresome, hysterical phonies I have ever met; I have knocked some of them down. But there are a few wonderful people here and there in the profession, and I believe I am working with those. The rest is unbelievable, enormous profits, embarrassing work, misery, insecurity—I'd rather be dead. I have a fine agent, she is intelligent, wise, and believes in good things; she has already helped me enormously and there are many good things ahead, but I must move wisely and make the right choices. Our old car is puffing and huffing, limping on its last leg—another problem. Without a car out here we are dead ducks. One has to drive thirty-five minutes to the station. The tires are slick as the palm of your hand, too. [. . .]

Every year gets harder, it seems, and more and more I yearn to sit and work quietly. Once this real push and purge is over, I believe I shall be able to do that, if I can make a fair sum and control its uses—that's all I want. I am prodigiously in debt—it's huge, what I owe; but what the hell, I'll stall them and appease them a little, bit by bit, and if ever I make a few thousand dollars, then it will start, the pump will be primed. I have never seen such bad, sleazy plays as there are on Broadway this season. This encourages me. And I want to write this screenplay. These two pieces of work consume me, the books can wait—I've done enough of that for a while. Perhaps I shall do a few television plays, too, but I look at that medium with a dim eye, it is, to me, still silly and quite loathsome. You've no idea what those TV people are like. [. . .]

The play: The Diamond Rattler. Excerpts were published in *Mid-American Review* 13, no. 1 (1992).
my first film: The Left-Handed Gun, produced by Fred Coe (1914–1979), directed by Arthur Penn (b. 1922), and released by Warner Bros. in May 1958. The screenplay was originally written by Leslie Stevens, after a television play by Gore Vidal (*The Death of Billy the Kid*). Goyen revised the screenplay and wrote the lyrics for the ballad used in the score.

To Dorothy Brett
TLS-1

Erwinna, Pa.
Feb. 15, 1958

My dearest Brett:
   Your long letter today—plus the *map*, showing all the changes in our territory. I was glad to hear. First off, let me tell you that I had a bad day when I received your letter about your house—I was in a storm of unhappiness about it, then a time of sadness. I wrote you two different letters, then mailed the short note which you received. I see now that I was feeling a combination of disappointment and sorrow—sorrow for the

passing of old days that might never come again, disappointment in a path I had long since established within myself. What it was, was a giving up, I guess, of an old way and, by far, the most joyous, free and beautiful of any I have known since: life in that country, my beginning work, all our pranks and energies and hopes and promises to each other. I don't think you know how deeply I feel about those years out there, about all of you (though I go on neglecting my old first friends of my freedom after the war: Spud, Ruth Swayne, Dotty and Tom, and the rest—even Angie [somehow I cannot write to him, that is strange]). At any rate, dear Brett, I am through it, and of course you are right to say don't rush it, and you are right about the disposal of your house, which is, nevertheless, still quite sacred to me. I remember that I rushed out one night to it, knocked on the door, you opened it in your nightie and holding an oil lamp, to tell you I had sold my very first story in the world—and we had a celebration at Sagebrush Inn with two helpings of ice cream. It was you who brought the building of our house into materialization, you who were a sort of guiding spirit over my whole new way of life that has, believe it or not, changed very little. Naturally I associate it all with your house, with the land there. Well—your letter was a kind of ending of it all, as only I know. Enough for sentiment.

I can still see myself returning there one day, an old man with a cane, to finish my days on that desert and against that mountain. But alas it will be so much changed. I like it here, find it serene and peaceful, it is, as you say, right for my work, for Joe's work. If the dream house becomes possible, then we shall get it if we can—but the only thing is my work and the continuity of that. I therefore do think we ought to sell the little house and let it all go, alas, and let the sentiment go, or bury it—as one has to do, over and over again. I do cling to that house, still, and to that land, and will always, though I may never live there again. Nothing has ever been quite as real, since, let me tell you. In the meantime, do not be disturbed, your dream was quite right—dreams are, usually; I had been unhappy. What I ask you, now, is that you leave me some little something of yours that is *really* yours, something you love, something I remember, something that will always be Brett and the glorious days of the past to me. Thank you for this.

I am working night and day, Joe too. His show opens on March 10. I wish you could see it. Please be well and please stay here a long time, to see what in God's name happens to all this. I love it all, all that has been, all that is, and I look to what might be. When the right buyer for our house comes, snap him up. You are right about beginning with $12,000. We are having a terrific blizzard at the moment that is supposed to go on for another 24 hours. It has been zero or thereabouts for two weeks. But we are warm inside, thank God; the house is simple and cozy. I understand what you have done, and I am with you in it. Please be well. I send my love, Joe too, May too, and to Reggie. Write again—

Bill

---

about your house: Brett had decided to dispose of her house outside of Taos and move elsewhere. Frieda Lawrence had died in August 1956.
Ruth Swayne: Owner of a small dude ranch at Talpa, New Mexico.
Dotty and Tom: Neighbors Dorothy and Thomas Duncan Benrimo (1887–1958). He was an illustrator, art director, and set designer, particularly active in the 1910s. In New Mexico he refused to exhibit.
Angie: Angelo Ravagli.
the dream house: A green house in nearby Ottsville, Pennsylvania, into which he was soon to move.
sell the little house: Brett found a buyer, and Goyen did not return.
His show: At the Catherine Viviano Gallery in Manhattan. Goyen wrote text for the exhibition catalog, "The People of Joe Glasco," and used some of the text of this pamphlet in his story "The Rescue" (*Collected Stories*, pp. 266–267).
May: Glasco's dog.
Reggie: Brett's dog.

To Helen Merkel
TLS-1

Erwinna (Bucks County), Pa.
June 10, 1958

Dear Miss Merkel:

Enclosed is the contract with Einaudi for the Italian publication of *The House of Breath*. As you will remember, this was negotiated by Fabio Coen through me because of a telephone conversation with his wife (Mrs. Coen) who out of the blue, started all this. Mrs. Coen said she had been unable to determine the owner of the rights to the novel, that Curtis Brown did not "seem certain about it," that Random House seemed to feel I owned them, etc. I simplified it, as I informed you, by telling her to draw up the contracts and publish the book in Italy, that I own the rights and that you are my agents.

So here is the contract—quite dusty with age: and where is the money due, I wonder? They beat me, these foreign publishers; I'm depressed

with them; the handsome royalty forwarded recently from Suhrkamp
($3.94!) makes one detest the writing of books. Anyway . . . my gratitude
for taking this over and for helping as you can. Please give my warm
greetings to Alan; tell him I miss seeing him; and that I have just finished
my first screen play—an original for Fred Coe.

Sincerely,
Bill Goyen

Helen Merkel: Of the foreign rights department of Curtis Brown, Ltd.
Alan: Alan Collins of Curtis Brown, Ltd.

To Elia Kazan
AL-4

Ottsville, Pa.
July 8, 1959

Dear Elly,

There is, I believe, a firmness in Son—not written—do you see? I want
to talk to you about this and other points you make—I'd like to see Son
played firmly in the last act, up to the death of Little Sister. He is a strong
man—life has run all through him and over him: he must *show* this (on a
stage) rather than in vocalization, no? This is one of the touchstones of
the character and one of the deep problems in trying to create such a
character; and you have put your finger right on it. I am grateful for your
good honest responses—all to be considered seriously. Above all, I love
your *participation* in the work along with me.

I want the world of the play to be a non-violent one—as I want Son to
be a man rendered *sensitive* by life, made *humble* by life, made *strong* in
these ways by life—Of course I have written scenes of murder—earlier
the play ended with Pennie's and Linsie's destruction—by Pennie's hand.
But that's wrong—I don't believe it—there are other kinds of destruction—other signs that are deeper and more terrible than that of death—
no? Even David Bell's constant near-violence is always broken by tenderness, struggle with self—you can see I am writing *against* violence as a
way through the enormous and beautiful complexities of life—is that the
un-firmness you feel? I'm so dissatisfied with the ways through dilemmas
in plays—murder, suicide, castration, lynching—there is, to my mind,

always a play to *follow* the final curtain of such plays—resolution (moral), reconciliation, penance, redemption, etc. A quieter play follows—maybe that doesn't make theatre?

Linsie is not evil. It was *Son's* fault—or inability to take his life through her because of the tragic sense of sin—that they did not come to fulfillment together. All his life (the seven years away) he's been looking for one woman—Linsie—but a Linsie without the shackles of "Sin" on her. He was, essentially, in love with two women—carnality, piety (or "saintliness")—each woman robbed the other of Son (Pennie & Linsie)—but they did not destroy *him*. Stella Gaines died—she was *the woman* instead of *the two women*. How could Son *hate* Pennie? Her secret is not known to him. He comes to understand her—and can one hate understanding? One *accepts*—the area of gentleness again; not violence of emotion or act. Pennie has destroyed herself—Ace *has*, finally, answered her—through Son.

Son has recognized that he is free of both women—and we ought to feel that whatever he does now, will be done in freedom and in knowledge (of himself). He has "lost" everything, including his witness—but, as he says quietly, "I did it. I *did* it." That is, "I have broken through. I can go on." There are those who can go on and those who can't. The two women who "created" Son have destroyed each other—and their "creation" has saved himself—but cannot, alas, save them. Terrible! How could one hate them? Do violence to them? Only pity them. So then, in this light, the play is a revelation of two women through Son—no? *He* is the light cast on them, *he* is the lantern—

[unsigned]

Elia Kazan: (b. 1909). Stage and film director.

Ottsville: Goyen, with Joe Glasco, had moved to his second Bucks County house.

Son, Little Sister, Pennie, Linsie, Stella Gaines, Ace: Characters in Goyen's play *The Diamond Rattler*.

murder, suicide, castration, lynching: Goyen may have had in mind the conclusion of Tennessee Williams's *Sweet Bird of Youth*, which opened in New York on March 10, 1959, and was still running. In the last act the character Chance Wayne is castrated by a group of men.

Hotel Webster
40 West 45th Street
New York, 36, N.Y.
Dec. 19, 1959

Dear Jay—
    Greetings after so long a time. I wonder if you'd be interested in
reprinting two books of mine, long since out of print and whose rights I
have bought for myself some time ago from Random House. They are
The House of Breath and *Ghost and Flesh* (stories). They're still, from what I
hear, very much in demand and by this time sort of collectors' items. You
can have them if you want them. Could we talk about this? [. . .]

----

two books of mine: Laughlin did not reprint the books.

To Charles Provine Goyen
and Mary Inez Goyen
ALS-3

124 East 57th St.
New York 22, N.Y.
Feb. 4, 1960

My dear Mother and Dad:
    Guess Lis got away all right, and I know you all are blue, but try to
manage it and it will all be all right, in time, I know. Poor Lis, it will be
hard for her, but she's had a hard time anyway, and this looks like a
chance for everything to change. Once again, all we can do is have faith
and endure.
    I am doing my best to do just that. When I called you—or asked you
to call me the other day—I was ready to throw it all over and try to make
a new start. I've been afraid of ruining my health and my mind, for it has
gone on so long. Life is still young for me, although I'll be 45 this
spring—and a lot lies ahead, if I can only make the right move and find
my true way. It seemed to me that the right and best thing to do was to
break away and start fresh.

Now I have decided, after thinking about it and talking it over with my doctor—who is still helping me—to give it one more good, last try. She feels, along with me, that it would be giving up to turn my back on all these years, without giving it another try. So I will. I'll give myself three months. I'll go on to Boston and work on the play there and go ahead and try it out there. It is scheduled to open on April 5. Rehearsals are scheduled to begin on March 15. If it goes well there, then the future is opened up for me. If not—I'll have to make other plans. I'll go on teaching and doing my best to live on $200 a month, which has been impossible. But, as the doctor says, I've gone this far and somehow made it, so why not go another distance and see. I'm sure you'll agree with her and with me, although I know you'll be disappointed that I won't be coming right away. Thank you for making me feel welcome there and for always being with me. Life has been hell for the past two years, without any let-up; and it's amazing how much of a beating a human being can take. The easy thing would be to run away from it. But I believe I wouldn't respect myself in the end, if I did so. So I must keep struggling and fighting and doing all I can to come to what I've given my life to. Stay with me, if you can, and understand.

Please try to stay well and meet life as it comes, as I'm trying to. There's still happiness ahead, I know, if we can only find it. It does, I believe, lie in ourselves.

I'll let you know about the play. I'll give everything I have to it—after all, I've worked two years on it. Send me news, and please wait with me if you can. I'll try to come home in April, after the play opens. I've *got* to come through this, dearest Mother and Dad. I can't fail myself, above all. God bless you. Write me here.

Goodnight,
Bill

---

124 East 57th St.: Goyen and Glasco had left Bucks County and returned to Manhattan.
Feb. 4, 1960: Goyen's literary correspondence is very much reduced after this date.
Lis: Goyen's sister, also referred to in the letters as Kat. Her problems at the time of the letter are unidentified.
the play: The Diamond Rattler, produced in 1960 at the Charles Playhouse in Boston.
go on teaching: Goyen was still instructor of the novel, drama, and short story at the New School for Social Research.

To Doris Frankel
ALS-2

Hotel Avery
Washington and Avery Streets
Boston, Mass.
May 26, 1960

My Dearest Doris:
    What puzzles me—and the *puzzlement* is worth living—is how what one feels is beautiful and true can take another shape in the presence of *audience*. Some distortion occurs—and then what to believe in? At least something *living* has happened—is happening tonight again, on that stage in Boston, at this very moment. The lines torment me.
    There is so much to know—*worth a lifetime*—so little to give; and the beauty and wonder of life can never matter whatever the illusion one might have of any other. Isn't that right? The physical beauty of this world—which the stage can show us—is the great wonder, the unmatchable wonder—isn't that right?
    I love you, Doris, and I bear it—the haunting distortion—because you and those I love, do—

BILL

Doris Frankel: (d. 1994). Manhattan-based scriptwriter.

To Charles Provine Goyen
and Mary Inez Goyen
TLS-3

323 East 58th Street
New York City 22, N.Y.
February 5, 1961

Dearest Mother and Dad:
    At last am moved in and somewhat settled. It is very nice and I like it. I have my own floor and Joe has his above. So believe it will work out. [. . .]
    The television play will be on Sunday night, Feb. 19th at 9PM—General Electric Theatre. Please call me afterwards—will want to know

how you liked it. Since they've filmed it out in Hollywood, I have no idea what they've done to it, but they sent me a telegram that they liked it very much, and Joan Fontaine, the star, is here in New York now, and she said she liked doing it. Just wish the movies would buy it. They've asked me to do another one for them, and I certainly will. So things look much better. But don't want to get over-confident, just be grateful for things changing a bit.

Mom, please be patient and help yourself wherever you can. You've had enough on you to kill a horse, but you are strong and have good faith and must pull yourself up, the way I have, and Sis has, and all of us, Dad too. I know you will, know that it takes time, and patience, and faith. Please hold on, for all our sakes, and for yours. Don't write if you can't, but do call once in a while, if you're blue, and we can talk. Hope I can come home in late April or early May. School is out then and I really need to see you all and be there with you. So let's try to count on that.

Did you know I was invited to Kennedy's Inaugural Ball? Had an invitation from him, and was very flattered. Apparently he's interested in writers and wants them to support him. Of course I didn't go! What do you all think of him? I think it's good to have a young man and his young wife up there. [. . .]

---

television play: A Possibility of Oil (1961). Dramatic adaptation of the seventh chapter of *The House of Breath*, first televised on General Electric Theatre on February 19, 1961. *Inaugural Ball:* President-elect John F. Kennedy had invited a number of writers.

**To Charles Provine Goyen
and Mary Inez Goyen
TLS-2**

*214 East 50th Street
New York 22, N.Y.
November 5, 1961*

My dearest Mom and Dad:
 Guess you think I'm gone forever, but have been writing night and day on a television show which I just finished on Friday night, and have been sleeping ever since. Feel fine and rested, now, and all is well. The show will be on ABC Network on Sunday, December 10 at one o'clock in the afternoon, on a program called *Directions '62.* So you must look at it. I

think it might be pretty good, but I don't know at this point. Anyway, it kept me going night and day for three weeks. Now that it's over, I can go back to the play, which is nearing completion, and the novel.

I tried to call you tonight (Sunday), but you were out. Anyway, I'm fine and in good shape and going along. Write me and tell me about yourselves, and about Uncle Arthur. I've thought about him and Aunt Lucy, and please give them my love and tell them I am praying for them.

About Germany: I'm going if I can. I'll read at the University of Berlin (West) on January 8, then read and lecture in a few other German cities like Munich and Frankfurt, and then in Zürich, Switzerland. I have friends there, and my publishers are very kind to me, and I'll stay with them. I hope I can stay for a few months, inasmuch as my round-trip transportation is paid and I should take advantage of the trip to Europe. There should be no problem, so don't worry. A number of distinguished writers will read there, and I'll be in good company. Will let you know more as the time approaches. I don't know my plans from here until then because I am working so hard to make my living, and I have taken a leave of absence from the New School this year, so must work doubly hard. If I can get the play right, then it will make me money; so will the novel. But that means work and little else. We must take it week by week and hold on with patience. Don't worry about me. Just wish I could see you all, I need to, and miss you: but we'll see how and when we can. Please take care of yourselves and send me the news. Forgive me for not writing—but I have tried to call. You call me sometime, please. Keep well, for I love you so much. Dad, the American Express thing is paid and settled. I made them wait, since they were so god-damned big-deal about it all. Forgive me, but I won't be treated like that any more. God bless you both, and write to me.

Love,
Bill

---

214 *East 50th Street:* Goyen and Glasco were no longer together about this time. *Directions '62:* A series of programs produced by Richard J. Walsh for the National Council of Catholic Men, in association with the Public Affairs Department of ABC. Goyen's segment, "The Mind," was hosted by anchor-artist Robert Gerringer and was a dramatization on the subject of man's memory. Goyen's script incorporated material from his story "The House and the Day Moth." The program closed with readings from the reflections of a mystic, Saint John of the Cross.
Germany: He had been invited abroad by the U.S. State Department to give a series of readings.

[New York, N.Y.]
June 6, 1962

My dearest Mother and Father:

It's better now, and I'm sorry for losing control of myself last night when you called. I had been waiting to hear from you and trying to call you, and in a state of shock and exhaustion after coming back so suddenly, and it all had built up in me. When you called I let it go. I left Kiel suddenly, after doing all I could to endure it. It was a disappointment to me to have to do this, since I was working for my country and wanted to give all I could. But Kiel was terrible, as I wrote you, and the people not pleasant and the whole thing was a dreadful mistake. They paid me so little and I used up all I had. So I came home broke and owing terrible bills, about $1000, including rent for three months. Naturally I have been feeling insecure and unhappy. I had counted on $1000 for the novel I finished over there, but now the publishers don't want to publish it until I've finished the second one, which is not finished, and so they are blocking the first. That knocked the hell out of me, but I'll get over it. The play is nearing completion, and I am working with my director to finish it this month. There'll be money from that. Money will come from other sources, too, if I just keep working and stay with it. So don't think me down and out that way. I'm just emotionally very wrecked after the experience in Germany and the last awful month in Kiel. Up till then it was very good. But I did wear myself out for it all, which I somehow can't help doing.

Never mind, I'll pull up. I have before. And I have faith in myself. Still, I need, as I always have, your faith and I still count on you to stand by me in hard times. At least not to criticize me but to accept, if you can, my way of life and what it brings—as I have. I have about $25 to my name at the moment, and it's been a fight to get money at once out of people in my business here in New York. That's discouraging, because in Europe I was treated like a fine writer and respected and admired everywhere. Here, it's still hard.

I really wanted to come on home at once, and I need you both and I need home, after all I've been through in Europe. But I can't come until I'm strong myself and feel sure of myself and my work here. Otherwise I'd just be delaying the whole thing, and I have to face it now and work it

out. I do have to earn my living here and can't get around that. I have a
good chance of doing that, *if* I'm here. Let me have the rest of the month
to try to finish this work, the play mainly, and get it going. Then I can
come and have some time at home with you all and try to look after
myself and be with you. Otherwise I'd be distracted and not really there,
as you know. [. . .]

Kiel: Kiel, West Germany. Goyen suffered something resembling a breakdown there.
the novel I finished: The Fair Sister (Garden City, N.Y.: Doubleday, 1963). When
published in London under the title *Savata, My Fair Sister* (London: Peter Owen, Ltd.,
1963), it appeared with important variations in chapter five.

To William M. Hart
TLS-2

214 East 50th St.
New York City 22, N.Y.
July 10, 1963

My dear Bill:

   Just now around to answering your letter—it's a bad summer for me,
work all stifled in me, no money, anticipation and anxiety over the play
and its goddamned problems, etc. I need desperately to get away, out of
this room, and under sun, away from this desk—but I see no chance. My
life is pulling to the right—somewhat against my reins—like a stubborn
horse that wants to go on some path I'm not sure of. But I think it's good.
I believe *The Fair Sister* has freed me, at long last, of my old web. I am in
process of devising a musical from the book, and that excites me. When
you read it you will see. Also I am involved in my *Six Women*, my first
non-fiction, and it bedevils me. You know most of the six, and God knows
I have a lot to tell. Margo is one, Frieda is another. And a past income tax
swoop out of the blue drained me down to my toes, so I have such money
anxieties as would kill the Aga Khan if he were so swooped. Fuck it, is all
I have come to be able to say, in my most ripe and wise middle-age. I am
so seasoned in distresses of the purse that the peculiar ache it brings is
like an old friend. Still, the work piles up and the work goes on, and fuck
it, Billy. [. . .]

   As for your sweet plans, dear Bill, I'd be delighted to talk at Rice as
well as at the Univ. of Houston, but they must pay me. I am, my dear, no

longer a gratuity—too many years of that. Nor am I any longer a sweet luxury. Good.

I think the gift of books and magazines to Rice is a lovely idea, and I'm honored. I might like to add some things, indeed. This we will discuss when I'm there. As for the letters, I'm not sure I want that, Billy. Perhaps secrets should always be secrets—what else? I've really made no secret of my real life—my printed work is witness to that. I'm not sure, no, about the letters. When I come, we'll discuss that, too. Nobody's going to die before October 1, that we know of, meaning you and me! I'm just in my prime, and intend to march very sprightly on in it, waving several flags of various nationalities. After all, one is always under several flags, like Texas. [. . .]

Well, we'll have much to say when I come. I'm eager to help wherever I can, I can do all that now and enjoy it. I believe, from all early portents, that this little one will sell and will find other expressions of itself beyond *book*. You'll see, I hope. Anyway, send me news, now, and remember my affection. We'll do it grandly, Billy. Be well. [. . .]

As for the letters: William Hart's gifts to the Fondren Library at Rice eventually included his letters from Goyen.
this little one: The Fair Sister (Garden City, N.Y.: Doubleday, 1963), the publication date of which was to be September 27.

To Granville Hicks
TLS-1

214 East 50th St.
New York City 22, N.Y.
August 4, 1963

Dear Mr. Hicks:

I've admired—and benefited from—your comments on my books for some years; they've clarified my work for me and given me, often, a sense of it. This is why I feel I must let you know that I've written another book, another short narrative in first person, called *The Fair Sister*, to be published on September 27 by Doubleday. I'm eager for you to read it, and in the light of my previous work; and it would please me if you could review it—however that's done—should you have something to say about it.

Could you see about the *New York Times* or the *Saturday Review?* Galleys are certainly available now, and the book copy should be ready shortly. My editor at Doubleday is Samuel Vaughan. Thanks for saying something to me about this little book, if you can and wish to.

May I wish you good things and good work. I hope you're having a pleasant summer. It would please me to hear from you.

Cordially,
William Goyen

Granville Hicks: (1909–1982). Critic and novelist who had reviewed Goyen in the *Saturday Review*.

To Dorothy Brett
TLS-1

277 West End Avenue
Apt. 2B
New York City 23, New York
June 6, 1964

My dearest Brett:

My God I've been trying to write to you for months. Married life has taken most of my time, as you can imagine. What a change! And what an adventure! I *love* it and can't imagine living any other way, although there are and have been large problems. But Doris and I battle through them and keep coming through. Doris is so wonderful and beautiful and dear and we love each other more and more each day. Little Michael grows more content and adjusted and he and I are great good friends. We have a lovely relationship. I am his "second daddy," and he considers it a luxury to have two. Besides, I am "the very best friend" he ever had. He is proud that I am a writer and tells everyone about my books. He has two small fierce turtles who bathe with him every night and threaten his little thing, of which he is most aware at 7. He has a most unlikeable cat named Princess who has been in heat for four months without let-up, poor wretch. And some six weeks ago he caught a most dreadful creature in the pond at Central Park which lives, thrashing in a pot of water over which the cat glowers, in his bedroom. The creature, to our horror, is slowly turning into a *frog*. God knows what we'll do with it, but Michael must have it, of course. One early morning we shall all hear a great croaking, and there the frog will be. That's a glimpse of our life here.

We have a charming and intelligent young woman named Carrie who lives with us. She loves Michael and he her, and she takes the strain off Doris and me, keeps us going. We have to struggle to pay for it all, but we must and so we will. I am working at various projects, will teach for six weeks at Columbia this summer, am in line for a position with a publishing house as part-time editor. That I would like. It would give us some security and enable me to write half a week and work with other writers half a week. You know I love to do this. Doris is probably going into rehearsal for a Broadway play middle August, opening late September. She's been free for a few months, and that has been lovely. We are scarcely apart. This is the great love of my life, Brett, and it came in time. We are like two children, madly, passionately, often painfully in love. It rages on. I am writing a novel from it, called *Another Man's Son*. I must put down what has happened to us over three and a half years. We've been married, incidentally, seven months today . . .

Love, as ever,
Bill

---

277 West End Avenue: In November 1963 Goyen married and moved to what was to become his last New York City residence.
Doris: Doris Roberts (b. 1930), who had appeared in Goyen's play *Christy* (1963). She went on to become a star on Broadway in such plays as *Last of the Red Hot Lovers* and *Bad Habits*, then moved into films (*A New Leaf, Hester Street*) and television (*Angie, Remington Steele*). She won an Emmy for her portrayal of a bag lady on *St. Elsewhere*.
Little Michael: Stepson Michael Cannata (b. 1957), son of Doris Roberts and Michael Emilio Cannata (1922–1989).
part-time editor: See Goyen's undated letter to Seymour Lawrence, proposing part-time work at Atlantic Monthly Press.

To Seymour Lawrence
TLC-2

[No address]
[No date]

Dear Sam:

I would like to associate myself with a publishing house as part-time Editor, Editorial Consultant, or Scouting Editor for new writers of quality. My academic training has been in Literature (Master of Arts Degree in Languages—Spanish, French, German—and Comparative Literature). I've made translations from German and French. Over a period of ten years I've conducted workshops in the writing of the novel, the short story, non-fiction, and playwriting, at The New School, New York City, New York University, and Columbia University. My work there was with young and new writers, several of whom I've brought to publishers. I've acted as story editor at various writers' conferences and for various publishers, reading manuscripts for and bringing new writers and material to them. I've been frequently asked over the years by publishers to give editorial opinion on first novels, among them *The Assistant* by Bernard Malamud, which I reviewed in the *New York Times Sunday Book Review; Wise Blood* and *A Good Man is Hard to Find* by Flannery O'Connor (which I reviewed for *The New York Times Book Review*); the work of Calvin Kentfield, Harold Brodkey, J. F. Powers (his first book of stories, which I reviewed for *The New York Times*); William Humphrey's *Home from the Hill; The Lost Country* by J. R. Salamanca; Elizabeth Hardwick, Truman Capote, and many other first works of now-established writers. I've been consultant and advisor for The Guggenheim Foundation Fellowships in Creative Writing, for the Ford Foundation Program for Novelists and Poets.

My natural ability to work with writers and to draw from them new and exciting work leads me to desire to work in such a capacity with a large publishing house which wants to publish work of quality, to discover work of merit; and I believe this ability, coupled with this long experience could be useful and profitable. There are some talented writers with whom I have worked and whose work-in-progress I have discussed editorially with them, including Edward Albee, Jack Richardson, Jack Gelber, William Inge (all novels); and there are several new writers whose manuscripts I have been working with and are so far undiscovered and without publishers. I'd like to help develop their talent. I also want to help attract, may I say, from other houses writers who may be discontented and restless there for want of the kind of editor I might be for them. I believe I am the kind of writer-editor who can do good work in this area.

I have worked with Book Page editors on *The New York Times Sunday Book Review* for many years, on *The Nation* and on the *Sunday Herald Tribune*. I've read for Macmillan, Random House, Harper's, Knopf, Farrar Straus, Harcourt Brace and Little Brown, among other publishers.

People who know of my ability and work include: Maggie Cousins,

Frank Taylor (Avon), David McDowell (*Saturday Evening Post*), John Mong, Peter Israel (Putnam), Samuel S. Vaughan, Robert Whitehead.

William Goyen

Seymour Lawrence: (1926–1993). At this time Lawrence was director of Atlantic Monthly Press.

TLC-2: A carbon copy, with the look of a draft, this letter might not have been sent.

The Assistant: Goyen's review appeared on April 28, 1957, p. 4. It was not a first novel, as Goyen states, but a second.

Wise Blood: May 18, 1952, p. 4. He does not appear to have published a review of *A Good Man Is Hard to Find*.

Harold Brodkey: (b. 1930). Goyen reviewed his *First Love and Other Sorrows* in the *New York Times Book Review*, January 12, 1958, p. 29.

Home from the Hill: Reviewed in the *New York Times Book Review*, January 12, 1958, p. 4.

Truman Capote: Goyen does not appear to have reviewed Capote's first work, *Other Voices, Other Rooms*; at the time of its publication (1948), Goyen had only recently published his first stories in magazines. He did review Capote's *The Grass Harp* for the *Houston Post*, October 7, 1951, sec. 4, p. 14; and *Breakfast at Tiffany's* for the *New York Times Book Review*, November 2, 1959, pp. 5, 38.

John Mong: Fiction editor at *Saturday Evening Post*, where Goyen published the story "Figure over the Town."

To Sam Vaughan
TLS-2

[No address]
April 4, 1965

Dear friend Sam:

Here's a work-copy of *Christy* which, as you know, was the first Work-In-Progress production at the American Place Theatre here in New York. The play received great interest, both as a play and as a motion picture. I decided, after working on the material for a couple of years, to re-form it into the shape of a novel so that I could encompass the large scope of it, then perhaps see it through a play version and, hopefully, a motion picture: that is my plan.

The buried story of the writer-poet (American, such as Agee, but within the Dylan Thomas image) and his wife; the disintegration of a regional section of America, the inheritance of a poet's vision *in money* (Hollywood)—the irony, contemporaneity of it all, have absorbed me for some several years. The play production was a clarification of the theme, situation and plot for me. Indeed, Ross Claiborne saw the play, as I remember, and spoke with me about it—unless I've lost my mind and memory. We'll talk more about this, if you like or need to.

Six Women should be no problem to sell to anyone. The third novel, *Another Man's Son*, which I thought you knew about but Phyllis tells me you didn't remember, is very close to me and might come off very fast. I need *time* to get all these down and shaped and controlled—as you know, Sam. I've talked, too, to Ross about this novel—about a step-father's passionate and romantic marriage to a woman who brings a young son into the marriage, the problems between the step-father and the step-son who brings an unseen intruder (his own father) into the household and the desperate relationship of the man and the woman. I am writing the novel in the form of letters from the step-father to his own father, so that two fathers and two sons are involved—but, above all, the story is a passionate and tormented love story between the man and the woman. I don't like or want to submit resumés of plots of novels, Sam; but I tell you this much—which I thought I'd already told you, forgive me—so that you may know the rest.

We'll talk soon. Good luck to you and you know how happy I am for your new success, and all my good wishes for you.

As ever,
Bill

Another Man's Son: A projected work, never finished.

To Dorothy Brett
TLS-2

277 West End Avenue
New York City 23, N.Y.
November 15, 1965

My dearest Brett:
    [. . .] I wish you'd tell me about yourself and what these days are like for you. Seems to me you have a Birthday somewhere along here, or just had. Now what does that make you? Whatever, I hope it was gay and bright, and I, and now Doris, wish you more and more. Doris had one on

the 4th of November, took it very lightly and festively, thinking she was 41—we had gone through her travail of reaching 40 last year during which she became very dramatic and even sad—only to have her mother arrive to proclaim that she was indeed 40 *this* birthday; but it was too late to worry and so we had a happy time. Also our Wedding Anniversary (the Second Year) was on November 10, and there was celebration all over again. We feel so accomplished at having got two years behind us. Dear Brett, marriage is a wonderful adventure, exciting and beautiful. Doris and I grow closer every day. Certainly there are bad times and difficult problems, but we have always been able to struggle through them and come to something good and beautiful. She is a most wonderful and beautiful human being, and I am truly possessed by her. We had an event in our life this August—we lost a baby. Doris was between three and four months with it, and suddenly she miscarried it. You know how much we want our own, but this was not to be and so we accepted it. It brought us very close and dear to each other; and now we are hoping for another soon. The worst thing of it was that we were on holiday and had to put Doris in a small-town hospital where she almost died, came very near to it. But she is strong and gay now, and that is behind us. She is hoping to work in a new play soon and that will be good for her.

I'm head over heels with work, so much bread-work to keep us going. But I like most of what I have done and keep trying to find a way to do the work I really need to do—a novel and stories. I'll find the way soon, and then I'll be freer. You know I'm slowly writing the book on my six Romantic Women, and you're one of them. I think it will be good . . .

Love as always,
Bill

Walter is living in Paris this year and Joe now lives in Athens, very happily.

---

her mother: Ann Roberts (1895–1975).
Walter: Walter Berns.
Joe: Joseph Glasco.

To Perry Knowlton
TLS-1

McGraw-Hill Book Company
330 West 42nd Street
New York, N.Y. 10036
February 4, 1966

Dear Perry:

You may have heard that I recently joined McGraw-Hill as Senior
Editor under Frank Taylor. I am very excited about it and have high
hopes of some good work. What I am looking for is new, bold, creative
writers of fiction and non-fiction.

I'll be in touch with you soon to see when we can get together to
discuss projects that may prove to be of mutual interest to us.

Best Regards,
Bill Goyen

Perry Knowlton: Agent at Curtis Brown, Ltd.
joined McGraw-Hill: Goyen's work at McGraw-Hill curtailed his own literary output—
and his correspondence about his writing—over the next five years. His professional
correspondence includes letters like this one and the next three which follow. An
additional note: His family correspondence, now in the manuscript collection of the
Fondren Library at Rice University, ends in 1963.

To William Inge
TLS-2

McGraw-Hill Book Company
330 West 42nd Street
New York, N.Y. 10036
August 22, 1966

Dear Bill:

Well, I have read your revision, and I must say I think it is much, much
better and that I am still haunted and moved by the story.

Chris is right in feeling that the landlady can get a little tiring, but I
suggest that you don't meddle with her so totally that we lose a sense of
her as a very real character, which she does, to my mind even with her
weaknesses, emerge as.

Of course Bennett would think these things about the story. I do not agree with him, but I do suggest that you re-examine some of the more sensational aspects of Vic's male sexuality, such as the photographs and any over-adulation of him by you as a male.

Now here are some thoughts I'm having. Could Vic be more fleshed out as a character? Is he still too passive in the story? Why does he continue to encourage sexual invitations? Does Marilyn persist as the battered victim out of self-punishment? Could you rethink Marilyn in terms of Vic, for they are such marvelous characters, and it seems to me that they are counterparts and each works in terms of the other. What is Marilyn's attraction to Vic? Don't you think you might clarify this? I'm concerned still about Marilyn's conversion. It works in principle, but don't we need further motivation for it?

Put these things through your mind and let me know your response. I really think you're on your way towards a marvelous story, but I ask you to re-examine the text with an eye to eliminating any sexual inferences that might be interpreted as just "queer," rather than deeper emanations of male sexuality. I ask you to be sensitive to this because I feel the book has a classic quality, a quality of power and universality, and any detail that lessens or weakens that quality we would want to clean out.

Now the last question: Am I to consider the book as a possibility for McGraw-Hill publication under my editorship? Am I now free to think of it in this way? I ask this because of my deep interest in the book and in you, because I should like to begin to think of it in those terms if you are so inclined at this point. As you know, this has nothing to do with my wanting to share the development of the book with you as a friend, and to help you in any way I can to make it a fine book and a fully realized one for you, no matter who publishes it.

Let me hear from you by phone or by letter whenever you need to call on me, and I'll wait for that. Meantime my love,

Bill
William Goyen

William Inge: (1913–1973). American playwright who wrote fiction late in his career.
your revision: Of an unpublished novel. Neither of Inge's two published novels have characters named Marilyn and Vic.
Bennett: Bennett Cerf.
re-examine the text: When Goyen's own *The House of Breath* was reprinted in 1975, he suppressed a passage on page 178 which had appeared on page 166 of the original (1950) edition. It involved homosexual graffiti.

To Granville Hicks
TLS-1

McGraw-Hill Book Company
330 West 42nd Street
New York, N.Y. 10036
August 22, 1967

Dear Granville Hicks:

I want to thank you for the time and attention you've given to our First Novel Program of 1967. We were all delighted with your essay in last week's *Saturday Review*. You've always been a staunch and loyal supporter of new and talented writing, and it's encouraging to all of us who write and edit and publish.

Needless to say, McGraw-Hill is continuing its promotion and publication of first novels, and in 1968 we shall introduce another group of talented writers whose work we believe in.

Thanks again for your good words, and my warmest personal regards.

As ever,
William Goyen
[dictated but not signed]

---

attention you've given to our First Novel Program: Hicks wrote about the McGraw-Hill First Novel Program, which Goyen helped develop, in his regular column, "Literary Horizons." As an editor at McGraw-Hill, Goyen discovered and published June Arnold, Michael Rubin, and nine other first novelists.

To Granville Hicks
TLS-1

McGraw-Hill Book Company
330 West 42nd Street
New York, N.Y. 10036
September 7, 1967

Dear Granville Hicks:

I'm sending you with pleasure and pride Elizabeth Spencer's new novel, and I hope you'll read it and let me know your feelings about it.

Miss Spencer is certainly one of our major American writers, and whenever new work of hers appears—and in this case a major work with which
I have been closely associated as her editor—I feel that those of us who
care about the growth and achievement of our best writers will want to
share in it.

I send you *No Place for an Angel* with great excitement. Do let me hear
from you when you've read it.

With warm personal greetings.

Sincerely,
William Goyen

Elizabeth Spencer's new novel: No Place for an Angel (1967). Elizabeth Spencer (b. 1921)
worked with Goyen on two other books as well: *Ship Island and Other Stories* (1968)
and *The Snare* (1972). Among Goyen's other authors at McGraw-Hill were Heinrich
Böll and Catherine Marshall.

To Dorothy Brett
ALS-3

277 West End Avenue
New York City 23, N.Y.
August 7, 1968

My dear Brett:
    Sad news—my dear father died on July 1 and we buried him in
Houston on July 2. He lies under a big live-oak tree in a beautiful
garden-like place. He had been ill for some months with a bad heart. I
spent two weeks with him and had a wonderful, sweet visit with him
before he went on. All his children, grandchildren, nephews and nieces
came to sit with him and he settled his accounts and made his peace with
all of them. I loved my father, as you know, and his death was harder for
me than I had ever thought it would be. My mother is alone and quite
disconsolate. Some words from you would be a great solace to her, for she
needs comfort and understanding from people like you who understand
death. On his deathbed, my father had visions of the desert and the
mountains of Taos—you remember how he loved that country—and he
longed to go back there. I have a feeling he's all around there—so try to
reach him. He has appeared before me several times since his death, and I

know he is peaceful and free. It is my mother who will not let him go, and
we must all work on her to free the good man. Her address:

    614 Merrill St.

    Houston, Texas

  Are you well, are you happy, are you painting? How I miss you and the
old, lovely times! Send me a hello? Doris and the boy Michael are happy
and beautiful and we are all full of love and marching along. I am writing
slowly and at my own pace, and for myself am enjoying my work at the
Publishing House, and thank God for *that*!

Love to all of my friends. Deaths like this bring us all closer together.
Love always,

Bill

---

the Publishing House: McGraw-Hill.

To Robert Phillips
ALS-2

277 West End Avenue
New York, N.Y. 10023
May 28, 1969

Dear Robert Phillips:

  What a startling and original way of looking at "The White Rooster"!
I'm excited by it, find it illuminating and revealing. I'm very grateful.

  It would please me so much—indeed honor me—if you could one day
find it possible to write about these other people of mine. So little has
been said about them. I feel you know them in a way I never could, since
obviously *they* created me, and the long bitter battle of the created is to
try to understand the creator—son and father, made and maker.

  But I'm almost shy about meeting you, the more I know what you
know about me, about my work. Before it goes too far, shouldn't we just
arrange for lunch? Say, sometime during the second half of June (except
Fridays, when I now work at home)? If you'll call, we'll arrange this.

  Once again, I'm glad, and stimulated, and grateful.

Cordially,
Bill Goyen

Robert Phillips: (b. 1938). Editor of the present volume. Goyen's correspondence with Phillips amounts to more than sixty items, now housed in the Phillips Papers, Arents Research Library, Syracuse University. Beginning with this letter in 1969, the correspondence continued until Goyen's death in 1983.

way of looking: Phillips had sent Goyen a copy of his essay "Samuel and Samson: Theme and Legend in 'The White Rooster,'" *Studies in Short Fiction* 6 (1969): 331–333.

these other people: Goyen's encouragement resulted in Phillips's book, *William Goyen*, which was published in Twayne's United States Authors Series (Boston, 1979).

work at home: Goyen had arranged a four-day schedule at McGraw-Hill. But the long weekends produced little of his own writing until he began *A Book of Jesus* in 1971. By this point he had become severely alcoholic, and this too made it nearly impossible for him to write.

To Clyde Grimm
ALS-11

Weston, Conn.
(Where I am working four days a week
until Sept.)
July 17, 1970

Dear Clyde Grimm:

1. The *Venture* piece, as I wrote to you (I think) is unpublished. It was only a survey of Regional Theatres, called "Off-Off-Broadway." When my editor at *Venture*, Arnold Ehrlich (who had commissioned the piece), left *Venture* for *Holiday*, the magazine canceled the piece. It's of no import, anyway—I'd forget it.

2. I'm sending scripts of *House of Breath* (the Providence production), *Christy*, and *The Bite of the Diamond Rattler* (based on two of my stories), "Rhody's Path," "Pore Perrie." None of these plays has been published.

3. The Providence production of *House of Breath* was produced in Nov. and Dec. of 1969 (6 weeks). I'll send the reviews.

4. *Christy* was produced by The American Place Theatre in April, 1964. It was not reviewed—was only a "Work-in-Progress."

5. It's possible that the Providence group will produce *The Bite of the Diamond Rattler* this fall or winter. No other production of this play or *Christy*, to date.

6. The musical adaptation of *The Fair Sister* is now being prepared by the composer Cy Coleman, who has optioned the book. The earlier production fell through during the ugly Watts period. Pearl Bailey was scheduled to play Ruby Drew. The comedian Bill Dana was to be the producer.

7. T.V. Productions: 1) "A Possibility of Oil" (with, of all people, Joan Fontaine [my God!]) was produced by Revue Studios, "Four Star Theatre" on CBS in 1959 or 1960. It had a lot of "Rhody's Path" in it, and *The Bite of the Diamond Rattler* grew out of it. 2) NBC ("The Catholic Hour"—I don't know why, I'm not Catholic) produced a strange adaptation of my story, "The Horse and the Day Moth," in, I believe, 1958, or '55.

8. Films—I wrote a long ballad called "The Left-Handed Boy," which was sung over the film *The Left-Handed Gun*, Paul Newman's first film produced by Warner Bros. It's now quite a famous underground film. Was Arthur Penn's first film. I worked closely with Penn and the producer, Fred Coe, on this film. Can be seen fairly frequently on television and the film is now considered a curious primitive masterpiece, the forerunner of contemporary films like *Easy Rider* and *Sundance Kid*. Also—a very odd experimental film adaptation of "The White Rooster" was made by some bright young fellow at Princeton in, say, 1955–6.

9. No, *The Fair Sister* is not the same book as *Half a Look of Cain. Half a Look* has long been scheduled for publication in Germany by my German publishers, Suhrkamp (who've published all my books in Germany), but I think they can't get a decent translation. Curtius had begun it shortly before he died. I am not satisfied with it and my American publisher, Random House, was not, either. I am still struggling with it and cannot yet get it right. Anyway, I'm not anxious to have it published until it's right.

10. *Six Women* is very much alive and I am always working on it (even now)—quite intensely at present. I'm not in a hurry to get it published. It's a good portion of my autobiography. "The Romantic Woman" is a kind of superficial spin-off from that material, yes. The sub-title of *Six Women* is "The Vanishing Romantic Woman" (God help me with the absurd Women's Liberation Movement!).

11. The Curtius preface is his own translation. It appears in the German edition (Suhrkamp) as Preface. It has never been published in English. You know, incidentally, that Curtius, along with Frieda, was a powerful force in my life—met him as a young man (me) while I was writing *The House of Breath*—he had read parts of the novel in *Partisan Review* ("A Bridge of Breath," the story of Folner Ganchion) and *Accent* ("Four American Portraits as Elegy"). We met in El Prado, New Mexico (1946–47?) where he had come as a guest of Helene Wurlitzer, after lecturing at the Goethe Centennial in nearby Aspen, Colorado. Years later I was with him in Switzerland shortly before he died. I had needed so much desperately to be with him, to *talk*, to share quandaries and

enigmas about literature, the life of writing, poetry. When I got to him in a small, dismal Alpine village, I found him speechless—he had suffered the stroke that took his life a few months later. But I talked and talked all one day and night, and he nodded, like a mechanical doll.

You are also aware that I traveled over most of Germany in several months of 1960, reading from my books at universities and "Amerika Hauser," as a guest of the U.S. State Dept. Young people followed me everywhere—their favorites were *The House of Breath* and *In a Farther Country*. Both books are popular paperbacks in Germany—out of print in our own country (all my books are O.P.).

12. There are many more critical studies—or comments on—my books. I'll send a list of as many as I'm aware of.

13. Now about Frieda. It had *nothing* whatsoever to do with all the D. H. Lawrence legend crap. I *loathed* all that—what little I knew of it when I came to New Mexico. What I learned of it after I got to N.M., I spat out and turned away from. I simply was *not* "literary," knew nothing of Salons, Writer's Groups, etc.—instinctively fled all that; was scared and inarticulate, anyway; *never* wanted to be around writers and the sophisticated literary world. Frieda's was my first deep, instinctual, primitive friendship with a woman. We did not talk books or writing. It was a long time before she ever read a word of what I was writing. Our friendship had nothing to do with writing or *my* writing—*any* writing. I was seeking the simplest life, a *ground* life; Frieda, despite her life with Lawrence, had always kept to that kind of life. Her life with Lawrence didn't—and still doesn't—interest me. I was never around when worshippers of Lawrence appeared at Frieda's doorstep—I vanished. Since she is one of my *Six Women*, I prefer to tell this, at length, in that book. (Please do not quote me.) I was with Frieda when she died. I buried her and read the Burial Service over her grave. Although my beloved Brett (Dorothy Brett) remained (she's now 88 and still there), I left El Prado not many months after Frieda died. Brett (another of my *Six Women*) was also an early influence on my life and work, in such a different way from Frieda's.

14. About the transit from aircraft carrier to desert and adobe house. During the interminable War—for me almost entirely at Sea—I determined, if I lived, to retreat and live in a basic, simple life of writing. I settled on someplace near San Francisco, which had excited me during my ship's (the Casablanca) two or three calls to that port. At war's end I left Houston for San Francisco—in an old car. Passing through New Mexico—Taos, Sante Fe, El Prado—I stopped at Taos, and I stayed (off and on over a 10 yr. period). I was not aware that Frieda—or Brett—lived there. It was a landscape I wanted, and needed. I stayed. I knew few

people there—as long as I lived there. It was a life-or-death fight to write
and to live from what I had to write (not, *absolutely not*, from what "income" my writing would bring me—for me, then, what had "income" to
do with writing? Writing was a Way of Life).

15. Which leads into your question about "a note of disappointment or
resentment about the business of authorship, the lack of sufficient
recognition" [. . .] I wrote compulsively and obsessively—it was simply
what I *had* to do. There are, naturally, disappointments that came with
lack of recognition—but that was, and is, my burden, along with the
burden of writing. I could never be involved with the "*business* of authorship," as you put it, although my occupation is, has been for 4 1/2 years at
this writing, as Senior Editor in a publishing house; that has nothing to
do with my own writing. I could *never* live as a "free-lance writer"—I'm
just not, by nature, "free-lance." I write what I *have* to write, or not at all.
It is misery waiting until something *forms* and takes firm, living root.

My marriage? It's one of my best books! "Decline" in publication since
1963. No "decline." There's been, simply, a change in *metabolism* in the
body of my work, vision of life, people, my *landscape* has changed. Writing
is no longer a way of life for me, day by day. It's slower, more careful. It
(writing) most certainly is *not* a "career"—how could an art be a "career"?.

A great change—painful, bewildering, enraging, voluptuous and
exhausting—has occurred in me. It is a change away from the four books
(including the fifth, *The Fair Sister*) I've written. They are done. They
have, for me, exhausted a landscape, a language, a people. We'll see what
comes next—if anything. Must Something come "next"?

I ask you to let me see what comes out of this "pamphlet." I do,
indeed, ask for "approval" of it, if you will. Otherwise, I'm not sure about
all of this. It's too much of a nest of hornets, friend Grimm.

Yours,
Bill Goyen

It's very important that it be clear that this is only *information* that I'm
giving you. Please do not *quote me in my own words*. I can't give you my
approval to do so. In other words, I am not writing these things for the
pamphlet or for you to quote. Thanks for understanding this; and I ask
you to write to me telling me that you will give me approval of the
manuscript when it is finished and before it is published. I'd also like the
right of approval of proof before the pamphlet is finally printed. Will you
write me a letter to this effect? Thanks.

W.G.

Also, it seems to me that you're writing a Life of me that I, myself, must write. Isn't that *another* book? [. . .]

Clyde Grimm: Clyde L. Grimm, Jr. (b. 1929). Bibliographer and critic. These responses were occasioned by a questionnaire submitted by Grimm to Goyen. It was his intention to publish a forty-page pamphlet on Goyen's life and work for an academic series. He died before its completion. He did publish, however, "William Goyen: A Bibliographic Chronicle," which appeared in *Bulletin of Bibliography* 35, no. 3 (1978): 123–131.
"The Romantic Woman": Drafts of this essay are in the Harry Ransom Humanities Research Center. It was Goyen's contribution to a symposium ("Who Is the American Woman?") in *Status* 2 (October 1965): 27, 28, 75–76.
several months of 1960: It was in 1962.

To Daniel Stern
TLS-1

McGraw-Hill, Inc.
330 West 42nd Street
New York, New York 10036
January 28, 1971

Dear Danny:

I've finished reading *The Rose Rabbi* and I do, indeed, think it is your most original work—a really impressive and, I think, distinguished narrative. I think you've never written better. It is certainly the style that tells the story, and Wolf Walker is the very style, itself.

The premise of the novel is very clear to the reader—that is, that it's Wolf's birthday and that on that day he is recapturing his life. Only a mild suggestion for you to ponder: be sure that the reader is aware of time, the immediate action and past action. I think all this is adroitly done, but it does involve the form of the novella and I would want the form to be impeccable. In other words, let us be sure that the reader knows time and time sequence. It is a beautiful raveling out of a man's experience and, moreover, a very intelligent novel and one that will, I believe, make the reader intelligent.

I love the title; although today when I spoke with Lynn to tell her how I feel about the book and that I'm sending on the last advance payment, she said she didn't like it much. I reminded her that besides being beautiful itself, titles with "Rabbi" in them sell. Let's do keep it, if there were ever any question in your mind.

Doris and I are leaving this Sunday for ten days in Mexico, our first vacation this year, but do please send a note to Cathy letting us know when you are due back in the City. We have scheduled *The Rose Rabbi* for September, and so I'll want to put it into production around the middle of February. Also, Danny, I need a second copy of the manuscript, and would you please put it in the mail to me at once so that I can get to work on it for production.

Congratulations on a beautiful, serene, and deeply thoughtful piece of work, and I hope we can get a lot of people to read *The Rose Rabbi*.

Faithfully,
William Goyen

Daniel Stern: (b. 1928). American novelist and short story writer. Goyen was his editor for two novels, *The Suicide Academy* (1968) and *The Rose Rabbi* (1971).
Lynn: Lynn Nesbitt, Stern's agent at International Creative Management.
titles with "Rabbi" in them sell: Goyen is thinking of Harry Kemelman's series of novels about a rabbi, *Friday the Rabbi Slept Late* (New York: Putnam's, 1964), and others, which were best-sellers.
Cathy: Goyen's assistant, Cathy Rockfol.
due back in the City: At the time Stern was living in Los Angeles and was Vice President for Publicity Worldwide for Warner Bros.

To Robert Phillips
ALS-3

July 26, 1971

Dear Robert:

This will be a jumble of things—I've been in Texas for two weeks, visiting mother and family and being on the staff of Southwest Writers' Conf. in Houston. It was good. Just back today. Before that—a ten-day lovely session in Martha Duffy's house in Bridgehampton doing work on the Jesus book, which is afire and wildly exciting. I've a contract with Doubleday for it—simultaneous paper and cloth; my deadline Sept. 15— not more than 100 pages; all just as I'd seen it. It happened quickly, Doubleday loved the idea and leapt to it. I'll do it simply, straightfor- wardly, it will be a little life, no more—except for a Prologue or Preface where I want to say something. Weston now falls into place; it is all very strange and sort of foreordained; I'm all ablaze and have illuminations. I'll take three straight weeks from mid-August and finish. This book must be published as soon as possible, I feel.

The *Southwest Review* arrived today and it's very impressive. Your piece is excellent, Robert, and I'm proud of it. We are set up so handsomely in the mag., you and I. I thank you from my heart. Doris is beaming. Bravo! [. . .]

Now you know why the delay. I rush this off—more later. Look for *Cain* (Suhrkamp in Frankfurt). Send more news. I'll do the same, as I can. [. . .]

Martha Duffy: Mrs. James Duffy, writer and editor at *Time.*

paper and cloth: Doubleday never did publish a paperback edition; a paper reprint appeared from New American Library as a Signet Book in 1974.

not more than 100 pages: The Doubleday edition has 143 pages.

to say something: In his brief "Author's Note," Goyen states, "I have wanted to uncover the strange, remarkable and sometimes hidden life of this man, as he walked through humanity from his baptism to his crucifixion, primarily for those who do not know it or who know it dimly. For those who know this life, it is always new.

"My intention has not been to interpret or analyze. The material preaches itself. I have hoped, simply, to try to tell again the story of the man, his world, his times, the people around him."

Weston: Goyen and Doris Roberts were guests of Alice De Lamar, who ran a private artists' colony at her estate in Connecticut, inviting those who interested her. The summer that Goyen was in residence other visitors included Paul Cadmus, the painter; Jon Andersson, the cabaret singer; and Tanaquil de Clerg, the ballet dancer and the last Mrs. George Balanchine.

Your piece: Phillips's essay "The Romance of Prophecy: Goyen's *In a Farther Country*" had appeared in *Southwest Review* 56, no. 3 (Summer 1971): 213–220.

you and I: Goyen's story "The Thief Coyote" was published in the same issue of *Southwest Review,* pp. 222–230. The story was appearing in America for the first time, but it was not a new work; it appeared in a bilingual *William Goyen: Short Stories,* edited and annotated by Erwin Helms (Göttingen: Vandenhoeck and Reprecht, 1964), pp. 17–25. At one time the story was titled "In the Pecan Grove." Goyen had not appeared in *SWR* in ten years and was eager to be represented in the issue.

Look for Cain: Goyen wanted to know if his German publisher had issued the book without telling him. Phillips and his wife, Judith, and son Graham had moved in July to Düsseldorf, West Germany, where they were to remain for two years.

To Robert Phillips
ALS-9

[Weston, Conn.]
Mon., Aug. 16 [1971]

Well, dear lad—

Forget Jesse Stuart. *Never* forget Margaret Hartley! She has been at my side since the earliest days (27 yrs odd), knows my life fully. One I love very deeply and for a long time. I am quite crazy as I write this. I have been 10 (ten) days in the country, alone, with my Jesus life, it is so strange and unsettling and so powerful, a *new* life, here again; I'm astounded. He gave me terrible problems while I tried to write his life. I was never (or seldom) more sensual or physical or less "spiritual." We're very close—he knows every thing about me. I wish he'd keep quiet. But we had ten days together—except for a great big goddamned bull frog in the pond—who—like the Weston ravens kept crying to me—something—My God, John the Baptist (see Matthew) was something. I'm on to something—"all things made new"—what we're all about: "Make it new." I'm quite crazy with so much coming into me—so different from the Weston craziness. Alone ten days with the life of this man—I'm strong—but I've got to understand why He did what He did that last week. And don't try to tell me what you think. But do, Judy. Do you realize that He and I came together—but I'm talking too much.

There are days and weeks that are tenuous (a word?) because I'm trying to keep to what came to me—about this strange person. How to figure out those last days? But let me alone with it. It's my book that I must give Him—and I'm not sure I *do* know that I love John, the water man. Oh John!

B

nach-wort—After-word
But it's not half enough. When it comes on us, Judy, Robert, my darlings, it's not half enough—what we write is never even *half* enough—Half Cain, half-life, half murder. It comes in so full—the Man is my meaning—always was/ See Folner—"Who draws thee, drawest me." "Where I go, you cannot follow." Why did I know this—in Texas? You're glad, my lovelies, to have a letter like this, in your first month in a beautiful, *deadly* country?

—B

Noch einmal ein Nach-Wort—
Can't stop. Full-World of publishing. Want to walk in sandals as I did at the beginning—and in a tunic—all hanging free—Want to—but I've other duties, at any rate, finally as much as I love you, it is all my very own—*mine.*

B.G.

Forget Jesse Stuart: Phillips had asked Goyen what he thought of the stories of Stuart (1906–1984), an American writer known for his books dealing with the mountain region of Kentucky and its people.
my Jesus life: A Book of Jesus.
the Weston ravens: Throughout his weeks in Weston, Goyen complained of the loud noises of the ravens distracting him.
See Folner: Character in *The House of Breath.*
beautiful deadly country: Goyen was drawing upon his mixed feelings about living in Germany in 1962.

To Robert Phillips
TLS-1

277 West End Ave., N.Y.C.
Oct. 26, 1971

Dear Robert:
    The silence means a lot of things. First, I am leaving McGraw-Hill at last—this Friday, Oct. 29th. Rejoice with me. I'll write for a while, find myself again. Rejoice. Second—we were in Italy for two glorious weeks, and in London for three—no doubt while you, of all things, were there—I can't quite remember when it was, but we're back only two weeks.
    The Jesus book has me completely driven and obsessed [*sic*]. The first draft is done, but now I need more time to really get it right. It will be.
    We are fine and well, therefore. More later. You can imagine these days, all the trailing authors, six years of roots in this office, Cathy away in Spain on her vacation, learning only by letter of my decision to leave swiftly. I shall be free, at last, of publishing and other authors; I shall try to do my own work, for as long as I can manage.
    Thank and bless you for your letters, your patience above all. Now I'll write more, once I'm through this madness of winding up affairs. Everybody I know hails me and stands behind me—it is so good and strengthening. [. . .]

Cathy away: Cathy Rockfol.

my decision to leave: Goyen wrote a letter dated October 19, 1971, which went to agents and authors he was handling. It stated, in part, "I am leaving for a time in order to do some of my own work; after that we will see what happens." But see the following. Apparently his obsession with completing *A Book of Jesus* had interfered with his properly executing his responsibilities at the office.

To Robert Phillips
TLS-2

277 West End Avenue, NYC
December 2, 1971

Dear Robert:

Awoke this morning to turn *NYTimes*—to Book Review Section to find your picture and the splendid review of the Alice book. Cheers and congratulations! We're very proud of you. Made me homesick for you. I do, really, miss you and still feel put upon that you would move away! I've really needed some good talks during this strange period. Fell apart a few times, once quite wildly, but—you know me—I spring up. Now the little Jesus book is delivered and my editors send word to Phyllis that they are "delighted" with it and that they plan to make it a beautiful book. I think, now, that they plan to make it a Fall book. I'll know more next week. It's a swift, striking (as in a blow), physical little thing, this book: quite gracefully rude, like some farm instrument to be used by hand, a sickle or a hoe; and my Jesus snorts and sighs and groans, curses, spits, sticks his fingers in the ears of deaf people; and he *handles* mortality, touches the flesh of hundreds, heals that way. The experience of writing it has been an extraordinary experience. My discoveries were so exciting, so personal, sometimes as ecstatic as few things I've known. I was never more carnal; the tension, the division, the strife was tremendous, and perplexing, and exhausting. I've kept notes about *that*.

I'll be a week at Brown Univ. starting Dec. 12, holding seminars, and informal rap sessions, etc. One evening I'll give a "public reading." It will be, to their astonishment, from the Jesus book. I'll discuss the problem and the experience of writing such a book, of writing about such a man. I find I'm evangelizing lots—unexpectedly, at dinner parties, among astounded old friends. I've been full of it, of the marvelous and beautiful and dramatic stories. More will come out of this strange adventure which has come to me, has been coming upon me since April. Can you believe that I have *written?* That I sat down every day and worked at writing, some days for 12 to 14 hours, as in the old days? A miracle. [. . .]

Cathy has left McGraw-Hill. She begins work at Ohrbachs, in the Exec. Div. next Monday. You do know that I was fired, most ignominiously. But my deep feeling is that I had asked for it, and that the Lord has pulled me out of the deadness, had forced me out. I asked Him to, promising I would do whatever He wanted me to do—I was that far gone. He done it, baby, oh He done it.

God I miss you and I do need your friendship. I'm so alone. But work is rich and alive and time is mine. I must work and keep well. I sink some, though. Work is dangerous for me, it can take me either way. But this, now, is what I'm supposed to do, and I have my guide and my leader, believe me. I'll go that way until there's no where else to go. [. . .]

---

review of the Alice book: Christopher Lehmann-Haupt's "Lewis Carroll in Criticland," review of *Aspects of Alice*, an anthology edited by Robert Phillips, in the *New York Times*, December 2, 1972, p. 8.
Phyllis: Goyen's agent, Phyllis Jackson.
A miracle: Goyen had not written for five or more years.
Cathy: Cathy Rockfol.

To Robert Phillips
TLS-2

New York
Dec. 30, 1971

Dear, dear Robert:

Don't be blue. I miss your friendship, too, and have been really blue and lonesome, with problems and madnesses, all gone, now; but they will return. Through Christmas, a sweet time, brief and asparkle and then out, as it should be. We are happy, Doris is so sweet and so much with me, my mainstay. [. . .] Michael, we adore, a young man of wit and sensitivity.

Brown was super. I was in residence for a week, during which time I held seminars, talked with students about their work in the Writing Program, read tons of mss, held two big seminars, one on publishing, the other on writing. The reading was marvelous, if I do say. We taped an hour and a half of it, but the best came after, when we talked together until three in the morning. All considered the little book, only about a third of which they heard (because of time) a personal witness, a deep, personal response to the "material." I kept speaking of the thing as a "writing problem." Imagine the personal experience of Jesus as ending up, simply, as a "writing problem"! But I wanted to keep out evangelism and emotion. I think I overturned a lot of heads. I learned very much about the little book and about how next to present it. Now I'm doing a little more work on it. Then I'll send you a copy. Wait. I'll go back to Brown for a three weeks' residency in April. A marvelous college. I'll want to do more, and I'll certainly get in touch with my friend Galen—as soon as there's time and the season is over. The Jesus movement is just beginning on campuses, and I believe our publication schedule is right: early Sept. with books in July: my visiting campuses in fall and winter, reading and holding rap sessions and seminars. Can you arrange one in Düsseldorf, ha! My German translator, harridan of the past, has reduxed (cf. Upjohn Dike), wants to make friends, do more of my work. We've forgiven each other, and that's good, since she is now just about the best translator from American into German (Elisabeth Schnack). The Jesus book should have a good reception in Germany. [. . .]

Oh the glory of being free again and at my desk. I'm still rearranging myself, I'm freeing myself, letting things come up from me as they will, to see what that *thing* in me that produced all that *other* will do, if free after all these years. I'm going to be an artist, and a poet, and be in life like that, for a while; to see. I'm hungry for so much, starved; I was near perishing from emptiness of work and staleness of daily deadly chores. *Now*, if I can thaw and loosen and limber and open, what will pour out? We'll see. It's a gift, a blessing, it was *given* to me as well as earned by me. I was pushed into it. I knew it was going to happen, I knew it in Italy, in London. I dreamt it. Now the page is turned. I love you all and miss you and wish you *life*. Doris, too. I'm *with* you.

Love,
Bill

Michael: Michael Cannata.
Galen: Galen Williams, the director of the Poetry Center at the YMHA (Young Men's Hebrew Association) in Manhattan. Goyen was hoping to give a reading from *A Book of Jesus*. He would not read at the Y until March 2, 1982, ten years later.
Upjohn Dike: John Updike (b. 1932), whose novel *Rabbit Redux* (New York: Fawcett, 1971) Goyen did not like.

To Daniel Stern
TLS-2

277 West End Ave.
New York City, 10023
February 3, 1972

Dear Danny:

Wait a minute! my good, petulant, childish, diva-esque, paranoic friend! Why on earth, if you think a minute, would I want to keep from you, or anyone, news of my leaving McGraw-Hill! Are you getting your mail? Do you not know that I wrote to you at the same time I wrote to Manès Sperber and all others; did you not have a Christmas note from me?

I was most viciously fired—by letter—by Albert Leventhal. I was asked to say that I was leaving to do my own work if I wanted separation pay, which I did. It really doesn't matter, since I was ready to leave and had been wanting to find the courage to stalk off and do my own work again—as you know. But the manner in which I was dismissed was appalling in its misjudgement and inaccuracies. It was, of all things, waiting for me in my mail when I returned home from Italy. I am surprised Robert Phillips, or some others, did not tell you this; although I told you in the note at Christmas. I did my best for my authors and their books in the short time they allowed me to stay; but Albert (and others, I'm sure, although I don't want to think about it anymore) seemed eager for me to get out; he'd already arranged for stop-gap editors (outside the house) to take over my best-selling authors, behind my back. But I did what I could. You (and I) are most certainly just as well out of that publishing house, and I'd like to think that my friends who are devoted to my work and welfare support and hurrah me. All of them—but you—have, and they do not yet know of my dismissal. It doesn't really matter any longer. Remember?

Sorry you took the time to be disgruntled and misinformed and couldn't write to me to say so. Love to Gloria and to *you*, bastard.

Bill

News:

The Jesus book is done and I and Dblday are very proud of it. It turned out to be what I'd hoped it would be. It will be published in September. I am now working on the novel and hoping to be able to stick with it through this year and deliver it by the end of the year. This depends on money, etc. It's, as you know, a time of rearrangement, first time in years I've lived a writer's day, day after day.

Doris in rehearsal for CBS-TV Special, "Look Homeward Angel," to be shown on February 25.

Send me your news—and for God's sake remember our friendship. Also check your fucking mail!

Yrs,
B.

They are now calling McGraw-Hill "Irving Trust Co." Too much.

---

your mail: Gloria and Daniel Stern were spending the year in Paris, France.
Manès Sperber: Manès Sperber (1905–1984). Austrian writer.
Albert Leventhal: A senior officer at McGraw-Hill Publishing, now deceased.
The Jesus book: Goyen's *A Book of Jesus.*
the novel: Come, the Restorer.
"Irving Trust Co.": McGraw-Hill had been duped into buying a fraudulent "autobiography" of Howard Hughes, penned by Clifford Irving.

To Anaïs Nin
TLS-*1*

277 West End Avenue
New York, N.Y. 10023
March 24, 1972

Dear Anaïs:

I have been wanting to write to you to give you news of myself which I think you will celebrate with me; and after seeing and experiencing your beautiful presence on television not long ago, I'd wanted to write to tell you how much I was impressed with you that evening.

I have left McGraw-Hill and am at last again writing fully. I left on November 1st and have been working at my desk and little more since then.

This new freedom is a joyous one, although a bit scary at times; but it must be done. I will, I hope, finish the novel by the end of this year. Once that novel is finished my publishers, Doubleday, will publish *The Collected*

Stories of William Goyen and then they promised to bring all my books back into print. I have finished a short and radical *Life of Jesus* which Doubleday will publish in January of next year, and already I have begun lecturing on this curious book and the strange and haunting material of it. I find young people in universities tremendously curious and eager to hear about it. I am therefore free to travel and speak to groups at universities or wherever, and maybe you will have some ideas for me.

Doris and I missed the gathering at Gotham Book Mart celebrating the last volume of your diary. We hated that, but we were in Italy.

I'm longing to see you and I feel so much more in myself, so much calmer and fuller since I am, once more, taking my chances as an artist. I send you my love as always and Doris too. Your constant growth and flowering delight me.

Love,
Bill

---

the novel: Goyen had begun writing *Come, the Restorer* (Garden City, N.Y.: Doubleday, 1974).
books back into print: Doubleday did not reprint Goyen's books.
Life of Jesus: Published as *A Book of Jesus* (Garden City, N.Y.: Doubleday, 1973).

To Margaret Cousins
TLS-1

277 West End Ave.
New York, 10023
July 11, 1972

Dear Maggie:
Aw come off it, for Christ's sake! I wasn't trying to tell *you* anything about Jesus—you knew the story before I did. But what about your readers? You're publishing for them, not for you or those like you. What a high-handed attitude to take, what an ugly feeling in this letter, copy of which I'm returning to you because it's very bad for the kind of work I'm trying to do, really a kill-joy.

Didn't you read the foreword to the book? Didn't you read what I announced as my intention? This is a dumb letter you wrote to Phyllis. And not the kind of spirit I need around the house these days in my work and life. Thanks a lot Maggie, for the kick in the behind. Point is, I'm returning one to yours. In the good old Christian spirit.

Bill

Margaret Cousins: Fiction/Books editor of *Ladies' Home Journal*, to whom Goyen's agent, Phyllis Jackson, had sent *A Book of Jesus*. Jackson made the mistake of sending Goyen a copy of Cousins's letter of rejection of the manuscript, in which she stated: "I'm afraid there is no possibility for it here, as it seems to me to be addressed to children. . . . The story is probably the most familiar story there is, and the problem, even for children, is to realize a time and a place and a people—to create a landscape and a climate which makes it all seem real. The New Testament makes fierce competition" (Cousins to Jackson, June 28, 1972).

To Samuel S. Vaughan and Stewart Richardson
TLS-2

277 West End Avenue
New York, N.Y. 10023
September 25, 1972

Dear Sam; Dear Sandy;

I'm just now telling you how much I appreciate your illuminating and supporting letter of August 25th. I've grown to expect and appreciate more and more your, what I call, encyclicals.

This is a rather special one, however, and it fingers my heart as well as my adrenal glands. It's still hard for me to see why The Jesus Book, for instance, must be an all-out hard cover book and not an accessible low-priced paperbound book for the racks, the high school and university book stores. I've just returned from my son's high school up in Northfield, Mass.—Mt. Herman School. There, in a school of 1100 young people between the ages of 14 and 19, was one of the most alive book stores I've seen. Do you know that all freshmen in most high schools are required to take a course called Religion? The text is the annotated Bible. But there are supplementary texts for this course and for more advanced courses in religion. All are in paperback costing from $.95 to $1.25. There is not one hard cover book in this exciting book store. *A Book of Jesus* should most certainly be one of the books in this book store next Spring—but as a hard cover book costing $3.50 it will hardly have a chance to be there. This is one book store out of hundreds of thousands where young people, for whom this book is passionately intended, should be able to find it and to buy it. May I suggest, again, that you all consider the possibility of publishing simultaneously, editions of hard- and soft covers? It could hardly be to your disadvantage as a publishing project. You might publish enough hard covers to satisfy reviewer and libraries— say, no more than 2500, and the rest, anywhere from 15 to 25,000 copies of paperback.

I earnestly want to be a part of the format and jacket design of *A Book of Jesus*. The final galleys, now being reset, were something of a shambles. *A Book of Jesus* should be a simple, eminently readable, and above all, *accessible*, book. It should be alive when the eye finds it and when the hand holds it. That is its very meaning and message. It should not look sacred, holy or antique.

A couple of weeks ago I met your new designer in Sandy's office and I am eagerly waiting to see what she comes up with. I mentioned then my hopes of seeing the jacket design as soon as possible, and mentioned again to Sandy my strong feelings about the use of a New Leaf design on the jacket and as ornamentation within the book. The New Leaf emblem is the very meaning of the man in the book. I have the very dry stalk with new green leaf astoundingly appearing right in my own flower box. There were three dry stalks which I kept meaning to pull out. When I finally went to do so, I found the tiny green of new life in the middle stalk. Doris took a Polaroid photo of the three stalks yesterday and I am sending you the picture so that you may see, as I did, that it makes a beautiful design and takes on the very meaning I had from it—and more—three cross-like figures as on Golgotha. The one in the middle, is alive, did not die. We must use this as we can, and I know you and Sandy will agree, if this picture is not useable, could not your photographer come here and take pictures? So much better than a drawing. This is out of Nature, out of Life! Then too the green leaf ornament could be used throughout the book, no matter how simple. I therefore see the book's color as green— life-green. If I sound taken, I am. What have I got to lose? [. . .]

Samuel S. Vaughan: (b. 1928). Editor-in-chief at Doubleday.

Stewart Richardson: Trade editor at Doubleday.

my son's: Goyen's stepson, Michael Robert Cannata.

your new designer: Eva Choremi.

color as green: The final jacket was yellow, pink, blue, and gray. The binding was blue. There was no leaf design.

New York City
October 25, 1972

My dear Robert:

We're not doing very well with the letters. For me it's total work, with little let-up except to chase Doris, who's on the road again (New Haven, Boston) with new Paul Zindel play (did I tell you?); she's coming home Sunday and they begin previews next week, open Nov. 14. Play has problems, so they're all unhappy and working twelve hours a day while performing at night. Doris is standing-by for Maureen and playing a strange, striking lady; also tap-dancing.

I'm determined to finish the novel by end of this year (did I tell you). Jesus book has had no end of fuck-ups, the totally re-set galleys are still not ready; I launched a wild demand for paperback; they pouted; they now promise paperback in the fall; are charging $4.95 for the book, which makes an entirely different kind of thing from what I began with. I'm disappointed with Doubleday; they talk a lot and forget what they said, feel they've done it when they've said it . . . baby.

At any rate this is a strange novel, haunting the hell out of me, about Jewel de Persia and Mr. de Persia and Addis. Three people who have moved in on my life. The book is not being written by me, it is revealing itself—the way all my books have done. I have to wait until the story shows itself. Pieces come—here, there; hang there, manifestly, without any apparent connections. What I write for is to find the connections. But I am pushing this, as I told you (did I?), running after it, trying not to brood over it, trying not to let it stab me to death, hurt me, make me sick.

Then I am with my St. Francis (*A Book of St. Francis*), trying to plan and design it and using Anne to help on that. After that, my plan is to write the autobiographical book, incorporating *Six Women*. I'll want a contract for *St. Francis*, the Autobiography, and probably my Paul book (*A Book of St. Paul*). I'm really not sure about Doubleday at this point. They've behaved badly. They love and they mean well, but they just don't do good, thorough work; and I need a passionate editor, one I can be passionate with, one who adores me and my work. Sandy is not that editor. He pretends to be. Sam Vaughan could be, and I went there for him. Now he's perched on the top trapeze, President and beyond all suffering. I have other ideas, but I'm not sure.

You? Why don't you write to this frogboy? When are you all coming home? Elisabeth Schnack is putting together a *Selected Works* for Manesse, a distinguished publishing house in Zürich. They have a Manesse Bibliothek. I believe there'll be 14 stories. Diogenes might do the *Collected Stories*, as you hope. I'm hoping to publish a *Selected Works* here, before the *Collected Stories*—probably under the guidance of my excellent nephew, Donald Gerrard, whose Bookworks–Random House imprint is now very fine and a vaunted one. He would design, select, and shape the volume, low-priced, for Universities, etc. Good?

The YMHA boycotted me on the *Jesus*, said they're too "orthodox." Ha! I'm now trying to organize a university lecture tour. Have you any ideas who could help me? The gal at Doubleday—typically—suddenly left; they now plan to suspend their lecture bureau for awhile. [. . .]

Paul Zindel play: Zindel (b. 1936) wrote the play *The Secret Affairs of Mildred Wilde*, produced on Broadway in 1972.
Maureen: Maureen Stapleton (b. 1928). American actress.
charging $4.95: Goyen had wanted a very inexpensive paperback that students could afford.
Jewel de Persia and Mr. de Persia and Addis: Characters in *Come, the Restorer*.
A Book of St. Francis: Never published.
A Book of St. Paul: Never published, perhaps never begun.
Sandy: Stewart Richardson, trade editor at Doubleday.
frogboy: Playful nickname for Goyen, based on character in *The House of Breath*.
a Selected Works: Selected Writings of William Goyen: Eight Favorites by a Master American Storyteller. Illustrated by Elizabeth Fairbanks. A Random House/Bookworks Book (New York and Berkeley, 1974).

To Elisabeth Schnack
TLC-1

277 West End Avenue
New York, N.Y. 10023
April 5, 1974

My dear Elisabeth:
    It's all very exciting and I rush to tell you that I would *love* to give a lecture at the British-Swiss Society. I have most recently given a rousing one at Brown University entitled "The Novelist Writing for the Theatre" or "The Novelist Loses his Privacy." This naturally has to do with the

theatre experience as suffered by the writer of books. People are very much interested in this topic and most novelists one finds are secretly yearning to write for the theatre; few are very good at it. This would give me a chance to talk about the American Theatre in which I have been working intensely during the last few years and about the American writer of books.

If this is not satisfactory, then another topic I have recently spoken on at the university is the American Writer and His Environment. This is particularly close to me since I, as you know, better than most people write from Nature and from the simplicity of Nature. Where is Nature? It is vanishing so rapidly in the American countryside that there is scarcely a Wilderness left. This, as you know, has been the theme of my work for thirty years. I could talk on and on about this—indeed, I'm almost an Evangelist on the subject.

Do, dear Elisabeth, please arrange for this, as it would please me very much and also help out. May I ask you please to arrange for a comfortable (I am not as poor as I once was) room at the Kurhaus Zureschberg beginning May 19th for a week. [. . .]

And last, dear Elisabeth, I want to help you with the novel. It is called *Come, the Restorer* and enclosed is the blurb for the jacket which the publishers will be using. Maybe this helps.

Thank you for everything, dear Elisabeth. Soon.

Love,

To Elizabeth Spencer
ALS-2

New York, New York
Dec. 4, 1974

Dear Elizabeth:

Thank you for all you've said. I'm very pleased. Doubleday seems to be too. Thanks for the effort and time you gave—and for what you saw in the book, and for the way you read it and approached speaking about it. People want all books to be like theirs, or to be a "novel" and therefore like all "novels." Even Pulitzer Prize laureates seem to want this, as though there were a strict genre called "The Novel." If not, they're adrift, poor things. The sad thing is (even disastrous sometimes) that, being adrift, these people are neither in the boat nor in the water.

I'm sorry you've lost your mother. But it seems she'd come round to something. Doris has lost her mother, Ann, in June. A great loss for all of us. We still grieve. She didn't want it and refused to come to terms with it. She signed a new three-year lease on her apartment on her deathbed—a ghostly scrawl taking half an hour. She had a choice of one, two, three years.

We voyaged, after that grief, to France on the *France*. Which sort of mutinied three miles off Le Havre and discarded us onto a tug, in cold rain. But once in Paris, it was lovely, my first return in 20 years. I had forsaken France for Italy. Now I love France again. Later a rather dreary London, but pleasant enough.

Since then I have kept myself in, to my schedule of 5 a.m. to 3 p.m. working on a *Memoir of Six Women*—which is really autobiographical. I rarely go out or fool with what is called "The World." What good? Doris works hard, a lot in California—the *Lily Tomlin Comedy Hour*. Do you know or see it? Very good, funny. Hope John is fine. Greet him for Doris and me. Keep working. And so many thanks for what you said and wrote. In the *Memoir* there is a section on "Publishing." I've been re-living a lot of McGraw-Hill days!

Love,
Bill

---

all you've said: Elizabeth Spencer, the novelist, had written Goyen's Doubleday editor in praise of the manuscript of his *Come, the Restorer*.
Ann: Ann Roberts, to whom Goyen dictated drafts of *Come, the Restorer*, a method of composition limited to this novel, which broke a silence of eleven years between works of fiction.
John: Spencer's husband, John Rusher.

To Maurice Coindreau
ALS-1

New York
Feb. 24, 1975

My dear Maurice:
Reviews of your *Memoires* are very fine indeed. Congratulations! Friends send me copies—one as far away as Vancouver, British Columbia! I hope you're happy and satisfied. I can't remember how many letters I

sent to you during the strike. Did you write to me? Apparently all that is lost. I would like to see some of the reviews of the *Memoires* if you can manage. Is Christian happy? I hope so, and please tell him, for me.

I have delivered *The Collected Stories of William Goyen* to my publishers for a Fall (Oct.) publication. I have written a Preface and I feel very pleased. This book means very much to me. *The House of Breath* 25th Anniversary Edition appears on April 7, with great celebration promised. People (critics, writers, editors) are writing from all over and a great ad will be published. This makes me feel proud, shy and older! Random House is publishing this edition—the "Silver Anniversary Edition." There will be a reception at the Gotham Book Mart, and pieces in the *New York Times Book Review* and *Publishers Weekly*. I wish you were going to be here with me: my baby is 25!

Maurice, perhaps Gallimard could publish *The Collected Stories?* It's quite a volume: 26 stories. Couldn't they—or somebody—do a distinguished edition of it? I must say I am smarting under the treatment they gave me concerning *Come, the Restorer.* No publisher, *even in America,* treats an author like that. I know you did your best, and it most certainly is not your fault—how could it be? But the arrogance! Never one word to me. And where was Michel Mohrt? I'm very sorry for this. It was a blight on my visit to France. Never mind, dear Maurice.

I am deep into my Memoires and finding many secrets I'd lost or forgotten. Then I am barely beginning a novel. And the play *Aimee!* goes on. I live only to work, I can't help it, it is my life.

Please be well, give my affections to my friends, and write.

Bill

Memoires: Coindreau's *Memoires d'un traducteur: Entretiens avec Christian Guidicelli* (Paris: Gallimard, 1974). Coindreau discussed Goyen's writing on pp. 76–85.

The Collected Stories of William Goyen: Robert Phillips had silently photocopied most of Goyen's published stories, assembled them as a typescript, and presented it to Goyen on his sixty-fifth birthday (April 24, 1975). Goyen then presented it to Doubleday, who accepted it in lieu of a novel or the autobiography *Six Women.* It was published in November 1975.

the arrogance: Come, the Restorer was rejected by Gallimard.

Michel Mohrt: Novelist and senior editor for Gallimard who wrote several essays on Goyen's work, including "Un Naturisme poétique" in *Le Nouveau Roman américain* (Paris: Gallimard, 1955), pp. 236–240.

my Memoires: Six Women, unpublished in book form, although the chapter on Margo Jones appeared as "Margo" in *William Goyen: New Work and Work-in-Progress* (Evanston, Ill.: Palaemon Press and *TriQuarterly,* 1983), pp. 22–26.

beginning a novel: Originally titled *Visitors*, this became *Arcadio* (New York: Clarkson N. Potter, 1983).

the play Aimee!: A musical which premiered at the Trinity Square Repertory in Providence, Rhode Island, on December 6, 1973. Goyen wrote the book and the lyrics. It was directed by Adrian Hall.

To James Leo Herlihy
ALS-2

New York
February 27, 1975

Dearest Jamie,

It is so good to be in touch with you again, my dear one. The years have not kept you out of my mind. I lost touch of you after Key West— and now I know where you are.

You've been beautiful about *The House of Breath*. Isn't it wonderful? A piece of me—the generating part—is being regenerated. It makes me very *young* again. That you are sharing it gives me joy. My memory of you is last laid in a New York apartment and involves a great luxuriant *fern*. What were we doing with it? You were moving out or in and the fern was the question. But what a green and fertile metaphor for my last sight and memory of you.

My work goes on day after day. Destiny has chosen (or my fucking publishers) that it lag on the way. I had not dreamt it would be so slow, but, after the initial (and early) shock, I am prepared for a slow dancer.

Jamie, I love you as always. Be with me as I am with you.

I had to touch you now.

As always,
BILL

---

about The House of Breath: Doris Roberts had written Herlihy requesting a blurb for the forthcoming 25th Anniversary Edition.

luxuriant fern: Herlihy had given the plant to Goyen when Herlihy was moving from New York to Key West in 1958.

To Robert Phillips
ACS-1

8968 Lloyd Pl.
Los Angeles, 90069
Aug. 13 [1975]

Dearest Robert:

Long silence denotes moving (a charming little house) and unhappiness. I've turned against this deadly place. Been very blue. Want my West End Ave. seclusion. Miss New York. Miss you and my few friends and all the old ways. But Doris works and wants to stay. She's in demand (mostly TV). So I'll do my best. But it's not for me. Suddenly I knew it. I find it very hard to work.

Is the interview now O.K.? I think it's probably very good. Why don't you write? Or call? I need news of you, news of home. Thanks for what you're doing for *The Collected Stories*. Tell me what's going on. I feel so lost, so out-of-touch. [...]

---

the interview: The forthcoming *Paris Review* interview with Goyen, which Phillips had conducted in June 1975 in Katonah, New York.

To Ellen Garwood
ALS-2

Inn of the Governors
Santa Fe, New Mexico
September 13, 1975

My dear Ellen:

I am so tired, but I must write to you. It will be difficult to tell where I am, what has happened; I can only give you a glimpse—and I need, above all, your sympathetic insights, even your advice, your dear friendship.

I am tonight in Santa Fe, as you see. I came suddenly last Monday upon a call from my beloved Dorothy Brett in my old beloved Taos. I had very privately reached a level of despair (I'm sorry to admit—but I can, to you) in Los Angeles. I have not been able to bear it; it has killed my vitality and my creative strength. I have wanted to die. I saw, forgive me, no way out. I could not leave Doris, and Doris said, "This is the most exciting time of my life." I have tried to hide my dying, I must try to stand behind my wife. But I have not been able to. Please, what I tell you is in utmost confidence, only between you and me. Doris must not know that I am telling you this. I decided to take my life. I tried. I did not have enough medicine. I called a friend (I had gone to Newport Beach), the friend came and got me through. But I am still afraid. I am searching for hope.

It was at this point that my Brett wrote for me to come (*Please* don't tell Warren Roberts about my coming to Taos). I must be brief. I came. We've had a beautiful time together. I stayed next door in my old beautiful, simple house that I built with Indians in 1946. A *great* mysterious vitality came into me, a *saving*, life-restoring power came, out of the great mountain near my house, out of the land, out of "my" house, out of the mysterious force in 92-year-old Brett. A man had bought the house and land and added an extravagant annex to my simple dwelling, but it is left intact. Brett had wanted to give me back a piece of my land, seeing that my salvation—all of this unexpected—was coming from it. Alas, she had willed everything to the man, her own house and land, even. Since the land is very valuable, he waits for Brett to go and then sell the land. Brett has begged for a piece of my own land to be deeded back to me. I can build a simple house again. It will bring me my *life* again, my *work*. Why should I—even if the man were willing—*buy* the land? But he is demanding that. I am exhausted with this and know that I should fight for it. I honestly do not have any money—another reason for my despondency. My books have made *no* money. What came from the sale of my mss. to the Univ. of Texas I've used to get us going in Calif. and to try to save to write on. But I wonder, should I persist in fighting? *Yes*. It is my hope and salvation. I can get there from Los Angeles in 2 1/2 hrs. and work while Doris is working. Don't you agree?

I'm here in Santa Fe (70 miles away from Taos) for the week-end to try to get a perspective. It is one of the most critical times of my life.

I'll go back to Taos on Monday 15th (this is Sat. night) and stay on for a few more days, until Wed. 17th. The light will come. Pray for me and help me as I know you will.

I will be at the residence of Dorothy Brett, El Prado, N.M. She is listed in the phone book. The man's name is John Manchester. Just in case you want to reach me.

The separation between Doris and me would be bad; but it has, obviously, become a life necessity. She must work where she can even as I. But I've never known such despair that nothing can reach. I had invested our money in coming to L.A.—I made a mistake, except that we did get Doris where she feels she must be. But the money I had wanted for a house out of N.Y. (from the mss.) misfired for me.

Think of me. Try to help me by giving me your mind. Shall I follow the pull, that draws one here [missing line]? Dear Ellen, thank you. God bless you and love.

Bill

Ellen Garwood: Austin, Texas, patron who had funded the acquisition of some of Goyen's papers in 1975 by the Harry Ransom Humanities Research Center.
ALS-2: This may be the draft of a letter that was not sent.
Warren Roberts: At the time of this letter, director of the Harry Ransom Humanities Research Center. No relation to Doris Roberts.

To Robert Phillips
ALS-2

L.A. (99 miles from)
November 29, 1975

Dear Robert:

My bride brings me brief news of you from her whirlwind visit to N.Y. (I think it did her good.) I'm ready to come back (for three days back into Los Angeles from that visit to New York, I suddenly died again: I can find no way to survive out here—it just kills me). So, although I dislike leaving Doris behind, I'll be returning Jan. 5. The apt. will be available, and I'll move in. It'll be marvelous to work in my old workroom again, although I'll be lonely without Doris.

I was overwhelmed by Joyce Carol Oates' review. (It was really an essay.) It's just too much for me to absorb so soon—so rich and full and tender. I read it all in one gulp; now I'll savor it piecemeal and slowly. I never expected such thorough, careful attention. The piece has brought me mail from all corners. Friends feel they must send me the piece, cut out, as a kind of gift to me from *them*, and a recognition. I've written a note back to Miss Oates but I'd forgotten about the strike—the letter came back. How does she receive her mail? How can I reach her?

There is a beautiful, loving review in the *Chicago Tribune* of Nov. 9 (Sun.) by Richard Rhodes. I sent him a note—he lives in Kansas City— and today he answered with an equally loving letter. He's written a good novel, *The Ungodly*, just out in paperback. He's marvelous—a new discovery. [. . .]

---

99 *miles from:* Goyen was much taken with Art Garfunkel's rendition of Hal David and Albert Hammond's song "99 Miles from Nowhere," from the album *Breakaway* (New York: Columbia Records, 1975).
Oates' review: Of *Collected Stories*, in the *New York Times Book Review*, November 16, 1975, pp. 4, 14.
by Richard Rhodes: (b. 1937). "William Goyen's World Is Enormous and Enormously Minute," *Chicago Tribune Book World*, November 9, 1975, p. 3.

To Robert Phillips
ALS-2

Los Angeles
Sunday, May 16, 1976

Anaïs has had someone write me asking me to come see her. She can't *write*. Something happened. I'll tell you. Have seen the charmer Jamie (Leo) Herlihy. Had an evening I'll tell you about.

Dear Robert:
    Thank you for the birthday book about St. Francis and his four ladies. I'm eager to read it. Is this the one you once told me about? At any rate, I was not reprimanding you, only wanting to be in touch with you on or near that occasion—which marked the end of an awful year: my Sixtieth, although marked by a constant hard-on (one of the most tormenting heats of my sixty years), was a just-about totally negative year. You know it all, so I'll save ink. What I thought was my most distinguished book and certainly one of the most distinguished American books in decades got not one distinction given it—Zero. This made me quite disinterested in writing at the moment, quite bitter about my peers, quite sorry about America and trying to live and work as a serious artist. Once again I doubt everything. My fear is that I missed some turning, or didn't take the right turning. My sense of it is that something was meant to climax, shoot off, didn't. Certainly there was a load on.
    Well, we need to talk. I can't write it all. I sit here with my pore eye and my curled hair and don't mind—I'm neither here nor there. Doris comes and goes and seems to be doing what I'd planned to do—here and

there. I've made a few desperate moves toward action—one a fast trip to Paris for a week. I needed Europe. Called Repusseau, who offered me his apt. I made my first-class (ha!) reservation. Next morning I canceled it. Then decided with Doris's O.K. to move back to N.Y. Then changed that. [. . .]

So I sit here, threatened by the earthquake, until (I guess) Sept. 1.

The *Nine Poems* limited edition is now signed and being bound. It's due to be published—226 copies—in May. It's *very* handsome. Don't worry, I have one for you. It's the Albondocani Press. [. . .]

There's a lovely review by Kirsch in the *L.A. Times.*

P.E.N. called & wanted to know if I'd be a candidate for President. I said no. Would I serve on the Board? Yes.

I'm very fond of Howard Moss—a friend since I first came to N.Y. He introduced me to Joe Glasco and John Malcolm Brinnin. And I'm so fond of Robert Carter. Please give them both my love. [. . .]

Anaïs: Anaïs Nin.

most distinguished book: His *Collected Stories.*

pore eye: Goyen was suffering a detached retina.

Repusseau: Patrice Repusseau (b. 1948). French scholar and translator of twentieth-century American literature, who was planning a Goyen issue of the literary journal *Delta.*

review by Kirsch: Robert Kirsch (1922–1980) reviewed *Collected Stories* in the *Los Angeles Times,* May 10, 1975, p. iv.

P.E.N.: P.E.N. American Center, headquartered in Manhattan.

Howard Moss: (1927–1987) Lyric poet and poetry editor of *The New Yorker.*

John Malcolm Brinnin: (b. 1916). Poet and biographer of Dylan Thomas and Gertrude Stein.

Robert Carter: Robert Ayres Carter (b. 1930). American author.

To John Igo
TLS-1

8968 Lloyd Pl.
Los Angeles 90069
May 21, 1976

Dear John:

What a stunning review! Surely one of the best essays on my work that's been written. How glad, how fortunate I am to have you. Live long!

Several people have sent xeroxes of the review to me, as well as those you wrote for *Choice*. So you're widely read. Bless you, love you.

I'm still having trouble from the eye operation (torn retina, did I tell you?) in Feb. My vision in that eye (rt) is still troubled. A bore and a discouragement. Keeps me somewhat limited. As for L.A. I've lost my loathing for it, miraculously, and a kind of acceptance has set in. This is good, since Doris is finding some dreams coming true here and is having fun working. She expects a very good year this year. . . .

But I'll be back in our apt. in N.Y. since I'm going to teach at Princeton for the Fall Semester (3 Fiction Writing Seminars).

Wish I could see you. I was working in the Humanities Research Center at the U. of Texas when the eye went funny, early Feb. Had hoped, had that not happened, to get over to see you for a week-end. Next time, for I still have a lot of work to do in that most marvelous collection (for my *Memoirs*).

Doris sends her love. She's at present working in a movie written and directed by Anne Bancroft. We miss you. Hello to my friends there. And I'm honored, instructed and enraptured by the superb essay on the *Stories*. May all be rich and rewarding for you . . . Send us news.

Faithfully,
Bill

---

stunning review: Igo's review of *Collected Stories of William Goyen* ("Texan Explores All Tribes of Man," *San Antonio Express*, April 18, 1976, sec. H, p. 7).
working in the Humanities Research Center: Goyen was consulting his own papers as he worked on *Six Women*.
my Memoirs: The unpublished *Six Women*.

To Robert Phillips
ALS-2

L.A.
Aug. 19 [1976]

Robert:

Sure Repusseau can use the Glasco drawing (he must have seen it in the Rice Univ. collection), but 1) I don't know Glasco's address and 2) the beautiful cat on the German edition of *Faces of Blood Kindred* (title,

Zamour und Anderen Erzahlen) is very similar. Would he not need only the permission of the Fondren Library to use the drawing (if that's where he saw it—I believe Joe drew it, for fun, on the ms. of the stories.) [. . .]

I'm eager to get there, and confused, divided. I have an urge, a call, sort of, to go back into publishing. I'm sick, heart-sick, of writing to publish, of writing at all; disillusioned and tired. Something is happening in me. We'll talk.

I haven't yet read your piece on the poems. If this is what you want to contribute, O.K. I love the title, "Exalted Times." Ahh—they got worse, my times.

B.

---

back into publishing: For a time Goyen was a free-lance "finder" of manuscripts for Doubleday.
your piece on the poems: Originally Phillips was to contribute an essay on Goyen's poetry to the issue of *Delta* edited by Patrice Repusseau. Instead, he published a piece on the stories in *Ghost and Flesh*.

To John Igo
ACS-1

Los Angeles
(Christmas 1976)

Dear John:

Merry Christmas.

We're in a new place, a charming little home . . .

I'm just beginning to tolerate (Los Angeles), which I hated for months. Suddenly it's better. Nevertheless I'll begin working in New York, trying to finish the new book by April 1 (ha!). I'll commute.

We've enjoyed hearing from you, dear one, forgive us for the silence. That truly was because I was so despondent and lost here. Wish we could all be together. Walk to some Mexican restaurant or something . . .

Bill and Doris

---

a new place: Goyen and Roberts had moved in November.
the new book: Unspecified. It was probably either *Six Women* or *Wonderful Plant*.

To Samuel Vaughan
and Stewart Richardson
TLS-2

277 West End Avenue
New York, New York 10023
July 10, 1977

Dear Sam and Sandy:

In my ripening years as a durable author I look for more loving care, more demonstrated respect from my publishers, signs of modest attention, reasonable spiritual support. Indeed, it has always been my simple conviction (as editor and author) that the life of publishing lies in the author-editor relationships: Not too much to expect, it seems to me. What other relationship matters? Publisher-bindery? Publisher-warehouse? The best thing for a publisher to have for himself is an author who supplies him a book to publish. That being is valuable to him—*very* valuable. To demonstrate a publisher's awareness of an author's value is the primary purpose of a publisher. Editors are appointed, as a publisher's representative, to do this. Since Christmas 1976 (and that at my instigation after repeated attempts at communication), I have neither heard from nor seen my editor. Since that time some cause for greeting from my editor and my publisher has made itself known: a major literary interview, an eminent literary distinction bestowed by an eminent university, a Birthday, significant notices of my work and literary worth in significant publications. What author among your thousands of authors would not be disheartened by such apparent irresponsibility, such plain bad taste, such—finally—arrogance?

My disappointment has grown over the years. I have repeatedly made it known to you. The physical quality of my books—the tiny type face, the slim appearance, the flimsy binding, the cheap paper have embarrassed me and the general reading public insofar as I have encountered it in book stores, universities where I have read, etc. The absence of advertisements, the failure to reprint my books, the pitiful handling of my last novel, *Come, the Restorer*; the lack of energy and interest invested in all my books, particularly the aforementioned novel and *The Collected Stories*, should be sufficient evidence to embarrass you and bring you relief at being shed of me. I have no energy with which to list grievances beyond these, nor to pile up details of further dissatisfaction. I just simply don't want to publish my books with Doubleday any longer; and what editor/publisher wants to publish books by an author so spiritless? I'm through, gentlemen.

My debt to Doubleday amounts to $12,500 on an existing contract. You will receive repayment of that debt shortly.

Sincerely yours,
William Goyen

---

major literary interview: The *Paris Review* interview (Winter 1976).
an eminent literary distinction: Goyen received the Distinguished Alumni Award from Rice University in 1977.
a Birthday: Goyen was sixty-two on April 15, 1977.
on an existing contract: An advance of $12,500 had been made for a manuscript of *Six Women.* The book was never completed.

To Patrice Repusseau
ALS-2

New York City
Jan. 24, 1978

Dear Patrice:

You are, again, a teacher. Welcome to the ranks. And where is your village? Never mind, keep on with your own work as you can, and fuck the Oil King crook. It's exciting that you have a new book of poems. Who will publish it? Will you send it to me?

Did you get, at last, the Oates review? I've finished a strange, apocalyptic story—it has moved me so deeply and strangely; it has come to me as a gift out of the mysteries, I suppose, since it is certainly not autobiographical. I have wept over it. I want you to see it. It is a part of this strange new work that is coming to me, about the drunken nurseryman in the icebound greenhouse of glass, the dear Hermaphrodite named Arcadio ("Nature's Quirk") who is called Sideshow, the hideous insect that lived at the heart of a Venetian peach and leapt out at the eater who broke the fruit open and was lost in the flowering bushes of Venice where in the night it spun over the path of that same man a jeweled web that shone in the morning dew; and these two loving brothers who tried to kill each other. Etc. I am enchanted by this world and care only for it and wish I could sink into it away from any other. It is totally mine, has nothing to do with any other world, really my own secret and to Hell with editors and publishers and reviewers and critics and booksellers.

Fuck them all, I must find a way to live without them and make my stories only for my self.

I am enclosing the check for the wonderful artist Mockel and I'm so grateful for the "l'inquiet." I haven't yet been able to get uptown to fetch the other engraving from the gentleman who called to tell me that he has it—we are more or less snowbound. But I'm so happy to have it. [. . .] I have not heard from Michel Place—nor M. Mohrt at Gallimard. How is my cut-worm? [. . .]

---

your village: Repusseau had moved from Paris to Laval.
Oil King: Character in *Come, the Restorer.*
the Oates review: Of Goyen's *Collected Stories.*
drunken nurseryman: From "In the Icebound Hothouse."
hideous insect: From "The Texas Principessa."
two loving brothers: From "The Precious Door."
Mockel: Francis Mockel (b. 1940). French painter and engraver. Goyen bought three of his gravures in 1977. An appreciation of his work by Goyen, "A propos de Suite Funèbre de Francis Mockel," was published in *Francis Mockel—Gravures* (Arcane 17, St. Nazaire, 1982) and reprinted in the exhibition booklet of the same title in 1986 (Centre de Development Culturel de Boulogne-Sur-Mer).
Michel Place: Jean-Michel Place, publisher who issued Repusseau's translations of *The Faces of Blood Kindred* (as *Zamour et autres nouvelles*) in Paris in 1977.

To Roberta Pryor
TLS-1

277 West End Ave.
New York, N.Y. 10023
March 26, 1978

Dear Roberta:
Please help with the following?
Insist from Sam Vaughan that the reversion of rights be assigned to me on the following:
A Book of Jesus, published in 1973
Come, the Restorer, published in 1974
You'll recall (from a copy of my letter to Sam and Sandy) that the remaindering of *Come, the Restorer* was one of the sources of, shall we call it, disenchantment with Doubleday and my editors: I came upon a mountain of the novel—a writer's bad dream—in Barnes and Noble,

heaped under a pert sign that said, "Books for a Buck"; what was so bad was that my photo covering the back was displaying leeringly. Oh well, the shock and the momentary bad feelings are gone, but the plain knowledge that the rights should now be officially mine persists. Please? [. . .]

Roberta Pryor: Goyen's agent at International Creative Management. She replaced Phyllis Jackson as agent for his book properties.

SEVEN

Los Angeles

New York

Los Angeles

1978–1983

To Margaret L. Hartley
ALS-2

Los Angeles
June 10, 1978

Dearest Margaret:

I'm out here for a while—a day at a time, since I'm not really very happy in Los Angeles—to be with Doris (who works most of the time here in films and TV). I hasten to tell you of my happiness that you'll publish "Precious Door" in *Southwest Review*. I feel I am in a new beginning in my work and the place to start again, in hope and trust, is with you and Allen and the *Southwest Review*, where I first began. I'm so happy to be with you.

Yes, the way you put it is right: I am, as it is turning out, writing a group of stories into a single piece. I hope, if I may, to show you more. There is a small mass of work already done.

Yes, please use "whom" on page 5. And on p. 6, do please change "heavy beard" to "thick beard." Thanks.

I'll be back at my New York address in a few weeks—certainly by July 1. Oddly, I work better there. I have utmost privacy. And do not feel isolated. Oddly, again, L.A. gives one little solitude. The air rings with stale TV plots and everything—which seems, to me, so little—is out in the "open." I have to be closed a lot. [. . .]

"*Precious Door*": Appeared in *Southwest Review* 63, no. 4 (Autumn 1978): 330–336.

To Joseph Savino and Mark Zipoli
ALS-2

Los Angeles
September 27, 1978

Dear Joseph Savino and Mark Zipoli:

I feel bad about the long silence between your wonderful letter (April 18, 1978) and mine of right now, September 27, 1978, written from my bed upon which I lie in temperature (the weather's not mine) that has ranged during the last five days between 102° and 107°, recovering from unexpected surgery three weeks ago and beginning to feel my good strength again.

I am not often here, since my wife is an actress working in films and television though I do not much care for the place and prefer my own apartment (i.e., my family's and mine) and workroom in New York. And I am here, because of my illness, when I had expected to be back in New York (where I shall return, doctor willing, in early November).

By now you have weathered five months in your new life and under your beautiful new commitment you wrote to me about. I hope you are still there; I am sure that you are; I pray that you are. Give it some more months, my friends. Writing is a lifetime's work and I have always seen it as that. It was just what I was going to do for the length of my life, no matter how cruelly it treated me, how "unsuccessful" I was, who tried to talk me out of it, counsel me about it, warn me, disparage me. I was no martyr or saint—though in memory it seems I sometimes took the stance of those (now I see, at those times when I was most afraid). I stayed away—in deserts, on mountains, in *Pensions*, backstreet bed-sitting rooms. It was the staying away that I think about now as I'm writing to you; staying away, more than hiding out or escaping. I see that I had to do this to stay *with* what I was writing, which took the life out of most everything else except Nature itself, took the life out of love affairs, family building, owning things, insurance, and so forth. Did I stay away when I should have been there? And those times when I was there, my God should I have stayed away? Well, I wrote and still do, lived as a man writing, and still do. The lifetime goes on, piling up memory and feeling, which is what I go on writing about. Simplicity helped. Can one live a life of simplicity now? More than ever I fight for it. Basic daily living, a day at a time. Living in many places (while staying away). Not getting *bound*. Keep the senses clean, and out of the head. Whitman (I'm reading him again right now) wrote "If the body is not the soul, then what is the soul?" Feeling and trying to keep feeling *true*, not to fuck up feeling, trying to write from *true* feeling, working to get that and to find true *words* for it. And telling people when you care, as you do me.

I'm so glad you wrote me what you did. If you're still there—and I know you are—send me a note to let me know. Forgive my silence. God speed!

Sincerely
William Goyen

Joseph Savino and Mark Zipoli: Both were twenty-three-year-old aspiring writers at the time of this correspondence. They had read Erika Duncan's profile of Goyen in *Book Forum,* which then sent them to *The House of Breath.* They were so taken by the prose that they wrote Goyen a "fan letter" and asked him if he would come to their apartment "for a good old-fashioned Italian dinner," which he did (letter from Mark Zipoli to Robert Phillips, June 4, 1990).

unexpected surgery: For dupetrends, knitted tendons in the hand which make it curl up like a claw.

your beautiful new commitment: Both young men had recently quit their jobs for "art"— determined to devote their lives to writing while sacrificing the security of the nine-to-five existence. "Needless to say, it was a mistake from which we learned a very grave lesson," Zipoli ironically reported (letter to Robert Phillips, June 4, 1990). They saw Goyen only one other time, at a reading at Books and Company in Manhattan. In awe of his public presence, they did not make themselves known.

To Robert Phillips
ALS-2

Los Angeles
October 3, 1978

My plane reservation is for Nov. 2, when Doc. says I can move.

Dear Robert:

Thanks for all the letters, the poems, the poem to me, and your good thoughts, and all. It's one month today since the surgery and I'm getting stronger, readier for the fray. Still hurts, but less. A long September. [. . .]

I work in my bed every morning for a couple of hours (early) then read most of the day. I go on blithely with *Arcadio,* letting it lead me. I've read all the Kerouac stuff and, as I told you, am drawn to the story for some unknown reason. It may be the Kerouac-Memere (his mother) relationship, which is heart-breaking, or the Kerouac-Cassady relationship, which is heart-breaking, for me. It's all very close to me, and somehow (yet for me to know) has to do with my Arcadio story. *Certainly* it has to do with my own life and history. I remember Kerouac standing in corners of a few parties Bob Giroux (then courting me away from Random House to him at Harcourt, Brace) took me to. You'll remember that I (with Walter Berns) was on the road and in San Francisco ten years before all the bunch got there. Driving across the country from Texas to California in a 1930's Chevrolet with all we owned piled in the back seat up to the top with layers of books on top. This is how we found Taos in 1945 (Jan.)

It was in 1947 that we first came into San Francisco & environs. Was with Rexroth. A life I still can't shape. I miss you.

Love,
Bill

Kerouac stuff: Goyen had asked Phillips to supply him with books about the life of Jack Kerouac (1922–1969), with whom he was fascinated.
Cassady: Neal Cassady, part of Kerouac's circle.
Bob Giroux: Robert Giroux (b. 1914). Author and publisher.
Rexroth: Kenneth Rexroth (1905–1982). Prolific American poet and essayist and the presiding figure of the San Francisco Renaissance.

To Patrice Repusseau
ALS-1

New York
May 26, 1979

Dear Patrice:
   I am here and pretty shattered, absolutely worn out. Florence was a madhouse of cars with insane drivers. One could scarcely walk in the streets and did not dare stop to look up at a Basilica. I have returned feeling that Europe is a disaster of inhospitable people and dreadful cities. I do not want to return for a very long time, if ever. The Europe I loved is ruined. I found America little better. The same insanity drives these people. I care little for the world right now and have been sitting very still and alone for three days. I have felt that I have not wanted to live on.
   Mme. Ballorain agreed to make the changes (of little extent, only some few words and sentences) I asked. The piece you receive from her will be acceptable. She was quite agreeable and I liked her, finally. But no more interviews for me.
   Thank you for your patience and loyalty and for your superb work. Had you not been there in Paris I'd have left, no doubt. I was on the verge of doing so anyway, on one bad day. Doris has raced to Los Angeles to work. I'll remain here in New York until June 15 when I'll return to Los Angeles. Love to Monique. Thank you again for everything.

Bill

Mme. Ballorain: Rolande Ballorain, French educator, whose interview with Goyen appeared in *Delta* 9 (November 1979): 7–45.

To John Igo
TLS-1

LA
Nov. 5, 1979

Dear John:

Thanks for your careful and loving help to Arcadio; he appreciates, she appreciates, I appreciate it. I feel more secure now, although I'll stick with *Tomasso*—got so used to it. He's suddenly, incidentally, emerging and so I am giving him his say.

You're terrific. And I'm glad you didn't tell me to burn it. I wouldn't have anyway. More later.

Yours,
Bill

I am, as you gather, living out here now—since June, that is *we* are; Doris is flourishing, a Star! and very popular and we are comfortable. For me it's another miracle my life of hate turning to love. I've come around. Therefore the New York address—though the apartment is still ours—no longer serves. Use this one please.

Maybe I could come to Texas this fall or winter. I want to do some more research on my own notebooks in the Humanities Research Center in Austin. It would be wonderful if I could dip down (does one dip down to San Antonio from Austin—I've forgotten—or up?) to San Antonio for a few days. In time. Right now I'm wishing you well, as faithfully as ever, and sending the same old friendship and affection of close to 30 years. We have survived.

Doris sends abrazos—and dear, mean Arcadio does, too.

So send the piece here, please, And thanks for all, dear John.

Yours,
Bill

---

he appreciates, she appreciates: The character is a hermaphrodite.
I'll stick with Tomasso: Name of character in *Arcadio*. Igo had suggested "Tomás" or

"Tomaso" instead. Igo helped Goyen with the many Spanish phrases in the novel.
the piece: The unrevised interview between Igo and Goyen for *Southwest Review,* later
published as "Learning to See Simply: An Interview with William Goyen," *Southwest
Review* 65 (Summer 1980): 267–284.

To Reginald Gibbons
ALS-3

Los Angeles
December 16, 1979

Dear Reg:

Yes, my Mescan friend in San Antonio wrote that "Camerado" is a
"good Spanish word." He also got me straight on all those like "larmas"
for "lágrimas," etc.

Your careful reading and comments from it were immensely impressive
and very helpful, though I was disturbed all last Sunday (this is another
one a week later) by your quibblings—it seemed to me then to be quibbling but later thoughtful and careful questioning: the 'twas and 'tis, for
example, etc.

Arcadio's father Hombre was an East Texas man; Arcadio's Mexican
speech is tempered a) by the speech of this father's region; b) ventrilo-
quistically by the narrator's speech (or Song). It is the narrator's ("the
Singer of the Singer's song") Song we are hearing—would have to be
since the Singer can't sing any more, he's dead!

You've made me think about (not wholly good) my ventriloquism, and
now it is clear to me that that is all I am, speaking through other peoples'
dead throats, using their dead tongues for *my* breath (Jesus now I've seen
about *The House of Breath* and what that was. Scary and final freedom for
me, to see this.) [In margin, in quotes: "Speech found for what was not
spoken"]. Those are the instruments (like a horn), dead until their sound
is blown by somebody. Shit it's too complex and I want to get away from
thinking about it, I'm getting crazy with it. But the voice from the
breather, the one with the breath generally is able to make like the dead
voice, imitates pretty well—almost humanly—what the breath-less voice
would sound like *if it could sing.* And occasionally—sorry, folks, but
deliberately, too—the breather's voice shows, breaks through, especially
when it's tired or wears thin. Ventriloquism, true ventriloquism, is a most
difficult art and a sublime art. But the voice gets tired.

Also—sometimes the ventriloquist so identifies with its mouthpiece that it sings out on its own for a little while. This is what I love most of all and seems too humanly wonderful and a beautiful thing of life—is when the singer becomes everybody he's making sing and breaks out into his own song; gets carried away—to his own reality, his own truth. I've seen this happen in opera, particularly Italian opera, in Verdi where Verdi himself suddenly starts singing (of homesickness, of love) through his character—a true "aria." I'm always interested in writing arias for others (and then upstaging them, moving into them, my voice into theirs—a duet?)

I feel quite mad with this, incensed. It's quite dangerous to get into; but then if everybody is everybody (sooner or later) and everything is everything, what's the problem?

But of course the Singer is Arcadio, is Uncle Ben, is his mother, father, brother from time to time.

All this from your good notes, *amigo, Camerado, corazón, dulce*.

But I'm back into *Arcadio*—for some weeks now. Tomasso has risen and taken Arcadio's voice. I can't go on with this. It sounds shitty. But deep thanks, Reg. While others are Christmas shopping. More later.

Yrs.,
Bill

Reginald Gibbons: (b. 1947). Poet and writer, and editor of *TriQuarterly* magazine beginning in 1981. Like Goyen, a Texan; he was later to become Goyen's literary executor.
my Mescan friend: John Igo.

To Reginald Gibbons
ALS-2

Los Angeles
January 13, 1980

Dear Reg:

Back here and had your loving letter, I had got a little crazy—or was on the verge—and went off to New York to my old beloved room and got somewhat restored there, stayed just about alone and quiet, reading and writing (some, not much, couldn't) and trying to get straight. I'm O.K., though still deeply ill at ease. Your letter so beautifully brought me some comfort and reminded me of the reality of work, and of friendships—and of the faith of friends; and of poetry. Thank you brother.

[. . .] So—I am of better spirit. Arcadio talks through it all, my ups and downs, the fucker keeps talking. So thanks Reg for the strokes, and the *abrazos* and, Jesus, the understanding. Often I've felt over the years of writing, that my work writes me farther and farther from the world— where is everybody, don't they know me any longer, don't they hear me? In bringing the world so close to myself I seem to further lose it. How could such intimacy so alienate?

Yours,
Bill

---

old beloved room: At 277 West End Avenue.

To Eve Caram
ALS-2

Los Angeles
March 10, 1980

Dear Eve:

Just now able to get a note to you, reminding you of your sweetness and kindness and good company during our week. And I've loved your two letters. I've gone right to work on a lot of things and days seem short. The rain *falls,* my God, Doris and I are up at night emptying pots and pans. But it's so *green* and everything keeps right on blooming—never saw such flowers, on *everything*—like Florida. I love the warmth. [. . .]

I love my little office and have just miraculously assembled— crooked—a new cabinet for books, to get them off the floor. I'm on a corner, look out on the old Hollywood Pantages Theatre (now housing Dick Van Dyke in *The Music Man*) and the Capitol Records Building. Across is old Hollywood Palace vaudeville theatre. In the distance, when it's clear, I see snow-covered mountains—what are they, where? I've never asked. I'm circled by palm trees, which I used to despise but now like. And most days Hollywood is a half-asleep tacky small town with empty shops and few people on the street. I like working in it. It's not unlike Main St. in Columbia when I walked to school in those mornings. Which was nice, as I remember it. The hotel was cozy, for me—like many I've stayed in, lived awhile in, always writing and hurting—in those days (which I never want again and out of which I got a lot down in books in stories). Columbia was, as I now recall it, a *place*. And the warmth and life of that floor in that building (English Dept.?) were quite unusual—have you been in others? Hamilton College, for example. Or even, God knows, Princeton. I liked that crazy corner where we all were—it was, as I said, a little like backstage—*during* a show. And *your* office, now that I recall it—what was it? Why its shape? Where does it go—in that sort of angle behind your desk? What's on the other side? Now that I think of it. It was all fun. I truly enjoyed it. And it was fun talking with you and rushing out in your little white car, always so hard to find.

I thought the interview good, the photo awful, and wished the reporter hadn't thought Arthur Bond a "freak." But she was very good—for a first job. [. . .]

We're off to New York on April 2, for two weeks, to get our apartment painted and to see if we can buy it. I'll—I hope—have some sessions with my (new) editor at my (new) publishers. [. . .]

Eve Caram: (b. 1934). Fiction writer, then an instructor of fiction writing at Stephens College in Columbia, Missouri.

our week: Goyen had visited Stephens College from February 18 to February 24, during which time he read part of "The Missouri Jail" section of *Arcadio* and also the story "Arthur Bond" and was interviewed for the American Audio Prose Library.

To Elizabeth Spencer
ALS-2

Los Angeles
May 24, 1980

Dear Elizabeth:

Glad to hear from you. I'm recovering from a somewhat ghastly operation on my left hand—two weeks ago—and it's been painful. I'm therefore slow with everything. Roberta and I are having a second honeymoon—I ditched Jed Mattes, he bungled my affairs with the new novel and I'm too old for that; anyway Roberta should have been doing it. But she was confused by my desires, etc. Now all's *good* and she's marching along with fine plans for me. I've asked Sandy Richardson to read *Arcadio* (the novel) and he's happily doing so. We'll see what that leads to.

Meantime I'm recovering and making plans to go to Greece in [illegible] via a week in London, on June 11 (in N.Y. for 3 days). Stay with your work. Remember how it comes and goes, turns on and off, for apparently *no* reason. I'm sure it's good, better than you know. It's exciting to me that you're writing. I think *Collected Stories* is exciting, too—an event. And with Miss Welty's preface. Especially since she now seems to be the Rose of American Literature. Good for her but I think it's a little too much, myself. But it'll be *good* for you, and I'm glad. [. . .]

---

recovering: Another operation for dupetrends.
Roberta: Roberta Pryor.
Jed Mattes: A literary agent, also of International Creative Management in Manhattan, who briefly handled Goyen's *Arcadio* typescript.
the Collected Stories: Misnomer for *The Stories of Elizabeth Spencer,* published by Doubleday in 1981.
Miss Welty: Eudora Welty.

To Robert Phillips
ALS-4

Los Angeles
August 19, 1980

Dear Robert:
    I lived in the cottage on the corner with a good workroom and a big long bedroom which holds memories. Those who lived around me and who often gathered in my workroom (I was finishing the stories in *Ghost and Flesh*—indeed finished the book there) were Elizabeth Bishop (next door), Calvin Kentfield, Katherine A. Porter, Eleanor Clark, Alexei Haieff. Elizabeth Ames was my dear friend and comforted me many times when I thought I had gone mad over some of the work in *Ghost and Flesh,* particularly "A Shape of Light." Walter was calling me a lot (we were then living in Chicago on Drexel Boulevard) (Walter was studying for doctorate at Univ of Chicago) to tell me that Irene, his fiancé, was pregnant; and Glenway Wescott was daily sending me word during one week about my candidacy (a surprise to me) for the *Prix de Rome* (didn't even know what that was) and finally about my having narrowly lost it by one vote to a poet, Anthony Hecht. I remember that I was emotionally quite badly disturbed then, during that Yaddo time (2 months?) and that

once Elizabeth thought I might have to leave—for help. It was a heavy white winter (Feb., March?) and one of the servants who waited on the breakfast table kept saying that it was "glare ice, just glare ice" on the roads. I loved Yaddo and love it now with very deep feelings. Please give my greetings to the Director (can't remember his name) and to Hortense, his wife. Maybe I could come there next winter (Feb. or March).

I called Truman while I was reading his charming *Music for Chameleons*. He was very sweet and had just been, he said, talking about my work in an interview with *Le Monde*. He asked about new work and I asked him to read *Arcadio*. He was delighted and said he was happy that Doubleday dismissed me. He was amusing and childlike, although his strange stammering bothered me. I was glad to reach back to him and I do love him and respect his work and I needed his acknowledgment, something, for I called quite desperately from my little office and was feeling rejected and passed-by. It has been a very bad time for me. I have absolutely no money, after 2 1/2 years or 3 of investing in *Arcadio* and all my work is out of print. Random House keeps sending me boxes of my books to clear their shelves, I guess. At any rate it is a very bad time. I've been sick and am now in the midst of lots of X-rays of my insides and have good doctors now. Silence from publisher, ex-editor, agent, is ringing. Who wouldn't feel abandoned?

But fuck it. I'm working again and will go on working—some stories for the new volume (publishers will be so happy to know this), seeds of a new novel. I want to write another short novel (fuck publishers). It is my form and my joy and fuck them! [. . .]

---

the cottage on the corner: West House at Yaddo. Goyen had been there in February and March 1951, directly after suffering from pleurisy.
Elizabeth Ames: Executive director of Yaddo during Goyen's stay.
by one vote: In 1976 Goyen was to lose another important award at the American Academy and Institute of Arts and Letters. This time the nod for the Rosenthal award went to fiction writer Richard Yates. Goyen was never voted into the institute.
the Director: Curtis Harnack (b. 1927). American novelist and memoirist.
Hortense, his wife: Novelist and story writer Hortense Calisher (b. 1911).
Truman: Truman Capote, from whom Goyen had been estranged ever since he wrote a critical review of Capote's *Breakfast at Tiffany's* (*New York Times Book Review*, November 2, 1958, pp. 5, 38).
to read Arcadio: Goyen sent the typescript to Capote. Capote did not reply.

To Audrey Wood
ALS-2

Los Angeles, Ca.
Nov. 11, 1980

Dearest Audrey:

Here's the piece on Katherine Anne Porter I promised you. Eventually
I'd want to publish it along with those little lives of Margo Jones, Frieda
Lawrence, and the others (my old *Six Women*) that I showed you last year.
And now I want to add some men to the book (my life has widened!)—
among them Jesus, St. Paul and St. Francis. What do you think of *that?*
Of course the Inge would be a book of its own, but something of the
same feeling and spirit would be there. I missed Roberta on Friday before
I left last week, but I hope you two will talk about the Inge book in terms
of the way Roberta spoke of it to me when we had dinner last week: I
thought she had exactly the right idea about the book and she literally
changed my mind about writing it.

I loved your presence. It was lovely to be with you. Stay as well as you
are, and on we go. We'll talk soon, I hope.

Love to you,
Bill

———————————————

Audrey Wood: Goyen's play agent.
on Katherine Anne Porter: "Katherine Anne Porter: An Appreciation," *Dallas Morning
News*, September 28, 1980, p. G1. Porter had died at the age of ninety.
the Inge: Goyen was contemplating writing a biography of his playwright friend
William Inge (1913–1973). Goyen's primary motive was to make money, but there is
no doubt he felt deep sympathy for Inge's life.
Roberta: Roberta Pryor, his book agent.

To Phyllis Jackson
TLS-2

277 West End Avenue
New York, N.Y. 10023
[Undated. March 1981?]

Dear Phyllis:

What an excitement to be writing about Bill Inge! We had so much in common, both being small-town men, teachers loving the young, writers who loved and feared the theatre (Bill came to it late, you know, and he needed a lot of encouragement: the times I've walked with him before an opening! Walked in cold speechless terror). We shared work a lot. He'd suddenly call up and tell me that he was going to read a play to a few of us. He *did* talk about his work. Like most playwrights he longed to write books, and finally, bless God, he did. But in those days Bill envied me my books while I was secretly envying him his stage.

It was Margo Jones who brought so many of us together and who gave so many of us early chances. Margo had produced the early version of *Picnic* called *The Women on the Porch*. I missed this, but when *Glass Menagerie* was playing in Chicago I found Bill. I was living in Chicago and had gone to see the play and to greet Tennessee who had been introduced to me by Margo some time before. There was Bill. When Tennessee introduced Bill and me, Bill knew some of my stories which he had published here and there. We talked a while and saw what we had in common: home, homesickness that couldn't be eased by going home, family feeling; our background was very similar. We both wrote about those things. Over the years we shared feelings and concern for family and hometown and local old-time friends. Bill knew that I understood his silences. We were able to talk—a rare relationship.

This will be a full-fledged biography, thoroughly researched and carefully documented (as a teacher—Visiting Prof. in English, Brown Univ. at present—and perennial graduate student: M.A. in Comparative Lit., and natural researcher, I'm well-disciplined in research). I am a natural interviewer. I particularly approach this material with love and respect and bring a lot of insight to it. I bring, then, to this biography my own recognizable talents as a creative and imaginative writer and those of a trained researcher and analyst of facts—plus the information coming from long-time friendship with Mr. Inge.

The life of Inge is a tragic one, but the Life is not going to be a downbeat one nor a bleak one. (Frost's life was not an Ode to Joy and Sunshine; nor Eliot's. Was Pound's? O'Neill's?) There must be a frank discussion of Inge's homosexuality—without, of course, doing any harm to his family or personal integrity. He was an alcoholic. His work did not succeed as he had hoped it to—and yet he was an immensely successful playwright. But his work degenerated; he seemed to lose sight of its center (the horror of all artists); it lost its vitality, its fibre. He could never find home. His loneliness was unbearable. He was cut off from humanity. He couldn't relate to people. He was always working, always producing; he had several writing projects going at one time. He wanted people around him (he was not a Solitary), yet when they were there he would not say anything to them. His life ended in suicide. Yet his work, which was about himself, his own preoccupations, his own intuitive sense of human relationships, his own work was his victory; and we are beginning to see the depths of meanings in it, its contemporary relatedness; his work is on its way toward refreshing itself. Another three to five years and we shall see its renascence, I firmly believe. There are signs.

This will be a big book, an important book, a distinguished book, and it will be a popular book. Students are inquisitive about Inge's plays. A revival of production of his plays is glimmering. Inge's life is interesting more people. I mean to write the biography as a book that will set down his life honestly and humanly and that will interest many many people. It can read like fiction; it should have a wide appeal (I've not been an editor in a publishing house for six years for nothing.) I truly see how to make this Life a popular and a distinguished one.

I intend to talk to the several friends who were close to Inge. They are friends of mine, easily accessible. I shall love giving William back to the world. I shall take great pleasure in showing those who did not know him the nobility of the man, the kind of awesomeness that surrounded him, his compassion, the vivid sense of life that resided in William Inge. And especially will I celebrate the opportunity to introduce and to speak of his work to the young, and to all who do not know it. [. . .]

---

bless God: Inge published two novels late in his career.
Margo Jones: Jones produced Inge's *Farther Off from Heaven*, an early version of *The Dark at the Top of the Stairs*, in her *Theatre '47* series.

To Patrice Repusseau
ALS-4

Los Angeles
March 18, 1981

Dear Patrice:

Arcadio is pure instinct. Of course there was no "research." The voice came and was unstoppable. I thought it went quite crazy at times, that voice; and sometimes I couldn't believe what it was telling me. But it was a true *telling* voice and it made me a *true listener*. So, again, for me writing is generally listening, not telling. And if the listening and telling are *one*, then it is true *ventriloquism*. Which I began to think about last year while finishing *Arcadio* and it drove me quite mad, or at least I felt unstable and deranged. The question, the *mystery* of Voice, the Telling Voice, must be let alone, not tampered with. So with *Arcadio*. I tried never to philosophize upon him or to analyze him—to psychoanalyze him. Can you imagine him with a psychoanalyst? Arcadio is out of the Bible, out of the Ancient Mysteries; he abides in the shadows of the Aztecs. But *very* accessible, too, very human. His near-insane escapades baffle me. I have tried to *discipline* the telling of them; I am a strict poet, not a tape machine; of course. But once the stories were given to me—like the flag-pole sitter artist—I had to get to work (slowly, for me) to keep them true. Nobody blurted out anything. Sometimes Arcadio seemed *very* careful. That behooved me to be so. And when he seemed not to be careful, I had to be careful for him. I see, again, the work and the responsibility of the artist. Once again I commit my life to Art (under and through God, my father). The life of Art is my life. I want to make beautiful things, out of life, as they continue to be shown to me, and given to me. I say this, once more, and on the eve of my 66th birthday. A fine round double of numbers: 66.

I read another new story (in work for many years—since 1972(3), when I was at Brown University in Rhode Island) at Harvard University last week. There was a small group, mostly students on the staff of *The Harvard Advocate*, an old (for America) and distinguished quarterly published since 1866. Eliot read there, and Faulkner and E. E. Cummings, many. I was honored, certainly. The story (one of three which I read: "Arthur Bond" and "The Texas Principessa"—another "new" or just finished story I've worked on, off and on, for many years being the other two) is a difficult one, titled "In the Icebound Hothouse." A few students talked with me afterwards. I felt very shy and pushed-down. The story gets passionate (within a cold framework or shell) and personal and I remember reading it passionately toward the end. I may have overwhelmed the young people—who are, themselves, withdrawn and pushed-down-seeming. The story—which I will send to you, along with "The Texas Principessa"—is, I feel, a turning point for me: some large, long-carried feeling is disemburdened of me—like Hombre from Arcadio's back.

I have read your stunning work *The House of Breath in the Work of William Goyen* for two days—since I've returned to Los Angeles from my two-month absence. I accept your insight, your interpretation of my work. Generally. It is *yours*, this perception. I am stunned by this perception; I am being enlightened by you. I am not here as a questioner or critic or editor of your *masterful* work, but as a fellow artist, a passionate admirer, a peer, a brother, even. Your gifts are enormous; you will find your place. Or maybe you *won't:* Who *has?* Who *can?* But you will accept praise and recognition and you will stay in—or get in—the struggle of art.

My beloved and remarkable, gifted friend, I love you! In the love that is in all poetry and the beauty of art and life.

I go on reading. I am hoping to be able to come to Paris in May (did I not foreswear that city when last I left it?). For a week and if I can stay in the apartment of friends. Even if you have not, by then, moved to Paris, you will be able to come in? I *hope* this can be worked out; I am only thinking of it now. Please tell me your plans.

In Houston—did I tell you—I finished yet another *Arcadio*—that is, additions, some small enlargements, an ending that may be right. I'll want to send it to you soon—if you will. I have shown this—or sent it off from Houston—three weeks ago—to a young editor who cared very much about the very *first* version (now called the "short" version), at a publishing house. While in New York this time I met and liked very much another young editor—to whom I shall right away send this final, I guess, version.

Please be aware of the triumph of your work, Monsieur. And please take some of the patience I have had, and lost, and found again, through the years. And give it back to me when I shall have lost it again. Thank you, Patrice Repusseau.

William Bill

The House of Breath in the Work of William Goyen: Repusseau's doctoral thesis, researched at Rice University and submitted for degree at the Université Paris VII.
young editor: Thomas Hart, of Houghton Mifflin. No relation to William M. Hart.
the "short" version: Goyen's first version of *Arcadio*, which he submitted to Doubleday, Vanguard Press, and Random House, was only eighty-five typed pages. When editors complained about its brevity for book publication, he then developed the subplot concerning Tomasso, and the book's length nearly doubled.
another young editor: Peter Hethers, of Random House.

Los Angeles
March 20, 1981

Dear Roberta:
   The situation:
   I would need money to travel and research—and for an assistant, at a
point—for a) the Inge biography and b) the biographies in *Six Women*
(*Six Lives, Lives,* with a subtitle like *Six Women* or *Seven Women and One
Man* [me]). I would want to talk with people (vanishing quickly, some of
them, so we better hurry up) who are close to my subjects—principally in
Texas, Kansas, New York, California, New Mexico.
   What we will have in *Lives* is really six (or more) separate but over-
woven or interlocking biographical narratives. You have in your possession six sort of "treatment"-narratives plus the published piece on
Katherine Anne Porter. The six (or more) biographical narratives really
ride over, or ride under, a larger encompassing autobiographical narrative
that will, in the whole, constitute a social, historical, literary document
covering, autobiographically, the years in which I knew the people (1945–
1981), but also covering the span of each life (i.e., Frieda Lawrence in
Germany, Mexico, etc.; Katherine Anne Porter in Texas, Paris, Mexico,
New York, etc.)
   I would estimate between $15,000 and $25,000 for travel, research, use
of an assistant, for the two biographical works. Subject to your advice.
   The novel is herewith delivered to you, March 20, 1981 (*Arcadio*).
Publication 1982?
   The stories (11 stories and a novella—*Wonderful Plant*—do you agree?)
or 12 stories without the novella. The book will be ready in a month, six
weeks. Bob Bender knows three of the stories and admires them. Deliv-
ered on or before June 1, 1981. Publish 1983?
   The Biographies-Autobiography will need a year's work, with help
from an assistant, at a point. Deliverable let's say September 1, 1982.
Publish 1983–4?
   The Inge will then take another year-and-a-half, deliverable on or
before September 1, 1983. Publish 1984? *If* I can be free to write the
book as I see it, without anybody's "approval" or right to launder.
   Also, I'm full of work—another novel in work; a little book on St.
Francis (*A Book of St. Francis*); a little book on St. Paul (*A Book of Paul*),
constituting a trilogy with *A Book of Jesus*.

What about paperback reprints of my out-of-print books, *Collected Stories, Come, the Restorer, The House of Breath, The Fair Sister, In a Farther Country?*

What a load to heap upon somebody! At any rate, this is a picture of my situation as it now stands.

Thanks, dear, for what can be done. If you and Mr. Bender want me there, I'll be there.

Love,
William Goyen

6225 Quebec Drive
Los Angeles, 90068

Bob Bender: Robert Bender, book editor at Washington Square Press.
paperback reprints: The House of Breath received a second paperback edition, this time from Persea Books, in 1986. It duplicated the slightly expurgated text of the 1975 Random House/Bookworks edition.

To Thomas Hart
ALS-3

Los Angeles
August 3, 1981

Dear Tom:

We've just talked. I hope we can work together. I'm full of work and hope for a place where there can be continuity of work and publication with an Editor who helps. Again, I appreciate the work you've done and respect your perceptions and judgments concerning the stories, the elimination of some, the re-designing of the group, the sharpening of *Arcadio*. I plan to have these *Arcadio* changes in your hands within the week. The old boy has had enough of my mind for the time being: his voice has tantalized me for three years. He, like Mr. de Persia and Cleon Peters, has got a language out of apocalyptic moments and the powerful influence of Biblical narrative speech, and sometimes just plain bullshit. It is my problem to justify that and to make the ring of it true. But it is, even as in the new novel I'm working on, an aspect of magical persons that keeps seizing and exciting me. I'll be sending you within the next days a discussion of the novel which, with Arcadio and *Come, the Restorer,* will form a *sort* of trilogy of short novels. Perhaps. It really doesn't matter.

1) Roberta is today sending you the sort of scenario of *Six Women* (still a tentative title). This I agree should be the third book—follow the stories. This is well because it keeps expanding as various of my subjects die, leaving their life now frameable and graspable: they can't do anything more. (Sad, but a relief for their biographer!)

2) You now have in hand the replacing stories and front matter.

3) You will shortly receive:

a) revision of *Arcadio*

b) material on the novel in work

I shall be working simultaneously, for the most part, on the novel and *Six Women.* Both should, I now guess and God willing, be done by summer 1985—that is this current plan of work from *Precious Door* to *Six Women* all completed by that time.

I hadn't planned to go on this long, but I see I need to get it out of my head. I so badly need to discuss my work, which overwhelms me sometimes without the focusing presence of an Editor.

Thank you for your guidance. Let's see what we can do.

Yours,
Bill
William Goyen

Mr. de Persia: The restorer in *Come, the Restorer.*
Cleon Peters: Wandering preacher in the same novel.
Precious Door: Title for a collection of stories Goyen planned to publish after *Arcadio* appeared. Most of the stories he would have included were published in the posthumous collection *Had I a Hundred Mouths* (1985).

To Thomas Hart
ALS-2

L.A.
August 10, 1981

Dear Tom:
I'll take the liberty of sending you this revision of the long tale *Arcadio,* in its present shape, since I fear a real foul-up in the U.S. Mail very

shortly. Please be indulgent with the number of pages and lousy typing. I've worked long and hard to get this to this present version of the tale. You will let me know what you feel and, hopefully, we can now put it in with the rest of the stories of *Precious Door*.

I want to say a word about Arcadio's language, or speech. Arcadio's speech is an amalgam of East Texas speech—rhythm and dialect (from his father Hombre), Mexican (from his mother Chupa), Biblical rhetoric (from the White Bible via the Dwarf), and street and whorehouse jargon (from the Show and from *The China Boy*) all washed over and enriched by a narrative elegance ranging from Cocteauesque (near-Camp) and the comic-folk hero's absurd of the *Pícaro*. Arcadio is *Pícaro-Fantástico!* He enjoys the gift of grandiosity mixed sometimes with (hopefully charming) self-pity and just plain bullshit. Under it all is a daemonic sensuality, born not only of psychic but a *genital* conflict of two sexes. His sense of sex is tragi-romantic. And Arcadio is blessed with a natural gift of tale-telling.

There! Thanks for looking at this. Next mail (before the collapse?) will bring notes on novel. Hope all is well.

Yours,
Bill

Arcadio: The book had been rejected by Random House and Morrow.
foul-up: A mail strike was threatened.
with the rest: Goyen vacillated between publishing the shorter version of *Arcadio* within the new book of stories or publishing the longer version as a novel.

To Thomas Hart
ALS-2

Los Angeles
August 12, 1981

Dear Tom:

You've been so fine and *with* me in my work, new and old, that I consider you already a companion to it; and I'd like you to have the enclosed, written by two people (one dead, alas: Clyde Grimm) who, I feel, have truly been with me and who are precious to me. And the KAP little memoir. I've just read the quite poorly-done book by someone named Hank Lopez. It's a bad all-around job, *I* think, of writing, editing, publishing. Thank *God* I'm not mentioned. But as a secret between you and me, there's a photograph of me and Miss Porter in the book. I'm wrongly called Albert Erskine, her second husband! (and for a time, my editor [*The Faces of Blood Kindred*] at Random House). I'm even more stimulated to write fully about the difficult/wonderful woman who I loved very much. The segment called "At Lady A's" in *Six Women* is a piece of an attempt to get down her speech rhythms. Thank God I'm spared in Lopez's book.

Hope you're fine. I'm at work on a discussion with you and my *Oyente* about the novel-in-work, which I'll shortly send to you.

Yours,
Bill

Clyde Grimm: Goyen probably forwarded to Hart the Grimm bibliography of his work.
KAP little memoir: He had been asked by the *Dallas Morning News* to write a response to Miss Porter's death.
poorly-done book: Enrique Hank Lopez, *Conversations with Katherine Anne Porter: Refugee from Indian Creek* (Boston: Little, Brown, 1981).

To Ned Rorem
ALS-1

Los Angeles
Aug. 17, 1981

Dear Ned:

Here's where we are, have been for six years although we're often in New York and keep an apartment there. Your card was finally forwarded here. I do thank you for caring enough to write to me—you know how we need to hear. Maybe there's a song or two in some of those stories— "Ghost, Flesh, Water and Dirt"? And a libretto; well, I've always wanted to do that. Perhaps we'll talk sometime. Where are you in N.Y.? I'm there every few months, it turns out. When I showed Doris your note about *Color of Darkness*, she went into a quite long memory of it. It *was* very special . . . We both send fond wishes, as always. Hope it's good for you, Ned.

BILL

Ned Rorem: (b. 1923). American composer and writer. He had written Goyen about
adapting his short stories as songs.
Color of Darkness: An evening of plays by James Purdy (b. 1923) produced in 1962, in
which Doris Roberts acted and for which Rorem wrote the background music.

To Thomas Hart
TLS-2

August 20, 1981

Dear Tom:

Your letter of August 18 today. I agree, certainly, that it is important
for us to proceed this way, through "comment and exploration," as you
say, and that we know what each other is thinking at each step. I believe
we have done just this up to this present letter. At the outset, again, I
thank you for your care and thoroughness.

First, *my* disappointment. *Six Women.* I believe you're being too hard
too soon. This is why I don't like to show work in progress and rarely do.
A glimpse of a little leg is not the whole body; and as you and I know,
often a bad leg sticks out of a good thigh. Your judgment may come too
early and forces me to justify, explain too early. Careful editing on
specimen material can be premature expenditure of energy. This *is*
specimen material, these *are* "brief glimpses." I offered nothing more
than the glimpse of a little leg. Some of these excerpts may "live on their
own," and will not be through until I've found them (a quality which you
surely suspect of me by now). Naturally some of the pieces seem "just
reportage." But I believe just reportage will be what I want in some
instances, a fresh way of seizing the nature of some of these people. The
Father piece *is* about Houston, which is the ground, the *venue* of my early
creative life. Having read it in public has nothing to do with its authentic-
ity as part of a body of work; you are judging a part as a whole. You're
making *finalist* judgments. I feel this is unfair and can be hindering. I
have, indeed, given you "overall summaries." The book is *in work.* The
method *is,* generally, that of the "Margo" and the "Lady A" sections. Read
your letter and you'll see (ll. 19 *et seq*) that you are describing my intro-
ductory note. All this clearly describes precisely what I *am* doing, the way
I *am* working on the book. Your very description of it excites and stimu-
lates me again! Makes it sound like the hell of a book it is! So I'm confused (also tired of this long paragraph and I'm sure you must be). I'm not
clear about your objections to the material, your disappointment. And

this is my disappointment and *my* hardest part: my concern about heavy and premature judgment of work being created—and hardest of all, having to justify or explain too soon.

For I'd like to work with you, once we get our positions and attitudes towards work straight. I feel that these exchanges between us have been necessary to our understanding each other and how each other works, feels about work. I truly appreciate your interest and careful thought—I keep telling you that. All of it has been and is immensely helpful and, as I've told you, stimulating to good work, better work. But I do need freedom. Having that and keeping that, God knows what I'll find for myself. I have to take flights, go wild, play around. It's not the time to "freeze" the production, as they say in the theatre. You will and can help me (have already) within that understanding. I believe. But I really feel that we are *one* on the intent, direction and quality of *Six Women!*

As for our good *Arcadio*, I am still willing to cut away the long Tomasso section and to follow your suggestion—which, indeed, has been my alternate plan. Let's go right from "La noche tumba" (p. 117) to "It is night . . ." (p. 118), as you've outlined it in your letter, deleting references to Tomasso and Hondo, of course.

I'll need your guidance on the autobiography-memoir, and your . . . overlook. But I'll have to have my freedom (and your trust) in the process of work—and not feel too judged too early, or too picked at. Thank you, Tom, for your thoughts. These are mine. I hope we can talk again.

Sincerely yours,
Bill

August 20, 1981: Draft of a letter to Hart.
my disappointment: Hart had written Goyen to express his disappointment in the specimen pages of *Six Women* he had asked to see.

To Robert Phillips
ALS-2

L.A.
August 28, 1981 (102°)

Dear Robert:
It is a fresh green little book. Congratulations! And the poems ride well (no pun) and keep their charm, light and melancholy, fun. There are

so many I admire. And thank you for the lovely sweet poem written for me. Where will the book be sold out here? Let me know.

The heat is staggering and I've not felt well these few days, nor been able to tolerate my little workroom. Just after I'd trotted all my work and books and manuscripts *back*, once more, from Quebec Drive (I'd toted them home to be safe during my long absence).

I'm still being "critiqued" and edited by Tom Hart at Houghton Mifflin. He continues to send 3-page letters of suggestions, objections. Comments on what he asks to see, mainly *Six Women*. I've written him a strong letter letting him know how I feel about showing unfinished work and about premature criticism. I'm educating him. But he still seems attractive as an editor, and certainly devoted to my work; and once we see clearly what each other is like to work with, we might have a good relationship. Now he's asked Roberta and me to wait until he returns from a holiday—around Sept. 11—for him to give us "something you can both react to." I've sent him material on both works in progress (4 pages of notes on the new novel, tentatively titled *The Archer*) and a final, *I hope*, edition of the "shorter" *Arcadio*, which would be included in the *Precious Door*. [. . .]

---

little book: Phillips's *Running on Empty* (Garden City, N.Y.: Doubleday, 1981).
poem written for me: "Everyone Recalls the Saints, But What of the Animals?," *Running on Empty*, pp. 61–62.
workroom: The office on Hollywood Boulevard that Goyen rented to use as a writing space.
Roberta: Roberta Pryor.
The Archer: A projected novel based on the myth of Philoctetes.

To Robin Moody
ALS-2

L.A.
September 8, 1981

Dear Robin Moody:
    Thank you for the long chilling story of *Come, the Restorer*. My first feeling—after the deep hurt—was "thank God Robin Moody has the salvaged books; now they're safe." These days a publishing house is the most dangerous place for one's books to be in. I have, in the past, told my criminal publishers that they destroy books, not publish books: their

publishing was an act of destruction! But I can rest with my past, now—but I do not forget. At last the story has come clear, thanks to you. I never, of course, knew. Countless letters over the years have availed me nothing. But the (my) editors have gone, have been pushed out in an afternoon; I go on. I've finished two books, one a group of tales and stories called *Precious Door* and a short novel, *Arcadio*. It appears that Houghton Mifflin will be my publishers. I am now working on an autobiography-biography-memoir, *Six Women*, and a novel. I feel full of work.

I feel so good, knowing my books are there with you. Thank you. Have you any way of acquiring copies of *The Fair Sister* (Doubleday, 1963) or *A Book of Jesus* (NAL, 1974)?

I read at universities quite often, and of course there are never any books—my audience, except for old admirers, have to take me on faith! And most universities—English (or American) Lit. classes and writing workshops—"teach" my work. They're always writing to me for information about *where* my books can be found. At some universities (even Harvard) I've autographed Xeroxed copies students have brought to me. Now I can tell people where a bunch of my books are. Do you advertise within Writing Programs in universities? A good idea, if you haven't.

Again, my thanks for all your help and for your time and care taken to write me that long bitter story. It *has* disturbed me but it has put the whole thing to rest in my head. Bless you!

And if I can help you with your venture there in any way, let me know. It's a terrific thing you're doing and may it and yours prosper. You're a lighthouse.

Cordially,
Bill Goyen

Robin Moody: Bookseller whose Daedalus Books was then located in Washington, D.C. Goyen had ordered five copies of his *Collected Stories* and as an afterthought added to a letter, "Also, there seem to me to be *no* copies anywhere of my favorite novel (among my own, that is), *Come, the Restorer* (Doubleday, 1974). Will you please let me know when you find some copies?" (letter to Robin Moody, August 25, 1981).

chilling story: Moody wrote Goyen that in 1977 Doubleday had offered 2,973 copies of *Come, the Restorer* for remainder sale at fifteen cents a copy. He bought 1,000 copies for Kramerbooks, a remainder outlet, of which he was at the time manager and buyer. He also offered to pay thirteen cents a copy for the last 1,973, but Doubleday insisted upon twenty cents a copy. He did not accept, and Doubleday proceeded to pulp all 1,973 remaining copies (letter of August 27, 1981).

a novel: The unfinished *Leander*.

To Robert Phillips
ALS-2

L.A.
Sept. 12, 1981

Robert—

Thanks but I wouldn't go *near* Miss Welty. She has, let us say, not sustained well, for me. And she's a tiresome legend. Diarmuid Russell, her devoted agent, was an early friend to my work—Eudora had sent me to him. I liked him. Volkening (Henry) was his other half. Jessamyn West had sent me to *him!*

I'm reading a book on Beckett, *Frescoes of the Skull*. Recognizing my image (p. 1 of *House of Breath*), I challenged the two British authors through their publisher, Grove Press, and got a long apologetic letter from them, acknowledging their use of my conceit and thanking me for its brilliance—the conceit had shaped their work. They had known that Martha Graham had used it in her new work, performed in London, and had read about it in the papers. Miss Graham wouldn't—or didn't answer their letter. Their whole preface praises their title and goes on to describe how important it is to a vision of art, etc.—as if it were their own. Now they promise to acknowledge me if the book is reprinted. What a long battle for simple recognition. Thank God I write for *myself*.

The Flaubert letters *are* fine. I've had them a long time. I've also relished *Flaubert in Egypt*. I have just read [the] Barthelme interview in new *Paris Review*. I cannot believe his arrogance and high-blown bullshit! Does anyone *believe* him? Pure *New Yorker*.

At last Gallimard will reissue the three books in Folio, their paperback edition—or did I tell you? Houghton Mifflin keeps wearing me down with delays. Now they've called me to give them sales figures on my books. Thank God I write for *myself* or I'd be dead or crazy or drunk all the time.

I've now met two classes at USC and the ten students seem eager, intelligent and productive. They're graduate students working for an M.A. I've said I'll take on the workshop only this term; talking about writing for too long a time makes me crazy. [. . .]

Miss Welty: The occasion for attempting to pair Welty and Goyen has been forgotten. Obviously Goyen was of two minds about her work; see his January 29, 1948, letter to Katherine Anne Porter. Also, in R. Ballorain's 1974 interview, Goyen stated in response to "What contemporary writers do you like?": "I appreciate Eudora Welty very much. I know her, like her writing. *Delta Wedding* and the early stories, *A Curtain of Green* . . ." (*Delta* 9 [1979]: 43). When Welty left Harcourt, Brace, Goyen was an editor at McGraw-Hill. He tried to lure her there, but she accepted Random House's offer instead.

Frescoes of the Skull: Critical study by John Knowlson and John Pilling, subtitled *The Later Prose and Drama of Samuel Beckett* (New York: Grove Press, 1979). On page 3 of *The House of Breath*, Goyen wrote: "Yet on the walls of my brain, frescoes: the kneeling balletic Angel holding a wand of vineleaves, announcing; the agony in the garden; two naked lovers turned out; and over the dome of my brain Creations and Damnations, Judgments, Hells and Paradises (we are carriers of lives and legends—who knows the unseen frescoes on the private walls of the skull?)."

Martha Graham had used it: (1900–1991). In her ballet *Holy Jungle* (1974).

Flaubert letters: The Letters of Gustave Flaubert, 1830–1857 and *The Letters of Gustave Flaubert, 1857–1880*, both volumes selected, edited, and translated by Francis Steegmuller (Cambridge: Harvard University Press, 1980, 1982).

Flaubert in Egypt: Trans. and ed. by Francis Steegmuller (London: The Bodley Head, 1972; Chicago: Academy Chicago Ltd., 1979).

To Eve Caram
ALS-2

Los Angeles
September 14, 1981

Try Univ. of Houston Writing Program—my friend Stanley Plumly is co-director with Cynthia Macdonald. Tell em I suggested you write. Do it *now.*

Dearest Eva:

Well I've just *got* to write to you now, for your letter came today (and so many other wonderful ones have come) and you make me realize how long it's been since I've written to you. That does not mean that I don't think of you and love you. Sometimes I can't write *out*—it's selfish or self-obsessive, but I can't get *out*. Other times I simply sit down and I do it. There've been some mean times, but, overall, full and alive and vulnerable, which is what we have to be—unless we want to lie doped or drunk somewhere, beyond it all. The publishing experience of the past year has been rough, hurtful, maddening. I've survived it and can hardly speak of it now. This is what you dreamed. I believe my publishers will now be Houghton Mifflin and the first book they'll publish will be the new book of stories, *Precious Door,* eight stories and tales. Among them will be

"Arcadio," a short (the original) version. Following—if all works out—will be a new novel (still untitled) and following that (at *last*) my *Six Women*. My (hoped-for) editor would be a young enthusiastic man with whom I had a one-day meeting in Boston this summer. Pray for me.

New York, for me, too, was not so hot. I struggled with the heat, noise, ugliness, greed, injustice of embittered editors, soured publishers. Our apartment was my refuge. I stayed in it many days and nights. I wrote, I read. I waited for editors to read my new work. Conglomerate-hounded and chain-bookstore whored, they were apologetic or rude or arrogant. May I never have to do with them again. Doris and I were in Europe for a month—with friends who live in Paris, with friends who were living for the summer in Cortena, above Sienna, in Rome (which was dirty and hot—it was July) and in beloved London.

I'm teaching one workshop (fiction) at Univ. Southern California for the fall semester *only*. I have to be free after that. After two classes—graduate students taking an M.A.—it's good. The students are mature, bright, committed, productive. I'll enjoy it. But I have a lot of work to do. Still have my little office. Doris is in a new series written by Erma Bombeck, *Maggie*. California is better; I feel at home. New York brought you and me "home" *this* time, didn't it? But Beckett said, *"l'artiste qui joue son être n'est pas de nulle part; et il n'a pas de frères."* I feel immensely freer—I see that you do, too. At last. Do you see dear Bill Peden? We've exchanged a few postcards over the past year. Can't I go to Stephens this winter or spring? (Invite me.) You and/or Bill. We'd have a ball of a reunion. Is there a reading program? I'll stop. We have *more* to tell. I'll do better—Wish we could talk. Love to you,

Bill

Try Univ. of Houston: Caram had only a part-time job at Stephens College, and Goyen was trying to get her placed elsewhere.

your letter: She had written praising the opening section of *Arcadio*, which had appeared in *Southwest Review*.

(hoped for) editor: Thomas Hart.

New York, for me, too: Both writers had spent part of the summer of 1981 in New York, although they did not contact one another. Caram was in Grace Paley's apartment in Greenwich Village, and Goyen was at his West End Avenue apartment.

Bill Peden: (b. 1913). Fiction writer and English professor at the University of Missouri and an editor of *Missouri Review*, which published several of Goyen's later stories.

Los Angeles
September 18, 1981

Dear Robin Moody:

Your letter is of help to me: it came on the very heels of a "corporate decision" (I'm hearing this phrase a lot these days, as I submit my work) by Houghton Mifflin *not* to publish my books. This is a shocker since they'd kept giving me good assurances weekly for over two months. I'd even made some changes in some stories following the editor's scrupulous queries and notes in 3–4 page letters. He, too, seemed shocked and surprised at a decision he'd not counted on from the powers—or power—above who decreed that "not enough copies could be sold." There'd been, over the 2 1/2 months, such a scrutiny of my past, my sales, my reviews, that I became—almost—a little paranoid. Contemporary publishing up to the moment, as I've experienced it—neurotic, paranoid, unreliable, deceptive.

So another door shut to all my new work, and after thirty years of writing and publishing. Thought you'd wanta know. I think you are *precisely* right about the publishing situation and hope your prophecy is fulfilled. I'm a *witness* to the degraded state of serious publishing in this country—and no newcomer.

Thanks for the support you, unwittingly at the moment, gave me in a rough hour yesterday.

I'm okay today.

Good hopes!
Bill Goyen

Yesterday, like a comment on what had happened, the 33 copies of dear old *Come, the Restorer* arrived from Strand, thanks to *you!*

"corporate decision": Goyen was informed that when his two manuscripts were presented before the editorial board at Houghton Mifflin, the editor Thomas Hart was told that "we cannot commit to an act of culture at this time" (conversation between Goyen and R.P.).

your prophecy: Moody had written Goyen that "publishers will begin to separate into types more than they have already—large houses who cannot profit from literary works, because they require a market larger than the *reading* public in this country, will

stop playing as if they are that kind of publisher, and the small and medium-small houses like Farrar, Straus & Giroux who are literary will maintain their identity and leave the self-help books to the other guys" (letter of September 11, 1981).
33 copies: Moody had located two cartons of the remaindered novel in the warehouse of the Strand Bookstore in Manhattan.

To Robin Moody
ALS-2

Los Angeles
December 5, 1981

Dear friend Robin Moody:

Your "presumptuousness" is accepted—heartily and gratefully. I appreciate—more than I can say—your letter of November 13. I've not heard from Farrar, Straus & Giroux, but had already sent the ms. of the stories, *Precious Door*, to them, maybe six weeks ago. Sometimes—or at least *this* time—it's seemed that when I've sent out my work to an editor it's as if it were a stone that's knocked him in the head, cold. Because such a long silence follows. I know more now about publishing as it is *now* than I did when I first finished these two pieces of work, the novel and the stories. Editors seem paranoic, and terrified that some great hand (of a marketing person, or even of an Editor-in-Chief) is going suddenly to appear and wipe out everything they've been doing. Some Houghton Mifflin hand seems to have done just this. I can't live or work in bitterness and that's gone, but *hurt* lasts longer (I can work with hurt, always have).

At any rate, your affirmation (and Daedalus Books) burns like one of those monastery lights in the Dark Ages. Thanks for the little light, Robin Moody. There are a few outposts in my present desert. Maybe there are always only a few, for some of us. But boy do I cherish them. Anyway, to hell with it, I'm working every day and having a good time with my stories and keep being amazed at them, how free they are, and oblivious of current events. They keep me free.

I don't mean to lean on you, but if you feel a hand on your shoulders sometimes when I'm getting up, that's mine. I've got a good shoulder for you if ever you need it. And I'm grateful for the *beautiful* space for my books in your Catalogue. You are, at present, my only publisher! I'm proud and grateful. Now—may all be well with you.

Bill Goyen

"presumptuousness": After receiving Goyen's letter of September 18, Moody wrote on November 13 that he had "been presumptuous" again, by attempting to interest an editor at Farrar, Straus and Giroux in Goyen's work.

**To Joyce Carol Oates
and Raymond J. Smith
ALS-2**

*Los Angeles
February 3, 1982*

Dear Joyce and Ray:

Thanks for reading the stories, which seem to have come to you rather sloppily—two stories (and one the title story!) missing! Please forgive me. Of course you may publish the story "Black Cotton" in *Ontario Review*, and I'm pleased. I'll so inform my agent, Roberta Pryor, who's been holding back these new stories until a publisher for the book is found—a notion with which I disagree and have taken steps to overturn: William Peden will publish "In the Icebound Hothouse" in the Spring issue of *Missouri Review*.

It'd be pleasant to work together sooner or later; and you know I wish you success with your fledgling.

I admire you both and send affections.

Yrs.,
BILL
William Goyen

I believe our birds are of a somewhat feather—yours winged and mine land-bound! He's called "Paisano" by the Mexicans of the Southwest, though we know him as Roadrunner—a creature of my childhood.

---

the stories: Goyen had sent the Smiths new stories from his collection-in-progress, *Precious Door*.

"Black Cotton": The story appeared in *Ontario Review* 17 (Fall–Winter 1982–1983): 80–86. The Smiths earlier had published Goyen's story "The Storm Doll" in *Ontario Review* 7 (Fall–Winter 1977–1978): 28–34.

your fledgling: Ontario Review Press, which was to begin publishing books.

our birds: Both the Ontario Review Press and Goyen had beige stationery with decorations of a black bird in the corner. Goyen's, as he explains, is a roadrunner—which figures prominently in the novel *In a Farther Country*; Ontario Review Press's bird is a Canada goose in flight.

To Eve Caram
ALS-2

Los Angeles
March 29, 1982

Dear Eve:

Your card. Don't—or try not to—feel you have to leave Yaddo with a
huge novel ready for the publisher. But I know the feeling. We say "a day
at a time" and that helps me. It's the old "sufficient unto the day . . ." I
feared it would be cold—that's a cold corner. But isn't it beautiful? Do
you *live* in the sun porch? How odd. Who's there? By now I'm sure
you're a lot more comfortable: I detected a sigh of lonesomeness and
some fear. My dear, I've just described *writing*. What we all have to bear.
I've been *full* of work and good feelings, raced down to Texas (Austin) last
weekend for that Seminar (2 days) on Biography, got real stimulated and
had a good, open time. Spring was there (it was a damnable 85°,
though—a freak hot spell) and the beautiful bluebonnets were in full, and
all remembered little wildflowers that just crop up in the grass, some so
frail, pale pink and deep blue (my mother called the blue ones "bluets")
and buttercups along the airport runway. I love Texas. Met some interesting people.

Now I'm struggling with this *speech* that I have to write and read at the
"Forum" (it turns out) on "The Uses of Autobiography in Fiction" for
the NYU affair on Tues., April 6. I'll get to N.Y. on Sunday night (April
4) and have Mon. to get the thing finally done. When they say *publish* I
clam up and start a prodigious revision. Wish I could change that. [. . .]

I'm done with my new story and have sent it to Roberta Pryor for her
to add to the book. I believe it's a good story. God knows I toiled on it—3
months. And then nobody buys these things. But it's what I do and I love
it. [. . .]

---

that's a cold corner: Caram was housed in Pine Garde Cottage at Yaddo.
this speech: "Autobiography in Fiction."

To Robin Moody
ALS-2

Los Angeles
June 21, 1982

Dear Robin:

I've been silently enduring a slow decision still trying to be made by Clarkson Potter for the novel and the book of stories. Somebody there seems to be fighting for me. Meanwhile I've continued work on the last two of the ten stories in the book and plan to have them done by early September. I remember promising to show you both books and will, still, when I finish the second. I believe both books are good and I see now how the stories have all rooted into each other—or sprang from the same bulb, which I'm separating; at any rate they've all been underground for a long time, and connected. Point is, I've tried to *write* them (not garden). One of them has just come out in *The Missouri Review* ("In the Icebound Hothouse").

Once again, I'm so glad to have you with me. Stay?

Yours,
Bill G.

Somebody there: Carol Southern, who was to become Goyen's last trade editor. She was the editorial director for Clarkson N. Potter, Inc.

To Carol Southern
ALS-1

Los Angeles
August 11, 1982

Dear Carol:

I am writing to you from of all places a hospital—which of course is no surprise or news to you now. I am stronger and on my way home tomorrow. So onwards and upwards.

It is needless to say how overjoyed I am that Clarkson Potter will publish our *Arcadio* and that you will be my editor. This makes me proud and happy.

I am finishing work on the last of the group of stories that all grow in upon and out of each otther (forgive hazy eyesight: two "t's" in other!) titled *Precious Door*.

I still hope to be in New York within a month; but at any rate I had to reach you now and tell you of my great pleasure. Thanks for your fortitude and *belief.*

Sincerely,
Bill Goyen

---

a hospital: Goyen was hospitalized for lymphoma.

To Carol Southern
ALS-2

Los Angeles
October 30, 1982

Dear Carol:
Here safely and at work again and remembering our very pleasant lunch and afternoon. I must say I was later a bit disappointed when it dawned on me that publication for *Arcadio* is now Fall 1983 and not Spring, as I'd expected. My real concern has been for the scheduling of publication of my other work, the stories (*Precious Door*), and the non-fiction (*Six Women*), how that might be now delayed. *My* hope had been to see the novel published in Spring and the stories in the Fall, 1983.

Still, I'm certainly not in favor of rushing the novel before thorough promotion can be done, and the September publication will give us ample time. Yet I'd hate to see us lose the current impetus for the novel and the enthusiasm which I felt when I met your salesman and Senior Editor and promotion lady.

I'll be sending the illustrations next week, along with the front matter for *Arcadio*. Also the long new story (Part II of "Had I a Hundred Mouths") which I promised.

Thanks for everything, Carol. I'll be waiting to hear how things go.

Best hopes!
Bill

Here safely: Goyen had flown to New York to meet his new editor.

Los Angeles
November 9, 1982

Dear Robin:

Just now thanking you for the beautiful *Housekeeping* by Marilynne Robinson. It's perfect and true and whole. I treasure it, relish it, have been startled by it.

I've been in New York and have met with my editor, Carol Southern, at Clarkson Potter. I was disappointed to learn that publication date for *Arcadio* had been moved to September 1983 (instead of May). This leaves my book of stories, *Precious Door*, hanging—or further delayed. I've asked that their (Clarkson Potter) option clause in the contract be deleted. Yet the little publishing house, nestled within the rich and gross Crown corporation, seemed at my visit, strong. One of their salesmen came to meet me and to tell me that he "loved *Arcadio*" and was going to "sell the shit out of it." Not like meetings with any other salesmen I've known in the past thirty years. Trouble is, will he love me as much in the fall of '83? All others I met show a lot of excitement over my strange Arcadio. I'm very keen on your reading the book if you'll have time to read early galleys.

We'll all wait until the right time arrives for your own publishing venture. Surely the hope lies in such people as you. We're all used to waiting and are willing to go on waiting with our books, although the times have been bitter and our disappointment in editors we once respected and leaned on hard to bear.

They are running or hiding.

I hope you can read one of the new stories from my *Precious Door*—"Had I a Hundred Mouths," published this month in *TriQuarterly*, Fall issue.

Thanks for all you do—and good wishes!

Bill

Housekeeping: Farrar, Straus, and Giroux, 1980.
own publishing venture: Moody had expressed hopes to establish someday a small literary house like North Point Press or David R. Godine.
TriQuarterly: "Had I a Hundred Mouths" appeared in *TriQuarterly* 55 (Fall 1982): 45–57.

November 16, 1982

Dear Carol:

For the jacket—something strange and extravagant, Aztec-an but also Picasso-like . . . ? The color would be important. Arcadio is a *mestizo*, a mixture of old (even ancient) and modern, or contemporary. I see flamboyancy and strangeness. Something like the attached . . . ?

Thanks for your letter. Sure, you're right not to crash the novel, rush it. My only concern—and still a very real one—is the second book—the 11 stories in *Precious Door*. It's important to me that this new work be published, not held back for so long.

Let me know when you need more from me. I'm enclosing front matter information. Is there a quotation in your ms. from a Whitman poem? If so, let's cut it and use none at all. OK with you? The dedication remains the same.

Onwards. I feel great and find enough time for the work that's pouring out of me!

The New York University Seminars (3) are now set for week of Feb 14th. I'll give 3 classes—or lead them—on (my tentative title) "Writing Life (the Writing of Fiction")".

But more later. Hope all's well.

Yours,
Bill

To Carol Southern

Los Angeles
January 17, 1983

Dear Carol:

Thanks for your very fine suggestion and for your careful reading of the manuscript *Arcadio*. I've carefully thought through your suggestions and done what I thought was right. I've written a page of "Author's Notes" which helps answer a lot of these queries. Also, I've had the manuscript vetted for the Spanish by a native Mexican of San Antonio, Texas, so it's O.K.

I don't agree with you about the tenuousness of the lost picture of "The Light of the World." That each who had it lost it makes it more illusory and mysterious, and it is quite typical that such a picture, of Jesus knocking on a vine- and cobweb-covered door (my soul and yours!) would be lost over and over again. The picture, incidentally, hung on our walls in my East Texas town and was a very popular sentimental painting (Pre-Raphaelite, by William Holman Hunt: I'm enclosing one I've torn from my book on the Pre-Raphaelites so please return it when you've seen it) of the turn of the century and all through the early 1900s—I love it very much and it is quite a dominant figure in *Precious Door*, as you recognize. I'd rather keep the construction of the last photograph as it is, if you please.

Please see that *all* final apostrophes indicating missing "g" are deleted but certainly not the apostrophe in can't and won't, only in *ing* words where the g is left off in the manuscript. Sometimes I have left the *ing* in so that the word has not seemed strange. Just follow the manuscript as typed, please.

I'd love it if the opening bars of "The Missouri Waltz" were done by an artist.

I've retyped pages 126–134 and made changes on that.

I do mean the flow to flow until it is almost maddening. Arcadio might have driven his listener quite crazy with the streaming unrelenting pouring down of his tale. I am therefore very careful about breaking up the flow into further paragraphs. Let the reader swoon. But I don't believe he'll have a hard time reading the story. Arcadio's speech has picked up words from all quarters and all kinds of people; and his education by Edna Pappas, who loved words, and her prissy brother Silvestro, the poet of the whorehouse, gave him many words and phrases which he himself probably didn't too well understand and certainly can't write, but used with *aplomb!*

Carol, thanks for your excellent help and care, and I never mean to offend you or take a high-hatted position toward readers. But I have done what I could. When you send me the galleys please, of course, send along the master. I have not been able to make a copy of the changed master, though I had hoped to. Doris' illness has kept me captive for over three weeks, depending on the kindness of neighbors. I'm fine and filled with work and keep something of a workday despite poor Doris' dependency on me (her pinched nerve has made an invalid of her).

Looking forward to the galleys. And I hope you'll soon decide if you want *Precious Door* since all that new work bristles to be published and

others should see it. Will you do this, soon? Thanks again, and good
hopes, Yours,

Bill

AUTHOR'S NOTE

On Arcadio the personage: The creature is a born story-teller; it loves
words and picks them up from all quarters; is a fabulist, a fantastico who
tells a wonder tale using words glibly and sophistically and auto-eroti-
cally, self-hypnotically. There is no "geography" or geographical reality in
this being's story. Arcadio is a fabricator (in the true sense of the word);
he is also a liar and a conperson; and Arcadio is also demonic and dark,
sometimes Satanic. Therefore we must allow this person's story wild
inconsistencies, absurdities and miraculous leaps and concepts of time
and distance. At times he shows an elegance of expression, puts on verbal
airs and speaks with the smoothness that one hears in some homosexual
high-camp raconteurs who are primitive and uneducated, especially in the
narration of Chupa's exploits with her lovers. I have noted this often in all
kinds of primitive but worldly people.

The *you wan hear:* The expression carries a variety of inflections. It is
almost never a question. It has equivalents of "you know," "you see," "you
know what I mean," "*n'est-ce-pas?*" I've worked very carefully to tune
these inflections.

Also, we must remember that the whole work is a ventriloquism. A gift to
Ben from the narrator (we presume it is his nephew). The narrator is
speaking *for* and *through* Arcadio, since he (the narrator) is imagining and
fabricating the whole thing. Through the narrator—a true "maker," the
true "artist"—through the narrator's speech Arcadio is created: the
creature is literally a creation from speech. This may sound too much for
some readers and needn't be mentioned at all; in the end it really doesn't
matter. *The House of Breath* exists only in speech, and in speech spoken
through the teller—or re-teller. But let's don't get too explanatory.
They're both damned good stories; and no matter the mechanics of
Arcadio's tale, so long as we let him speak.

W.G.

---

native Mexican of San Antonio: John Igo.

*To Joyce Carol Oates
and Raymond J. Smith
ALS-2*

*Los Angeles
November 24, 1982*

Dear Joyce, dear Ray:

I'm so pleased with *Night Walks* which has just handsomely arrived, and happy to be among those inside. And now I'm looking forward to *Ontario Review* 17. Add to these pleasures that I'm engrossed in *A Bloodsmoor Romance* and deeply taken, once more, by Joyce's marvel. Thank you both for this abundance.

I'm sorry I had to miss those two events that closely followed my departure (from the East): Richard's and Robert's reading—such *polar* opposites! Next time I can spend more time there. It was especially fine for me (however short) to have the luncheon visit with you and Robert. I realized later that I hadn't even had time to say hello to some old friends; but when I saw the bus for New York, I felt I'd better take it, early though it was. New York was quite tiring for me this time, and I visited with most of my other friends by phone. But I had good meetings with my two editors and agent.

I'm stronger every day and my work-day extends itself more each week. Reg came down from a conference at Stanford and we had a three-day intensive interview-conversation which I believe is rich and good. It will appear in the Winter ('83) issue of *TriQuarterly*. We spoke often of you and he seemed *very* much alive and involved in his work at the magazine—which pleased me and will please you to hear of it, I'm sure. He's sobering and stabilizing now. Please be well and fruitful and thanks for the loving visit—and all,

Yours,
Bill

Night Walks: Subtitled "A Bedside Companion," it was an anthology of literature on insomnia, edited by Oates (Princeton, N.J.: Ontario Review Press, 1982).
Ontario Review 17: It contained Goyen's "The Storm Doll."
A Bloodsmoor Romance: Novel by Oates (New York: E. P. Dutton, 1982).
Richard's and Robert's reading: Poetry readings on the Princeton University campus by Richard Howard and Robert Phillips.
stronger every day: Goyen was diagnosed as having leukemia in July 1982.

Reg: Reginald Gibbons.
Winter ('83) issue: TriQuarterly 56 contained "An Interview with William Goyen," by
Reginald Gibbons, with the assistance of Molly McQuade (pp. 97–125). The issue also
featured an excerpt from *Arcadio*, an excerpt from *Leander* ("Tongues of Men and of
Angels"), and the stories "The Texas Principessa" and "Where's Esther?" A shortened
version of the interview is appended to *Had I a Hundred Mouths: New and Selected
Stories 1947–1983.* Introduction by Joyce Carol Oates (New York: Clarkson N. Potter,
1985), pp. 251–275).

To Elizabeth Spencer
ACS-2

Los Angeles
Christmas 1982

Dearest Elizabeth:

So glad to hear from you and to have the *Three Stories*, my old favorites. And congratulations on the novel. *Why* have I been forbidden to read
it? Why don't you send it on—please—to me, *now*. It means very much to
me to read your new work. Send it! I'll read it soon.

I am well and on my way, though still under treatment. I had a leaping
recovery—into swimming and inspired daily work: I'm full of new work.
I've finished the twelve stories in the collection, *Precious Door*, and keep
prodding Roberta not to hold up the manuscript because of the slowness
of my publishers of the novel (*Arcadio*). I've waited *three* years for the
novel to get going—and now another pub. date—September 1983! Also
I'll probably be working again with the tremendous Sam Vaughan at
Doubleday, my old editor, on *Six Women*, who are perking again. I'm
happy about Sam but *not* about *Doubleday*. But happy about the book. [. . .]

Three Stories: Trois Contes, by Gustave Flaubert, which Spencer had sent Goyen for
Christmas.
the novel: The manuscript of Spencer's novel *The Salt Line*, which was not published
until 1984.
under treatment: For leukemia and lymphoma.

Los Angeles
January 30, 1983

Dear Allen:

   Your letter came yesterday and it's been with me ever since. I feel your
pain and know it well. I share it with you; I pray that it will pass. [. . .]
Long—or not so long—ago I was told that there is a gift in every painful
time. This was hard for me to believe. And anyway, what gift could I
possibly care about? Yet I have seen this to be true: the gift will come,
sooner or later. It will be deeper insight, richer feeling, a new kind of
freedom, deeper love; or it may come in the figures of other human
beings—closer, more beautiful. At any rate you will be restored, Allen,
you will be healed, renewed. I pray that you can be patient, feel the pain
and bear it. I wish I were closer, I wish I was in Texas, I wish we could
talk. In many ways—in most—I have only felt safe in Texas. There
everything is all right, or will be. I feel this as deeply today as ever, and I
suppose I'll always be homesick for Texas. So it gives me good feelings to
know that you are there, though in such sad circumstances. But I still
believe that Texas heals! How many times in the early days did I go home
to get well. I pray that you were brought there to get well again, to see
things clearly, and to *accept* what you are given.

   Allen, I am all right. I almost lost my life in July and August, but I
didn't. I got such a gift out of that bad time—more work, deeper work.
Since August I have been so full of new work that my energy can't handle
it. It comes from me naturally and fully. Though I tire easily, I work as
long as I can every day. My mornings are full of work. This all began to
come when I was at my lowest. I had real visions of it. The first part of
the new work, which had been going on all during my summer sickness
and which was completed after I got home from hospital, has already
appeared in *TriQuarterly* (current issue). The second part will appear in
the March issue. I am now finishing the third part. It is called *Had I a
Hundred Mouths* and it will be a novella as *Arcadio* is (which will be
published in September). And I have finished a volume of 12 stories,
called *Precious Door*, which I hope will follow *Arcadio* (Clarkson Potter is
the publisher). So Allen there is more life, more vigour and creative force
in us than ever we know. *Life.* I know it may be hard for you to work now
(yet it may not be), but hold to that clarity in you that has brought your

work to you; and *wait*, if you have to. The word is "abide", a beautiful meaning. *Abide*, my boy.

And we'll live. It's really up to *us*. I found that out, again. I want to live. I'll be finished with these treatments in early March and then I'm sure I'll be O.K. It is not terminal cancer, be assured. What I have is treatable and controllable. *I'm fine*. I beg you to be open and accepting as you can be. You'll have to weather all this passion—the only way out is *through* it. But I hope you can *stay in the current of life* and keep moving with it. As you abide, think of me as being with you in it. I pray for your peace and for your fine work.

Faithfully,
Bill

Allen Wier: (b. 1946). Fiction writer and author of the novel *Blanco* (1978) and the collection of stories *Things about to Disappear* (1978).
in Texas: Wier and Goyen had met at Hollins College in 1978, when both taught there. At the time of this letter, Wier was visiting novelist for a semester at the University of Texas in Austin. He was living in a cabin on the Blanco River near Wimberley, about forty-five miles from Austin in the Texas Hill Country.
appeared in TriQuarterly: "Had I a Hundred Mouths," *TriQuarterly* 55 (Fall 1982): 45–57.
the second part: "Tongues of Men and of Angels," *TriQuarterly* 56 (Winter 1983): 76–90.

To John Igo
TLS-1

Los Angeles
Feb. 1, 1983

Dear John:

Thank you for the excellent help. Now I feel secure. The corrected ms. has gone back to the publisher and now I wait for galleys. Publication is in September.

And thank you for what you say about the work. I *hope* it's reached you. For you are one of the ones, for me.

I'm *fine*, recovering beautifully and filled with new work, producing like a laying hen. It's remarkable, the new work that comes.

Please be well and remember my love. Doris sends hers.

Faithfully,
Bill

excellent help: Igo had corrected Spanish phrases in *Arcadio*.

new work: At this time Goyen was at work on the new short novel *Leander*, which was to follow *Arcadio* in publication, but which Goyen did not complete. After Goyen's death, the two chapters, previously published in *TriQuarterly*, were collected as stories in the volume *Had I a Hundred Mouths*.

To Roberta Pryor
ALS-2

Los Angeles
February 10, 1983

Dear Roberta,

Thanks for the sweet letter and the good thoughts. I haven't said much to anybody about the treatments because they sound gruesome and make people think I'm dying, which I most certainly am *not*. I've had four chemotherapy treatments, one every three weeks, and have two to go. I'll be finished March 9. This is for a lymph disorder and is called Lymphoma—a lovely word. I'm responding beautifully and the doctor seems satisfied. Occasionally the treatments have interfered with my work, but generally I've been working as usual, and then resting. I'm tremendously full of new work, as you know. I haven't been this productive in some years. So—my condition is chronic, *not* acute and terminal. It can be treated and *remissed*—a good word. I feel very hopeful and the only fear I have is that I won't be able to get impatient occasionally when my new work waits around. Of course I feel a shortage of time and I'd love to see my work back in print and new work published before I move on. I want to get *Six Women* done (for Sam), write more stories or another novel.

I know you'll be careful about discussing this with others. I did one day tell Jed—I was worried and he called at the right moment; and I believe I wrote to Anne Heller and Eileen Schnurr, my pals at Doubleday. But if word gets around that you've got "something," attitudes change. Anyway, I don't want to be thought of as an invalid or dying. But *time* is important and I know you'll give my work an extra push, as you offer to do. I'm filled with exciting new works. The *Leander* story has grown to novella length. Thanks for your love and help.

As always, love,
Bill

for Sam: Samuel Vaughan at Doubleday.
Jed: Jed Mattes.

To Patrice Repusseau
ALS-2

Los Angeles
Feb. 24, 1983

Dear Patrice:

The *NRF* has arrived—so *fast!*—and the story is superb. Such a beautiful translation. I'm immensely proud of it, and I thank you again. What have you thought of the Part II of the story? I'm now finishing Part III. The whole thing will be called *Leander*. It may be close to the length of *Arcadio*. I'm full of new work and write most every morning. You know I am not well and am undergoing treatment for a form of Leukemia, a malignancy of the blood which is treatable and can be arrested. Still, it is not a pleasant thing to have and the treatments are not too jolly, although I've been luckier than most because I've not been too sick. The treatments are over on March 7 and six weeks from then they'll re-evaluate to see what's happened. I believe I will be all right, and have no fear. [LINE OBSCURED] a sense of time hangs over me and I want to finish as much work as I can—there is much to do. Poor Doris has been crippled by a back ailment for over two months. She's in constant pain and can only walk with a cane and not very far. So she can't work. We are very distressed and hardly know what to do. She may have to undergo surgery—a frightening prospect. We have been saving our money to come to France in June. God and all our ailments willing. We'd stay with our friends again and rent a car and drive about France, perhaps to Brittany. Goyen territory. Will we be able to see you then—around early to mid-June? Or will you be rocking the new cradle? I hope Monique is doing all right. And I hope, dear friend, that your papa is now well again and that *you* are somewhat happy and doing your own work. We have not seen each other for a long time in the world. So let us try to see each other. Would you write to me about "Tongues of Men and of Angels"? I am very much alone [in my work] under the palms. Doris and I send love to *la famille*.

Bill

N.R.F.: Nouvelle revue française, which included Repusseau's translation of Part I of Goyen's *Leander* (i.e., "Had I a Hundred Mouths").

To Carol Southern
ALS-2

March 3, 1983

Dear Carol:

Living a little longer with the being on the wonderful *Arcadio* jacket, I feel more strongly that it's too feminine and should be masculinized a bit more. I like the hair, eyes, mouth—all except that I get in the body the feeling that Arcadio is wearing more of a skirt than trousers. Could the wonderful artist make the masculine thigh more muscular and the arm, too?

It's the *body* that's too feminine. [. . .]

Thank the artist for me, and thank you. Don't do *too* much to the strange *presence*.

Yours,
Bill

---

the artist: The jacket illustration for *Arcadio* was painted by a New York illustrator and designer who goes by the single name of Bascove, who was also to do the art for the jacket of the posthumous *Had I a Hundred Mouths*.

To Edward J. Osowski
ALS-2

Los Angeles
March 31, 1983

Dear Edward:

I'm sorry for my silence and grateful that you keep writing to me. I've been ill and thought I'd send you a card telling you so—Since July I've been having a bout with Leukemia and undergoing chemo-therapy. This has been tolerable and I have generally felt good and have continued to work (and to teach one day a week), but my activities have slowed down. My work, however, has been more alive than ever and I have finished two books and now working, once again, on the autobiography, and far into another short novel. The novel *Arcadio* will be published in September by Clarkson Potter. And, I hope, the stories (*Precious Door*) will come out in the winter. Maybe you can pass this word on to Liz Bennett.

Thanks for the reviews you are sending. You are growing and writing better and better, and I'm *proud* of you. I'm not an admirer of Joan Didion, can never quite believe her, think she's pretentious and a bit phoney—and *Salvador* sounds like it falls right in line—self-pitying, self-proclaiming and "sensitive." But *your writing* about it is perhaps your *best*.

And your jaunts to New Mexico! How I envy you. Again I've missed another round of seasons there. Spring is a dream. Give a hug and kiss to dear Tress. Tell her I will be well. And happy birthday! Your life sounds good and thank God. Doris and I go to New York on Easter Sunday and I'll speak on "Recovering and Writing" at NYU on April 13th. Please stay in touch.

Love, Bill

Edward J. Osowski: National Endowment for the Humanities Project Director at Houston Public Library.
Liz Bennett: Elizabeth Bennett, book editor at the *Houston Post*.
Salvador: By Joan Didion (New York: Simon and Schuster, 1982).
Tress: Patricia Trescott (Tres) Ripley, an actress.

To Carol Southern
ALS-1

April 27, 1983

Dear Carol:

I've today mailed notes to Erica Jong, Truman Capote, and Bill Styron (RFD Roxbury, Conn.), advising them that they'll be receiving the ms. of *Arcadio* shortly. Also left phone messages for Rex Reed and Truman and Joyce Carol Oates. Hope you get the ms. to them right away.

Thanks—
Bill

Erica Jong . . . Joyce Carol Oates: When the novel was published, the jacket carried blurbs by Oates, Reed, and Christopher Isherwood, but none by Capote, Jong, or Styron.

To Patrice Repusseau
ALS-2

Los Angeles
June 14, 1983

Dear Patrice and Monique:

Congratulations on your new beautiful son from me and Doris. How happy you must be! And such a beautiful name.

Alas, now, the sad news: we shall not be coming to France. I have to continue my treatments—in fact they must be changed to another direction. I have not improved through the long chemo-therapy treatment, alas. Doris and I have been very upset but we are better now—and will be *fine* when you read this. And we have assurances that the treatment will not be too bad.

We'll miss you. But we *will* come to France—perhaps in the autumn.

Happiness and love to the whole family.

Bill and Doris

---

son: Loïs Repusseau.

To Edward J. Osowski
ACS-1

Los Angeles
July 10, 1983

Dear Edward:

Slow in writing to you and please forgive. I've been busy getting well and trying to write when I can. This new novel, *Leander,* is well on its way and I'm very excited about it. It also takes my mind off *Arcadio,* which soon comes out. Your letters always make me homesick for New Mexico. I see how you, too, love it. And your reviews are so fine. You're into the *flow* of it and are gaining authority rapidly. Your life sounds full and good. Please stay with me. I'll probably be in Houston in September–October for the book. Can't wait to see you!

Love, Bill

in Houston . . . for the book: Goyen died in Los Angeles on August 30, 1983. He saw bound galleys of *Arcadio* but did not live to see the finished book, which was published in October. After Goyen's death, Carol Southern, Goyen's editor at Clarkson N. Potter, preferred to publish a larger book of Goyen's stories rather than the new collection *Precious Door,* and *Had I a Hundred Mouths: New and Selected Stories 1947–1983* was the result.

AFTERWORD *by*

Stephen
Spender

I met William Goyen first in the summer of 1948 when, during the vacation that followed a year of teaching at Sarah Lawrence College, my wife, Natasha, and I made a tour of the West. We had, I think, several introductions from various Huxleys to Frieda Lawrence, so Taos was high on the list of places to be visited. There we met Frieda and her lover Angelo, who introduced us to Mabel Dodge Luhan and Dorothy Brett, whose little house stood midway between Frieda's and an adobe house which two young men—recent additions to the post-Lawrencian circle there—had built with their own hands. These were Walt—Walter Berns—and Bill—William Goyen.

The two were inseparable, and they loved one another, but they were not lovers. That is to say, Walter was completely—and, one might say, wonderfully—"normal," "straight"—whereas Bill appeared at this period of his life, to be predominantly homosexual. The wonder of their relationship was that it transcended sexual differences which might have caused them not to live together. Their friendship, which seemed more important to each of them than any other possible relationship, began during the war, when they were both sailors on an American battleship. As Goyen puts it in one letter: "His friendship was formed in the violent smithy of war and fear and shipboard craze. He stood by my bunk and held my body with his giant's hands when I was pretty goddamned ill and almost out of control. . . . And he is fine and noble and right, and he believes unyieldingly in me. He would give his life for me. And, my friend, he is no lover (to use the vernacular); he is—have you ever really *known* the definition of this word?—a comrade. And that is worth all the lovers, men and women, I have ever known." In these circumstances, Berns acted as a protector to the hypersensitive and physically weak Goyen, and Goyen acted, in some respects, as the teacher of Berns.

On the face of it, there was something almost monastic about this friendship between book-reading scholar and hefty toiler. Indeed, they looked dramatically different, a kind of sublimated version of Laurel and Hardy—Goyen almost comically slender, Berns strong and upright. But, looking back now, I wonder whether Goyen did not dramatize the difference, which made Walter seem the unlettered Man of Action in contrast to himself as contemplative, learned Creator. Walter, as his subsequent history as a professor and scholar showed, had a very good mind. Undoubtedly Bill widened the range of Walter's interests from the purely practical to the poetic and imaginative. Their living room was a library where they studied the novelists and poets. Walter's practicality was dedicated to the support of the extremely impractical Bill.

When we all met, Bill was writing intensively, but as I remember, he had great difficulty in getting published. I was able to help a bit by sending to Cyril Connolly at *Horizon* his story "The White Rooster," which had some success when it was published in London. Bill was writing at this time his novel *The House of Breath*, which he completed in my house in London in 1949. He dedicated *Nine Poems* to me in 1976.

The reader of these letters may feel, as I certainly do, surprise at the extent of Goyen's comparative failure to support himself by his writing. One reason perhaps for this is that he was so obsessed by his own vision—and, indeed, by his idea of himself as the totally isolated genius, the self-dedicated artist. Moreover, his dealings with agents, publishers, and editors seem imprudent, being based on the idea that they must become involved in all his problems as an artist; also, in his view, since they were not artists but businessmen or women, they had to accept the idea that they belonged to a lower order of humanity than the artist.

Another reason is that his work—his vision of the world—really is very idiosyncratic. He was one of those romantics—encountered more often in non-English-language European literature than in English—a Georg Büchner or a Gérard de Nerval—who is appreciated by very exceptional, very few readers. Therefore even when, toward the end of his life, his work was translated into French and German and enjoyed prestigious success, sales were limited.

In Goyen's letters we encounter several versions of the man—the dedicated artist forever complaining how alone he feels, yet cultivating aloneness; the friend or colleague who embraces almost to excess his correspondent; the lover or near-lover with whom he seems to be playing an elaborate game. The most striking example of the last is Katherine Anne Porter, with whom, on internal evidence provided by the letters, he appears to have had some kind of love affair. Yet reading Goyen's side of the correspondence, it is possible to think that the excess of his expressed affection conceals a considerable evasiveness in a game they both play and in which she is perhaps as elusive as he.

Writing this, though, I may be influenced by the description Bill once gave me of Katherine Anne Porter: "She lies in bed in her room with, on a shelf, her unfinished novel wrapped in a brown paper parcel, like a bleeding limb." Not exactly the remark of a fervent lover, but at least a reminder of how extraordinarily funny Bill could be.

There are many other examples of his humor in these letters. Those to Dorothy Brett remind us that Goyen could be simple and straightforward, extremely funny and rather malicious. He was often all these things in conversation, when he was not on his high horse of being the loneliest artist in the world. In many of these letters Goyen is at his conversational best—the young man who, together with Walter Berns, built the adobe house in the desert.

INDEX OF RECIPIENTS

GENERAL INDEX